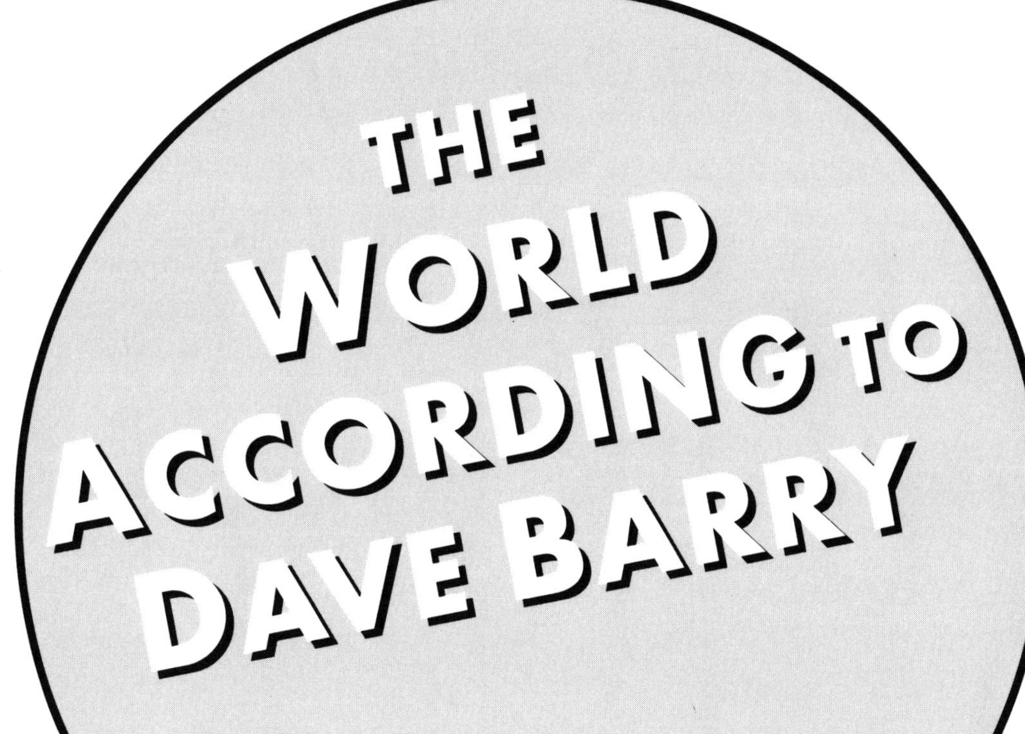
THE
WORLD
ACCORDING TO
DAVE BARRY

Dave Barry Turns 40

Dave Barry Talks Back

Dave Barry's Greatest Hits

THE WORLD ACCORDING TO DAVE BARRY

by Dave Barry

Cartoons by Jeff MacNelly

WINGS BOOKS
New York • Avenel, New Jersey

This omnibus was originally published in separate volumes under the titles:

Publisher's Note: Many of the products and services mentioned in these pieces are trademarks of their respective companies. Every effort has been made to identify these trademarks by initial capitalization. Should there be an omission in this respect, we shall be pleased to make the necessary corrections in future printings.

This edition contains the complete and unabriged texts of the original editions. They have been completely reset for this volume.

This 1994 edition is published by Wings Books,
distributed by Random House Value Publishing, Inc.,
40 Engelhard Avenue, Avenel, New Jersey 07001,
by arrangement with Crown Publishers, Inc.

Random House
New York • Toronto • London • Sydney • Auckland

Printed and bound in the United States of America

Library of Congress Cataloging-in-Publication Data
Barry, Dave.
The world according to Dave Barry / by Dave Barry.
p. cm.
Contents: Dave Barry talks back – Dave Barry turns 40 – Dave Barry's greatest hits.
ISBN 0-517-11870-X
1. American wit and humor. I. Title.
PN6162.P298 1994
814'.54–dc20 94-8402
CIP

8 7 6 5 4 3 2

Contents

DAVE
BARRY
TALKS
BACK

This book is dedicated to all the Alert Readers who take the time to send me newspaper items about exploding toilets when they could be doing something meaningful with their lives.

Acknowledgments

I thank the *Miami Herald* and all the other newspapers that run my column, except for the papers that cut out the booger jokes, which I bet they never do to George Will. I also thank my various editors, Tom Shroder, Gene Weingarten, David Groff, and Beth Barry, for telling me when things are NOT funny; and I thank Judi Smith and Doris Mansour for plausibly denying, when people call the office, that I even exist.

Contents

Introduction

I am always getting letters from people who want my job.

"Dave," they start out. They always call me Dave.

"Dave," they say, "I want your job, because my current job requires me to be a responsible person doing productive work, whereas your job requires you mainly to think up booger jokes."

This kind of thoughtless remark really gets my dander up. Because although the reading public sees only the end product of my work, the truth is that I often spend many hours researching a particular topic before I make booger jokes about it. Take the Middle East. This is a very troubled region, a region fraught with complex and subtle issues of major international significance. You can't just sit down and dash off a column that says:

"The Middle East! Ha ha! What a bunch of boogerheads!"

No, there is a lot more to it than *that.* As a respected commentator, I am expected to produce a column that is thoughtful, insightful, profound, and —above all—800 words long. Whereas the column above is only nine words, counting each "ha" as a separate word. So as a respected commentator I have to come up with another 791 words' worth of insights about the Middle East, such as: where it is* and how come it is fraught with all these things, and what exactly we mean when we say our "dander" is up. According to the dictionary, "dander" means "temper," which would make sense except that I distinctly remember that a former editor of mine named Bob Shoemaker used to wear a little medallion around his neck that said:

*** Not around here, I can tell you that.**

I AM ALLERGIC TO HORSE DANDER.

Bob said he wore this so that in case he was ever rendered unconscious in an accident, the paramedics would realize that they should not expose him to horse dander. But if the dictionary is correct, Bob's medallion was actually saying that he should not be exposed to angry horses. You'd think the paramedics would already know this. You'd think that one of the first rules they learn in Paramedic School is, "Never expose an unconscious patient to an angry horse." Sheep, yes. We can all readily imagine situations where it would be necessary, even *desirable,* to expose an unconscious accident victim to an angry sheep. But as a respected commentator I am deeply concerned about this horse thing, which is just one more example of the kind of subtle and complex issue that we must come to grips with if we are ever to achieve any kind of meaningful understanding regarding these boogerheads in the Middle East.

Another question readers frequently ask is: "Dave, what specific system of writing do you use?"

Like many great writers such as Fyodor Dostoevsky and William Shakespeare, I use the Two-Dog System of writing. This system gets its name from the fact that it involves two dogs, one of which is your main dog and the other of which is your emergency backup dog, in case for any reason your main dog is unavailable. My main dog's name is Earnest, and my emergency backup dog is named Zippy. Every morning I get my coffee and say: "You want to go to WORK?" And the two of them charge for the door. Sometimes they charge right *into* the door, because they have the combined IQ of mayonnaise.

So the three of us go to my office, where we all take our positions:

- I sit in front of the computer and try to have insights;
- Earnest lies directly under my desk and periodically emits aromas;
- Zippy lies several feet away, ready to step in and emit aromas if Earnest experiences technical difficulties.

That, along with occasionally barking insanely at invisible beings, is the sum total of the dogs' contribution to the column effort. In the years we have worked together, neither dog, to the best of my recollection, has ever come up with a *single idea.* Sometimes I get just a little ticked off about this. "Hey Earnest!" I'll say. "How about you come up here and have insights while I go down there and emit aromas?" This causes Earnest to look at me and, drawing on the shrewd instincts that have made dogs so successful as a species despite having no marketable skills, wag her tail. So the real burden of production rests entirely upon my shoulders, just as it rested upon the shoulders of Dostoevsky and Shakespeare, both of whom, you will notice, are currently dead.

My point is that, counting all the research, the fact-checking, the trips to the veterinarian, etc., there's a lot more to being a respected commentator than meets the eye. So as you read this book, I'll thank you not to pause every few sentences and remark: "Hey! *I* could write this crap!" Remember the wise words of the old Indian saying: "Before you criticize a man's collection of columns, walk a mile in his moccasins, bearing in mind that this is a good way to catch a fungus."

About Jeff MacNelly

I'm very pleased that Jeff MacNelly's illustrations will appear in this book, because he is, in my opinion, of all the illustrators in the world today, probably the tallest. Also he draws pretty well. He does some of his best work in bars. I've seen this a number of times. We'll go into a bar, and because Jeff is too modest to say anything, I'll take people quietly aside and say, "Do you know who that is? That's *Jeff MacNelly*."

And the people, clearly impressed, will say, "Who?"

So I'll explain that Jeff has won about 17 Pulitzer Prizes and also draws the "Shoe" comic strip. This always gets a reaction. "Oh yeah!" they'll say. "Shoe! I love that one! Especially Opus the Penguin!"

Jeff is very gracious about this kind of adoration and will frequently take some place mats and do drawings for his fans, which is amazing to watch because *he never opens his eyes*. Really. I'm not even sure that he *has* eyes, because nobody I know has ever seen them. He just sits there with his eyes closed, drawing things for people in the bar, and they get all excited and buy him beers. This makes me jealous because, as a writer, I can't do the same kind of thing. Usually I can't even bring my dogs *into* a bar. But at least my eyeballs are visible.

Introducing: Mr. Humor Person

I frequently get letters from readers asking me to explain how humor works. Of course they don't ask in exactly those words. Their actual wording is more like: "Just where do you get off, Mr. Barry, comparing the entire legal profession to flatworms?" Or: "How about if I come down to that newspaper and stick a wastebasket up your nose?"

People come to me with this kind of probing question because I happen to be a major world expert on humor. I deal constantly with sophisticated humor questions such as: Would it be funnier to have the letter say, "How about if I come down to that newspaper and stick an IBM Selectric typewriter up your nose?" Or should I maybe try to work in a subtle political joke, such as: "How about if I come down to that newspaper and stick Vice President Quayle up your nose?" This is the kind of complex philosophical issue that I am forced to wrestle with, hour after hour, until 10:30 A.M., when "Wheel of Fortune" comes on.

After years of pursuing this regimen, I've learned certain fundamental truths about humor. One of them is that "weasel" is a funny word. You can improve the humor value of almost any situation by injecting a weasel into it:

WRONG: "Scientists have discovered a 23rd moon orbiting Jupiter."
RIGHT: "Scientists have discovered a giant weasel orbiting Jupiter."
WRONG: "U.S. Rep. Newt Gingrich."
RIGHT: "U.S. Rep. Weasel Gingrich."

But the most important humor truth of all is that to really see the humor in a situation, you have to have perspective. "Perspective" is derived from two ancient Greek words: "persp," meaning "something bad that happens to somebody else," and "ective," meaning "ideally somebody like Donald Trump."

Take for example funerals. Funerals are not funny, which is why we don't laugh during them unless we just can't help ourselves. On the other hand, if a funeral occurs way on the other side of the world, and it involves the late Mr. Ayatollah "Mojo" Khomeini, and the mourners are so upset that they start grabbing garments and souvenir body parts off the deceased to the point where what's left of him could be laid to rest in a standard Good & Plenty box, then we have no choice but to laugh until our dentures fall into our laps.

An even better example of humor perspective involves a masseuse named Danette Sadle I met in San Francisco. (Let me stress, for the benefit of those readers who happen to be my wife, that I met her in a totally nonmassage situation.)

Danette had a regular client who decided to give her husband a professional massage as a gift, thinking that he would enjoy it. When the husband showed up, however, he was very nervous: He said he'd never had a massage before and he was concerned about getting undressed, and specifically whether he was supposed to leave his underpants on. Danette assured him that she was a professional and that he'd be covered at all times by a sheet, but he was still very concerned. So Danette said look, leave your underpants on, take them off, whatever makes you comfortable. Then she left the room while he undressed.

When she came back, the man was under the sheet looking as relaxed as a person being strapped down for brain surgery via ice pick. So Danette, trying to be as calm and nonthreatening as possible, walked up to him, reached out her hand, and touched the man's back at *exactly the moment* that the famous World Series earthquake struck.

Let me stress that there was *nothing funny* about this earthquake, unless you have the perspective of hearing Danette describe how the man's entire body, in defiance of gravity, twitched violently into the air like a trout on amphetamines and landed on the other side of the room.

"It's usually more relaxing than this," said Danette.

"It's a good thing I kept my underpants on!" said the man.

These are words that a lot of people could stand to remember more often, but that is not my point. My point is that by having perspective on things we can find humor in virtually any situation, except of course for genuinely tragic events that cause serious trouble for large numbers of people. Or anything involving my car.

Dave's HUMOR TIPS:

(This Column is Funny)

Today we're going to attempt a ground-breaking medical experiment in an effort to help those unfortunate readers who suffer from a tragic condition called: Humor Impairment. Don't laugh! Humor Impairment afflicts Americans from all walks of life. Look at Richard Nixon. Here's a man whose sense of humor was so badly stunted that he was forced, at White House social functions, to wear special undershorts equipped with radio-controlled electrodes so that his aides could signal him, via electric shocks, when he was supposed to laugh. Sometimes, if the guests were unusually witty, the chief executive wound up twitching like a fresh-caught mackerel as dangerous voltage levels were reached in his boxers.

So it is possible for a Humor Impaired person, through courage and determination, to overcome his handicap, and maybe even someday, like Mr. Nixon, attain the ultimate political achievement of not getting indicted. But before we can treat Humor Impairment, we have to be able to recognize it. It can affect anyone. YOU could have it. To find out whether you do, ask yourself this: *What was your reaction to the first paragraph of this column?* Did you think: "Ha ha! That Nixon sure is a geek, all right!" Or did you think: "This is offensive, cheap, crude, and vicious humor, making fun of a former president of the United States, a major public figure, an internationally recognized elder statesman, just because he is a geek."

If you had either of those reactions, you are not Humor Impaired, because you at least grasped that the paragraph was *supposed* to be funny. The Humor Impaired people, on the other hand, missed that point entirely. They are already writing letters to the editor saying: "They wouldn't use electric shocks! They would use hand signals!" Or: "Where can I buy a pair of undershorts like that?" Trust me! I know these people! I hear from them all the time!

In fact, that's how I got the idea for the ground-breaking experiment. I had received a large batch of Humor Impaired letters responding to a column I wrote about Mister Language Person, and I was asking myself: How can I respond to these people in a humor column, when they don't understand that it's supposed to be humorous? That's when I came up with my ground-breaking idea. You know how some TV shows are "closed-captioned for the hearing impaired," meaning that if you have a special TV set, you can get subtitles? Well, I thought, why couldn't you do that with humor?

So the rest of this ground-breaking column will be *closed-captioned for the Humor Impaired.* After each attempted joke, the humor element will be explained in parentheses, so that you Humor Impaired individuals can laugh right along with the rest of us. Ready? Here we go:

Many readers were upset about a recent column by "Mister Language Person," the internationally recognized expert (NOT TRUE) who periodically answers common language questions submitted by imaginary readers (HE MAKES THE QUESTIONS UP). All of Mister Language Person's answers are intended to be as accurate (NOT TRUE) and informative (NOT TRUE) as is humanly possible while still containing words such as "booger." ("BOOGER" IS FUNNY.) No item is ever allowed to appear in Mister Language Person until trained grammarians have indicated their approval by barking at it in an excited manner. (THOSE ARE NOT GRAMMARIANS. THOSE ARE HIS DOGS.)

Although I had thought that the Mister Language Person column met the usual high standards of accuracy (EVERYTHING IN IT WAS WRONG), it contained an item that attracted a very large amount of mail from astute readers (SARCASM: THESE PEOPLE APPEAR TO BE MISSING KEY BRAIN LOBES) (NOT LITERALLY) who saw that, in one of the items, *something was wrong.* Yes! In a column that was basically a teeming, writhing mass of wrong answers, these keen observers were somehow able to detect: a wrong answer. (HEAVY SARCASM.)

The item that virtually all of these readers focused on was the one where an imaginary airline employee asked whether it was correct to say "A bomb has been placed on one of you're airplanes" or "A bomb has been placed, on one of you're airplanes," (THIS IS NOT REALLY HOW AIRLINES HANDLE BOMB THREATS) (AS FAR AS WE KNOW) and Mister Language Person replied that the correct wording was "A bomb has been placed IN one of you're airplanes." (GET IT? IT'S *STILL* WRONG!! HA HA!) Many readers felt this answer was incorrect and took time out from their busy and

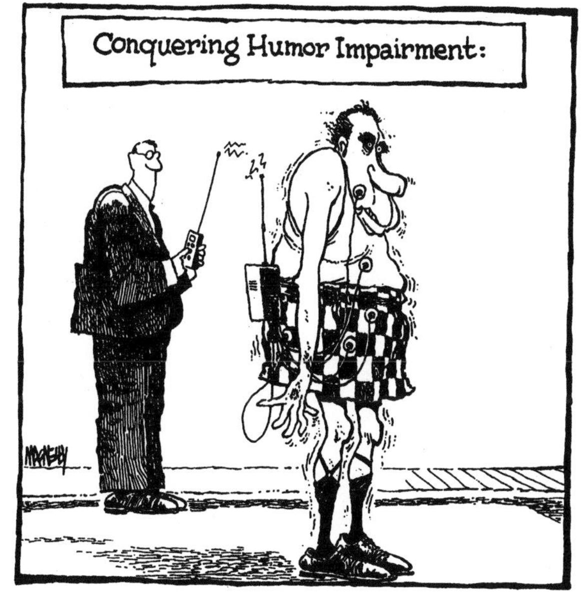

rewarding careers in the demanding field of food chewing (PROBABLY NOT TRUE) to write letters containing quotes such as—I am not making these up (HE IS NOT MAKING THESE UP)—"I was shocked with the grammar" and "Never have I seen such a mistake in grammer" and "I sure hope you remember this small bit of information, being as you are a writer you should have known it already."

Well, readers, I've researched this issue carefully (NOT TRUE: HE DRANK A BEER), and although this is not easy for me to say, I have to admit it: Your right. Thanks for "straightening me out." This job would not be the same without you. I mean it. (HE MEANS IT.)

READER ALERT

Exploding Things

I don't wish to toot my own horn, but I definitely deserve to win several Nobel Prizes for the ground-breaking scientific work I've done in the field of exploding things. Since I wrote my first report, several years ago, about a snail that exploded in a restaurant in Syracuse, New York, I have received literally thousands of letters from alert readers sending me newspaper clippings about exploding ants, pigs, trees, yogurt containers, potatoes, television sets, finches, whales, municipal toilets, human stomachs, and of course cows. In accordance with standard journalism accuracy procedures, I never pass any of these reports on to the public without first reading it, saying to myself, quote, "Huh!" Using this process, I've determined that we have a worldwide exploding-thing epidemic on our hands, and until further notice we should all take the sensible precaution of avoiding things whenever possible. For example, you should never have bought this book.

Blow-Up

Here at the Consumer Command Post ("Working To Make Your World More Threatening") we continue to receive alarming news items clipped out by alert readers who have somehow obtained scissors from their ward attendants. In accordance with our rigorous standards of accuracy, we have checked all of these submissions carefully to determine whether they contain any money, and now we are passing them along to you, the public, in hopes that you will be better able to make wise consumer choices and live a safer, healthier, and happier existence until such time as you burst into flames.

This is a very real possibility, according to a *Science Digest* article alertly mailed to us by Thomas Miller of Des Moines, Iowa ("More Than Just Pigs"). The article concerns spontaneous human combustion, which is when people, with no apparent cause, suddenly start burning like campfire marshmallows, reaching temperatures of thousands of degrees and being completely reduced to ashes. This is often fatal.

There are more than 200 reported cases of spontaneous human combustion, which can happen to anybody, anytime. "Persons have ignited while walking, driving, boating, and even dancing," notes *Science Digest,* reminding us of a number of evenings in the ninth grade when we, personally, came extremely close to erupting in flames right in the Harold C. Crittenden Junior High School cafeteria while dancing the Dirty Dig with Barbara Smayda to the song "Unchained Melody." Strangely, in many spontaneous human combustion cases, the area immediately around the victim is unaffected by the fire, although the ceiling and walls of the room are covered with oily soot.

No doubt you are asking yourself: "Is there anything that I, as an individual consumer, can do about this alarming problem?" Fortunately, there is. We've done some tests here at the Consumer Command Post, and we've found that you can get those walls looking "spick-and-span" again simply by scrubbing them with a mixture of detergent and warm water.

We feel we should warn you, however, that it is not a wise idea to put too many beauty products in your hair. We base this warning on a news article from *The State* of Columbia, South Carolina, sent in by Phyllis Wainscott, concerning a South Carolina woman who has filed a lawsuit claiming that her hair burst into flames because of the effect of the sun shining on two hair-care products that she was wearing. One of her attorneys is quoted—we are not making this up—as offering the following explanation:

"The whole thing is that she just put them on her head, both products, and—it was a hot day that day—and her head just spontaneously combusted."

Here's what gets our goat: Right now, the world scientific community is having multiple laboratory orgasms, just because some scientists *might* have discovered a "cold fusion" process whereby if you put atoms into a jar according to a certain recipe you *might* get a reaction that *might* someday be an important new energy source, but not until—trust us on this—the scientific community obtains a *large* amount of tax money donated by interested consumers. Meanwhile, here we have a South Carolina woman who, acting on her own, has apparently stumbled upon a proven energy-producing reaction requiring only a couple of readily available personal-grooming substances plus a human head! Think of the possibilities! We could see the day, in our lifetimes, when a city the size of Baltimore, such as San Francisco, could have all of its electrical power needs met for a decade simply by harnessing the latent hairstyle energy of a single Republican Women's Club.

But we must not start rejoicing yet, not while we still face an ongoing epidemic of exploding items, a story we have been covering relentlessly for several months now in an unselfish effort to win a large cash journalism prize. So far we have reported the mysterious explosions of a snail, a cow, numerous pigs, and a human stomach, and we were asking ourselves: What next? And sure enough the answer was: municipal toilets. These were located in a courthouse in Seattle, where, according to news items sent in by approximately 40,000 alert readers, somebody connected an air compressor to the water line, so that when people attempted to flush, they were suddenly attacked by the Geyser From Hell. We can only hope that these people were not attorneys about to make important court appearances. ("Your Honor, may I approach the bench?" "No.")

And if you think that this is just an isolated incident, you are, no offense, an idiot. According to an Associated Press article alertly sent in by Lisa Hoffman, three people in Fordyce, Arkansas, were injured when somebody accidentally allowed propane to get into the city water supply, thus essentially transforming some toilets into bombs. Here is an actual quote from one of the victims: "Whomp, the commode burst into flames."

Well, consumers, we're out of space here, so unfortunately we can't report some of our other items, such as the one sent in by Charles Popelka concerning the woman in Ottumwa, Iowa ("It's Flat, But It's Quiet"), who encountered the exploding potato. But rest assured that, in the months ahead, we will continue to provide you consumers with information that will enable you to become sufficiently alarmed about the lethal threats that are all around us in everyday objects such as this keyboard that we are typing on, which we notice seems to be emitting some kind of WHOM.

Moby Yuck

Here at the Exploding Animal Research Institute we have received two very alarming news items that we are passing along today in the hopes that you, the generalized public, will finally break out of your apathetic, selfish, materialistic life-styles and send us some large cash contributions.

Item One, submitted by numerous alert readers, concerns the recent criminally insane vote by the U.S. Senate AGAINST having the federal government monitor methane emissions from cows. I am not making this vote up. As you may be aware, cows emit huge quantities of methane, which contributes to global warming, which has gotten so bad in some areas that brand-new shirts are coming out of the factory with armpit stains already in them. So the U.S. Senate (motto: "White Male Millionaires Working For You") was considering an amendment to the Clean Air Act, under which the government would monitor methane emissions from various sources, including "animal production."

Well, as you can imagine, this did not sit well with the senators from those states where cow flatulence is a cherished way of life. Leading the herd of opposition senators was Senator Steve Symms of Idaho ("The Exploding Potato State"), who took the floor and stated that the amendment would—this is an actual quote—"put the nose of the federal government in almost every place it does not belong."

So the Senate took out the part about monitoring animal methane, which means there will be no advance warning when, inevitably, there is some kind of cow-interior blockage, causing a potentially lethal buildup of flammable gasses and transforming one of these normally docile creatures into a giant mooing time bomb which, if detonated, could cause the dreaded Rain of Organs. Have you ever, in a supermarket, accidentally encountered a cow tongue

—a large sluglike slab of gray flesh that you couldn't imagine anybody purchasing for any purpose other than to nail it to the front door in hopes of scaring off evil spirits? Well, I'd like to know what Senator Symms would say if one of those babies came hurtling out of the sky and struck him at upwards of 100 miles per hour. "Yuck," would be my guess.

I base this statement on a similar situation in Oregon where innocent civilians were struck by falling whale parts. I am absolutely not making this incident up; in fact, I have it all on videotape, which I obtained from the alert father-son team of Dean and Kurt Smith. The tape is from a local TV news show in Oregon, which sent a reporter out to cover a 45-foot, eight-ton dead whale that washed up on the beach. The responsibility for getting rid of the carcass was placed upon the Oregon State Highway Division, apparently on the theory that highways and whales are very similar in the sense of being large objects.

So anyway, the highway engineers hit upon the plan—remember, I am not making this up—of blowing up the whale with dynamite. The thinking here was that the whale would be blown into small pieces, which would be eaten by sea gulls, and that would be that. A textbook whale removal.

So they moved the spectators back up the beach, put a half-ton of dynamite next to the whale, and set it off. I am probably guilty of understatement when I say that what follows, on the videotape, is the most wonderful event in the history of the universe. First you see the whale carcass disappear in a huge blast of smoke and flame. Then you hear the happy spectators shouting "Yayy!" and "Wheee!" Then, suddenly, the crowd's tone changes. You hear a new sound, the sound of many objects hitting the ground with a noise that sounds like "splud." You hear a woman's voice shouting "Here comes pieces of . . . my GOD!" Something smears the camera lens.

Later, the reporter explains: "The humor of the entire situation suddenly gave way to a run for survival as huge chunks of whale blubber fell everywhere." One piece caved in the roof of a car parked more than a quarter of a mile away. Remaining on the beach were several rotting whale sectors the size of condominium units. There was no sign of the sea gulls, who had no doubt permanently relocated to Brazil.

This is a very sobering videotape. Here at the Institute we watch it often, especially at parties. But this is no time for gaiety. This is a time to get hold of the folks at the Oregon State Highway Division and ask them, when they get done cleaning up the beaches, to give us an estimate on the U.S. Capitol.

The Bovine Comedy

We do not wish to create a panic, but we are advising those of you who live in the Midwest to evacuate the area immediately and stay out until we can get to the bottom of this matter concerning the exploding cow.

We found out about this thanks to alert reader Dale Clemens, M.D., who sent us a very troubling article from the *Sun*. This is the same publication that broke the story three years ago about the rampage of the Giant Vampire Fleas, which were mutant fleas capable of sucking all the blood from small dogs within minutes and jumping 50 feet straight up, as the *Sun* put it, "without warning."

But as alarmed as we were by that article, we were even more alarmed by this new one, which is headlined: COW EXPLODES, HORRIFIED FARMER SUES. The story concerns a New Zealand farmer who purchased a cow, which he and his family were admiring, when suddenly—without warning, we bet—the cow "exploded before their eyes, spattering into a million bits of flesh and bone and drenching them all in blood."

Now, for most of us, when we hear of a shocking tragedy of this nature, our natural reaction is extreme sorrow that we were not able to observe it firsthand while wearing goggles. We estimate that, just from our immediate circle of friends, we could fill a municipal stadium with people willing to pay $50 apiece to see a cow spontaneously explode. But apparently this family prefers a cow that engages in more traditional cow behavior, such as a standing around exhibiting the intelligence of coleslaw, because the farmer is suing the breeder for selling him a "defective" cow. The article quotes a veterinarian as saying that cows produce up to three quarts of gas per minute. "If it can't burp," the veterinarian says, "its stomach can explode within the hour."

This is exactly the kind of story the Founding Fathers had in mind when they put the clause in the Constitution stating that the press has the right to run up enormous long-distance telephone charges. So we called up New Zealand, which is in the Mars Time Zone, but we were unable to locate any of the people named in the exploding cow story. We were actually starting to wonder if the *Sun* story was untrue when suddenly, without warning, an alert reader named Donald McEwan sent us *another* frightening cow-related news item. This one came from the *Washington Post,* and it stated—we are not making any of this up—that a Colorado State University animal-nutrition professor named Donald Johnson has been studying cow flatulence for 20 years, and has determined that the average cow emits 200 to 400 quarts of methane *per day,* resulting in a total annual world cow methane output of 50 million metric *tons.*

(Campers: This is yet another argument for NEVER allowing a cow inside your sleeping bag.)

So, of course, we called Professor Johnson, who seemed remarkably normal considering his chosen field, and we asked him whether cows can explode.

"I've never heard of it," he said. "It's rather unlikely that a cow would actually explode, although there is considerable methane gas and in some cases it could be present in concentrations that could ignite."

In fact, Professor Johnson revealed that on more than one occasion, in college classrooms, he has used a candle to set fire to emissions being emitted by live cows, one of whom was able to sustain the flame *without the candle.*

Ask yourself this question: What if such a cow were to fall into the wrong hands? Picture this: You're on a seemingly routine commercial airline flight, rummaging around your breakfast tray in search of an implement sharp enough to penetrate your "omelet," when suddenly, without warning, from back in the smoking section, you hear sharp cries of:

"Look out!"

And:

"He's got a cow!"

You whirl around, and there, in the aisle, stands: a terrorist. In one hand he holds a Bic lighter; in the other he holds a fuse, which is attached to Professor Johnson's high-output cow—which by the way would not be detected by any airport metal detector currently in use—and in the next instant the entire cabin is filled with the chilling, unmistakable sound of: The Death Moo.

What can we do to prevent this chilling scenario from becoming a reality or—even worse—a made-for-television "docu-drama"? Clearly what is

called for is a federal task force, ideally headed by Dan Quayle, who seems to have a lot of spare time, assuming that he is not called upon to suddenly, without warning, become president of the United States. We urge you to write a letter about this to your congressperson, bearing in mind that if he is an average adult, he produces, according to the *Washington Post,* about one liter of methane per day.

Apocalypse Cow

I have wonderful news for those of you who were disappointed when the world failed to end last year.

In case you missed it, what happened last year was that a man named Edgar Whisenant, who is a former NASA rocket engineer, came out with a booklet in which he proved via exact mathematical calculations based on the Bible that the world was going to end in 1988, most likely on September 12. I first heard Mr. Whisenant explain this on a radio show one morning when I was in New Orleans for the Republican convention. At the time I was thrilled, because I had spent the previous evening with some other trained journalists at an establishment named Nick C. Castrogiovanni's Original Big Train Bar, which features a specialty drink that comes in a large foam container shaped like a toilet, and as far as I was concerned the world could not end soon enough. A lot of other True Believers around the country also got very excited over Mr. Whisenant's prediction, so you an imagine what a letdown it was when September 12 rolled around and—as you know if you keep up with the news—the world did not end, which meant among other things that we had to go ahead with this presidential election.

Well, guess what. Mr. Whisenant has just come out with another booklet, and in Chapter 1 (entitled "What Went Wrong in 1988") he graciously admits that there was an error in his calculations. He now scientifically calculates that the world will probably end on—mark it in your appointment calendar—this coming September 1. Yes! *Before the World Series.*

So you need to get ready. You need to prepare for The End by doing some real "soul searching" and asking yourself this hard question: "If the world ended tomorrow, could I honestly say that I have done everything I could, as a spiritual person, to run up my VISA balance?" Think about it! Because come September 1 it's all over. All the people who have led moral lives will go straight to heaven, whereas you and your friends are going to suffer through seven years of wars, plagues, famines, and sitting in a small room while a man named "Nate" explains the advantages of time-sharing. And then you will go to hell, which as you frequent fliers know is located in Concourse D of O'Hare International Airport. See you there!

Please bear in mind, however, that just because the world is coming to an end does NOT mean that you are relieved of your civic responsibility to be alarmed about the ongoing international epidemic of exploding organisms. I regret to report that the situation has worsened drastically, to the point where we here at the National Exploding Organism Alarm Bureau (B.O.O.M.) are declaring a Condition Red Alert Mode Status Condition.

As you know if you read this column regularly but have retained some brain functionality, over the past year we have gone through an escalating series of Alert Conditions in response to documented reports of organisms exploding, as follows:

1. CONDITION YELLOW: Snail.
2. CONDITION BROWN: Pig, Cow.
3. CONDITION YUCK-O-RAMA: Human stomach, municipal toilets.
4. CONDITION POTATO: Potato.

But we are now forced to declare Condition Red in response to a recent deluge of letters from readers who want to know the proper pronunciation of "deluge." Also we have received many alarming new reports of exploding organisms. For example, each of the following items was submitted by several Alert Readers:

- The *Chicago Tribune* reported that a bison at the Atlanta Zoo "was overfed and then transported in a truck. Its stomach exploded en route, killing the animal."
- The *Baltimore Sun* reported that when a 40-ton whale carcass turned up in Baltimore harbor, sightseers were kept away because, according to a federal official, the decomposing whale "might explode."
- The *National Law Journal* reported that a man is suing the Arm & Hammer baking soda company, claiming that after he took some baking soda for indigestion, his bison exploded. No! Wait! He claims his *stomach* exploded. Sorry if we alarmed you.
- The *Virginian-Review* in Covington, Virginia, published a column entitled "Aunt Mary's Letter Box," at the top of which is a drawing of a sweet-looking elderly lady with wire-rimmed

glasses. The first letter asks how to get rid of pesky black ants. Here's Aunt Mary's answer, which I swear I am not making up: "Make a small ring of jelly and in the center place some yeast. The ants will eat through the jelly and then get to the yeast. After they eat the yeast they will explode." Ha ha! That Aunt Mary! I'd love to find out how she got rid of pesky Uncle Bill.

But this is no time for speculation. No, this is a time for courage. There's an inspirational saying that high-school football coaches use to send their young "gladiators" out onto the "battlefield" to have their knee cartilage turned into "gumbo," and it goes like this: "When the going gets tough, everybody should crawl under the dinette table of his or her choice and commence whimpering." If you have no dinette table, you should purchase one, scheduling your payments to start sometime after September 1.

Pop Goes the Weasel

This is getting scary.

I am referring to the alarming increase in the number of spontaneously exploding animals. If you read this column regularly, you definitely need to get some kind of therapy, but you also are aware that we have repeatedly presented documentary proof of explosions involving the following broad spectrum of animal life:

1. A snail.
2. A cow.

The snail, you will recall, exploded in a restaurant in Syracuse, New York, whereas the exploding cow was in New Zealand. So clearly we are looking at a Global Trend, yet our so-called "leadership" remains silent. What is it going to take? Must we wait until the president of the United States, demonstrating his concern for Agriculture, poses for a photo opportunity at a dairy farm, and suddenly the air is

filled with the unmistakable sound ("whumph") of detonating beef, and the leader of the Free World is caught in a hail of bovine organs, including up to four stomachs, traveling at up to 350 miles per hour? Wouldn't that be *great?* Ha ha!

Fine, go ahead and have your cheap sophomoric laughs. But perhaps you will not be so amused when we report the shocking information we have obtained recently concerning:

Exploding Pigs

Yes. *Pigs*. This was brought to our attention by several alert readers who sent us an article from the *Weekly World News,* a respected supermarket-checkout publication whose journalism motto is *"Licentia Vatun Veritatis"* (literally, "Leech Boy Eats Mom"). The article concerns farmers in Brazil who are upset because their pigs, as the *News* sensitively puts it, "are exploding like bombs." In case anyone might have the slightest doubt about the accuracy of this story, there is an actual photograph of a pig, which has been cut in half (we're talking about the photograph), with the word "BANG!" realistically inserted between the two halves. Case closed!

So we now have solid evidence of explosions in *three* species of animals. And that, we fear, is not all. This whole animal situation is turning out to be a lot like an iceberg, where you see only a small portion sticking up in the air, but when you look below the surface, you discover a huge quantity of exploding penguins. Because lately we have been receiving a *lot* of alarming animal-related news articles, such as the one concerning the:

Violent Sportswear-Obsessed Attack Owl

Alert reader Joyce Schwettman sent in this article, from the *Anchorage Daily News,* concerning a man named Bruce Talbot who was skiing in a park, minding his own business, when a great horned owl swooped down and, over the course of the next few minutes, relieved the increasingly alarmed Mr. Talbot of the following articles of clothing: his hat, his gloves, his coat, his vest, and finally his *shirt.* We are not making this up. The owl would get his talons into a garment, and the only way Mr. Talbot could escape was to remove the garment, and then the owl would latch on to *another* garment, and so on until the owl had assembled almost a complete ski-wear ensemble and Mr. Talbot was half-naked and skiing for his life, hoping to make it to safety before the owl developed a hankering for his pants.

The article quotes a wildlife official as saying that great horned owls "regularly" attack people. "They have very powerful feet," the official says, leading us to believe that it is just a matter of time before these creatures are employed by automobile dealerships ("No thanks really, I was just look . . . HEY! Let GO!!").

But we don't want to think about that now. Right now we want to devote all our mental energy to trying to comprehend an article from the Montgomery County, Maryland, *Journal,* alertly sent to us by C. H. Breedlove, Jr., concerning a:

Dramatic Lobster Rescue

You're going to be *sure* that we made this up, but we didn't. It seems that a Rockville, Maryland, restaurant called The House of Chinese Gourmet installed a lobster tank, which greatly upset some customers who belong to a group called the People for the Ethical Treatment of Animals, whose members apparently have (1) a deep respect for all living things and (2) a tremendous amount of spare time. They bought seven lobsters from the restaurant for $40, removed them from the tank (according to the article, a PETA member "talked softly and rubbed the lobsters to reassure them"), and then paid $200 to fly the lobsters to Portland, Maine, where they (the lobsters) were released in the ocean, where we are sure they will live happy, productive lives until they are recaptured by lobstermen, who will re-sell them to The House of Chinese Gourmet, which will re-sell them to PETA, and thus will the Great Cycle of Life continue until the lobsters become so airsick that they deliberately hurl themselves into boiling water.

Our final alarming item is an Associated Press photograph, sent in by various readers, showing an Afghan Freedom Fighter using a rocket-propelled grenade launcher—no doubt paid for with our tax dollars—to shoot at *fish*. We thought you PETA members should know.

Cheep Sex

Many, many of you have written to me asking the following question: "Dave, are there any new developments in the field of artificial falcon insemination, and could these developments help improve the American electoral process?"

I am pleased to report that the answer to both questions is "yes." I have received some very exciting information on this subject from alert reader Lance Waller, who sent me an article from the April issue of *Smithsonian* magazine concerning the World Center for Birds of Prey in Boise, Idaho. The Center is engaged in the preservation of falcons, fierce birds of prey that are named after the Ford Falcon, which holds the proud title of Slowest Car Ever Built. In certain areas of the country you can go to a stoplight and find Falcon drivers who pressed down on their accelerators in 1963 and are *still waiting* for their cars to move.

Anyway, the scientists at the Center are trying to breed falcons, sometimes via artificial insemination, which means they (the scientists) have to get hold of some falcon semen, which you cannot simply pick up in your local supermarket. (Well, OK, you CAN, but it's not fresh.)

So according to *Smithsonian* magazine, these scientists obtain the semen via a process so wondrous that you will insist I made it up, but I did not. Here, according to the article, is how it works: First, a falcon handler hand-feeds a baby male falcon, which eventually "regards its handler as another falcon." Then, when the falcon matures, the handler goes into a chamber with it and they engage in a courtship ritual, wherein they bow their heads and make cheeping sounds. "The two of them provide an amazing spectacle," states the article, "man and bird bowing and cheeping, affectionate lovers arousing each other."

Then the handler puts on—remember, I am not making this up—"a nondescript fedora with a rubber dam around the crown to catch the semen." He turns around, and the falcon "flies to the hat and, with much cheeping and fluttering of wings, copulates with it."

The magazine has an actual photograph of this, showing a man with his arms folded, wearing a facial expression that would look somber and dignified, suitable for a portrait painting of a bank president, except that the man is wearing an extremely comical hat, on top of which is this large, wildly excited bird experiencing a Climactic Moment. (The article doesn't say what happens next, but I like to think they smoke tiny cigarettes.)

Anyway, looking at this picture, I couldn't help but think about the American electoral process. You know how your top political figures traditionally demonstrate their qualifications for high government office by putting on virtually any form of cretin headwear that is handed to them? Well, think how it would be if, during the 1992 presidential campaign, some leading presidential contender was making an appearance in Iowa, and some innocent-looking Girl Scout handed him what she claimed was a special ceremonial headdress, and he put it on, and his head suddenly became a highly erotic stimulant for major birds of prey ("In a surprise campaign development that raises delicate legal issues, Rep. Dick Gephardt was carried off today by a large, cheeping flock of lust-crazed, federally protected falcons").

Wouldn't that be wonderful? Wouldn't that transform the presidential campaign from an endless droning bore into something you'd genuinely look forward to on the TV news? Oh, I know what you're thinking. You're thinking, "But what if the politicians *like* it? What if they start wearing their hats *all the time?* What if, say, the vice president starts wearing one to formal foreign funerals? Where would he get a hat small enough? Certainly these are large hurdles, but I am certain that, as a nation, we will find a way to overcome them. But not right now. Right now I have to go. Rex is chirping for me.

Death by Toothpick

Here at the Bureau of Medical Alarm, we continue to receive shocking new evidence that being human is an extremely dangerous occupation that probably should be prohibited by law.

For example, consider the alarming article sent in by alert reader Jessica Bernstein from the August 10, 1984 issue of the *Journal of the American Medical Association,* entitled "Toothpick-Related Injuries in the United States, 1979 Through 1982." This article notes with concern that although toothpicks "are long, slender, hard, sharp, and indigestible, they are rarely considered objects of potential injury and death." Yes! Death! The article reports that during the period studied, there have been thousands of toothpick-related injuries and three actual fatalities.

What gets our goat, here at the Bureau of Medical Alarm, is that these needless tragedies could be avoided if the government would simply require all toothpicks to carry this printed message:

WARNING: THE SURGEON GENERAL HAS DETERMINED THAT YOU SHOULD NOT SWALLOW THIS TOOTHPICK OR STAB YOURSELF IN THE EYEBALL WITH IT WHILE TRYING TO READ THIS WARNING.

Why hasn't this been done? When will the politicians stop knuckling under the powerful toothpick lobby, with its easy money, fast boats, and loose women? How come powerful lobbies never send loose women down here to the Bureau of Medical Alarm? These are some of the questions that were very much on our minds until we were distracted by an even more alarming article, sent in by alert reader Betsy Powers, from the July 5, 1980 issue of the *British Medical Journal.* Unfortunately we cannot be too specific about this article, because this is a family newspaper (it has a wife newspaper and two little baby newspapers at home). All we can say is that the article involves an upsetting development that can occur when a well-known male bodily part gets too close to a working vacuum cleaner. This seems to be a fairly common occurrence, at least in Britain. The article contains the following quotations, which we swear we are not making up, although for reasons of tastefulness, the bodily part will be referred to as "Morton" (not its real name):

"Case 1—A 60-year-old man said that he was changing the plug of his Hoover Dustette vacuum cleaner in the nude while his wife was out shopping. It 'turned itself on' and caught his Morton. . . ."

"Case 2—A 65-year-old railway signalman was in his signal box when he bent down to pick up his tools and caught his Morton in a Hoover Dustette, 'which happened to be switched on.' "

These quotations definitely touched a nerve here at the Bureau of Medical Alarm. Clearly males need to be more careful, especially if they get naked anywhere near a Hoover Dustette, which is apparently auditioning for a role as a major appliance in *Fatal Attraction II.*

What you are no doubt saying to yourself now is, "Hmmmm, I wonder if there have been any similar incidents involving lobsters." We regret to report that the answer is yes, as we learned from an article alertly sent in by Janice Hill (notice that it is women who are sending these articles in).

This article concerns a man who attempted to steal a lobster from a Boston fish market by stuffing it (the lobster) down the front of his pants. The lobster had been wearing those rubber-band handcuffs, but apparently they slipped off, and the lobster, with revenge on its tiny mind, angrily grasped hold of the first thing it found, and we will not go into what happened next, except to say that, if you are a guy, it makes a toothpick to the eyeball sound like a day at the Magic Kingdom.

We actually have MORE alarming medical items here, including a really good one about a moth that flew into a noted Denver attorney's ear canal and refused to come out voluntarily. But we're running out of space, so we'll just close with this Health Reminder: Don't smoke or drink. Or eat. Or go outside. Or breathe. And men: If you MUST change a major-appliance plug in the nude, PLEASE wear a condom.

What Has Four Legs and Flies

People often say to me, "Dave, when you say you're not making something up, does that mean you're really and truly not making it up?" And the answer is yes. Meaning no, I am not making it up. I mention this so you'll believe me when I say that I'm not making up today's topic, which is: the Head-Smashed-In Buffalo Jump.

The Head-Smashed-In Buffalo Jump is a historical site and tourist attraction in Alberta, Canada. Canada, as you know, is a major important nation boasting a sophisticated, cosmopolitan culture that was tragically destroyed last week by beavers.

Ha ha! Don't mind me. I like to toss out little "zingers" about Canada from time to time because I enjoy getting mounds of letters from irate Canadians who are Sick and Tired of Americans belittling Canada and who often include brochures full of impressive Canadian Facts such as that Canada is the world's largest producer of magnesium dentures as well as the original home of Michael J. Fox, Big Bird, Plato, etc.

The thing is, I like Canada. It's clean, and it makes good beer. Also it has a spirit of general social cooperation that you find lacking in the States, a good example being the metric system. You may recall that a while back we were all supposed to convert to the metric system from our current system of measurement, which is technically known as the "correct" or "real" system. The metric conversion was supposed to result in major economic benefits deriving from the fact that you, the consumer, would suddenly have no idea how the hell much anything cost. Take coleslaw. Under the current system, coleslaw is sold in easily understood units of measurement called "containers," as in "Gimme one of them containers of coleslaw if it's fresh." In a metric supermarket, however, the deli person would say, "How much do you want? A kilometer? A hectare? Hurry up! My break starts in five liters!" You'd get all confused and wind up buying enough coleslaw to fill a wading pool, and the economy would prosper.

So the metric conversion was clearly a good idea, and when the government started putting up metric highway signs (SPEED LIMIT 173 CENTIPEDES) Americans warmly responded by shooting them down. Thus the metric system did not really catch on in the States, unless you count the increasing popularity of the nine-millimeter bullet.

Meanwhile, the Canadians, being cooperative, quietly went ahead and actually converted. I know this because I was on a Canadian radio program once, and the host announced that the temperature was "8." This was obviously a lie, so I asked him about it, and he confided, off the air, that the real temperature, as far as he knew, was around 40. But then his engineer said he thought it was more like 50, and soon other radio personnel were chiming in with various other interpretations of "8," and I was struck by the fact that these people had cheerfully accepted, in the spirit of cooperation, a system wherein *nobody really knew what the temperature was.* (The correct mathematical answer is: chilly.)

The point I am making is that Canada is a fascinating and mysterious country, which is why we should not be surprised to learn that it is the location of the Head-Smashed-In Buffalo Jump historical site and tourist attraction. I found out about this from an extremely alert reader named Sandy LaFave, who sent me an article from the *Fort McLeod Tourist Greeter* that explains the whole buffalo-jump concept.

It seems that many moons ago (in metric, 14.6 megamoons) North America was occupied by large and fortunately very stupid herds of buffalo. Certain Native American tribes used to obtain their food by disguising themselves in buffalo skins and going from tepee to tepee shouting "Trick or Treat!"

No, seriously, according to the *Fort McLeod Tourist Greeter,* they disguised themselves so they could lure a buffalo herd closer and closer to a cliff, then stampede it over the edge. That's where the "Buffalo Jump" part of the name comes from. The "Head-Smashed-In" part comes from a native legend, which holds that one time a young brave (probable tribal name: "Not Nuclear Physicist") decided to watch the hunt while standing *under* the cliff. According to the *Tourist Greeter,* he "watched the buffalo topple in front of him like a mighty waterfall. . . . When it was over and the natives were butchering the animals, they found him under the pile of dead buffalo with his head smashed in."

Even thousands of years later, it is difficult to ponder this tragedy without choking back large, moist snorts of anguish. But some good has come of

it. The Head-Smashed-In Buffalo Jump has been declared a World Heritage Site ("as are the pyramids in Egypt and the Taj Mahal in India," notes the *Tourist Greeter*). The Alberta government has constructed an interpretive centre (note metric spelling) where activities are held. "There's always something to see and do at the Head-Smashed-In Buffalo Jump Interpretive Centre and this summer is no exception," states an official schedule. I have called the centre, and when they answer the phone, they say, very politely—I absolutely swear this is true—"Head-Smashed-In, may I help you?"

And the scary part is, I think maybe they *can*.

Flying Fish

We certainly do not wish to cause widespread panic, but we are hereby warning the public to be on the lookout for falling trout.

We base this warning on an alarming article from the *Bangor Daily News,* sent in by alert reader Jane Heart, headlined TORPEDO APPROACH USED TO STOCK LAKES WITH TROUT. According to the article, the Maine Department of Inland Fisheries is restocking lakes by dropping trout from airplanes. A hatchery official notes that the trout, which weigh about a pound each, drop from 100 to 150 feet "like hundreds of little torpedoes."

This article should cause extreme concern on the part of anyone who is familiar with gravity, which was discovered in 1684 by Sir Isaac Newton, who was sitting under a tree when an apple landed on his head, killing him instantly. A one-pound trout would be even worse. According to our calculations, if you dropped the trout from 150 feet, it would reach a speed of . . . let's see, 150 feet times 32 feet per second, at two pints to the liter, minus the radius of the hypotenuse, comes to . . . *a high rate of speed.* Anybody who has ever seen a photograph showing the kind of damage that a trout traveling that fast can inflict on the human skull knows that such photographs are very valuable. I paid $20 for mine.

And yet here we see Maine, which we usually think of as a quiet, responsible state known primarily for sleet, deliberately causing potentially lethal fish to hurtle at high velocities toward Earth, residence of many members of the public.

Oh, I realize the program is not *designed* to harm the public. But even highly trained pilots are not perfect. Consider the three pilots who were recently convicted of flying drunk on a commercial flight, during which they aroused suspicion by instructing the passengers to fasten their seat belts be-

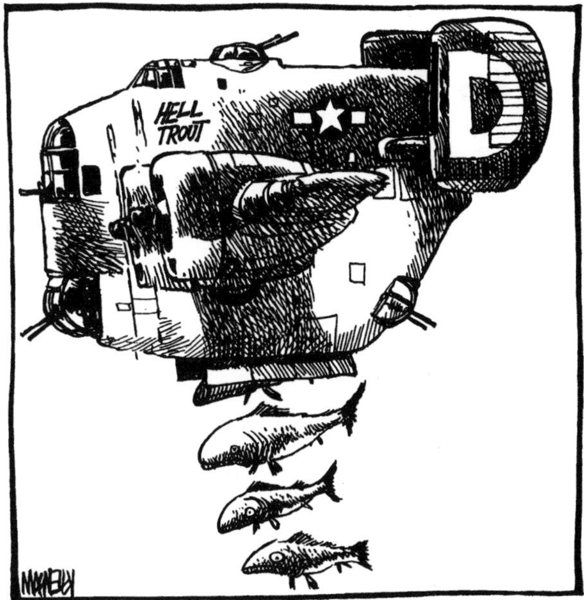

cause of "snakes in the engine." I am not accusing the Maine Department of Inland Fisheries of using drunk pilots, but if one of them *did* have a few, and happened to fly over, say, a Shriners convention while carrying a full load of trout, the temptation to let those babies go would be irresistible. To us, anyway.

What is especially alarming is that this is not the first time that government agencies have dropped potentially lethal creatures from planes. An even scarier example is discussed in an article in the October 1990 issue of *Air Force* magazine, which was alertly sent to us by John Breen. The article, by C. V. Glines, is entitled "The Bat Bombers," and we urge you to read the whole thing yourself, because otherwise you are not going to believe us.

In brief, here's what the article says:

In December 1941, shortly after Pearl Harbor, a Pennsylvania dental surgeon named Lytle S. Adams thought of a way that the United States could fight back against Japan. It will come as no surprise to anyone who has undergone dental surgery that the idea he came up with was: attaching incendiary bombs to bats and dropping them out of airplanes. The idea was that the bats would fly into enemy buildings, and the bombs would go off and start fires, and Japan would surrender.

So Dr. Adams sent his idea to the White House, which laughed so hard that it got a stomachache.

No! That's what you'd *expect* to happen, but instead the White House sent the idea to the U.S. Army, which, being the U.S. Army, launched a nationwide research effort to determine the best kind of bat to attach a bomb to. By 1943 the research team had decided on the free-tailed bat, which "could fly fairly well with a one-ounce bomb." Thousands of these bats were collected and—remember, we are not making any of this up—placed in ice-cube trays, which were then refrigerated to force the bats to hibernate so bombs could be attached to them. On May 23, 1943, a day that every schoolchild should be forced to memorize, five groups of test bats, equipped with dummy bombs, were dropped from a B-25 bomber flying at 5,000 feet. Here, in the dramatic words of the article, is what happened next:

"Most of the bats, not fully recovered from hibernation, did not fly and died on impact."

Researchers continued to have problems with bats failing to show the "can-do" attitude you want in your night-flying combat mammal. Also there was an incident wherein "some bats escaped with live incendiaries aboard and set fire to a hangar and a general's car."

At this point the Army, possibly sensing that the project was a disaster, turned it over to the Navy. Really. "In October 1943, the Navy leased four caves in Texas and assigned Marines to guard them," states the article. The last thing you want, in wartime, is for enemy agents to get hold of your bats.

The bat project was finally canceled in 1944, having cost around $2 million, which is a bargain when you consider what we pay for entertainment today.

But our point is, the government has a track record of dropping animals out of airplanes, and there is no reason to believe that this has stopped. Once the government gets hold of a truly bad idea, it tends to cling to it. For all we know, the Defense Department is testing bigger animals, capable of carrying heavier payloads. We could have a situation where, because of an unexpected wind shift, thousands of semi-frozen, parachute-wearing musk oxen come drifting down into a major population center and start lumbering confusedly around with high explosives on their backs. We definitely should have some kind of contingency plan for stopping them. Our best weapon is probably trout.

Amphibious Assault

You can imagine how alarmed I was when I found out that I had been swimming in the same waters as the Giant Perverted Turtle. Unless of course you have not yet heard about the Giant Perverted Turtle, in which case please be advised that, until we get this thing cleared up, you should avoid submerging yourself in any body of water unless it has a drain and a soap dish.

I found out about this story when numerous alert readers sent me an article from the *Reporter,* a newspaper published in the Florida Keys, headlined TURTLE ATTACK IS REPORTED. Immediately I interrupted my regular journalism routine of staring fixedly at individual pieces of ceiling dirt, because it just so happens that my major hobby, aside from turning off lights and appliances that have been turned on days earlier by my son, is scuba diving off the Florida Keys. You go out to the reef, bouncing over the waves, then you dive in and admire the incredible variety of marine life that is attracted by other diving enthusiasts barfing over the side of the charter boat.

No, really, you see some fascinating things down there. I once got to see what fishing looks like from the fish end. There, dangling in the current, was a largish hook, to which had been attached a disgusting thing such as you might be served in a sushi restaurant. Staring at this thing was a small formal gathering of filefish, which is a fish with pursed lips and a bulging forehead that make it look very serious, as though it should be carrying a little briefcase and doing the other fishes' tax returns. As the other filefish watched, the first one would swim forward, take the sushi in its mouth, spit it out immediately, then swim to the end of the line. Then the next fish would repeat this procedure, and the next, and so on ("Yuck! You try it, Norm!" "OK! Yuck! You try it, Walter!" "OK! Yuck! You try . . ."). If I'd had a waterproof pen and paper with me, I'd have stuck a little note on the hook saying, "THEY DON'T LIKE IT."

This experience gave me an idea. Remember when President Bush was taking his biweekly vacation up in Kenneth E. Bunkport IV, Maine, and he failed to catch any fish, day after day, until it became a national news story of greater urgency than Lebanon, and the whole federal government apparatus seemed to shudder to a halt while the Leader of the Free World, the man most responsible for dealing with pressing and increasingly complex national and international issues, was off somewhere trying to outwit an organism with a brain the size of a hydrogen atom? Well my idea is, next time we have this problem, we send some U.S. Naval frogpersons down there to attach a fish manually to the presidential hook. These would have to be trusted frogpersons, not pranksters, because America would definitely be a laughingstock among nations if the president were to engage in a fierce three-hour angling struggle and finally, triumphantly, haul out, say, a sheep.

But before we implement this program, we need to do something about the Giant Perverted Turtle. According to the *Reporter* article, written by outdoor writer Bob T. Epstein, there's a very aggressive male 300-pound loggerhead turtle that lurks in the water under one of the bridges in the Florida Keys and—I am not making this up—keeps trying, very forcefully, to *mate with human divers.* What is worse, Epstein says, in at least one case the turtle actually *succeeded.* I'm not going to give details of this occurrence in a family newspaper, except to say that if we ever decide we need some form of punishment harsher than the death penalty, this would be a strong candidate.

JUDGE: I sentence the defendant to be put in the lagoon with Bart.

DEFENDANT: NO! NOT THE TURTLE!

I called up one of the divers who'd reportedly been attacked, a real estate agent named Bruce Gernon, who confirmed the whole thing, but asked me to stress that he successfully fought the turtle off. So let the record show that the turtle did not get to first base with Mr. Gernon. But clearly we have a serious problem here. Bob Epstein told me that, since his story appeared, he has been contacted almost daily by people who have been molested by large sea creatures but never told anybody. "This is a sensitive area," Epstein said. "People are reluctant to talk about that aspect of their relationships with turtles or seals or dolphins or walruses."

Did you hear that? *Walruses.*

(**DEFENDANT:** NOOOOO!!)

Fortunately this alarming story is getting attention from leading science authorities: Epstein told me he had been contacted by both the Letterman and Sajak shows. So action is being taken, and not a moment too soon, either, because—this appears to be a related story—several alert readers have sent me an Associated Press article stating that two marine biologists in a submarine 690 feet deep, far off the coast of Alaska, discovered, lying on the ocean floor: a cow. I am still not making this up. Needless to say the cow was deceased. God alone knows how it got there. One obvious possibility is prankster frogpersons, but we cannot rule out the possibility that the cow was abducted by lust-crazed walruses. Fortunately the biologists were able to make a videotape, starring Rob Lowe, so we should have some answers soon. Until then, I'm not going to even take a shower. Not that this is anything *new*.

Children May Be Hazardous to Your Health

It's time for Alarming Medical News Items, the popular feature that can strike at any time without warning symptoms. For your protection, this column undergoes a rigorous fact-checking procedure under which, before we will print an item, it must first be delivered to us by the United States Postal Service. Don't bother to thank us: We aren't listening.

Speaking of which, our first alarming item concerns the recently discovered:

Ear Problem From Hell

We learned about this thanks to alert reader Diane Eicher, who sent in an American Medical Association newsletter containing an article about a North Carolina man who went to his doctor complaining of a "full sensation" in one ear, accompanied by a hearing loss. The doctor checked it out, and found that the man's ear canal was blocked by—we are not making this up—a plug of hardened Super Glue.

Now some of you are scratching your heads and wondering, "How does a person with an IQ higher than pastry get Super Glue in his EAR and not know it?" But you parents out there are no doubt nodding your heads and saying: "It would not surprise me to learn that this man has a three-year-old son."

And, of course, you're right. according to the AMA newsletter, the son "squirted the glue into the father's left ear while the man was sleeping." Fortunately surgeons were able to unclog the man's ear, but as medical consumers we can prevent this kind of near-tragedy by remembering to take these safety precautions:

1. Never keep three-year-old children around the house.
2. If you do, never sleep.

Also: You older children should remember that Super Glue is a serious household repair substance and NOT a toy to be used in such pranks as applying it to the toilet seats in the Faculty Men's Room, taking care to first prepare the surface by wiping it clean of oil and dirt.

Our next item was brought to our attention by Debbie and Lindsey Mackey, who alerted us to an article in the British medical journal the *Lancet* with the title:

"Exploding Head Syndrome"

Quite frankly we were disappointed by this syndrome. We naturally assumed, from the title, that it would involve the actual explosion of a person's head, ideally Barry Manilow's in concert. But it turns out to be just this weenie syndrome where you wake up in the middle of the night having "a violent sensation of explosion in the head." Big deal. We get that all the time, but you don't see us whining to the *Lancet*. You see us making a mental note to drink gin from smaller containers.

But not right now. Right now we want to tell you about the exciting new:

Advances in B.O. Measurement

We found out about this through alert readers James McNab and Shelley Owens, who sent us an article from the *Journal of the American Society for Heating, Refrigeration and Air-Conditioning Engineers* written by a man named—we are still not making this up—"P. Ole Fanger." Mr. Fanger, who hails from Denmark, has done a LOT of research in the field of measuring exactly how much a given human being tends to stink up a given room, and he has come up with a unit of air pollution called the "olf" ("from the Latin *olfactus*, or olfactory sense"). To quote the article: "One olf is the emission rate of air pollutants (bioeffluents) from a standard person (Figure 1)."

We sincerely wish that we could show you Figure 1, which is a truly wonderful drawing of a standard person with dozens of little Smell Arrows shooting out of his body. Looking at this drawing reminded us of one of the highlights of our life, which is the time that we were with two friends of ours, Randall and George, in a bar that was empty except for two women at the far end of the room, and George, after maybe 17 Miller High Lifes, decided to Make a Move, which was pretty funny because George, even on those occasions when he has total control over his dentures, is not exactly Paul Newman, or even Mr. Ed.

But he went lunging over there and, with all the subtlety of Hurricane Gilbert, attempted to strike up a conversation, which the two women were clearly not interested in. So they were quiet, and after a while George got quiet, and we were listening quietly, so the whole bar was very quiet when George had an unfortunate bodily event. It's the kind of event that can happen to anybody, except maybe Margaret Thatcher, but it rarely happens with the magnitude that it happened to George. You talk about Hurricane Gilbert. Of course, in those days we did not have modern measurement techniques, but we're sure that this event was completely off the scale on the Olf Meter. We're only sorry that we didn't get to see the two women virtually sprint from the bar, because we were lying flat on the floor laughing so hard that we thought we were going to suffer a heart attack, which every American should know the Six Warning Signs of.

TODAY'S MEDICAL TIP: Never undergo any kind of major surgery without first making an appointment.

Attack of the Cartoon Animal Heads

It's a Sunday evening, and we're driving home from Orlando, where we have taken our son, Robby, and his friend, Erik, for a special birthday weekend of fantasy and fun and hurling money at random around the Official Walt "You Will Have Fun" Disney Magical World of Theme Kingdoms and Resort Complex.

We're taking what the American Automobile Association has designated as the "scenic route" back to Miami, through south-central Florida, a region that used to cater primarily to frogs but that has in recent years sprouted dozens of "adult" (which we used to call "retired person") communities with names like Belle Harbour Vista Manour Downes Estates Centre West II, consisting of what we used to call "trailers," and later we called "mobile homes," and still later we called "manufactured houses." I don't know what we call them now. Probably something like "countrie townehome villas," as in "Hey, Ed! Lester's cow knocked over your countrie townehome villa again!"

We've been driving for three, maybe eight hours. In the backseat, the boys have finished writing on their forearms with Official Walt Disney World souvenir felt-tipped markers, and are now passing the time with a little game they have invented with their soaring childhood imaginations: spitting on each other.

Ptooo, goes Robby.

Ptooo, goes Erik.

Ptooo, goes Robby.

This little game of saliva tennis is clearly audible in the front seat, but Beth and I, the Parental Authority Figures, say nothing. We are both thinking the same thing: *At least they are taking turns.* That is how low we have sunk on this car trip. We frankly would not mind if they were back there shooting a high-

powered rifle out the window, as long as they shared it. But, of course, they wouldn't.

"No fair!" Robby would shout. "Erik got three shots and I only got two but he won't give me back the rifle!" And Erik would say, "But Robby hit the farmer and I didn't hit anybody!" And Robby would say, "You did too! You hit the policeman!" And Erik would say, "Only his hat!" And finally one of us Authority Figures would whirl around and snap, "If you can't share the rifle, we're going to take it away and and then NOBODY WILL BE ABLE TO SHOOT ANYBODY."

We always get irritable like this when we return to harsh reality after a couple of days in Walt "You Are Having Some Fun Now, Yes?" Disney Resort and World and Compound, a place where your dreams really do come true, if you dream about having people wearing enormous cartoon-animal heads come around to your restaurant table and act whimsical and refuse to go away until you laugh with delight. This happens to you constantly at Disney World. I think it's part of a corporate discipline program for Disney executives. ("Johnson, your department is over budget again. You know what that means." "No! Please!" "Yes! *Into the Goofy suit!")*

We saw a lot of Goofy. Every time we sat down to eat, there he would be, acting whimsical. It got so that Robby and Erik, busily playing with their action figures, hardly even noticed him.

"Look, boys!" we would say, food dribbling down our chins. "Here comes Goofy! Again!"

Robby, not even looking up, would thrust one of his figures toward Erik and say: "This guy sends out a laser beam that can MELT YOUR EYEBALLS."

"Oh yeah?" Erik would say. "Well this guy makes a noise like, mmmmmmPAAAAAH!, that goes through your ears and EXPLODES YOUR WHOLE HEAD."

Meanwhile, right behind them, encased in a heavy costume, this poor person, probably the executive vice president for group sales, would be writhing around, trying desperately to fulfill the boys' innocent childhood fantasies. Finally we grown-ups would have to let him off the hook. "Ha ha, Goofy!" we would say, speaking directly into the saltshaker, which is where we figured the microphone had been hidden by the Walt Disney World Whimsy Police. "You sure are causing us to laugh with delight!"

Don't get me wrong. I like Disney World. The rest rooms are clean enough for neurosurgery, and the employees say things like "Howdy, folks!" and actually seem to mean it. You wonder: Where do they get these people? My guess: 1952. I think old Walt realized, way back then, that there would eventually be a shortage of cheerful people, so he put all the residents of southwestern Nebraska into a giant freezer with a huge picture of Jiminy Cricket on the outside, and the corporation has been thawing them out as needed ever since.

Whatever the secret is, it works, and I urge you all to visit Disney World several dozen times. Afterward, I recommend that you drive down to Miami on the "scenic route," although if you notice two boys, ages 6 and 7, standing on the side of the road spitting at each other, my advice is not to pick them up.

Don't Box Me In

We're moving again. We're not going far: Maybe two miles, as the heat-seeking radar-equipped South Florida Stealth Mosquito flies. It's hard to explain why we're doing this. Call it a crazy whim. We just woke up one morning and said, "I know! Let's put everything we own into boxes!"

And that's what we're doing. The giant cardboard mines of Peru are working overtime to meet our box needs, because we have a LOT of stuff that we need to take, including many precious heirlooms such as our calculator in which all the keys work perfectly except the "4," and our complete, mint-condition set of 1978 VISA statements (try replacing THOSE at today's prices). Stuffwise, we are not a lean operation. We're the kind of people who, if we were deciding what absolute minimum essential items we'd need to carry in our backpacks for the final, treacherous ascent to the summit of Mount Everest, would take along these aquarium filters, just in case.

The humorous part is, we never finished *unpacking* from when we moved in here. The other day I watched my wife, Beth, as she opened a box that has been sitting around, unopened, since our last move, removed the contents, and carefully packed them, every last one, into a *new* box. I grant you that these are not the actions of a sane person, but you wouldn't be sane, either, if you'd spent the last few weeks doing what Beth has been doing, namely trying to get hold of workmen. The workmen are playing an elaborate prank wherein they come to our house and do a tiny smattering of work and then run off and hide in the Everglades for days at a time, breathing through hollow reeds and refusing to return Beth's phone calls. Every now and then one of them will come sneaking into our kitchen, frogs clinging to his hair, and shout, "nyah nyah nyah" at her, then sprint off before she can hurdle the boxes and grab him.

We need the workmen because we're trying to make our current house look domestic so that somebody will want to buy it. We're making a lot of simple, obvious improvements that never would have occurred to us to make while we actually lived here, because, tragically, we both happen to be domestically impaired. If we were birds, our nest would consist of a single twig with the eggs attached via Scotch tape. We lived for 11 years in a house with a light fixture that we both agreed was less attractive than if we had simply suspended a urinal from the ceiling. But of course we never did anything about it until we moved, just as in our current house we waited until now to clear out the giant tropical spiders who live next to the front door, subsisting on Federal Express men; or to replace the electrical ceiling-fan switch that has three positions, "Low," "Medium," and "Burn Down House"; or to eliminate the violently pink carpet that made our bedroom look as though an Exxon tanker had run around there and spilled millions of gallons of Pepto-Bismol. Yes, we have plenty to do, and we're doing everything we can to attract workmen, including tying a string around a small bundle of money and placing it on the lawn as bait. When a workman approaches, we tug it slowly toward the house, and when he gets close enough we slam a box over him.

During this difficult time we have received a large mound of assistance from our two dogs. Using their keen, nearly asphalt-level intelligence, they have sensed that something important is happening, and have decided that their vital contribution will be to kill anybody who comes near our house. This means they have to spend a lot of time shut away in my office, barking. They've reached the point where they automatically start barking as soon as we shut them in there, whether or not there's anybody to bark at yet. It's their job, barking in my office. Somebody has to do it! They produce approximately one bark apiece every two seconds, so if I leave them in there for, say, 45 minutes, then open the door, I get knocked several feet backward by the escaping force of 2,700 accumulated barks.

Sometimes prospective buyers come to our house to look at it, and we have to go hide in the Everglades with the workmen. Buyers don't want you hanging around when they look at your house, because they feel free to make frank observations such as, "What are these? *Toenails?*" They would make this remark in my office, which contains many large unexplored toenail deposits that have built up over the years because I'm a professional writer, which means I spend as many as five hours a day engaged in foot maintenance while waiting for professional sentences to appear in my brain. But the

rest of the house is looking real nice, thanks to Beth. In fact, she's starting to make me nervous: Yesterday she put some magazines on a table *in a fan arrangement.* This is of course one of the early symptoms of the dread June Cleaver Disease, which ultimately leads to the appearance, in your bathroom, of soap shaped like fruit. So I'm hoping we sell this house soon. Make us an offer. We're motivated. We're reasonable. We're accommodating. You get the dogs.

Un Nintended Benefits

OK, I bought my child a Nintendo video-game system. I realize I should not admit this. I realize the Child Psychology Police may arrest me for getting my child a mindless addictive antisocial electronic device instead of a constructive old-fashioned educational toy such as an Erector Set. Well let me tell you something: All my childhood friends had Erector Sets, and although I am not proud of this, I happen to know for a fact that, in addition to the recommended educational projects such as the Truck, the Crane, and the Carousel, it was possible to build the Bug Pulper, the Worm Extender, and the Gears of Pain.

And speaking of pain, you have no idea how hard my son made my life before I caved in and bought Nintendo. The technique he used was Power Wistfulness. Remember the old comic strip "Dondi," starring the little syndicated orphan boy who always looked heartbreakingly sad and orphanous and never got adopted, possibly because he had eye sockets the size of manhole covers? Well, my son looked like that. He'd start first thing in the morning, standing around with Dondi-like eyes, emitting armor-piercing wistfulness rays and sighing over the fact that he was the only child outside of the Third World who didn't have Nintendo. Pretty soon I'd be weeping all over my toast, thinking how *tragic* it was —my own son, an orphan—until finally I just had to go to the Toys "Я" Approximately a Third of the Gross National Product store, because after all we're talking about a child's happiness here, and you can't put a price tag on . . . What? It cost HOW MUCH? What does it DO for that kind of money? Penetrate Soviet airspace?

No, really, it's worth every penny. I know you've probably read a lot of articles by Leading Child Psychologists (defined as "people whose children probably wet the bed through graduate school")

telling you why Nintendo is a bad thing, so let me discuss some of the benefits:

Benefit No. 1—Nintendo enables the child to develop a sense of self-worth by mastering a complex, demanding task that makes his father look like a total goober.

The typical Nintendo game involves controlling a little man who runs around the screen trying to stay alive while numerous powerful and inexplicably hostile forces try to kill him; in other words, it's exactly like real life. When I play, the little man becomes highly suicidal. If he can't locate a hostile force to get killed by, he will deliberately swallow the contents of a little electronic Valium bottle. So all my games end instantly, whereas my son can keep the little man alive through several presidential administrations. He is always trying to cheer me up by saying "Good try, Dad!" in the same sincerely patronizing voice that I once used to praise him for not getting peas in his hair. What is worse, he gives me Helpful Nintendo Hints that are far too complex for the adult mind to comprehend. Here's a verbatim example: "OK, there's Ganon and miniature Ganon and there's these things like jelly beans and the miniature Ganon is more powerfuller, because when you touch him the flying eagles come down and the octopus shoots red rocks and the swamp takes longer."

And the hell of it is, I know he's *right.*

Benefit No. 2—Nintendo strengthens the community.

One evening I got an emergency telephone call from our next-door neighbor, Linda, who said, her voice breathless with urgency: "Is Robby there? Because we just got Gunsmoke [a Nintendo game] and we can't get past the horse." Of course I notified Robby immediately. "It's the Liebmans," I said. "They just got Gunsmoke, and they can't get past the horse." He was out the door in seconds, striding across the yard, a Man on a Mission. Of course he got them past the horse. He can get his man all the way to the bazooka. *My* man dies during the opening credits.

Benefit No. 3—When a child is playing Nintendo, the child can't watch regular television.

Recently on the local news, one relentlessly personable anchorperson was telling us about the murder at a Pizza Hut, and when she was done, the other relentlessly personable anchorperson got a frowny look on his face, shook his head sadly, and said—I am not making this quotation up—"A senseless tragedy, and one that I am sure was unforeseen by the victims involved."

I don't want my child exposed to this.

Benefit No. 4—A child who is playing Nintendo is a child who is probably not burping as loud as he can.

I mention this only so I can relate the following true exchange I witnessed recently between a mother and her eight-year-old son:

SON: Burp. Burp. Burp. Burp. Bu . . .
MOTHER: Stop burping!
SON: But, Mom, it's my *hobby*.

So, Mr. and Ms. Child Psychologist, don't try to tell me that Nintendo is so terrible, OK? Don't tell me it makes children detached and aggressive and antisocial. In fact don't tell me anything. Not while the octopus is shooting these rocks.

Licking the Drug Problem

What with the recent unsettling developments on the world political scene, particularly in the Middle East, I imagine that most of you are eager for a report on our yard.

We've moved to a new yard, which contains an alarming amount of nature. And I'm not talking about the friendly kind of yard nature that you get in, for example, Ohio ("The Buckeye State"), such as shrubbery and cute little furry baby buckeyes scampering around. I'm talking about the kind of mutant terroristic nature we get here in Florida ("The Assault Roach State"). For example, we have a kind of toad down here that, if you lick it, can kill you.

Now you're saying to yourself, "Yes, but who, aside from Geraldo Rivera seeking improved ratings, would lick a toad?" The answer is: More and more people. According to news articles that alert readers keep sending me, there's a brand of toad (not the kind here in Florida) that secretes a hallucinogenic

substance when it gets excited, and licking this toad has become a fad in certain circles. Which raises a couple of questions in my mind, such as: Does this occur in social settings? Do you have a group of sophisticated people sitting around a dinner table, finishing their coffee, and one of them reaches suavely into his jacket pocket, pulls out this thing that looks like a giant wart with eyeballs, and then, lowering his voice suggestively, says, "Anybody want to do some *toad?*" Also, how do they get the toad excited? Show it movies? Give it a tiny marital aid? Also, will Free Enterprise try to cash in on this? Will Anheuser-Busch come out with a TV commercial wherein some rugged-looking workmen, exhausted from a hard day of not showing up at people's houses, relax by taking some man-sized slurps off a Toad Lite?

Unfortunately I can't answer these questions, because I'm busy worrying about being killed by our mango tree. Our new yard has a mango tree, which I bet sounds like exotic fun to those of you who live in normal climates, right? Just think of it! All the mangoes you need, right in your own yard!

The problem is that, mangowise, you don't need a whole lot. You take one bite, and that takes care of your mango needs until at least the next presidential administration. But the mangoes keep coming. They're a lot like zucchini, which erupts out of the ground far faster than you could eat it even if you liked it, which nobody does, so you start lugging hundreds of pounds of zucchini to your office in steel-reinforced shopping bags, hoping your co-workers will be stupid enough to take some home, except of course they're lugging in their zucchini, all summer long, tons of it coming in, until the entire office building collapses in a twisted tangle of girders and telephone message slips and zucchini pulp, out of which new vines start to spring immediately.

Mangoes are even worse, because (a) they grow on trees, and (b) they're about the size of a ladies' bowling ball, only denser. They're the kind of fruit that would be designed by the Defense Department. They hang way up in our tree, monitoring the yard and communicating with each other via photosynthesis, and whenever they see me approaching they fire off a Warning Mango, sending one of their number thundering to Earth, cratering our lawn and alarming seismologists as far away as Texas ("The Silly Hat State"). Even on the ground, the mango remains deadly, because it immediately rots and becomes infested with evil little flies, and if you try to kick it off the lawn, it explodes, a mango grenade, covering your body with a repulsive substance known to botanists as "mango poop" that stays on your sneakers forever, so that when you go out in public, your feet are obscured by a cloud of flies, and the Florida natives snicker and say to each other, "Look! That idiot kicked a mango!"

So I keep a wary eye on the mango tree at all times, which means I am in constant danger of falling into the Scum Vat. This was originally intended to be a small decorative pool with maybe a couple of cute little goldfish in it, but at some point a gang of aggressive meat-eating algae took over. If you tried to put some goldfish in there, you'd never get close. A tentacle of algae would come swooping up and grab them out of your hand, and then you'd hear an algae burp. The only thing that can survive in there is the Giant Arguing Frogs. We've never actually seen them, but we hear them at night, when we're trying to sleep. They have a microphone hooked up to a 50,000-watt amplifier, and all night long they broadcast the following conversation:

FROG ONE: BWAAARRRRPPPP.
FROG TWO (disagreeing): BWAAARRRRPPPP.

You can tell they're never going to work it out. Some nights, lying in bed and listening to them, I've thought about going out there to mediate, but of course the algae would get me. You'd have to be some kind of dumb mango kicker to pull a stunt like that. Better safe than sorry, that's my motto, which is why I'd like to remind all my readers, especially you impressionable young people, that if you *must* lick a toad, make sure it's wearing a condom. Thank you.

A Brush with Gardening

It will probably come as no surprise to you that I got the idea of painting my lawn from an agency of the federal government.

When I say "painting my lawn," I don't mean my whole lawn. I just mean this one circular spot that suddenly, mysteriously turned brown, as though it had been visited by a small UFO or a large dog. I ignored the spot at first, but it started to grow, and I realized that it was similar to international communism: If you let it get a toehold in, say, Nicaragua, it will start to spread to the other strategic nations down there such as El Labrador and Costa "Ricky" Ricardo, and the next thing you know your entire lawn is brown.

So I was wondering what to do, when fortunately I received a letter from an alert reader named Dick Howard, who enclosed a news article from the *Roanoke* (Virginia) *Times and World News* about some National Forest Service rangers who painted a group of federal rocks to make them look more natural. I am not making this up. It happened in the Jefferson National Forest, where the Forest Service had built a mountainside road that was designed, according to the article, "to blend in with the environment." It had a darkish color scheme, because, as you campers know, the environment consists primarily of dirt.

Unfortunately, there was an unscheduled flood, which exposed some large tacky white quartz rocks that frankly did NOT fit in with the natural road design. You can imagine how this offended the fashion sensibilities of the Forest Service personnel, who decided to do exactly what you would do if you were in charge of a national forest and had accidentally consumed a massive overdose of prescription medication: Paint the rocks. They did a few tests to select just the color they wanted, then they spent two days spraying paint on the rocks, and before you could say "massive federal budget deficit," the hillside looked just the way God would have created it if He had received the benefits of Forest Service training.

As a professional journalist, I have always been fascinated by people who appear to have even more spare time than I do, so I called up one of the men involved in the rock-painting, District Ranger Bob Boardwine, who turned out to be a friendly individual. He told me that the rangers had taken a fair amount of ribbing over the rock-painting, but as far as he was concerned the project had come out real nice. I told him I was thinking about painting the brown spot on my lawn, and he gave me some fashion tips. "Make sure you use a dark green," he said. "When we painted the rocks, we went into it thinking in terms of a moss green and a light brown, but they weren't dark enough."

Thus advised, I asked my eight-year-old son if he wanted to help me paint the lawn, but he and his friend Erik were deeply involved in an urgent Nintendo game that is not expected to be completed during my lifetime. Fortunately Erik's six-year-old brother, Tyson, was able to make some room in his schedule, so we got my son's watercolor set and went out to paint the brown spot. We were working on a blade-by-blade basis, and after a while we got tired of dark green, so at Tyson's suggestion we switched over to purple, then red, then orange, and when we were done we had converted what had been a dull and unattractive area of the lawn into an area that looked as though somebody had just thrown up several pounds of semi-digested jelly beans. Tyson and I were standing there admiring our work when—this really happened—up drove a pizza deliveryman, apparently sent by the God of Comedy Setup Lines.

"Looks like rain!" he said.

"Yes," I said, "and wouldn't you know it, I just painted my darned lawn!"

I added a friendly "Ha ha!" to reassure him I was a normal person unlikely to suddenly chop him into fragments with a machete, but he was already accelerating down the street. Nevertheless the lawn-painting was a critical success, and it got me thinking about other ways I might be able to improve nature around our house, especially the yard crabs. Since we live in South Florida, geologically a giant swamp with shopping centers, we have these crabs who live in holes in our yard, and I do not care for them. Being from the North, I prefer yard critters that are furry and cute, whereas crabs look like body parasites magnified 1,000 times. During mating season, they become outright hostile. I'll go out in my yard, and there, blocking my path, will be a crab, adopting a karate stance, and waving his pincers menacingly to prevent me from mating with his woman.

"I don't want to mate with your woman," I tell him. "Your woman is a *crab,* for God's sake." But this only makes him angrier, because I think he knows,

deep inside his slimy little heart that I'm telling the truth.

So anyway, my idea is that the crabs should wear costumes. I'm thinking specifically chipmunk costumes. I could look out the window and watch them scuttling around the lawn in their furry finery, and it would be just like being back up North on a brisk fall day following a nuclear accident that had caused all the chipmunks to develop extra legs and walk sideways. My only question is where I'd get chipmunk costumes for crabs, but I'm sure the federal government can help me out. Assuming it's not too busy touching up federal rocks.

Captains Outrageous

The reason we bought a motorboat is, we needed a new kitchen. Our current kitchen has a lot of problems, such as a built-in Colonial-era microwave that we think might not be totally safe because it can cook food that is sitting as far as 15 feet away. We had spent months striding around our current kitchen, making sweeping gestures and saying things like, "We'll move the sink over there!"

What a pair of goobers. As you experienced renovators know, it's easier to construct a major suspension bridge than to move a residential sink. Thousands of homeowners who embarked on sink-relocation projects during the Eisenhower administration are still washing their dishes in the bathtub. My wife and I kept running into people like this, people with plaster dust in their hair and hollow eyes from spending their wretched nights sleeping in the garage and their bleak days waiting desperately for workmen who inevitably made things worse. "We have no telephone or electricity or water," the Renovation People would say, "and on Monday a man is supposed to come and take all our oxygen."

This was discouraging, but we really needed a new kitchen. Finally we said, "OK, if we don't do it now, we're never going to do it," so we decided to bite the bullet and: Buy a motorboat. Our reasoning was, "Hey, if we have a motorboat, we'll have Family Outings where we can experience Togetherness and possibly crash into a reef and sink, and then it won't matter about our kitchen."

But reefs were not our immediate problem. Our immediate problem was something much worse, a daunting nautical challenge that has tested the courage of mariners since ancient times, namely: backing the boat into the carport. The trick to remember here is, if you turn your car wheels to the right ("starboard"), the boat trailer will actually go to the LEFT

("forecastle") until your wife ("Beth") announces that you ran over a sprinkler head ("$12.95"). Using this procedure I was able to get the boat into the carport in no more time than it took for Magellan to reach Guam.

We kept the boat moored in the carport for several weeks, after which we decided—call us bold adventurers—to try it on actual water. We met at the marina with our salesperson, Dale, who showed us how to launch the boat via a terrifying procedure wherein I had to back the trailer down a scary ramp right into the bay. I have since learned that, here in Miami, on weekends, amusement-seekers will come to the marina, set up folding chairs, and spend a highly entertaining day watching boat owners perform comical maneuvers such as forgetting to set their parking brakes and having their cars roll down the ramp and disappear, burbling gaily, below the surface. In the generous nautical tradition of rendering assistance to those in need, Miami boat owners sometimes—this is all true—get into gunfights over whose turn it is to use the ramp.

Fortunately we had Dale with us, so we had no trouble getting out on the water, where he taught me the basics of seamanship. Here's how it went:

DALE: OK, you see that shoal over there?
ME: No.
DALE: OK, you see that marker over there?
ME: No.
DALE: Do you want to take the wheel for a while?
ME: No.

Finally, when I was fully confident that, if necessary, I could take the boat out myself and get everyone killed, we returned home to spend a carefree evening washing our hull. You have to do this because it turns out that—get ready for a fascinating nautical fact—seawater is very bad for boats. I'm serious. Ask any boat owner. Seawater contains large quantities of barnacles and corrosives, which will rapidly turn your boat into a giant piece of maritime crud.

So while I was scrubbing my hull, I had this blinding insight: The smart thing to do, clearly, is never put the boat into the water. I shared this insight with some other boat owners, and they all agreed that, definitely, putting your boat into the water is asking for trouble. Most of them have had their boats sitting in their driveways long enough to be registered historical landmarks.

A group of us boat owners were discussing this one evening at a party featuring beer, which is how we decided to hold a Driveway Regatta. Really. I have the whole thing on videotape. We had it on our driveway, and we had four boats, on trailers, secured via anchors in the lawn, trees, etc. The judges awarded First Prize to a dentist named Olin, whose boat not only contained golf clubs and a croquet set, but also had a spider web containing a certified spider that had apparently died of old age. It was a fine afternoon, and nobody got seasick, and we even—try this at sea—had pizza delivered. I would have cooked, but we really need a new kitchen.

Ship of Fools

We wanted to have a relaxing family vacation, so we got together with two other families and rented a sailboat in the Virgin Islands. There is nothing as relaxing as being out on the open sea, listening to the waves and the wind and the sails and voices downstairs yelling "HOW DO YOU FLUSH THESE TOILETS?"

It takes a minimum of six people, working in close harmony, to successfully flush a nautical toilet. That's why those old ships carried such large crews. The captain would shout the traditional command—"All hands belay the starboard commode!"—and dozens of men would scurry around pulling ropes, turning giant winches, etc., working desperately to avoid the dreaded Backup At Sea, which is exactly the problem that the captain of the *Titanic* was downstairs working on, which is why he didn't notice the iceberg.

We had a competent captain in our cruise group, but just to be on the safe side we hired a local captain for the first afternoon to demonstrate the finer points of seamanship. He was on our boat for a total of three hours, during which he demonstrated that he could drink six of our beers and two large direct-from-the-bottle swigs of our rum and still not fall headfirst into the Caribbean. He was definitely the most relaxed person on the boat. His major piece of nautical advice was: "No problem." We'd say: "Which Virgin Island is that over there?" And he'd squint at it knowledgeably and say, "No problem." Then he'd go get another beer.

So this was pretty much how we handled it, and the cruise was problem-free, unless you count my Brush With Death. For this I blame the children. We started the cruise with only five children, but after several days on the boat there appeared to be several hundred of them, all of whom always wanted to sit in exactly the same place, and no two of whom ever wanted to eat the same thing for lunch.

So one afternoon a group of them were playing an incredibly complex card game they had invented, wherein everyone had a different number of cards

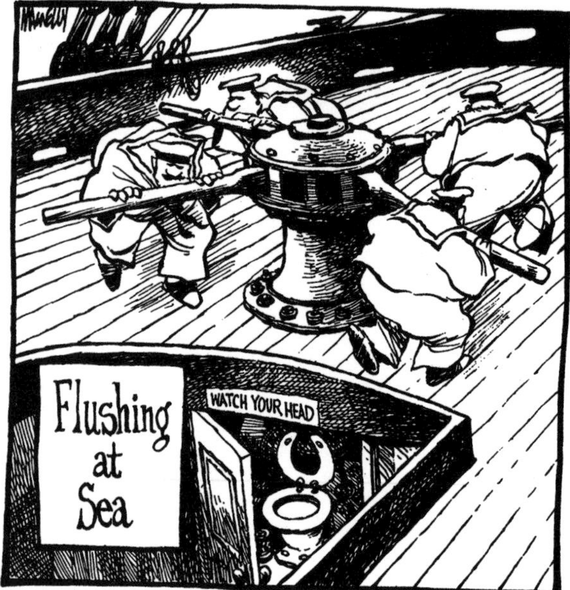

and anyone could change the rules at any time and punching was allowed and there was no possible way to end the game but everybody appeared to be winning, and suddenly a card blew overboard.

Until this kind of emergency arises, you never know how you're going to react. I happened to be nearby with a group of grown-ups who had smeared their bodies with powerful sun-blocking agents and then, inexplicably, gone out to lie in the sun, and when I heard the chilling cry ("Card overboard!") I leaped to my feet and, without thinking, in fact without any brain wave activity whatsoever, jumped into the water, dove beneath the surface, and saw: a barracuda the size of a nuclear submarine. The other people claimed it was only about three feet long, but I was right there, and this barracuda had actual torpedo tubes. It was examining the card closely, as if thinking, "Huh! A two of hearts, here in the Caribbean!" I used this opportunity to exit from the water by clawing violently at air molecules and ascending vertically, Warner Bros.–cartoon style, back into the boat.

Fortunately that was my only Brush With Death on the relaxation cruise, except for the other one, which occurred when I attempted to pull up the anchor. You have to pull up the anchor from time to time on a sailboat so that you can put up the sails, which causes the boat to lean over, which allows water to splash in and get all the clothes wet. It's a basic rule of seamanship that everybody's clothes have to be wet all the time. If there's no wind, you are required by maritime law to throw your clothes overboard a couple of times a day.

So I was standing on the deck, hauling up the anchor. You have to be careful on the deck, because of the "hatches," which are holes placed around a sailboat at random to increase the insurance rates. From the moment we got on the boat, I had been warning the children about the danger of falling into the hatches. "Don't fall into those hatches!" I'd say, in the stern voice that we wise old parents use to tell our children the ludicrously obvious. And so, as you have already guessed, when I was pulling on the anchor rope, walking backward, poof, I suddenly became the Incredible Disappearing Man. It was a moment of high relaxation, a moment that would definitely win the grand prize on the popular TV show "Boneheaded Americans Injure Themselves On Home Video," and I'm sure I'll have a good laugh about it once I'm out of surgery.

No, seriously, all I got was a bruise that is actually larger than my skin surface area, so that parts of it extend into the atmosphere around me. But other than that it was a swell cruise, and I strongly recommend that you take one. Make sure you go to the bathroom first.

Death Wormed Over

The key to a successful Summer Vacation Adventure is: preparation. For example, if you're planning a trip to Europe to visit historic sites such as the Hunchback of Notre Dame Cathedral, you should prepare *right now* by setting fire to your airline tickets. I'm advising against vacationing in Europe this year because Europe contains England, which is currently being invaded by the Alien Flatworms of Death.

I found out about this thanks to several alert readers who sent me a *Manchester Guardian* article that begins: "Killer flatworms from New Zealand which drug earthworms and devour them are invading Britain." The article quotes a scientist as saying: "They're weird; it is like something out of science fiction. They excrete an enzyme that paralyzes the worm like a narcotic drug. Then they excrete another one that dissolves the worm before your eyes like soup, then they suck it up. In about 30 minutes all that is left is a trace of old soil from the worm's stomach."

It is not definitely known how the killer flatworms got from New Zealand to England. Possibly they smuggled themselves aboard a commercial airplane disguised as attorneys. We can only imagine what might have happened if they had become hungry en route:

FIRST AIRLINE PASSENGER: Have you seen Nigel?

SECOND AIRLINE PASSENGER: No, but what's this on his seat?

FIRST AIRLINE PASSENGER: Hey! That looks like Nigel's complimentary breakfast omelet!

You don't want this kind of tragedy to spoil your Vacation Adventure. So this year you should take an old-fashioned Family Fun Vacation, wherein you get into the family car and drive and drive and drive until you come to an interesting local attraction, and then you drive past it at 78 miles per hour. I'm assuming here that Dad is driving. Dad likes to

cover a lot of ground on a vacation. His ideal vacation itinerary would look like this:

6 to 6:15 A.M.—Eat breakfast.

6:15 to 6:30—Yellowstone National Park.

6:30 to 7—Canada.

And so on. Dad wishes he had auxiliary gas tanks so he could vacation all the way to, say, Argentina and back without ever stopping the car. Unfortunately, he has to refuel roughly every 600 miles, so sometimes Mom and the kids are able to escape and, running with their foreheads almost touching the ground because their bodies have been permanently molded into the shape of a car seat, flee into the underbrush in search of a local attraction.

For my money, the best attractions are small arts and crafts fairs. We once stopped at a fair in Pennsylvania Dutch country where a grim-looking woman was demonstrating how to make an authentic local dish from—this is true—the stomach of a pig. It was the scariest-looking thing I have ever seen that was not featured in a major motion picture, and the woman was gripping it with both hands, as if she were afraid that it might get loose and attack the other crafts. People would stop by, stare at it for a while, and ask, "What does it taste like?" And the grim-looking woman, not looking up, would reply, "A lot of people don't like it."

There are thousands of equally attractive attractions all over the country, but if you asked me, as a travel authority, which was No. 1, I would have to say it was the maggot races at the Town Club Bar in Three Forks, Montana. I am not making this up. Alert readers Bill and Julie Hudick sent me an article about it from the *Bozeman Daily Chronicle,* with a photograph of men hunched over a miniature racetrack, watching maggots race.

I immediately called the Town Club Bar and spoke to one of the people who conceived of this concept, Darrel Raffety, owner of Raffety's Fishbait Company, which sells maggots for bait. He explained that one day in the bar, a customer complained that there weren't enough maggots in the container he had bought, so they poured them out and counted them right on the bar, and some of the maggots (possibly disguised as attorneys) started crawling away, and suddenly, *eureka* (Greek, meaning "They probably had a few beers in them"), the maggot-racing idea was born.

So they held a race to raise money for charity, and it was a large success. Town Club Bar owner Phil Schneider told me he'd do it again if enough tourists come by and create a popular demand. So you will definitely want to include Three Forks in your summer vacation plans. Fortunately, it's only 357,000 miles from wherever you live. Dad is very excited.

They Might Be Giants

OK, fans. Time for Great Moments in Sports. The situation is this: The Giants are playing a team whose name we did not catch in the hotly contested Little League Ages 6 and 7 Division, and the bases are loaded. The bases are always loaded in this particular Division for several reasons.

First off, the coach pitches the ball to his own players. This is because throwing is not the strong suit of the players in the Ages 6 and 7 Division. They have no idea, when they let go of the ball, where it's headed. They just haul off and wing it, really try to *hurl* that baby without getting bogged down in a lot of picky technical details such as whether or not there is now, or has ever been, another player in the area where the ball is likely to land. Generally there is not, which is good, because another major area of weakness, in the Ages 6 and 7 Division, is catching the ball.

Until I became a parent, I thought children just naturally knew how to catch a ball, that catching was an instinctive biological reflex that all children are born with, like knowing how to operate a remote control or getting high fevers in distant airports. But it turns out that if you toss a ball to a child, the ball will just bonk off the child's body and fall to the ground. So you have to coach the child. I go out in the yard with my son, and I give him helpful tips such as: "Catch the ball!" And: "Don't just let the ball bonk off your body!" Thanks to this coaching effort, my son, like most of the players on the Giants, has advanced his game to the point where, just before the ball bonks off his body, he winces.

So fielding is also not the strong suit of the Giants. They stand around the field, chattering to each other, watching airplanes, picking their noses, thinking about dinosaurs, etc. Meanwhile on the pitchers' mound, the coach of the opposing team tries to throw the ball just right so that it will bounce off the bat of one of his players, because hitting is another major area of weakness in the Ages 6 and 7 Division.

The real athletic drama begins once the opposing coach succeeds in bouncing the ball off the bat of one of his players, thus putting the ball into play and causing the fielders to swing into action. It reminds me of those table-hockey games, where you have a bunch of little men that you activate with knobs and levers, except that the way you activate the Giants is, you yell excitedly in an effort to notify them that the ball is headed their way. Because otherwise they'd probably never notice it.

"Robby!" I'll yell if the ball goes near my son. "The ball!" Thus activated, Robby goes on Full Red Alert, looking around frantically until he locates the ball, which he picks up and—eager to be relieved of the responsibility—hurls in some random direction. Then, depending on where the ball is headed, some other parent will try to activate his child, and the ball will be hurled again and again, pinball-style, around the field, before ultimately bonking off the body of the first baseman. Of course at this point the batter has been standing on the base for some time. Fortunately, in this league, he is required to stop there; otherwise, he could easily make it to Japan.

This is why the bases are always loaded, which is what leads us to today's Sports Moment. Standing on third base is James Palmieri, who is only 5, but who plays for the Giants anyway because his older brother, T.J., is on the team. James got on base via an exciting play: He failed to actually, technically, *hit* the ball, but the Giants' wily coach, Wayne Argo, employed a classic bit of baseball strategy. "Let's let James get on base," he said. And the other team agreed, because at this point the Giants were losing the hotly contested game by roughly 143–57.

So here it is: James is standing on third, for the first time in his entire life, thinking about dinosaurs, and next to him, ready to activate, is his mom, Carmen. And now Coach Wayne is throwing the pitch. It is a good pitch, bouncing directly off the bat. Bedlam erupts as parents on both teams try to activate their players, but none is shouting with more enthusiasm than Carmen. "Run, James!" she yells, from maybe a foot away. "Run!"

James, startled, looks up, and you can almost see the thought forming in his mind: *I'm supposed to run*. And now he is running, and Carmen is running next to him, cheering him on, the two of them chugging toward the plate, only 15 feet to go, James about to score his first run ever. Then suddenly, incredibly, due to a semirandom hurl somewhere out in the field, there appears, of all things: the ball. And—this is a nightmare—an opposing player actually *catches* it, and touches home plate and little James is OUT.

Two things happen:

- Carmen stops. "S-word," she says, under her breath. A mom to the core.
- James, oblivious, keeps running. Chugs right on home, touches the plate smiling and wanders off, happy as a clam.

You can have your Willie Mays catch and your Bill Mazeroski home run. For me, the ultimate mental picture is James and Carmen at that moment: the Thrill of Victory, the Agony of Defeat. A Great Moment in Sports.

READER ALERT

England

I happen to like England a lot, and when I wrote this column, I thought it was clear that I was just poking some good-natured fun at one of our best international buddy countries. However, I got a lot of mail from angry Englishpersons, who made the following points:

1. **I am a jerk.**
2. **The food in England isn't so bad.**
3. **What about the food at McDonald's?**
4. **England hasn't decapitated any members of royalty for a long time.**
5. **What about American crime?**
6. **Why don't I just shut up?**
7. **Boy, am I ever a jerk.**

And so on. I was genuinely surprised by this hostile reaction, and all I can say to these people, in all sincerity, is: I humbly apologize for offending you, and I promise that I will never, ever again, even in jest, say anything remotely insulting about England, and I especially will not make note of the obvious defects in the royal gene pool.

Blimey! Frognal Cockfosters!

Recently my family and I spent a week in London, which is a popular foreign place to visit because they have learned to speak some English over there. Although frankly they have a long way to go. Often, when they get to the crucial part of a sentence, they'll realize that they don't know the correct words, so they'll just make some silly ones up. I had a lot of conversations that sounded like this:

ME: Excuse me. Could you tell us how to get to Buckingham Palace?

BRITISH PERSON: Right. You go down this street here, then you nip up the weckershams.

ME: We should nip up the weckershams?

BRITISH PERSON: Right. Then you take your first left, then you just pop 'round the gorn-and-scumbles, and, Jack's a doughnut, there you are!

ME: Jack's a *doughnut?*

BRITISH PERSON: Right.

Also they have a lot of trouble with pronunciation, because they can't move their jaw muscles, because of malnutrition caused by wisely refusing to eat English food, much of which was designed and manufactured in medieval times during the reign of King Walter the Mildly Disturbed. Remember when you were in junior high school, and sometimes the cafeteria workers would open up a large Army-surplus food can left over from the Spanish-American War and serve you a scary-looking dish with a name like "Tuna Bean Prune Cabbage Omelet Casserole Surprise"?

Well, they still have a *lot* of food like that over in England, on permanent display in bars, called "pubs," where people drink for hours but nobody ever eats. We saw individual servings of pub food that we recognized from our last visit, in 1978. Some dishes—no effort is made to conceal this fact—contain *kidneys*. We also saw one dish with a sign next to it that said—I swear I am not making this up—"Spotted Dick."

The English are very good at thinking up silly names. Here are some actual stations on the London underground: Marylebone, Tooting Broadway, Piccadilly Circus, Cockfosters, Frognal, Goodge Street, Mudchute, Barking, and East Ham. Londoners are apologetic about their underground, which they believe has become filthy and noisy and dangerous, but which is in fact far more civilized than the average American wedding reception. At the height of rush hour, people on the London underground actually say "excuse me." Imagine what would happen if you tried an insane stunt like that on the New York City subway. The other passengers would take it as a sign of weakness, and there'd be a fight over who got to keep your ears as a trophy.

Our primary cultural activity in London was changing money. We had to do this a lot because the dollar is very weak. Europeans use the dollar primarily to apply shoe polish. So every day we'd go to one of the money-changing places that are all over London, and we'd exchange some dollars for British money, which consists of the "pound" and a wide variety of mutant coins whose sizes and shapes are unrelated to their values, and then we'd look for something to eat that had been invented in this country, such as pizza, and we'd buy three slices for what we later realized was $247.50, and then we'd change some money again. Meanwhile the Japanese tourists were exchanging *their* money for items such as Westminster Abbey.

In the interest of broadening our ten-year-old son's cultural awareness, we visited some important historic sites, including the Tower of London, the London Dungeon, and Madame Tussaud's Wax Museum, all of which are devoted to explaining in clinical detail how various historic members of royalty were whacked into small historic pieces. English history consists largely of royal people getting their heads chopped off, which is why members of the royal family now wear protective steel neck inserts, which is why they walk the way they do.

Needless to say, this brand of history was a hit with our son. He especially enjoyed the guided "Jack the Ripper" tour that we took one dark night with a very intense guide. "Right on this spot is where they found the victim's intestines," she'd say. "And right here is where they found the liver, which is now part of the food display of that pub over there."

Another cultural activity we frequently engaged in was looking the wrong way before attempting to cross streets. The problem is that in America, people drive on the *right* side of the street, whereas in Lon-

don, they drive on *both* sides of the street, using hard-to-see cars about the size of toaster ovens. The best way to handle this, as a tourist, is to remain on one side of the street for your entire visit, and see the other side on another trip.

But I definitely recommend London for anybody who enjoys culture and could stand to lose a few pounds. I learned many things that will be of great value to me, not just personally, but also professionally, and I'm not saying that just to be polite to the English. I'm saying it because of Internal Revenue Service regulations.

Dentists in Paradise

I want to stress that I did not go to Hawaii just to sit around the beach drinking giant comical drinks with names like the Wahine Martini that arrive at your table festooned with six kinds of fruit and a live parrot. No, I went to Hawaii for *sound journalism reasons*. Hawaii happens to be a hotbed of important news topics (FERDINAND MARCOS: HAS DEATH CHANGED HIM?), and as a trained journalist I felt it was my duty to "get the story," even though I knew I was running the very real risk that my entire trip would be tax-deductible.

First, some background. The Hawaiian Islands were discovered by hardy Polynesian sailors, who crossed thousands of miles of open ocean in primitive canoes, braving violent storm-tossed seas for months at a time. My family and I arrived by modern commercial aviation, which was infinitely worse. We flew on Halloween. "Never Fly on Halloween," this is my new aviation motto, because it took us 21 hours to get from Miami to Honolulu. We had two planes develop mechanical problems, one of them well out over the Pacific Ocean, which is famous for not having places to land on. At one point, just before we took off from San Francisco for Honolulu the first time, the pilot—I am not making this up—said, "Hopefully, this one will fly all the way." Of course it didn't. The second time we took off from San Francisco, the flight attendant said, I swear, "If you gotta go, go with a smile." The flight was violently bumpy, and the movie was—this is still true—*The Dead Poets Society*. To apologize for all the inconvenience, the airline gave us coupons good for discounts on future flights, although they knew full well that we were all planning to return to the mainland via primitive canoe and never go near an airplane again.

But I don't want to dwell on the flight. I want to talk about Hawaii, "The Aloha State." "Aloha" is an all-purpose Hawaiian phrase meaning "hello," "good-bye," "I love you," and "I wish to decline the collision damage waiver." The Hawaiian language is quite unusual because when the original Polynesians came in their canoes, most of their consonants were washed overboard in a storm, and they arrived here with almost nothing but vowels. All the streets have names like Kal'ia'iou'amaa'aaa'eiou, and many street signs spontaneously generate new syllables during the night. This confuses the hell out of the tourists, who are easily identifiable because they're the only people wearing Hawaiian shirts.

Things were very exciting when we were in Honolulu because the American Dental Association was holding a giant convention there. "Dentists in Paradise," is how I would describe it. There were 25,000 dental professionals wandering around, wearing shirts that appeared to be radioactive and looking at dental exhibits featuring large color illustrations of wonderful technical advances in dentistry that make you get down on your knees and pray they will never happen to you. I imagine the dentists probably also had some kind of large formal dental ceremony, where they gave out awards and took large ceremonial hits of nitrous oxide and drank a special wine toast and, in a solemn and moving tribute to those dental professionals no longer with us, spat the wine out into a giant ceremonial dental spittoon.

We missed this, but we did attend a "luau," which is Hawaiian for "a beach picnic featuring a large cooked pig who still has his eyeballs and stares at you while you're trying to eat him." Our pig's name was Bob. "Never eat anything that still has its eyeballs," that's my new culinary motto.

We also saw the famous Bonzai Pipeline, where brave or possibly just insane surfers ride on waves the size of Central American nations. My wife and son and I were standing on the beach, marveling at these waves, saying things like "Look at the SIZE of these waves! Look at this wave right HEEEAAAIIIEEEEE" and the next thing we knew we were being washed up the beach like the Jetsam Family, tourists in Full Bozo Mode.

This is why we were so wet when we ran into Imelda Marcos. This really happened. We were driving by the memorial park where Ferdinand was staying temporarily until Imelda could figure out a way to get him back to the Philippines, and we thought we'd stop and take a quick, unobtrusive gander. But when we got into Ferdinand's little private building, our shoes squishing as we walked, there was Imelda and her retinue. It was pretty awkward because they were dressed in full mourning attire and we were dressed like we just got off the Log Flume Ride at Disney World. Fortunately I am a trained journalist who knows how to handle himself in the presence of a major world figure. "Guck," I said, or some noise like it, way down in my throat, as I grabbed my son, who was wandering cheerfully over to the casket,

and we squished the hell out of there. So I can't give you a detailed report on the Marcos situation, except to say that Ferdinand seems to be doing as well as can be expected, under the circumstances.

Satisfied that our trip now contained a very high percentage of business-related activity, we returned to Waikiki Beach, where we relaxed with a few tax-deductible drinks and watched the gorgeous sunset Pacific sky change colors behind the silhouettes of gently swaying dental professionals. Aloha. And I mean it.

This Takes Guts

Today we present the exciting results of a Scientific Taste Test that we ran recently here at the Institute of Scary Foods. This test was inspired by alert consumers Ken Weidner and Eric Simonson, who sent us a label from a canned food named—we are not making this up—"Armour Potted Meat Food Product." The ingredients listed on the label include: Beef Tripe, Beef Hearts, Cooked Fat Tissue Solids, and Partially Defatted Beef Fatty Tissue, which is always a popular family favorite ("Mom, I'd like another heaping mound of Partially Defatted Beef Fatty Tissue!")

Also on the label is a color picture labeled "SERVING SUGGESTION," which shows a brownish substance with parsley and an olive sitting on it. Here at the Institute of Scary Foods we are highly suspicious of olives, which, in our opinion, are the eyeballs of giant frogs. We believe that if you stood outside an olive factory, you'd hear the unmistakable tragic sound (RIBBETT-THUMP; RIBBETT-THUMP) of terrified sightless frogs leaping into things.

So we were not exactly insane about the Potted Meat Food Product label. However, our job is to keep you, the food-eating consumer, informed, so we called up the manufacturer's Consumer Information Center, where we spoke with a perky and helpful person named Barbara.

"What is 'beef tripe'?" we asked.

"Well, it's a part of the cow," said Barbara. "I'm trying to think of what part it is."

She put us on musical hold for a few minutes, then came back with a solid answer.

"The tripe is part of around the stomach area of the cow," she said.

Thus reassured, we set off for the convenience store. This is the same store where we once bought an amazing digital wristwatch that cost only $1.99, yet told the time. And when we say "the time," we mean it. If you set this watch at 2:14, it would keep saying "2:14" until you changed it to another time. This watch was so convenient that you didn't even have to wear it, because you always knew what it said.

Sure enough, this store had Armour Potted Meat Food Product, so we bought some, as well as *another* brand, Libby's Potted Meat Food Product. In addition to the beef tripe, the Libby's label says it contains pork stomachs, which could be a real selling point ("Now With TWO KINDS Of Stomachs!").

To round out our Taste Test, we purchased:

- A can of Spam;
- A can of Mighty Dog-brand dog food;
- A can of Bonton-brand "natural" snails;
- A can of something called "Beanee Weenees."

We also bought some tortilla chips, because we were concerned about an article we received from alert reader Stuart Ritter about a woman who ate an improperly chewed chip, which ripped a five-inch gash in her esophagus. The article quotes the woman's doctor as saying: "A poorly chewed tortilla chip can produce serious injury."

For the Taste Test, we offered the various food products to a five-member Expert Taste Panel, consisting of me; my wife, Beth; our son, Robert; our large main dog, Earnest; and our small emergency backup dog, Zippy. The results were as follows:

- Spam ranked highest, earning the title of "The Rolls-Royce Car Product of Canned Meat Products."
- The Potted Meat Food Products had the same appetizing look and texture of internal-organ-colored wood filler, but did not taste as good. They were definitely a cut below the Mighty Dog, which was grainy but at least tasted as though it had once been organic matter.
- Robert spat everything into the garbage except Spam and Beanee Weenees.
- Earnest licked everything a LOT and continued to lick the floor for several minutes after all detectable food molecules had disappeared.
- Nobody except Beth and Earnest would eat the snails, which look like little Jabba the Hutts and are clearly being sold as a prank.
- Zippy got so excited about the sudden unforeseen onslaught of food products that he had a little accident in the kitchen.

For safety reasons, we did not attempt to eat the Tortilla Chips of Doom. But we did establish, in a chilling experiment, that a single chip is capable of

ripping a large, ugly gash in a personally computerized fund-raising letter we got from the Rev. Oral Roberts. Our advice to you consumers is: Don't try these experiments at home. Not without plenty of carbonated malt beverage product.

READER ALERT

Dogs

I've learned to live with the fact that my two dogs, Earnest and Zippy, are way more popular than I am. I always get a lot of mail when I write about them, and people are always asking me to write more, which is kind of puzzling inasmuch as all of my dog columns basically boil down to the following statement: "Boy, are dogs ever stupid!" Perhaps this reassures people. Perhaps they say, "Well, I may have missed out on that big promotion, and I may have screwed up my personal life, but at least I've never run headfirst into a tree at 37 miles per hour while chasing a squirrel. At least not while I was sober."

Taking the Zip Out of Zippy

I regularly get letters from irate MacNeil-Lehrer-watching readers who ask: "With all the serious problems facing the world, how come you write about your dogs?" To which I answer: Because I don't know anything about *your* dogs. Also—you can call me an idealist if you want, but this is my opinion—by writing about my dogs, I believe that I can bring my readers—rich and poor, young and old, intelligent and "lite"-beer drinking—to a greater awareness of, and appreciation for, my dogs. I want my dogs to someday be at least as famous as Loni Anderson. I want them to receive lucrative offers for major motion pictures based on their True Life Adventures.

This week, for example, our adventure is entitled:

Zippy and Earnest Get Operated On

This adventure began when Zippy went through puberty, a biological process that a small dog goes through in less time than it takes you to throw away your Third Class mail. One minute Zippy was a cute little-boy puppy, scampering about the house playfully causing permanent damage to furniture that is not yet fully paid for, and the next minute he was: A Man. When the new, mature version of Zippy sauntered into a room, you could almost hear the great blues musician Muddy Waters in the background, growling:

I'm a MAN
(harmonica part)
Yes I AM
(harmonica part)

A FULL-GROWN man.

Of course in Zippy's case, "full-grown" means "the size of a Hostess Sno-Ball, yet somehow less impressive." But in his own mind, Zippy was a major stud muffin, a hunk of burnin' love, a small-caliber but high-velocity Projectile of Passion fired from the Saturday Night Special of Sex. And his target was: Earnest.

Earnest is a female dog, but she was not the ideal choice for Zippy, because all of her remotely suspicious organs had been surgically removed several years ago. Since that time she has not appeared to be even dimly aware of sex, or much of anything else. Her lone hobby, besides eating, is barking violently at nothing. Also she is quite large; when she's standing up, Zippy can run directly under her with an easy six inches of clearance. So at first we were highly amused when he started putting The Moves on her. It was like watching Tommy Tadpole hit on the Queen Mary.

But shortly the novelty wore off and we started feeling sorry for Earnest, who spent the entire day staring glumly off into dog hyperspace while this tireless yarn-ball-sized Lust Machine kept leaping up on her, sometimes getting as high as mid-shin, and emitting these presumably seductive high-pitched yips ("What's your sign? What's your sign?"). So we decided it was time to have the veterinarian turn the volume knob of desire way down on the stereo system of Zippy's manhood. If you get my drift.

The next morning Earnest was limping, so we decided to take both dogs to the vet. They bounded enthusiastically into the car, of course; dogs feel very strongly that they should always go with you in the car, in case the need should arise for them to bark violently at nothing right in your ear. When we got to the veterinarian's office they realized they had been tricked and went into Full Reverse Thrust, but fortunately the floor material there is slippery enough to luge on. So when we last saw Zippy and Earnest that morning, they were being towed, all eight legs scrabbling in a wild, backward, futile blur, into: the Back Room.

When we picked them up that night, they were a pair of hurtin' cowpokes. Earnest, who had a growth removed, was limping badly, plus we had to put a plastic bag on her leg so she wouldn't lick her stitches off. And Zippy, to keep him from getting at *his* stitches, was wearing a large and very comical round plastic collar that looked like a satellite dish with Zippy's head sticking out in the middle. He had a lot of trouble getting around, because his collar kept hitting things, such as the ground.

For the next week, if you came to our front door, here's what happened: You heard the loud barking of two dogs going into Red Alert mode, but you did not see any immediate dogs. Instead you

heard a lot of bumping and clunking, which turned out to be the sound of a large dog limping frantically toward you but suffering a major traction loss on every fourth step because of a plastic bag, combined with the sound of a very small dog trying desperately to keep up but bonking his collar into furniture, doorways, etc. And then, finally, skidding around the corner, still barking, there appeared the dynamite duo: Bagfoot and Satellite Head.

During this week we were not the least bit worried about burglars, because if anyone had tried to break into our house, we would have found him the next morning, lying in a puddle of his own drool. Dead from laughter.

Yellow Journalism

If you were to ask me, "Dave, what are the two words that summarize everything that you truly believe in, other than that beer should always be served in a chilled glass?" I would have to respond: "Dog obedience." I own two dogs, and they have both been trained to respond immediately to my voice. For example, when we're outside, all I have to do is issue the following standard dog command: "Here, Earnest! Here, Zippy! C'mon! Here, doggies! Here! I said come HERE! You dogs COME HERE RIGHT NOW!! ARE YOU DOGS LISTENING TO ME?? HEY!!!" And instantly both dogs, in unison, like a precision drill team, will continue trotting in random directions, sniffing the ground.

This is of course exactly what I want them to do. Dogs need to sniff the ground; it's how they keep abreast of current events. The ground is a giant dog newspaper, containing all kinds of late-breaking dog news items, which, if they are especially urgent, are often continued in the next yard. We live next to an aircraft-carrier-sized dog named Bear, who is constantly committing acts of prize-winning journalism around the neighborhood, and my dogs are major fans of his work. Each morning, while I am shouting commands at them, they race around and scrutinize the most recent installments of the ongoing Bear *oeuvre,* vibrating their bodies ecstatically to communicate their critical comments ("Bear has done it AGAIN!" "This is CLASSIC Bear!" etc.).

Of course you cannot achieve this level of obedience overnight. You have to take the time to understand dogs as a species, to realize that they have not always been peaceful domesticated animals who fulfill their nutritional requirements primarily by sidling up to the coffee table when you're not looking and snorking taco chips directly out of the bowl. Millions of years ago dogs were fierce predators who roamed in hungry packs; if some unfortunate primitive man got caught out in the open, the dogs would surround him, knock him to the ground, and, with saliva dripping from their wolflike jaws, lick him to within an inch of his life. "Dammit, Bernice!" he would yell to primitive woman. "We got to get these dogs some professional obedience training!" This is still basically the situation today.

We had our larger dog, Earnest, professionally trained by a very knowledgeable woman who came to our house and spent several hours commanding Earnest to "heel." Wouldn't it be funny if it turned out that animals actually had high IQs and understood English perfectly, and the only reason they act stupid is that we're always giving them unintelligible commands? Like, maybe at night in the stable, the horses stand around asking each other: "What the hell does 'giddyap' mean?"

But the trainer had no trouble getting Earnest to comprehend "heel." Her technique was to give commands in a gentle but firm voice; to consistently praise Earnest for obeying properly; and to every now and then, as a reminder, send 75,000 volts of electricity down the leash. At least that's how I assume she did it, because in no time she had Earnest heeling like Vice President Quayle. Whereas when *I* take Earnest for a "walk" I am frequently yanked horizontal by dog lunges of seminuclear force—Earnest could tow a bulldozer across Nebraska—so that my body, clinging desperately to the leash, winds up bouncing gaily down the street behind Earnest at close to the federal speed limit, like a tin can tied to a newlywed couple's car.

But "heel" is not the only obedience skill our dogs have mastered. They also know:

ANSWER THE DOOR—When a person, real or imagined, comes to our house, both dogs charge violently at the front door barking loudly enough to shatter glass, because they know, through instinct, that there is a bad guy out there and they *must protect the house*. So when we open the door, no matter who is standing there—a neighbor, a delivery person, Charles Manson holding a four-foot machete—the dogs barge *right past him* and race outside, looking for the bad guy, who for some reason is never there, a mystery that always causes the dogs to come to skidding four-legged stops and look around with expressions of extreme puzzlement. Foiled again! He's a clever one, that bad guy!

GO TO SCHOOL—The highlight, the absolute pinnacle, of our dogs' entire existence is riding in the car when we drive our son to school, an activity that gives them the opportunity to provide vital services such as barking at policemen and smearing dog snot all over the rear window. So every morning they monitor us carefully, and the instant we do some-

thing that indicates to them that our departure is imminent, such as we wake up, they sprint to the garage door and bark at it, in case we've forgotten where it is, then they spring back to us and bark some more, to let us know they're ready to go, and then they spring back to the garage door, then back to us, and so on, faster and faster, until they become barely visible blurs of negative-IQ canine activity rocketing through the house at several hundred revolutions per minute, and you can just imagine how difficult it can be for us to make them understand the concept of "Saturday." One nonschool morning my wife felt so sorry for them that she went out in her bathrobe and drove them around the neighborhood for a while, looking for things they could bark at. So don't try to tell me dog training isn't worth it, OK? I can't hear you anyway, because there's a bad guy at the door.

Just Say No to Rugs

Everybody should have a pet. And I'm not saying this just because the American Pet Council gave me a helicopter. I'm also saying it because my family has always owned pets, and without them, our lives would not be nearly so rich in—call me sentimental, but this is how I feel—dirt.

Pets are nature's way of reminding us that, in the incredibly complex ecological chain of life, there is no room for furniture. For example, the only really nice furnishing we own is an Oriental rug that we bought, with the help of a decorator, in a failed attempt to become tasteful. This rug is way too nice for an onion-dip-intensive household like ours, and we seriously thought about keeping it in a large safe-deposit box, but we finally decided, in a moment of abandon, to put it on the floor. We then conducted a comprehensive rug-behavior training seminar for our main dog, Earnest, and our small auxiliary dog, Zippy.

"NO!!" we told them approximately 75 times while looking very stern and pointing at the rug. This proven training technique caused them to slink around the way dogs do when they feel tremendously guilty but have no idea why. Satisfied, we went out to dinner.

I later figured out, using an electronic calculator, that this rug covers approximately 2 percent of the total square footage of our house, which means that if you (not you *personally)* were to have a random diarrhea attack in our home, the odds are approximately 49 to 1 against your having it on our Oriental rug. The odds against your having *four* random attacks on this rug are more than *five million to one.* So we had to conclude that it was done on purpose. The rug appeared to have been visited by a group of specially bred, highly trained Doberman Poopers, but we determined, by interrogating both dogs, that the entire massive output was the work of

Zippy. Probably he was trying to do the right thing. Probably, somewhere in the Coco Puff-sized nodule of nerve tissue that serves as his brain, he dimly remembered that The Masters had told him *something about the rug.* Yes! That's it! *To the rug!*

At least Zippy had the decency to feel bad about what he did, which is more than you can say for Mousse, a dog that belonged to a couple named Mike and Sandy. Mousse was a Labrador retriever, which is a large enthusiastic bulletproof species of dog made entirely from synthetic materials. This is the kind of dog that, if it takes an interest in your personal regions (which of course it does) you cannot fend it off with a blowtorch.

So anyway, Mike and Sandy had two visitors who wore expensive, brand-new down-filled parkas, which somehow got left for several hours in a closed room with Mousse. When the door was finally opened, the visibility in the room had been drastically reduced by a raging down storm, at the center of which was a large quivering down clot, looking like a huge mutant duckling, except that it had Mousse's radiantly happy eyes.

For several moments Mike and Sandy and their guests stared at this apparition, then Mike, a big, strong, highly authoritative guy, strode angrily into the room and slammed the door. He was in there for several minutes, then emerged, looking very serious. The down clot stood behind him, wagging its tail cheerfully.

"I talked to Mousse," Mike said, "and he says he didn't do it."

People often become deranged by pets. Derangement is the only possible explanation for owning a cat, an animal whose preferred mode of communication is to sink its claws three-quarters of an inch into your flesh. God help the cat owner who runs out of food. It's not uncommon to see an elderly woman sprinting through the supermarket with one or more cats clinging, leechlike, to her leg as she tries desperately to reach the pet-food section before collapsing from blood loss.

Of course for sheer hostility in a pet, you can't beat a parrot. I base this statement on a parrot I knew named Charles who belonged to a couple named Ed and Ginny. Charles had an IQ of 260 and figured out early in life that if he talked to people, they'd get close enough so he could bite them. He especially liked to bite Ed, whom Charles wanted to drive out of the marriage so he could have Ginny, the house, the American Express card, etc. So in an effort to improve their relationship, Ginny hatched (ha ha!) this plan wherein Ed took Charles to—I am not making this up—Parrot Obedience School. Every Saturday morning, Ed and Charles would head off to receive expert training, and every Saturday afternoon Ed would come home with chunks missing from his

arm. Eventually Ginny realized that it was never going to work, so she got rid of Ed.

I'm just kidding, of course. Nobody would take Ed. Ginny got rid of Charles, who now works as a public-relations adviser to Miss Zsa Zsa Gabor. So we see that there are many "pluses" to having an "animal friend," which is why you should definitely buy a pet. If you act right now, we'll also give you a heck of a deal on a rug.

Things That Go Hornk in the Night

These are indeed exciting times we live in, what with the radical political changes in Eastern Europe, the dramatic developments in South Africa, and of course the long-overdue Illinois Owl Vomit Study. This was alertly brought to my attention by reader Paul Baker, who sent an article from the *Wisconsin State Journal* headlined LAWMAKERS CHOKE ON OWL VOMIT STUDY. It seems that some Illinois legislators are upset because the state is funding a $180,000 study wherein researchers go around collecting owl vomit to see what they (the owls) eat, which could have important implications.

"Owls spit up pellets of hair, bone, and teeth . . . at least once or twice a day," states the article.

This is also true of our small auxiliary dog, Zippy. His hobby is throwing up lizard parts when we're trying to eat dinner. He'll get that look of total concentration that dogs get when they have a really important task to perform, then he'll hunch his body

over and walk around in a circle making a noise that sounds like "hornk." If you put him outside, he'll sit patiently by the door until you let him back inside, then he'll resume hornking. "Never throw your lizard parts up outside" is Rule No. 1 of the Dog Code of Ethics.

So as you can imagine our dinners have a very appetizing ambience:

MY WIFE: Would you like some more stew?
ME: Sure, I'd love . . .
ZIPPY: Hornk.
ME: On second thought . . .
ZIPPY: HORRRRNNK.
MY SON: Look! A tail and a leg!
ME: I think I'll just lie down.

And I'll tell you something else that is not helping my appetite any: Our refrigerator currently contains a jug of pond water infested with mosquito larvae, which are so unappetizing as to make semi-digested lizard parts look like Chicken McNuggets. The reason we have mosquito larvae in our refrigerator, as you parents have already deduced, is that our son is doing a science-fair project, which involves seeing what happens to larvae when you put them into various environments such as the refrigerator environment, the hall-closet environment, etc. Here are our key findings:

1. In the hall-closet environment, the larvae turn into mosquitoes and wait in the dark until you open the door, when they hurl their little bodies pathetically up against the side of the jar and, with their whiny little voices, go, "Please let me out please please PLEASE I won't suck your blood I SWEAR." But they are lying.

2. In the refrigerator environment, the larvae do nothing, and after a while you don't even notice them, leading to the danger that their jar will become part of the general population of Mystery Refrigerator Items like the leftover takeout Chinese food from the Carter administration, and then one day Grandpa Bob will come to visit, and in the middle of the night he'll get thirsty and tiptoe out to the refrigerator, reach in, pull out what looks like a nice refreshing jug of iced tea, take a big swig and GAAAAAACCCCCKKKK thud to the floor. And then Zippy will throw up on him.

But I will say this for our dogs: They never shot anybody. This is more than I can say for the dog in Lyngdal, Norway, that shot a man. According to a news article sent in by many alert readers, the man was hunting rabbits, and he set his gun down, and his dog "accidentally" hit the trigger, causing the gun to go off. Fortunately, the man suffered only minor injuries. Unfortunately, the rabbits saw the whole thing and have obtained a mail-order assault rifle.

Just kidding, of course! But I am NOT kidding about the Arson Cat. According to an Associated Press story also alertly sent in by numerous readers, investigators concluded that a house fire in Lima, New York, was caused by "a cat playing with matches," prompting us to once again ask ourselves, as concerned citizens, WHEN the government is going to come to its senses and order the mandatory sterilization of ALL cat owners.

On a brighter note, the *New Zealand Herald* reports that a woman in Adelaide, Australia, received a hefty out-of-court settlement "after she was hit in the back by an eight-kilogram frozen tuna during the world tuna-tossing championships." The story adds that the organizers of this annual event "are now trying to make the sport safer for spectators by developing a rubber tuna."

So there is Hope for Tomorrow. In fact, things are looking better already: Alert reader Perry Bradshaw sent me a news item stating that the governor of Minnesota, whose name (I am not making this governor up) is "Rudy Perpich," has declared 1990 to be "The Year of the Polka." I wouldn't be surprised if this exciting event drew music enthusiasts from as far away as Illinois ("The Owl Vomit State"). I'd be there myself, but I have to taunt the hall-closet mosquitoes.

READER ALERT

Eat Bugs for Money

I got hundreds of responses to this column, including dozens from people who were willing to eat bugs for free. Bear in mind that, under our system of government, these people can vote.

Beetlejuice

There comes a time in the life of every American citizen when Duty calls. "Hey! YOU!!" are Duty's exact words, and unless you're some kind of flag-desecrating pervert, you're going to stand up, as Americans have stood up for more than 200 years, and you're going to say, "Yes, I will participate in the Arbitron television-ratings survey."

I answered The Call one recent afternoon. The phone rang, and it was a person informing me that I had been selected to be an Arbitron household based on an exhaustive screening process consisting of being home when my number was dialed at random. As you can imagine, I was deeply moved.

"Do I get money?" I asked.

The reason I asked this is that a couple of years ago I was a Nielsen-ratings household, and all they paid me was two lousy dollars, yet they wanted me to write down *every program I watched,* which was

virtually impossible because I'm a guy and therefore I generally watch 40 programs at once. Guys are biologically capable of keeping track of huge numbers of programs simultaneously by changing the channel the instant something boring happens, such as dialogue. Whereas women, because of a tragic genetic flaw, feel compelled to watch only *one program at a time,* the way people did back in the Middle Ages, before the invention of remote control.

Anyway, it turns out that $2 is also all you get for being an Arbitron household. But I agreed to be one anyway, because, let's face it, when anybody connected with the television industry asks you to do something, no matter how stupid or degrading it is, you do it. This is why people are willing to openly discuss their secret bodily problems in commercials that are seen by the entire nation. These people become *famous* for having secret bodily problems. When they go out to dinner, large celebrity-worshiping crowds gather to stare and point and whisper excitedly to each other, "Look! It's Elston V. Quadrant, Hemorrhoid Sufferer!"

At least these people get paid, which is more than you can say for the people who go on the syndicated TV talk show and seek to enhance public understanding of various tragic psychological disorders by candidly revealing that they are total wackmobiles ("I'm Geraldo Rivera, and these men are commercial-airline pilots with live trout in their shorts").

So I figured the least I could do, for television, was be an Arbitron household. This involves two major responsibilities:

1. Keeping track of what you watch on TV.
2. Lying about it.

At least that's what I did. I imagine most people do. Because let's face it: Just because you watch a certain show on television, that doesn't mean you want to *admit* it. Let's say you're flipping through your 8,479 cable channels, and you come across a program called "Eat Bugs For Money," wherein they bring out a large live insect, and the contestants secretly write down the minimum amount of money they would have to be given to eat it, and whichever one has the lowest bid has to actually do it. Admit it: YOU would watch this program. In fact, right now you're saying to yourself, "Hey, I wonder what channel that's on." Unfortunately, at present it's still in the conceptual stage. It's based on an idea from my editor, Gene Weingarten, who has publicly stated that he would eat a live adult South Florida cockroach (average weight: 11 pounds) for $20,000.

My point is that you'd watch this program, but you wouldn't tell Arbitron. You'd claim that you watched a *National Geographic* special with a name like "The Amazing World of Beets." In my Arbitron diary, I wrote that our entire household (including Earnest, who is, legally, a dog) mainly watched the network news, whereas in fact the only remotely educational programming we watched that week was a commercial for oat bran, which by the way is clearly no more intended for human consumption than insects are.

Speaking of which, here is a Late Bulletin: My wife—this is the wonderful thing about Free Enterprise—has considered Gene Weingarten's bid and announced that *she* would eat a live adult cockroach for just $2,000. If you sincerely feel you can beat that price, drop me a line c/o The Miami Herald, Miami, FL 33132, because I'd like to produce a pilot episode of "Eat Bugs For Money" with an eye toward—call me a Cultural Pioneer—advancing the frontiers of my income. I would also appreciate your lowest price on eating a nonpoisonous but hair-covered spider. Thank you.

Skivvying Up the Profits

Recently—I bet this has happened to you—I ran out of clean underwear in Los Angeles. So I wandered into the men's clothing department of an upscale department store, the kind of store where the salesclerks all have sharp haircuts and perfectly tailored suits that are far nicer than anything YOU own, and, although they act very deferential, you know they're secretly watching to see which clothes you touch so they can have them burned later as a precaution against vermin.

So I was skulking around, looking for the underwear section, and I came across the Ralph Lauren Exhibit, which, in addition to clothes, featured an old saddle, croquet mallets, and various other props associated with rich people. Ralph uses these to create a fashion look that has made him several zillion dollars, a look that I would describe as "Wealthy Constipated WASP." His magazine advertisements feature Lauren-clad people with their hair slicked

back, standing around in large antique-infested houses, looking grim, as if they have just received the tragic news that one of their key polo ponies had injured itself trampling a servant to death and would be unavailable for an important match.

I myself am of WASP heritage, and although my family was not even close to wealthy, we knew WASPs who were, and I frankly cannot understand why any fun-oriented person would want to imitate their life-style. Wealthy WASPs have less fun in their entire lifetimes than members of other ethnic groups have at a single wedding reception. Trust me. I have been to both WASP and non-WASP weddings, and your WASP couple can get married, go on their honeymoon, come home, pursue careers, have children, and get divorced in less time than it takes for a non-WASP couple to get to the part of their reception where everybody drinks champagne from the maid of honor's brassiere.

Nevertheless, the WASP look has been very good to Ralph Lauren. So has another clothing line of his that I would describe as "Pretend Cowboy," which is advertised via photographs of rugged male models, wearing designer cowboy outfits and authentic Wild West male fragrances, fixin' to ride their tastefully color-coordinated horses down to the Old Tradin' Post to purchase a heap o' stylin' gel.

So anyway, I was looking at the Lauren Exhibit, and I came across this T-shirt. It was a regular white T-shirt such as you might use to mow the lawn in or mop up spilled Yoo-Hoo with, except for two things:

1. On the front, in large letters, it had the words RALPH LAUREN STATE FAIR SEPT. 26-OCT. 1 and a large picture of a cowboy on a horse that was bucking wildly (perhaps because the cowboy was wearing too much male fragrance).

2. The price was $57.50.

Yup. Fifty-seven dollars and fifty cents. I once bought an entire *suit* for less than that. I admit that it was not an elegant suit. It was made from what appeared to be the same material they use to cover mattresses. I think it actually had a tag on the lapel that could not be removed under Penalty of Law. I was afraid to wear this suit late at night for fear that tired people would try to lie down on me. (Rim shot.) But at least it was a whole suit, for less than Ralph charges for a *T-shirt.*

Not that I mean to be critical. Hey, people are *buying* these things, just as they are paying top dollar for jeans that appear to have been ripped to shreds by crazed wolverines. You know why? Because garments like these make a *statement.* You wear a Lauren State Fair T-shirt, and you are telling the world: "I paid $57.50 for this T-shirt. God alone knows what I would pay for an official Ralph Lauren jockstrap."

So I am all in favor of the designer T-shirt concept, and I am only sorry that the Lauren Exhibit didn't feature any men's briefs for $38.95 per leg hole, or whatever Ralph would charge. I wound up having to go elsewhere and purchase another famous designer underwear brand. A French one. Le Mart du K.

Rotten to the Core

You residents of rustic, tractor-intensive regions such as Ohio will be pleased to hear that New York City has decided to become polite. Really. There's a new outfit called New York Pride, which is attempting to get New Yorkers to at least pretend that they don't hate everybody. This program resulted from a survey in which researchers asked tourists how come they didn't want to come back to New York, and the tourists said it was because there was so much mean-spiritedness. So the researchers spat on them.

No, seriously, I think New York is very sincere about this. I was in the city recently, and right off the bat I noted that the Teenage Mutant Ninja Taxi Driver who took me to the hotel was very thoughtfully allowing pedestrians as much as .3 nanoseconds to get out of his way, which many of them graciously did even though a taxi does not, technically, have the right-of-way on the sidewalk. The driver was also careful to observe the strict New York City Vehicle Horn Code, under which it is illegal to honk your horn except to communicate one of the following emergency messages:

1. The light is green.
2. The light is red.
3. I hate you.
4. This vehicle is equipped with a horn.

Even very late at night, when there were probably only a few dozen vehicles still operating in the entire city, they'd all gather under my hotel window every few minutes to exchange these vital communications.

Another example of politeness I noticed was that nobody ridiculed my clothes. Everybody in New York, including police horses, dresses fashionably, and whenever I'm there, even in my sharpest funeral-quality suit with no visible ketchup stains, I feel as though I'm wearing a Hefty trash bag. And it's *last year's* Hefty trash bag.

On this trip I also became paranoid about my haircut. After 20 years of having the same haircut, I recently got a more modernistic style that's a little longer in the back, and I was feeling like one hep "dude" until I got to New York, where the fashionable guys all had haircuts in which the hair is real long on top, but abruptly stops halfway down the head, forming a dramatic Ledge of Hair that depressed lice could commit suicide by jumping from. Nobody has had my haircut in New York since 1978. Pigeons were coming from as far away as Staten Island to void themselves on it. But the New Yorkers themselves politely said nothing.

Aside from this courtesy epidemic, the other big story in New York is that—get ready for a Flash Bulletin—the United Nations *still exists.* Yes! Like you, I thought that the UN had been converted to luxury condominiums years ago, but in fact it's still there, performing the vital function that it was established to perform in this troubled, turmoil-filled world: namely, hold receptions.

In fact, using the advanced journalism technique of having a friend give me his invitation, I was able to get into a reception hosted by the U.S. ambassador, who is, in my candid assessment, a tall man named "Tom" with a lot of armed guards. After shaking hands with Tom, I proceeded into the reception area, which was filled with representatives of nations large and small, rich and poor, from all over the world; and although I sometimes tend to be cynical, I could not help but be deeply moved, as a journalist and a human being, by the fact that some of these people had haircuts *even worse than mine.* This was particularly true of the Eastern Bloc men, who looked as if they received their haircuts from the Motherland via fax machine.

But the important thing was, everyone had a good time. People would arrive filled with international tension, but after several drinks and a couple of pounds of shrimp, they'd mellow right out, ready to continue the vital UN work of going to the next reception.

I decided that, since I was there, I might as well use proven journalism techniques to find out if any World Events were going on. So I conducted the following interview with a person standing next to me:

ME: So! Who are you?

PERSON: I'm a [something about economics] from [some country that sounded like "Insomnia"].

ME: Ah! And how are things there?

PERSON: Better.

ME: Ah! (Pause.) What continent is that in, again?

Unfortunately at that point the person had to edge away, but nevertheless I had what we journalists call the "main thrust" of the story, namely: Things are better in Insomnia. It was definitely a load off my mind, and as I walked out into the brisk New York evening, I experienced a sense of renewed hope, which was diminished only slightly by the knowledge that taxis had been sighted in the area, and I would never make it back to the hotel alive.

Well Endowed

Obscenity. Pornography. Naked people thrusting their loins. Should these things be legal? What is obscenity? What is art? What exactly are "loins"? How come nobody ever calls the office and says: "I can't come to work today because I have a loinache"? These are some of the serious questions that we must ask ourselves, as Americans, if we are going to get away with writing columns about sex.

These issues are relevant right now because of the raging national debate over the National Endowment for the Arts, which was established to spend taxpayers' money on art, the theory being that if the taxpayers were allowed to keep their money, they'd just waste it on things they actually wanted. Because frankly, the average taxpayer is not a big voluntary supporter of the arts. The only art that the average taxpayer buys voluntarily either has a picture of Bart Simpson on it or little suction cups on its feet so you can stick it onto a car window.

So if you left it up to the public, there would be hardly any art. Certainly there would be no big art, such as the modernistic sculptures that infest many public parks. You almost never hear members of the public saying, "Hey! Let's all voluntarily chip in and pay a sculptor upwards of $100,000 to fill this park space with what appears to be the rusted remains of a helicopter crash!" It takes concerted government action to erect one of those babies.

The taxpayers also cannot be relied upon to support performing arts such as opera. As a taxpayer, I am forced to admit that I would rather undergo a vasectomy via Weed Whacker than attend an opera. The one time I did sit through one, it lasted approximately as long as fourth grade and featured large men singing for 45 minutes in a foreign language merely to observe that the sun had risen.

My point is that the government supports the arts for the same reason that it purchases $400,000 fax machines and keeps dead radioactive beagles in freezers: Nobody else is willing to do it. The question is, should we carry this concept further? Should the government require taxpayers not only to pay for art, but also to go and physically admire it? This program could be linked with the federal court system:

JUDGE: Mr. Johnson, you have been convicted of tax evasion, and I hereby sentence you to admire four hours of federally subsidized modern dance.

DEFENDANT: NO! NOT MODERN DANCE!!

JUDGE: One more outburst like that, Mr. Johnson, and I'm going to order you to also watch the performance artist who protests apartheid using a bathtub full of rigatoni.

So federal art is good. But now we must grope with the troubling question: Should the government support smut? And how do we define "smut"? You can't just say it's naked people, because many famous works of art, such as the late Michelangelo's statue of David getting ready to fight Goliath, are not wearing a stitch of clothing. Which raises the question: Why would anybody go off to fight in the nude? Was it a tactic? Perhaps this explains why Goliath just stood there like a bozo and let himself get hit by a rock. "Hey!" he was probably thinking. "This guy is naked as a jaybird! What's he trying to AWWRRK."

Some people argue that a work is not pornographic as long as it has redeeming social value. But you can find people who will testify in court that almost anything has redeeming social value:

PROSECUTOR: So, Professor Weemer, you're saying that this video depicts an ecology theme?

WITNESS: Yes. The woman displays a LOT of affection for the zucchini.

On the other end of the spectrum, some people think that just about everything is evil. For example, the Reverend Donald Wildmon, a leading anti-pornography crusader, once mounted a crusade against a Mighty Mouse cartoon. I swear I am not making this up. In this cartoon, Mighty Mouse took a whiff of something; the cartoon makers said it was clearly flower petals, but the Reverend Wildmon was convinced that Mighty Mouse was snorting cocaine.

Of course it's difficult to believe that Mighty Mouse, even if he is a cocaine user, would be stupid enough to snort it on camera. But, as parents, we have to ask ourselves: What if the Rev. Wildmon is right? And speaking of cartoon characters with apparent drug problems, how come Donald Duck has been going around for 50 years wearing a shirt but

no pants? Flashing his loins! Right in front of Huey, Dewey, and Louie, his so-called nephews, if you get my drift! And consider this: If you call up the Walt Disney public relations department, they'll tell you that Mickey and Minnie Mouse are not married, despite having the same last name. Come to think of it, they also have "nephews."

My point is that the obscenity-art issue involves many complex questions, and we owe it to ourselves, as Americans, to give them some serious thought. You go first.

Pranks for the Memories

I love Halloween. And not just because it gives us a chance to buy a new mailbox. No, what I love most is the fun of opening our front door and hearing a group of costumed youngsters happily shout out the traditional Halloween greeting: "(Nothing)."

At least that's what traditionally happens at our house. The youngsters just stand there, silent. They have no idea that I have opened the door. They are as blind as bats, because their eyes are not lined up with the eyeholes in their costume masks.

Poorly aligned eyeholes are an ancient Halloween tradition, dating back at least as far as my childhood in Armonk, New York. My early Halloween memories consist of staggering around disguised as a ghost, unable to see anything except bed sheet, and consequently bonking into trees, falling into brooks, etc. The highlight of my ghost career came in the 1954 Halloween parade, when I marched directly into the butt of a horse.

Today's children, of course, do not wear bed sheets. They wear manufactured costumes representing licensed Saturday-morning cartoon characters and purchased from the Toys "Я" A Billion-Dollar Industry store, but I am pleased to note that the eyeholes still don't line up. So when I open the door on Halloween, I am confronted with three or four imaginary heroes such as G.I. Joe, Conan the Barbarian, Oliver North, etc., all of whom would look very terrifying except that they are three feet tall and facing in random directions. They stand there silently for several seconds, then an adult voice hisses from the darkness behind them: *"Say 'Trick or Treat,' dammit!"*

This voice of course belongs to good old Dad,

who wants more than anything to be home watching the World Series and eating taco dip in bulk, but who must instead accompany the children on their trick-or-treat rounds to make sure I don't put razor blades in the candy. This is a traditional Halloween danger that the local perky TV news personalities warn us about every year, using the Frowny Face they put on when they have to tell us about Bad News, such as plane crashes and rainy weekends.

So I understand why good old Dad has to be there, but he makes me nervous. I can feel him watching me suspiciously from somewhere out there, and I think to myself: What if he's armed? This is a reasonable concern, because I live in South Florida, where *nuns* are armed. So I am very careful about the way I hand out treats.

"Well, boys or perhaps girls!" I say to the licensed characters, in a voice so nonthreatening as to make Mr. Rogers sound like Darth Vader. "How about some NICE CANDY in its ORIGINAL PACKAGING that you can clearly see when I hold it up to the porch light here has NOT BEEN TAMPERED WITH?" Alerted by the sound of my voice, the licensed characters start lurching blindly toward me, thrusting out trick-or-treat bags already containing enough chocolate to meet the nation's zit needs well into the next century.

Of course there is more to Halloween than massive carbohydrate overdoses. There is also the tradition of bitching about pumpkin prices, a tradition that my wife and I enjoy engaging in each year after paying as much as $20 for a dense inedible fruit so that some pumpkin rancher can put a new Jacuzzi in his Lear jet. This is followed by the tradition of scooping the insides, or, technically, the "goop," out of the pumpkin, a chore that always falls to me because both my wife and son refuse to do it, and not without reason, what with the alarming increase in pumpkin-transmitted diseases. (Get the facts! Call the American Pumpkin Council! Don't mention my name!)

But I consider the risk of permanent disfigurement to be a small price to pay for the excitement that comes when I finally finish carving Mr. Jack O'Lantern and put him out on the front porch, there to provide hours of pleasure for the trick-or-treating youngsters except that (a) they can't see and (b) Mr. Jack O'Lantern immediately gets his face kicked into mush by older youngsters playing pranks.

Pranks—defined as "activities that struck you as truly hilarious when you were a teenager but, now that you are a property owner, make you wish you had a high-voltage fence"—are another ancient Halloween tradition. The first Halloween prank ever, played by a group of Druid teenagers, was Stonehenge ("HEY! You kids GET THOSE ROCKS OFF MY LAWN!!"). I can't really complain about the

pranks, because as a youth I played several thousand myself. In fact, I figure there must be a God of Prank Justice, who keeps track of everything we do when we're young and then uses Halloween to settle the score ("OK, that's his 14th mailbox. He has 57 to go."). Vastly enjoying this spectacle, I bet, are the ghosts of all my former victims. Assuming they can see through their eyeholes.

Silent Night, Holy %&?c*

The Holiday Season is here again, and there's "something special" in the air. It's the aroma being given off by our mailperson, who expired in our driveway several days ago while attempting to deliver 300 pounds of Holiday Greeting cards. These were mostly from businesses sending us heartfelt pre-printed bulk-mailed holiday wishes like:

> *'Tis now a time for Peace on Earth*
> *And Joy for all Mankind*
> *So let us know if we can help*
> *Unclog your sewer line.*

But we don't have time to read all our holiday wishes. We're too busy engaging in traditional holiday activities such as Setting Up the Electric Train That Doesn't Work. I bought this train set for my son on his first Christmas, when he was two months old and the only way he knew to play with it was by putting it in his mouth. So it developed some kind of serious train disorder, probably drool in the motor, and every year, when we finally get it hooked up and plugged in, it just sits there, humming. The Little Engine on Valium.

But we can't spend too much time playing with the train, because we have to get on with the tradition of Replacing All the Bulbs in the Christmas Tree Lights. We save big money by buying very inexpensive lights that were manufactured by Third World residents who have no words in their language for "fire code." These lights use special bulbs that are designed to stand up under virtually any kind of punishment except having electricity go through them. If the train isn't humming too loud, we can actually hear the bulbs scream when we plug them in, telling us it's time once again to troop down to the drugstore, where we spend approximately $14,000 per holiday season on replacement bulbs, many of which have been pre-burned-out at the factory for our holiday convenience.

But we can't spend too much time enjoying our tree, because we have to get down to the mall to watch the traditional and highly competitive Holiday Shoppers' Hunt for One of the Four Remaining Department Store Salesclerks in North America. "Ho ho ho!" we shout as a clerk is flushed out of Housewares and makes a desperate dash through Small Appliances, pursued by a baying pack of holiday shoppers, slashing the air with sharpened VISA cards.

Jingle bells! Jingle bells! sings Mister Low-Fidelity Mall Loudspeaker as loud as he can right in our ear. He sings it over and over and over, because he knows it's the kind of traditional holiday song that we can listen to for an entire nanosecond without growing tired of it. *Jingle bells!* it goes. *Jingle BELLS! Jingle BELLS*, DAMMIT! *JINGLE BANG* . . .

Uh-oh! It looks like Mr. Low-Fidelity Mall Loudspeaker has been shot by another important holiday tradition, the Increasingly Desperate Guy Shopper. He's trying to find something for that Special Someone in his life, who has made it clear that this year she'd like something a little more personal than what he got her last year, which was a trailer hitch. So he's edging warily through the aisles of what is, for guys, a very dangerous section of the department store, a section where sometimes women wearing scary quantities of makeup lunge out from behind pillars and spray you with fragrances with names like Calvin Klein's Clinical Depression. All around are potential gift items, but there's no way for the guy shopper to tell which ones would be thoughtful and appropriate, and which ones would cause that Special Someone to place an urgent conference call so she could inform all her friends simultaneously what a bonerhead she is hooked up with.

Last holiday season I went to a department store with a friend of mine named Joel, who was trying to buy something for Mary. He became badly disoriented in the scarf section, which featured a display of tiny fragile cloth wisps that had no imaginable function and that cost as much per wisp as a radial tire. It looked to me like some kind of holiday prank, but Joel, rapidly losing brain function from breathing a department-store atmosphere that was 2 parts oxygen and 17 parts cologne, grabbed one basically at random and actually *bought* it. But that was not his major gift purchase. His major gift purchase was something totally romantic, something that represents the ultimate in traditional holiday gift giving: a jogging bra. I am not making this up. "She'll love it!" he said. I agreed, but only because I knew that if he didn't finish shopping soon he'd start throwing money directly into wastebaskets.

Speaking of which, I need to get my holiday

butt over to the Toys Sure "Я" Expensive Considering How Fast They Break store before they run out of Giant Radioactive Nose Worms from Space or whatever popular heavily advertised holiday toy concept my son is hoping Santa will bring him. I doubt that Santa will to come to our house personally this year. The reindeer would go berserk if they got a whiff of the mailperson.

Garbage Scan

Monday morning. Bad traffic. Let's just turn on the radio here, see if we can get some good tunes, crank it up. Maybe they'll play some some early Stones. Yeah. Maybe they . . .

—POWER ON—

". . . just reached the end of 14 classic hits in a row, and we'll be right back after we . . ."

—SCAN—

". . . send Bill Doberman to Congress. Because Bill Doberman agrees with us. Bill Doberman. It's a name we can trust. Bill Doberman. It's a name we can remember. Let's write it down. Bill . . ."

—SCAN—

". . . just heard 19 uninterrupted classic hits, and now for this . . ."

—SCAN—

". . . terrible traffic backup caused by the . . ."

—SCAN—

. . . EVIL that cometh down and DWELLETH amongst them, and it DID CAUSETH their eyeballs to ooze a new substance, and it WAS a greenish color, but they DID not fear, for they kneweth that the . . ."

—SCAN—

". . . followingisbasedonan800yearleaseand-doesnotincludetaxtagsinsuranceoranactualcarweget-yourhouseandyourchildrenandyourkidneys . . ."

—SCAN—

"NINE THOUSAND DOLLARS!!! BUD LOOTER CHEVROLET OPEL ISUZU FORD RENAULT JEEP CHRYSLER TOYOTA STUDEBAKER TUCKER HONDA WANTS TO GIVE YOU, FOR NO GOOD REASON . . ."

—SCAN—

". . . Bill Doberman. He'll work for you. He'll *fight* for you. If people are rude to you, Bill Doberman will *kill* them. Bill Doberman . . ."

—SCAN—

". . . enjoyed those 54 classic hits in a row, and now let's pause while . . ."

—SCAN—

". . . insects DID swarm upon them and DID eateth their children, but they WERE NOT afraid, for they trustedeth in the . . ."

—SCAN—

". . . listening audience. Hello?"

"Hello?"

"Go ahead."

"Steve?"

"This is Steve. Go ahead."

"Am I on?"

"Yes. Go ahead."

"Is this Steve?"

—SCAN—

"This is Bill Doberman, and I say convicted rapists have *no business* serving on the Supreme Court. That's why, as your congressman, I'll make sure that . . ."

—SCAN—

". . . a large quantity of nuclear waste has been spilled on the interstate, and police are trying to . . ."

—SCAN—

". . . GIVE YOU SEVENTEEN THOUSAND DOLLARS IN TRADE FOR ANYTHING!!! IT DOESN'T EVEN HAVE TO BE A CAR!!! BRING US A ROAD KILL!!! WE DON'T CARE!!! BRING US A CANTALOUPE-SIZED GOB OF EAR WAX!!! BRING US . . ."

—SCAN—

". . . huge creatures that WERE like winged snakes EXCEPT they had great big suckers, which DID cometh and pulleth their limbs FROM their sockets liketh this, 'Pop,' but they WERE not afraid, nay they WERE joyous, for they had . . ."

—SCAN—

". . . just heard 317 uninterrupted classic hits, and now . . ."

—SCAN—

"Bill Doberman will shrink your swollen membranes. Bill Doberman has . . ."

—SCAN—

". . . glowing bodies strewn all over the road, and motorists are going to need . . ."

—SCAN—

". . . FORTY THOUSAND DOLLARS!!! WE'LL JUST GIVE IT TO YOU!!! FOR NO REASON!!! WE HAVE A BRAIN DISORDER!!! LATE AT NIGHT, SOMETIMES WE SEE THESE GIANT GRUBS WITH FACES LIKE KITTY CARLISLE, AND WE HEAR THESE VOICES SAYING . . ."

—SCAN—

"Steve?"

"Yes."

"Steve?"

"Yes."

"Steve?"

—SCAN—

"Yes, and their eyeballs DID explode like party favors, but they WERE NOT sorrowful, for they kneweth . . ."

—SCAN—

Bill Doberman. Him good. Him heap strong. Him your father. Him . . ."

—SCAN—

". . . finished playing 3,814 consecutive classic hits with no commercial interruptions dating back to 1978, and now . . ."

—SCAN—

". . . the radiation cloud is spreading rapidly, and we have unconfirmed reports that . . ."

—SCAN—

". . . liquefied brain parts did dribbleth OUT from their nostrils, but they WERE not alarmed, for they were . . ."

—SCAN—

". . . getting sleepy. Very sleepy. When you hear the words 'Bill Doberman,' you will . . ."

—POWER OFF—

OK, never mind. I'll just drive. Listen to people honk. Maybe hum a little bit. Maybe even, if nobody's looking, do a little singing.

(Quietly)

I can't get noooooooo
Sa-tis-FAC-shun . . .

Where You Can Stick the Sticker Price

We are attempting to purchase a new car, and I have just one teensy little question: WHY WON'T THEY TELL YOU HOW MUCH IT COSTS?

I mean, let's say you're in the market for a rutabaga. You go to the supermarket and there, plain as day, is a sign stating the price of the rutabaga, allowing you to decide instantly whether it is in your price range. If it is, you simply pay the amount and take your rutabaga home, and you hurl it into your garbage disposal. At least that's what I would do, because I hate rutabagas.

But when you walk into a car dealership, you are entering Consumer Hell. There is no easy way to find out what the actual true price of any given car is. Oh, sure, there is a "sticker price," but only a very naive fungal creature just arrived from a distant galaxy would dream of paying this. In fact, federal law now requires that the following statement appear directly under the sticker price:

**WARNING TO STUPID PEOPLE:
DO NOT PAY THIS AMOUNT.**

The only way to find out the real price is to undergo a fraternity-style initiation. First you squint at the sticker, which lists the car's 163 special features, none of which you could ever locate on the actual car because they all sound like rocket parts, as in "transverse-mounted induced-torque modality propounders." Then a salesperson comes sidling toward you in an extremely casual fashion (do not attempt to escape, however; an experienced car salesperson can sidle great distances at upwards of 45 miles per hour) and chatters on at length about the many extreme advantages of whatever car you are looking at ("It has your obverse-shafted genuine calfskin bivalve exuders"). But if you ask him the true price, he will make some vague, Confucius-type statement like: "Dave, we are definitely willing to go the extra mile to put a smile on your face."

"But how much does it cost?" you say.

"Dave," he says, lowering his voice to indicate that you and he have become close personal friends. "Frankly, Dave, (name of whatever month it is) has been a slow month, and I think, Dave, that if we sit down and cut bait, we can come up with a number that we can play ball with."

"WHAT number?" you say. "TELL ME THE NUMBER."

"Dave," he says, "I think if we both pull on our oars here, we can put the icing on the cake while the iron is still hot."

The easiest solution, of course, is to simply pull out a loaded revolver and say, "Tell me how much this car costs or I will kill you," but unfortunately it is still a misdemeanor in some states to shoot a car salesperson. So eventually you have to start *guessing* at the price ("Is it more than $9,500?"). It is very similar to the childhood game Twenty Questions, only it takes much longer, because instead of saying "yes" or "no," the salesperson always answers: "Let me talk to my manager."

The manager is comparable to the Wizard of Oz, an omnipotent being who stays behind the curtain and pulls the levers and decides whether or not the Cowardly Lion will get a free sunroof. I have never heard a conversation between a manager and a salesperson, but I assume it goes like this:

SALESPERSON: He wants to know if it's more than $9,500. Can I tell him?

MANAGER: How many times have you called him "Dave"?

SALESPERSON: 1,672 times.

MANAGER: Not yet.

So it can take hours to determine the true price, and this is just for one car. If you want to find out the price of another brand of car, you have to go through the entire fraternity initiation all over again. And there are hundreds of brands of cars out there. *Thousands* of them. Back when I was a child and Abraham Lincoln was the president, there were only about four kinds of cars, all of them manufactured by General Motors, but now you see new dealerships springing up on a daily basis, selling cars you never heard of, cars whose names sound like the noise that karate experts make just before they break slabs of concrete with their foreheads ("Hyundai!!").

So far, the cars we have looked at include: the Mimosa Uhuru 2000-LXJ. The Mikado Sabrina Mark XVIXMLCM, and the Ford Peligroso, which is actu-

ally the same as the Chevrolet Sombrero, the Jeep Violent Savage, and the Chrysler Towne Centre Coupe de Grace, and which is manufactured partly in Asia (engine, transmission, body) and partly in the United States (ashtray). They are all fine cars, but at the present time, based on our discussions with the various salespersons, we find ourselves leaning toward the rutabaga.

Lemon Harangue

Today's Consumer Topic is: How to Buy a Car.

The First Rule of Car Buying is one that I learned long ago from my father, namely: Never buy any car that my father would buy. He had an unerring instinct for picking out absurd cars, cars that were clearly intended as industrial pranks, cars built by workers who had to be blindfolded to prevent them from laughing so hard at the product that they accidentally shot rivets into each other.

For example, my father was one of the very few Americans who bought the Hillman Minx, a wart-shaped British car with the same rakish, sporty appeal as a municipal parking garage but not as much pickup. Our Minx also had a Surprise Option Feature whereby the steering mechanism would disconnect itself at random moments, so you'd suddenly discover that you could spin the wheel all the way around in a playful circle without having any effect whatsoever on the front wheels. Ha ha! You can imagine how I felt, as an insecure 16-year-old with skin capable of going from All-Clear Status to Fully Mature Zit in seconds, arriving at the big high school pep rally dance, where all the cool guys had their Thunderbirds and their GTOs with their giant engines and 23 carburetors, and there I was, at the wheel of: the Hillman Minx. A car so technologically backward that the radio was still receiving Winston Churchill speeches.

You don't see many Minxes around anymore, probably because the factory was bombed by the Consumer Product Safety Commission. You also don't see many Nash Metropolitans, another car my father bought. The Metropolitan was designed by professional cartoonists to look like the main character in a children's book with a name like *Buster the*

Car Goes to Town. It was so small that it was routinely stolen by squirrels. It was not the ideal car for dating, because there was room for only one person, so the other one had to sprint along the side of the highway, trying to make casual conversation and sometimes dropping from exhaustion. Being a gentleman, I always made sure my dates carried flares so I could go back and locate them at night.

Of course today's cars are much more sophisticated, by which I mean "expensive." This is because modern cars employ all kinds of technologically advanced concepts such as measuring the engine in "liters." Let's say you buy a car with a "5.7-liter engine": This means that when it breaks, you should not ask your mechanic how much it's going to cost until you've consumed 5.7 liters of a manufacturer-approved wine.

The most important consideration, in buying a new car, is the rebate. This is one area of automotive technology where America still reigns supreme. A lot of Japanese cars don't even *have* rebates, whereas some American car dealerships have become so sophisticated that *they no longer even sell cars.* You just go in there and sign legal papers for a couple of hours and get your rebate and your zero-percent financing with no payments due until next Halloween, and you drive home in your same old car. Ask your automotive sales professional for details. He's clinging to your leg right now.

NO! JUST KIDDING! The last time I jokingly suggested that there was anything even slightly unpleasant about buying a car, several million automotive sales professionals wrote me letters threatening to take all their advertising out of the newspaper and jam it up my nasal passages. So let me state in all sincerity that as far as I am concerned these people are gods, and car-buying is the most legal fun that a person can have while still wearing underwear.

But it can also be confusing. There are so many brands of cars today, with new ones constantly being introduced, not only from domestic manufacturers but also from foreign countries such as Mars. I refer here to the "Infiniti," a car that was introduced by a bizarre advertising campaign in which—perhaps you noticed this—*you never actually saw the car.* Really. All you saw in the magazine ads was ocean waves, leading you to wonder: Is this a submersible car? Or was there some kind of accident during the photo session? ("Dammit, Bruce, I TOLD you the tide was coming in!")

But no, the Infiniti ads were done that way on purpose. They wanted you to spend $40,000 on this car, plus whatever it costs to get the barnacles off it, but they *refused to show it to you.* Why? Because the Infiniti is actually: the *Hillman Minx.*

No, just kidding again. The truth is that the Infiniti ads are part of an exciting new trend called

"Advertising Whose Sole Purpose Is to Irritate You." The ultimate example of this is the magazine ads for Denaka vodka, where a haughtily beautiful woman is staring at you as though you're the world's largest ball of underarm hair, and she's saying, "When I said vodka, I meant Denaka." What a fun gal! I bet she's a big hit at parties. ("*Pssst!* Come into the kitchen! We're all gonna spit in the Denaka woman's drink!")

My point is that there's more to buying a car than just kicking the tires. You have to really know what you're doing, which is why, all kidding aside, I recommend that you carefully analyze your automotive needs, study the market thoroughly, and then purchase the car that you truly feel, in all objectivity, has the most expensive advertisement in this newspaper. Don't thank me: I'm just keeping my job.

Traffic Infraction, He Wrote

Probably the greatest thing about this country, aside from the fact that virtually any random bonerhead can become president, is the American system of justice. We are very fortunate to live in a country where every accused person, unless he has a name like Nicholas "Nicky the Squid" Calamari, is considered innocent until such time as his name appears in the newspaper. Also you have the constitutional right (the so-called Carmen Miranda right) to be provided—at the taxpayers' expense, if you cannot afford one—with an enormous fruit-covered hat. But the most important right of all is that every criminal is entitled to a Day In Court. Although, in my particular case, it occurred at night.

Let me stress right out front that I was as guilty as sin. I was driving in downtown Miami, which in itself shows very poor judgment because most Miami motorists graduated with honors from the Moammar Gadhafi School of Third World-Style Driving (motto: "Death Before Yielding").

So I probably should never have been there anyway, and it served me right when the two alert police officers fired up their siren, pulled me over, and pointed out that my car's registration had expired. I had not realized this, and as you can imagine I felt like quite the renegade outlaw as one of the officers painstakingly wrote out my ticket, standing well to the side of the road so as to avoid getting hit by the steady stream of passing unlicensed and uninsured motorists driving their stolen cars with their left hands so their right hands would be free to keep their pit bulls from spilling their cocaine all over their machine guns.

Not that I am bitter.

When he gave me the ticket, the officer told me that I had to appear in court. I had never done this before, so I considered asking my attorney, Joseph "Joe the Attorney" DiGiacinto, to represent me. Unfortunately, Joe is not a specialist in traffic matters, in the sense that—and I say this as a friend—he is the worst driver in the history of the world. I figured he might not be the ideal person to have on my side in traffic court:

JOE: Your Honor, my client . . .

JUDGE (interrupting): Wait a minute. Aren't you Joseph DiGiacinto?

JOE: Um, well . . .

JUDGE: The person who had driver licenses revoked by *three different states?*

JOE: *Well, I . . .*

JUDGE: The person who once, during a crowded street festival in New York's colorful Chinatown district, attained a speed of almost 45 miles per hour on the *sidewalk?*

JOE: Well, yes.

JUDGE: I sentence your client to death.

So I thought I'd be better off representing myself. I've watched "The People's Court" for years, and I pride myself on my ability to grasp the issues involved, even in complex cases involving highly technical points of law such as, does the dress shop have to take back the defective formal gown if the buyer got B.O. stains on it. In fact, I have always secretly wanted to be a lawyer. I could picture myself in a major criminal case, getting the best of my opponent through clever verbal sparring and shrewd courtroom maneuvers:

ME: So, Mr. Teeterhorn, you're telling us that you "can't recall" why you happened to bring a flame-thrower to the bridge tournament?

WITNESS: That's right.

ME: Well, perhaps THIS will help refresh your memory.

WITNESS: NO! GET THAT THING AWAY! OUCH!! IT'S BITING ME!!!

OPPOSING ATTORNEY: I object, Your Honor! Mr. Barry is badgering the witness!

ME (coolly): Your Honor, as these documents clearly prove, Rex here is a wolverine.

JUDGE (examining the documents): OK, I'll allow it.

By the night of my traffic court appearance, I had worked out a subtle yet crafty defense strategy: groveling. My plan was to beg for mercy and ask for the judge's permission to buff his shoes with my hair.

Only there was no judge. They herded us traffic violators into a courtroom with flags and a judge's bench and everything, but instead of an actual hu-

man, they had a judge *on videotape*. Really. I could have just stayed home and *rented* the American system of justice.

The video judge welcomed us to Traffic Court and explained our various legal options in such careful detail that by the time he was done none of us had the vaguest idea what they were. Then some clerks started calling us, one by one, to the front of the room. I thought this would be my opportunity to grovel, but before I had a chance, the clerk stamped my piece of paper and told me to go pay the cashier. That was it. Within minutes I was back out on the street, another criminal release with a "slap on the wrist" by our revolving-door justice system.

The first thing I did, back on the Outside, was make an illegal U-turn.

The Do-It-Yourself Deficit-Reduction Contest

I'm thinking maybe we should do something about this pesky federal budget deficit. Of course this is not our job. We have a political system called "democracy" (from the ancient Greek words "demo," meaning "white men," and "cracy" meaning "wearing blue suits") under which we, The People, do not personally govern the nation because we have to work. So we elect representatives who go to Washington on our behalf and perform the necessary governmental functions that we ourselves would perform if we were there, such as sending out newsletters, accepting large contributions, and becoming involved in a wide range of sex scandals. My favorite part is when the scandal becomes public and the congressperson, in accordance with congressional tradition, attacks the press:

CONGRESSPERSON: Are you media people perfect? Have you never committed an immoral act?

REPORTER: Not involving agricultural products, no.

SECOND REPORTER: At least not *soybeans.*

So there's no need for us to become involved in the government, unless of course we have a good reason, which is why, about a year ago, I called up the U.S. Treasury Department in an effort to get it to stop making pennies.

Pennies were invented during the Great Depression, a grim era that was filmed entirely in black and white. The nation needed a very small unit of money, because back then—ask anybody who lived through it—the average salary was only four cents per year, and houses cost a dime, and a dollar would buy you a working railroad.

Today, however, nothing costs a penny. Even shoddy, worthless products such as stale gum balls, rest-room condoms, and newspapers cost at least a quarter, the result being that pennies have become nothing but a nuisance, the Mediterranean fruit flies of the coin world. Everybody hates them. Stores deliberately palm them off on you by programming their cash registers so that no matter what you buy, the total comes to something dollars and 61 cents, allowing the clerk to dump upwards of 17 pennies into your hand, knowing that you can't prove that the amount is incorrect because, thanks to the electronic calculator, no normal American outside the third grade remembers how to subtract.

All these pennies end up in your home. In my household alone we have several penny deposits easily the size of brutally persecuted minority group Zsa Zsa Gabor. At risk of suffering fatal hernias we have lugged them from household to household, watching them grow, unable to turn them back into money because the bank won't take them unless you wrap them in those little paper sleeves, a job that we estimate would take us, assuming we did not stop for lunch, until the end of time.

So as a concerned citizen, I called the Treasury Department, where I was eventually connected with an official spokesperson, who told me that the reason the government keeps making pennies is—she really said this—the public *wants* pennies.

"No we don't," I pointed out.

But the spokesperson insisted that yes, we did. She cited several scientific surveys, apparently taken on the Planet Weebo, proving that pennies are highly popular, and assured me that the government plans to keep right on cranking them out.

It is at times like this that we should remember the words of President John F. Kennedy, who, in his stirring inaugural address, said: "Ask not what your country can do for you. Ask whether your country has been inhaling paint-thinner fumes." I mean, look at the federal budget deficit. Everybody in the known universe agrees that the deficit is way too big, so the government's solution is to make it *bigger,* by means of innovative programs such as the savings-and-loan industry bailout. Here we have an industry that managed to lose hundreds of billions of dollars because the people who run it apparently have the financial "know-how" of furniture, so our government's solution is to give them *hundreds of billions more dollars,* which they'll probably rush out and spend on shrewd investments such as worm farms.

So I'm thinking maybe it's time that we, The People, swung into action. Just sitting here scratching my armpit I've already come up with several practical ideas for reducing the deficit:

- Hire men named Vito to kidnap federal pandas Hsing-Hsing and Ling-Ling so the government will stop spending millions each year trying to make them (the pandas) reproduce.

- Require each congressman to sell $17 billion worth of cookies door to door.
- Pass a constitutional amendment requiring a balanced budget.

Well, OK, I admit that last one was "off the deep end." But my point is, our government needs help, which is why I've decided to hold:

A Deficit-Reduction Contest

I want you to think up an idea, write it down on a POSTAL CARD (remember, it has to be short enough that even top federal officials can grasp it) and mail it to me c/o The Miami Herald, Miami, FL 33132. If you win, I'll print your name and suggestion in a column, and armed federal employees with dogs will come to your house at night. Not only that, but if yours is the BEST idea, I'll send you a *CASH PRIZE*. I'm totally serious here. This will be such a massive cash prize that it will be shipped from my house to yours by *truck*. I'm sure it will bring you much happiness, once you get those sleeves on it.

The Shocking Solution to the Budget Deficit

Today we announce the winners in our big Deficit Contest, in which we asked you, the ordinary taxpaying citizens who make up the backbone and pelvic structure of this great nation, to see if you could come up with helpful suggestions for getting rid of this pesky federal budget deficit. As you know, our congresspersons have been unable to work on this because they've been busy passing an Ethics Bill, under which we're going to pay them more money, in exchange for which they're going to try to have some ethics. I think this is a terrific concept, and if it works with Congress, we should also try it with other ethically impaired groups such as the criminally insane.

Speaking of whom, you readers did a heck of a job responding to the Deficit Contest. As I write these words, my office floor is covered with thousands of contest entries, carefully arranged in mounds and in many cases welded together with dog spit supplied by my two research assistants, Earnest and Zippy, who were a major help. But it was you readers who really came through, proving once again that when the American people decide to "get involved" in a problem, it is best not to let them have any sharp implements. Because quite frankly, reading between the lines, I detected a certain amount of hostility in these entries, especially the ones proposing a nuclear strike on the U.S. Capitol.

Some hostility was also directed toward me. In some versions of my original contest column I had proposed, in a lighthearted manner, that we reduce the deficit by "selling unnecessary states such as Oklahoma to the Japanese." This caused a number of Oklahomans to send in letters containing many correctly spelled words and making the central lighthearted point that I am a jerk. They also sent me official literature stating that Oklahoma has enormous quantities of culture in the form of ballet, Oral

Roberts, etc., and that the Official State Reptile—I am not making this up—is something called the "Mountain Boomer." So I apologize to Oklahoma, and as a token of my sincerity I'm willing to sell my state, Florida, to the Japanese, assuming nobody objects to the fact that Japan would suddenly become the most heavily armed nation on Earth.

But most of the hostility in the Deficit Contest entries was directed toward our elected federal officials. This is especially true of:

The Contest Winner

This is Geoffrey Braden of Seattle, Washington, whose idea is that we convert the federal budget deficit to electrical voltage—the bigger the deficit, the higher the voltage—and then run the current through our congresspersons. Geoffrey recommended that we run the current through a specific section of the congressional anatomy that I will not identify here, except to say that besides eliminating the deficit, this proposal would put a real dent in all these sex scandals. Geoffrey therefore wins the big Cash Prize, consisting of all the pennies in my closet, estimated street value $23 million if put into paper sleeves, which will never happen.

Speaking of pennies, about a thousand of you suggested that we eliminate the deficit by sending all our accumulated hateful penny deposits to the government. This is a brilliant idea except for one minor flaw: It's stupid. What it boils down to is giving the government more money, which of course the government would immediately convert into things like accordion subsidies. Which is too bad, because some of you had excellent ideas for increasing government revenue, such as:

- "A $10 million Roman numeral tax on movies. For example, *Rambo IV* would cost Stallone $40 million. I'm not sure whether reducing the number of movie sequels would be a side benefit or the main benefit." (Ed Goodman, Waterbury, Connecticut)
- "Fine people $50,000 for each unnecessary education-related letter attached to the end of their names. For example, 'Robert H. Monotone, B.A., M.B.A., Ph.D.' would be fined $400,000 annually." (Ron DiCesare, Troy, Michigan)
- "The U.S. government should sell its secrets directly to the Russians and cut out the middlemen." (Leslie Price, Hibbing, Minnesota)
- "Rent the Stealth bomber out for proms." (Jimmy Muth, Haverstraw, New York)
- "Sell live film footage of George Bush showering

with his dog." (Leslie Gorman, Fort Worth, Texas)

- "Mug Canada." (Kyle Kelly of Dubuque, Iowa, and Mike Orsburn of Gainesville, Texas)

We also got a lot of suggestions that we do not totally 100 percent understand but that we are presenting here as a reminder of the importance of remembering to take our prescription medication:

- "Make deer legal tender." (Jon Hunner, Tesuque, New Mexico)
- "Arbitrarily and capriciously eliminate every other word in government documents." (George Garklavs, Golden, Colorado)
- "Sell manure (all kinds) at North and South poles." (Sharon Rice, Oologah, Oklahoma) (Really)
- "Substitute politicians for road barriers." (Steven Lenoff, Deerfield Beach, Florida)
- "I have a secret plan. Make me president and I'll tell you." (Richard Nixon)
- "Put it in the bunny." (Travis Ranney, Seattle, Washington)

You wacky readers! I love you! Please stay away from my house!

But all kidding aside, the time has come for us to work together on this deficit thing. What can you do? You can write to your congressperson. Tell him you're fed up with government irresponsibility. Tell him you don't want excuses. Tell him you want action.

Tell him these are going to be *very sharp* electrodes.

Bug Off!

I am sick and tired of our so-called representatives in Washington being influenced by powerful special-interest groups on crucial federal issues. As you have no doubt gathered, I am referring to the current effort to name an Official National Insect.

This effort, which I am not making up, was alertly brought to my attention by Rick Guldan, who's on the staff of U.S. Representative James Hansen of Utah, at least until this column gets published. Rick sent me a letter that was mailed to congresspersons by the Entomological Society of America. (An "entomologist" is defined by Webster's as "a person who studies entomology.") The letter urges Representative Hansen to support House Joint Resolution 411, which would "designate the monarch butterfly as our national insect." The letter gives a number of reasons, including that "the durability of this insect and its travels into the unknown emulate the rugged pioneer spirit and freedom upon which this nation was settled."

The letter is accompanied by a glossy political-campaign-style brochure with color photographs showing the monarch butterfly at work, at play, relaxing with its family, etc. There's also a list entitled "Organizations Supporting the Monarch Butterfly," including the Friends of the Monarchs, the National Pest Control Association, the Southern Maryland Rock and Mineral Club, and the Saginaw County Mosquito Abatement Commission.

Needless to say I am strongly in favor of having an official national insect. If history teaches us one lesson, it is that a nation that has no national insect is a nation that probably also does not celebrate Soybean Awareness Month. I also have no problem with the monarch butterfly *per se.* ("Per se" is Greek for "unless it lays eggs in my salad.") Butterflies are nice to have around, whereas with a lot of other insects, if

they get anywhere near you, your immediate reaction, as an ecologically aware human being, is to whomp them with a hardcover work of fiction at least the size of *Moby Dick*.

But what bothers me is the way the Entomological Society is trying to slide this thing through Congress without considering the views of the average citizen who does not have the clout or social standing to belong to powerful elite "insider" organizations such as the Saginaw County Mosquito Abatement Commission. Before Congress makes a decision of this magnitude, we, the public, should get a chance to vote on the national insect. We might feel that, in these times of world tension, we don't want to be represented by some cute little flitting critter. We might want something that commands respect, especially in light of the fact that the Soviet Union recently selected as its national insect the Chernobyl Glowing Beetle, which grows to a length of 17 feet and can mate in midair with military aircraft.

Fortunately, we Americans have some pretty darned impressive insects ourselves. In South Florida, for example, we have industrial cockroaches that have to be equipped with loud warning beepers so you can get out of their way when they back up. Or we could pick a fierce warlike insect such as the fire ant, although this could create problems during the official White House National Insect Naming Ceremony ("WASHINGTON—In a surprise development yesterday that political observers believe could affect the 1992 election campaign, President Bush was eaten.")

Other strong possible candidates for National Insect include: the gnat, the imported Japanese beetle, the chigger, the praying mantis, Jiminy Cricket, the laughing mantis, the lobster, the dead bugs in your light fixture, the skeet-shooting mantis, and Senator Jesse Helms. I could go on, but my purpose here is not to name all the possibilities; my purpose is to create strife and controversy for no good reason.

And you can help. I recently acquired a highly trained, well-staffed, modern Research Department. Her name is Judi Smith, and she is severely underworked because I never need anything researched other than the question of what is the frozen-yogurt Flavor of the Day at the cafeteria.

So I'm asking you to write your preference for National Insect on a POSTAL CARD. (If you send a letter, the Research Department has been instructed to laugh in the diabolical manner of Jack Nicholson as The Joker and throw it away unopened.) Send your card to: National Insect Survey, c/o Judi Smith, The Miami Herald Tropic Magazine, 1 Herald Plaza, Miami, FL 33132.

Judi will read all the entries and gradually go insane. Then I'll let you know which insect is preferred by you, The People, and we can start putting serious pressure on Congress. If all goes well, this could wind up costing the taxpayers millions of dollars.

In closing, let me stress one thing, because I don't want to get a lot of irate condescending mail from insect experts correcting me on my facts: I am well aware that Senator Helms is, technically, a member of the arachnid family.

Insect Aside

I wish that the critics who claim the average American doesn't care about the issues could see the response we got to our survey about the Official National Insect. We have been flooded with postal cards from all over the United States and several parallel universes. Just a quick glance through these cards is enough to remind you why this great nation, despite all the talk of decline, still leads the world in tranquilizer consumption.

As you may recall, this issue arose when the Entomological Society of America, realizing that troubled times like these call for bold government, began lobbying Congress to name the monarch butterfly as the Official National Insect. Congresspersons received a glossy full-color promotional brochure pointing out that the monarch is attractive, ecological, educational, and courageous, having on several occasions disregarded its own personal safety to pull little Timmy out of the quicksand.

Or maybe that was Lassie. Anyway, the monarch butterfly appeared to have a lock on the National Insectship, because the Entomological Society of America is a powerful outfit. More than one person who has dared to challenge the society on a piece of insect-related legislation has found his automobile ignition wired to a hornet's nest in the glove compartment.

Well, you can call me a courageous patriot with cruel yet handsome eyes if you wish, but I happen to think that when our Founding Fathers froze their buns at Valley Forge, they were fighting to create a nation where the National Insect would be chosen by a fair and open process, not in some gnat-filled back room. That's why I asked you, the average citizen with no ax to grind and way too much spare time, to write in and voice your opinion.

All I can say is, it's a good thing that some of you *don't* have axes, if you get my drift. I refer partic-

ularly to the person who wrote: "My choice for Official National Incest is mother-son. Thank you for asking."

Many of you voted for the dung beetle, the mosquito, and the leech, all of which were inevitably compared to Congress. I'm sorry but that's a low blow: Our research indicates that no dung beetle has *ever* accepted money from a savings-and-loan operator.

Other insects receiving votes include: the earwig; the gadfly; the tarantula hawk wasp (which kills tarantulas for a living and is already the Official Insect of New Mexico); the maggot; the killer bee (as one reader put it, "We better start sucking up to them while there's still time"); the scorpion; the pissant; the stink bug; the termite; "men"; the tick; the Stealth bomber; the nervous tick; a dead bug named Hector that was actually mailed to us; the screw worm; the fly ("Zip up, America!"); the weevil; the dust mite ("I want a National Insect I can unknowingly inhale"); the worm at the bottom of the tequila bottle; the spittle bug; "Those little moths that get into your cabinets and lay eggs in your Stove Top Stuffing which hatch and cause you to eat the larvae"; the pubic louse; the horned fungus beetle ("because it strongly resembles ex-president Richard Nixon, which makes stomping one into oblivion a special American experience"); Johnny Mantis; the Ford Pinto; Mothra; "any 13-year-old or my ex-husband"; the contact lens borer; the booger, the bug that goes splat on your windshield; and Ted Kennedy.

Without question the most thoughtful vote came from eight-year-old David Affolter, a student at the Spruce Street School in Seattle, who wrote: "I want the National Insect to be the ladybug, because the ladybug can do about everything a bug should do. It can be a board-game piece."

It's hard to argue with that. But it's also hard to argue with the numbers, and there were 213 votes for the monarch butterfly, versus 87 for the ladybug, 72 for the praying mantis, 65 for the bee, 43 for Senator Jesse Helms, and 37 for the cockroach. Beetles, as a group, got 261 votes, but the beetle vote was badly divided, with no clear "take-charge" beetle emerging.

This is a shame, because one beetle, which received several dozen votes, clearly deserves further consideration. This is the bombardier beetle, which —I am not making this up—has an internal reaction chamber where it mixes chemicals that actually explode, enabling the beetle to shoot a foul-smelling, high-temperature jet of gas out its rear end with a distinct "crack." It reminds me of guys I knew in college. The Time-Life insect book has a series of photographs in which what is described as "a self-assured bombardier beetle" defeats a *frog*. In the first picture, the frog is about to chomp the beetle; in the second, the beetle blasts it; and in the third, the frog is staggering away, gagging, clearly wondering how come it never learned about this in Frog School. I would be darned proud, as an American, to be represented by this insect. An engraving of a bombardier beetle emitting a defiant blast from his butt would look great on a coin.

My point is that, although the monarch butterfly is clearly the frontrunner and has a slick, well-financed campaign, we need to give this National Insect thing a lot more thought. Maybe, as reader James Buzby (his real name) suggests, Congress should appoint a Stop-gap National Insect while we make our final determination.

But whatever happens, I intend to follow this story, even though I may irritate the powerful Entomological Society of America, which for all I know could try to . . . hey, what are these things crawling out of my keyboard? OUCH! HEY!! OUCH!!!

Tax Fax

Income-tax time is here again, and I'm sure that the Number One question on the minds of millions of anxious taxpayers is: Do we have a new Internal Revenue Service commissioner named "Fred"?

I am pleased to report that yes, we do. In fact, if you look on Page 2 of your IRS Form 1040 Instruction Booklet Written by Nuclear Physicists for Nuclear Physicists, you'll find a nice letter from Commissioner Fred, in which he states, on behalf of all the fine men and women and attack dogs down at the IRS: "Let us know if we can do more."

I know I speak for taxpayers everywhere when I say: "NO! Really, Fred! You've done enough!" I am thinking of such helpful IRS innovations as the Wrong Answer Hotline, wherein, if you're having trouble understanding a section of the IRS Secret Tax Code, all you have to do is call the IRS Taxpayer Assistance Program, and in a matter of seconds, thanks to computerized electronics, you are placed on hold for several hours before finally being connected to trained IRS personnel dispensing tax advice that is statistically no more likely to be correct than if you asked Buster the Wonder Horse to indicate the answer by stomping the dirt.

Ha ha! Speaking as a married person filing jointly, let me stress that I am JUST KIDDING here, because I know that the folks at IRS have a terrific sense of humor. Down at headquarters they often pass the time while waiting for their cattle prods to recharge by sending hilarious tax-related jokes to each other in triplicate on IRS Humorous Anecdote Form 1092-376 SNORT.

IRS HUMOR EXAMPLE A: "A lawyer, a doctor, and a priest were marooned on a desert island. So we confiscated their homes."

IRS HUMOR EXAMPLE B: "What do you get when you cross Zsa Zsa Gabor with a kangaroo?" "I don't know, but let's confiscate its home."

What a wacky bunch of personnel! But all kidding aside, it's very important that taxpayers be aware of recent mutations in the tax law. For example, this year everybody connected with the savings-and-loan industry gets a free boat. Also there are strict new regulations concerning how taxpayers should cheat. "If a taxpayer wishes to deduct an imaginary business expense," states the IRS instruction booklet, "then he or she MUST create a pretend financial record by clumsily altering a receipt from an actual transaction such as the rental of the videotape *Big Nostril Mamas.*

When preparing your return, you should be sure to avoid common mistakes. The two most common taxpayer mistakes, states the IRS booklet, are (1) "failure to include a current address," and (2) "failure to be a large industry that gives humongous contributions to key tax-law-writing congresspersons."

All of us, at one time or another, have been guilty of these mistakes, but I'm sure that this year we'll try to cooperate fully with the IRS, because, as citizens, we feel a strong patriotic duty not to go to jail. Also we know that our government cannot serve us unless it gets hold of our money, which it needs for popular federal programs such as the $421,000 fax machine. I am not making this program up. I found out about it from alert readers Trish Baez and Rick Haan, who faxed me an article by Mark Thompson of Knight-Ridder newspapers concerning a U.S. Air Force contract to buy 173 fax machines from Litton Industries for $73 million, or about $421,000 per machine. Just the paper for this machine costs $100 a roll.

If you're wondering how come, when ordinary civilian fax machines can be bought for a few hundred dollars, the Air Force needs one that costs as much as four suburban homes, then you are a bonehead. Clearly, as any taxpayer can tell you, the Air Force needs a special kind of fax machine, a *combat* fax machine. The article quotes an Air Force spokesperson as making the following statement about it:

"You can drag this through the mud, drop it off the end of a pickup truck, run it in a rainstorm, and operate it at 30 below zero."

The spokesperson also said (I am still not making this up): "I was looking at a picture of a squirrel it produced this morning, and if you wanted to sit there long enough you could count the hairs on the squirrel."

1. The Air Force is using a $421,000 fax machine to send pictures of *squirrels?*
2. Are these *enemy* squirrels?

3. Or does the combat fax just start spontaneously generating animal pictures after you drop it off the end of a pickup truck?

The answers are: None of your business. You're a taxpayer, and your business is to send in money, and if the Air Force wants a special combat fax machine, or a whole combat office with combat staplers and combat potted plants and combat Muzak systems capable of playing Barry Manilow at 45 degrees below zero, then it will be your pleasure to pay for them. Because this is America, and we are Americans, and—call me sentimental, but this is how I feel—there is something extremely appealing about the concept of Barry Manilow at 45 degrees below zero.

READER ALERT

Mister Language Person

I like writing Mister Language Person columns, because I always get wonderful mail from irate people who have detected errors in Mister Language Person's grammar. Yes! "Perhaps, Mr. Barry," these letters say, "before you set yourself up as an 'expert,' you should make sure that your OWN grammar is correct." Often the letter-writer rips my column out of the newspaper and sends it back to me with angry corrections written all over it in red ink. You can just imagine how I feel.

English, as it Were

Once again we are pleased to present Mister Language Person, the internationally recognized expert and author of the authoritative *Oxford Cambridge Big Book o' Grammar.*

Q. What is the difference between "criteria" and "criterion"?

A. These often-confused words belong to a family that grammarians call "metronomes," meaning "words that have the same beginning but lay eggs underwater." The simplest way to tell them apart is to remember that "criteria" is used in the following type of sentence: "When choosing a candidate for the United States Congress, the main criteria is, hair." Whereas "Criterion" is a kind of car.

Q. What is the correct way to spell words?

A. English spelling is unusual because our language is a rich verbal tapestry woven together from the tongues of the Greeks, the Latins, the Angles, the Klaxtons, the Celtics, the 76ers, and many other ancient peoples, all of whom had severe drinking problems. Look at the spelling they came up with for "colonel" (which is actually pronounced "lieutenant"); or "hors d'oeuvres" or "Cyndi Lauper." It is no wonder that young people today have so much trouble learning to spell: Study after study shows that young people today have the intelligence of Brillo. This is why it's so important that we old folks teach them the old reliable spelling rule that we learned as children, namely:

"I" before "C,"
Or when followed by "T,"
O'er the ramparts we watched,
Not excluding joint taxpayers filing singly.
EXCEPTION: "Suzi's All-Nite E-Z Drive-Thru Donut Shoppe."

Q. What the heck are "ramparts," anyway?

A. They are parts of a ram, and they were considered a great delicacy in those days. People used to watch o'er them.

Q. How do you speak French?

A. French is very easy to speak. The secret is, no matter what anybody says to you, you answer, "You're wrong," but you say it with your tongue way back in gargle position and your lips pouted way out like you're sucking grits through a hose, so it sounds like this: "Urrrrooonnngggg." Example:

FRENCH PERSON: *Où est la poisson de mon harmonica?* ("How about them Toronto Blue Jays?")

YOU: Urrrrooonnngggg.

FRENCH PERSON: *Quel moron!* ("Good point!")

Q. I know there's a difference in proper usage between "compared with" and "compared to," but I don't care.

A. It depends on the context.

Q. Please explain punctuation?

A. It would be "my pleasure." The main punctuation marks are the period, the coma, the colonel, the semi-colonel, the probation mark, the catastrophe, the eclipse, the Happy Face, and the box where the person checks "yes" to receive more information. You should place these marks in your sentences at regular intervals to indicate to your reader that some kind of punctuation is occurring. Consider these examples:

WRONG: O Romeo, Romeo, wherefore art thou Romeo?

RIGHT: O Romeo! Yo! *Romeo!!* Wherethehellfore ART thou? Huh??

ROMEO: I art down here! Throw me the car keys!

Q. Does anybody besides total jerks ever use the phrase "as it were"?

A. No.

Q. What is the correct form of encouraging "chatter" that baseball infielders should yell to the pitcher?

A. They should yell: "Hum babe hum babe hum babe HUM BABE HUM BABE."

Q. May they also yell: "Shoot that ball in there shoot it shoot it SHOOT SHOOT SHOOT WAY TO SHOOT BABE GOOD HOSE ON THAT SHOOTER"?

A. They most certainly may.

Q. What is the difference between "take" and "bring"?

A. "Take" is a transitory verb that is used in statements such as "He up and took off." "Bring" is a consumptive injunction and must be used as follows:

"We brung some stewed ramparts to Aunt Vespa but she was already dead so we ate them ourselves."

Q. What is President Bush's native language?

A. He doesn't have one.

TODAY'S LANGUAGE TIP: A good way to impress people such as your boss is to develop a "Power Vocabulary" by using big words. Consider this example:

YOU: Good morning, Mr. Johnson.

YOUR BOSS: Good morning, Ted.

(Obviously you're not making much of an impression here. Your name isn't even "Ted." Now watch the difference that a couple of Power Vocabulary words can make:)

YOU: Good morning, Mr. Johnson, you hemorrhoidal infrastructure.

YOUR BOSS: What?

YOU GOT A QUESTION FOR MISTER LANGUAGE PERSON? We are not surprised.

It's a Mad, Mad, Mad, Mad World

Today's Self-Help Topic is: Coping with Anger.

There is definitely too much anger in the world today. Pick up almost any newspaper, and the odds are you'll get ink smeared all over your hands. We use a special kind of easy-smear ink, because we know how much it irritates you.

But that's not my point. My point is that if you pick up almost any newspaper, you'll see stories of anger raging out of control, of people actually shooting each other over minor traffic disputes. Can you imagine? Can you imagine feeling so much hostility that just because you're in a traffic jam on a hot day, and you've been stuck for an hour waiting in a long line of cars trying to exit from a busy highway, and along comes one of those line-butting jerks, some guy who's talking on his cellular phone and figures he's *too important* to be waiting in a line with common rest-room bacteria like yourself, so he barges past the entire line and butts in *right in front of you,* so you honk your horn, and he shows you his Mister Digit hand puppet, so you haul out a pistol large enough for antiaircraft purposes and LET THE SCUMBALL HAVE IT HAHAHAHAHAHAHAHA WOULDN'T THAT BE GREAT??

I mean terrible. "Wouldn't that be terrible," is what I mean. And this is why it's so important that we learn to understand what anger is, and how we can cope with it. As you know if you ever studied the famous Greek philosopher Aristotle, he was easily the most boring human being who ever lived. Thousands of college students suffer forehead damage every year from passing out face-forward while attempting to read his books. But it was Aristotle who

identified anger as one of the Six Basic Human Emotions, along with Lust, Greed, Envy, Fear of Attorneys, and the Need to Snack.

We know that primitive man felt anger, as is evidenced by the deep kick marks that archeologists have found in prehistoric vending machines. We also see evidence of anger in the animal kingdom. The great white shark, for example, periodically gets furious at the small seaside resort town of Amity and tries to eat all the residents, possibly in an effort to prevent another sequel. And dogs are for some historical reason *extremely* angry at cats. I once watched a dog named Edgar spot a cat roughly a hundred yards away and go tearing after it, faster and faster, gaining ground with each step until he was just inches away, at which point the cat made a very sharp right turn, leaving Edgar to run directly, at Dog Warp Speed, into the side of a house. Fortunately he absorbed the entire impact with his brain, so there was no damage, but this incident teaches us that anger is very self-destructive, and that we must learn to control it.

Let's take the case of the line-butting driver. The trick here is to put things into perspective. Ask yourself: Does it really matter, long-term, if this guy butts in front of you? Is it really more important than serious world problems such as Ethiopia or the Greenhouse Effect? Yes. No question. You don't even know where Ethiopia is. This is why psychologists recommend, when you feel your anger getting out of control, that you practice a simple yoga technique: Imagine that you're in a peaceful, quiet setting such as a meadow, then take a deep breath, then exhale slowly, then gently s-q-u-e-e-z-e that trigger. See how much better you feel? In Advanced Yoga we use grenades.

Aside from traffic, the leading cause of anger is marriage. No matter how much you love somebody, if you spend enough time with that person, you're going to notice his or her flaws. If Romeo had stayed long enough under the balcony staring up worshipfully at Juliet, he'd have become acutely aware of her nasal hairs. So most married couples, even though they love each other very much in theory, tend to view each other in practice as large teeming flaw colonies, the result being that they get on each other's nerves and regularly erupt into vicious emotional shouting matches over issues such as toaster settings.

Professional marriage counselors agree that the most productive and mature way to deal with marital anger is to stomp dramatically from the room. The key here is timing. You want to make your move *before* your opponent does, because the first person to stomp from the room receives valuable Argument Points that can be redeemed for exciting merchandise at the Marital Prize Redemption Center. Of course you have to be on the alert for defensive maneuvers. A couple I know named Buzz and Libby were once having a Force Ten argument in their kitchen, and Buzz attempted to make a dramatic exit stomp, but Libby, a former field-hockey player, stuck her foot out as he went past and tripped him, so he wound up stumbling from the room, trying desperately to look dignified but actually looking like a man auditioning for Clown School. Libby won 5,000 bonus points, good for a handsome set of luggage.

Ultimately, however, anger benefits nobody. If you keep it bottled up inside, it eats away at you, until eventually you turn into a bitter, spiteful, hate-ridden person working in Customer Service. So take my advice: Lighten up. Don't let your anger get the best of you. Don't lose your humanity, or your sense of humor. Don't *ever* try to butt in front of me.

Getting M*A*S*H*E*D

Recently my wife, Beth, was ravaged by a sudden, unexpected outbreak of modern medical care.

Well, OK, technically she also had a medical problem, which I won't go into here except to say that it quickly faded into dim memory once the treatment began. Which is exactly the point. As you know if you've ever been subjected to modern medical care, the whole theory is that if they can make you feel awful enough, you'll begin to look back on your original ailment with actual fondness. They take out all your blood and put you in a tiny room where they expose you repeatedly to daytime television, and every few hours total strangers come in to give you Jell-O and stab you with small medical harpoons and insert tubes at random into your body. Then they say, "Are you feeling BETTER NOW? Or perhaps we should give you some MORE MEDICAL CARE HAHAHAHAHA." Pretty soon you're on the floor, using whatever limbs they forgot to disable or remove to scrabble toward the elevator, your butt sticking into the air through a hospital garment no larger than a standard Handi-Wipe, your tubes dragging out 15 or 20 feet behind you and spewing a telltale trail of Jell-O that enables the hospital people to track you down and capture you in the parking lot and haul you back to the tiny room and MAYBE RUN A FEW TESTS HAHAHAHAHAHAHA.

Actually, Beth's doctor, technically know as Doctor Bob, was very nice. In fact everybody at the hospital was nice. But you never really know, with the medical profession. A lot goes on behind closed doors. Just a week before Beth went into the hospital, an alert reader named Pat Wilson in New Delhi, India, sent me an article from the *Hindustan Times* about a doctor at a medical college over there who

wanted to determine the "effect of human blood on the stomach when taken orally," so he whipped up a bunch of sandwiches made out of

WARNING:
DO NOT READ THE REST OF THIS SENTENCE IF YOU ARE OPERATING HEAVY MACHINERY

human bone marrow. I am not making this up. According to the article, the doctor fed the sandwiches to an unsuspecting colleague, claiming that they contained "a special sauce sent by his sister from America." The doctor was suspended from the college. The colleague is reportedly still off his feed.

This article kept popping into my brain while Doctor Bob and the other skilled professionals were explaining to us in detailed scientific terms how come Beth needed an onslaught of preventive medical care even though she was feeling perfectly fine.

"Do you have any questions?" they kept asking. I had two main ones:

1. "How about we just forget this whole thing?"
2. "You guys definitely eat *regular sandwiches* at this hospital, right?"

But I never found a good time to ask these questions, and so early one morning I drove to the hospital and surrendered Beth, who—this particular detail sticks in my mind, for some reason—was still feeling perfectly fine. They took her away and put masks on and committed acts of medical care on her, and when they brought her back, she was experiencing what the medical community likes to call "discomfort." This is like saying Hiroshima experienced "urban renewal." I have not seen Beth experience so much discomfort since the time she experienced the Joy and Wonder of Natural Childbirth, during which she left inch-deep grip marks in the steel bedrail.

So I kept lunging out into the corridor and tackling medical professionals around the ankles and dragging them in to look at Beth. "Yes," they'd explain helpfully, while Beth was thrashing around and making sound track noises from *The Exorcist* and, in her occasional moments of rationality, asking to be taken outside and shot, "she is experiencing some discomfort."

Finally I was able, without medical training, to figure out myself what was wrong.

"No wonder she's in pain!" I exclaimed. "Some maniac has put *staples into her!*"

I'm serious. Right into her body. If you, like so many of us, were ever stapled in the hand by Walter Gorski in the fourth grade, you know that even *one* staple is very painful; Beth had enough to supply a bustling legal practice. So you can imagine my shock when I learned that this had been done by, of all people, Doctor Bob. Yes! He was *charging us* to staple

Beth! What is more, he had installed a *drain.* In my *wife.* I realized right then that Beth had to recover quickly, because God knows what they would do to her next. I might come in one morning and find a kazoo sticking out of her forehead.

Fortunately she got out, and she's going to be fine. Someday she may even feel as good as before they started medically caring for her. So all's well that ends well, and although I've been "poking some fun" here at the medical community, I'm sure you realize that, deep down inside, I have a large inflamed cyst of respect for it. Really. Trust me. Have a sandwich.

P.S. The bill for staples—just the staples—was $63.

Taking the Manly Way Out

Today we're going to explore the mysterious topic of How Guys Think, which has baffled women in general, and the editors of *Cosmopolitan* magazine in particular, for thousands of years.

The big question, of course, is: How come guys never call? After successful dates, I mean. You single women out there know what I'm talking about. You go out with a guy, and you have a great time, and *he* seems to have a great time, and at the end of the evening he says, quote, "Can I call you?" And you, interpreting this to mean "Can I call you?", answer: "Sure!"

The instant you say this, the guy's body start's to dematerialize. Within a few seconds you can stick a tire iron right through him and wave it around; in a few more seconds he has vanished entirely, gone into the mysterious Guy Bermuda Triangle, where whole squadrons of your dates have disappeared over the years, never to be heard from again.

Eventually you start to wonder if there's something wrong with you, some kind of emotional hang-up or personality defect that your dates are detecting. Or possibly foot odor. You start having long, searching discussions with your women friends in which you say things like: "He really seemed to like me" and "I didn't feel as though I was putting pressure on him" and "Would you mind, strictly as a friend, smelling my feet?"

This is silly. There's nothing wrong with you. In fact, you should interpret the behavior of your dates as a kind of guy *compliment* to you. Because when the guy asks you if he can call you, what he's really asking you, in Guy Code, is will you marry him. Yes. See, your basic guy is into a straight-ahead, bottom-line kind of thought process that does not work

nearly as well with the infinitely subtle complexities of human relationships as it does with calculating how much gravel is needed to cover a given driveway. So here's what the guy is thinking: If he calls you, you'll go out again, and you'll probably have another great time, so you'll probably go out again and have *another* great time, and so on until the only possible *option* will be to get married. This is classic Guy Logic.

So when you say "Sure!" in a bright cheery voice, you may think you're simply indicating a willingness to go out again, but as far as he's concerned you're endorsing a lifetime commitment that he is quite frankly not ready to make after only one date, so he naturally decided he can never see you again. From that day forward, if he spots you on the street, he'll spring in the opposite direction to avoid the grave risk that the two of you might meet, which would mean he'd have to ask you if you wanted to get a cup of coffee, and you might say yes, and pretty soon you'd be enjoying each other's company again, and suddenly a clergyman would appear at your table and YOU'D HAVE TO GET MARRIED AIEEEEEEE.

(You women think this is crazy, right? Whereas you guys out there are nodding your heads.)

So my advice for single women is that if you're on a date with a guy you like, and he asks whether he can call you, you should give him a nonthreatening answer, such as:

"No."

Or: "I guess so, but bear in mind that I'm a nun."

This will make him comfortable about seeing you again, each time gaining the courage to approach you more closely, in the manner of a timid, easily startled woodland creature such as a chipmunk. In a few years, if the two of you really do have common interests and compatible personalities, you may reach the point where he'll be willing to take the Big Step, namely, eating granola directly from your hand.

No matter how close you become, however, remember this rule: Do not pressure the guy to share his most sensitive innermost thoughts and feelings with you. Guys hate this, and I'll tell you why: If you were to probe inside the guy psyche, beneath that macho exterior and the endless droning about things like the 1978 World Series, you would find, deep down inside, a passionate, heartfelt interest in: the 1978 World Series. Yes. The truth is, guys don't *have* any sensitive innermost thoughts and feelings. It's time you women knew! All these years you've been agonizing about how to make the relationship work, wondering how come he never talks to you, worrying about all the anguished emotion he must have bottled up inside, and meanwhile he's fretting about how maybe he needs longer golf spikes. I'm sorry to have to tell you this. Maybe you *should* become a nun.

Anyway, I hope I've cleared up any lingering questions anybody might have regarding guys, as a gender. For some reason I feel compelled to end this with a personal note: Heather Campbell, if you're out there, I just want to say that I had a really nice time taking you to the Junior Prom in 1964, and I was a total jerk for never, not once, mentioning this fact to you personally.

Life's a Hitch, and Then You Cry

We're getting into Wedding Season again. This is good for America. We may be falling behind Japan in other areas, such as being able to produce cars or televisions or high school graduates capable of reading rest-room symbols without moving their lips, but we still have the world's largest and most powerful wedding industry.

If you want proof, pick up the February-March issue of either *Bride's* or *Modern Bride* magazine, and right away you'll be struck by the fact that you have sustained a major hernia. Each of these magazines is large enough to have its own climate. *Modern Bride* is over 800 pages long; *Bride's* is over 1,000. Almost every page features a full-color photograph of a radiant young bride, her face beaming with that look of ecstatic happiness that comes from knowing, deep in her heart, that her wedding costs as much as a Stealth bomber, not including gratuities.

"Money can't buy you happiness, so you might as well give your money to us," that is the sentimental motto of the wedding industry. The pages of *Bride's* and *Modern Bride* are crammed with advertisements for silverware, glassware, crystalware, chinaware, ovenware, fondueware, Tupperware, underwear, and all the other absolutely mandatory weddingwares that will become Treasured Lifetime Family Heirlooms until they have to be sold to pay the divorce lawyers.

Because let's face it, a lot of marriages just don't work out. Many newlyweds are hurling crystalware within days. Even Donald and Ivana Trump, a couple who seemed to have everything—hair, teeth, most of Manhattan Island—have been having marital problems so tragic that even the most hardened observer is forced to laugh until his gums bleed.

This is why more and more smart engaged couples are avoiding costly future court disputes by means of a legal arrangement called a "prenuptial divorce," under which they agree to get married and divorced simultaneously. This eliminates problems down the road, yet enables the couple to go ahead and have the kind of enormous, ware-intensive wedding that America needs to remain competitive in the world economy.

Weddings also enable us to continue certain cherished traditions, such as the tradition of the bride's family and the groom's family hating each other so much that sometimes, at the reception, the two opposing mothers wind up wrestling in the cake. Of course you can avoid this kind of interfamily tension by means of a new matrimonial wrinkle, the one-family wedding, which was invented by a woman I know named Ginny.

Ginny was in the mood to hold a big wedding, but her only remaining nonmarried child, Edward, wasn't engaged to anybody. So she hit upon the idea of holding a wedding anyway, with the role of the bride played by Tiffany, a life-size bikini-wearing inflatable doll. Tiffany had spent several months floating around the pool, smiling, and everybody thought she was very nice despite a minor algae problem. Of course there was always the danger that she'd turn out to have a bunch of obnoxious inflatable relatives, but as far as anybody knew she was an orphan.

So we were all very excited about the wedding, when suddenly Edward—you know these headstrong kids—got engaged to Carey, an actual human being. Let me state for the record that Edward made a wonderful choice, but you have to feel bad for Tiffany, who quickly went from the role of Beautiful Bride-To-Be to the role of Deflated Wad in a Closet, which is a tragic waste when you consider that she is more than qualified to be vice president.

But we can't be thinking about tragedies, not with Wedding Season coming. We need to be thinking about the following quotation, which I am not making up, from the Beauty News section of *Bride's* magazine:

"DILEMMA: My brows are too bushy; my bridesmaids' are too sparse. How can we get them in shape by wedding day?"

Unfortunately the solution is too long to reprint here, so you brides-to-be had better pick up a copy of *Bride's*, using a rental forklift, and read the article pronto, because otherwise, as you walk down the aisle on your Very Special Day, you're going to hear people whispering, "What are those things on her forehead? Sea urchins?"

By the way, the rental forklift is the responsibility of the groom.

Getting Physical

I started aging rapidly last week. Until then, I had been aging steadily at the rate of about one year per year, with a few exceptions, such as during the party where I drank bourbon from John Cooper's shoe while standing in the shower. When I woke up on the lawn the next morning, I discovered that I had aged nearly a decade.

But after that I felt pretty good until last week, when I went in for my annual physical examination. I get an annual physical exam about once every six years. I'm reluctant to do it more often because of the part where the doctor does A Horrible Thing.

You middle-aged guys know what I mean. You're in the examining room, and the doctor has been behaving in a nonthreatening manner, thumping on your chest, frowning into your ears, etc., and the two of you are having a normal guy conversation about how George Steinbrenner should get, at minimum, the electric chair, and you're almost *enjoying* your physical examination, when, without warning, the doctor reaches into a drawer and pulls out: The Glove.

Suddenly you notice that the doctor looks vaguely like Vincent Price, and the room lights are flashing, and the music system, which had been playing "Wonderful World," is now playing the theme from *Jaws.* And now the doctor is holding up his hand, which has grown to the size of a mature eggplant and has sprouted eight or nine extra digits, and he's struggling to pull on The Glove, which has developed a life of its own, snarling and writhing like some kind of evil mutant albino squid. And now the doctor is turning to you, his eyes glowing like beer signs, and he's saying "Turn around

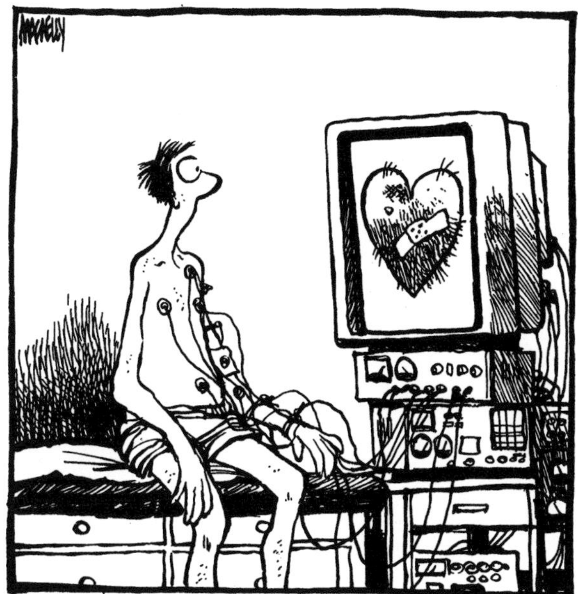

hahahaHAHAHAHA" and you're thinking OH NO PLEASE NOOOOOOO.

Once I was getting examined, and when it came time for The Glove the doctor brought in, for training purposes, *another* doctor, who happened to be a member of the extreme opposite sex, and the two of them were back there chatting away about various Points of Interest like a pair of guides on a glass-bottom-boat tour. When it was over, all I wanted was a grocery bag to wear over my head until I could get a new identity through the Federal Witness Protection Program.

But last week I got through The Glove OK. In fact I got through almost everything; the only problem the doctor found—this was NOT during the glove exam—was excessive earwax, which in many cultures is considered a sign of virility. So I was feeling good, ready to schedule my next appointment for late 1996 and sprint for the exit, when the doctor looked at my cardiogram and made that "hmmmm" noise that doctors are taught in medical school so they won't come right out and say "UH-oh!"

"You have an abnormal cardiogram," he said.

He said a lot of stuff after that, but I missed most of it because I was looking around the room for a good place to faint. I do remember the doctor gesturing at an explicit diagram of the human heart and talking about a condition called a "branch bundle blockage" (or maybe he said "bundle branch blockade"), which is caused by the heart valves being connected improperly to the distributor wires. Or something like that. I wasn't really following him. I felt the way I do when the guys at my service station, Sal and Bill, are attempting to explain what's wrong with my car.

"Look at this!" Sal will say, picking up a filth-encrusted object that for all I know is a fragment of Mayan pottery. "Your postulation valve has no comportment!"

"No comportment at all!" affirms Bill, genuinely disgusted that such a thing could happen in 20th-Century America.

"And look at this here!" says Sal, thrusting the thing toward me.

"Your branch bundle is blocked!" says Bill.

"You have two weeks to live!" says the doctor.

No, the doctor didn't really say that. He said that an abnormal cardiogram is perfectly normal, and it's probably nothing to worry about, but just in case, he wanted to schedule a test where I run on a treadmill and then they inject atomic radiation into my body and frown at the results.

"Fine!" I said, trying to appear composed, which was difficult because by that point I was sitting on the floor.

So now I'm waiting to take my test, and I'm

feeling *old.* I'm experiencing every one of the 147 Major Warning Signs Of Heart Trouble, including Chest Pains, Shortness of Breath, Tendency to Not Notice That the Traffic Light Has Changed, and Fear of Ordering French Fries. Also my heart has taken to beating very loud, especially late at night. Perhaps you have heard it. "STOP BEATING YOUR HEART SO LOUD!" is what I am sure the neighbors are yelling. Fortunately I cannot hear them, on account of my earwax condition.

Stress for Success

It's 8:30 A.M., and I'm in a small, brightly lit room with a tube in my arm, and a woman I have never met before named Bette is scrubbing my chest with what feels like sandpaper.

"Some people really scream when I do this," Bette is saying.

I'd scream, too, but I'm too busy pretending that there's no tube in my arm.

"There's no tube in my arm," is what I am telling myself in a soothing voice. "There's no tube in my arm. There's a TUBE in my arm. There's a tube IN MY ARM. OMIGOD THERE'S A TUBE STUCK RIGHT INTO MY ARM AND I'M GOING TO . . ."

"I need to lie down," I say.

"You *are* lying down," Bette points out.

I suppose it goes without saying that this is happening in a hospital. Specifically, it's in the Stress Department. That's the real name. When Bette gets on the phone, she says, "This is Bette, in Stress."

I'm here to get what is called a Thallium Stress Test on my heart. The reason for this, according to my doctor, is that there is probably nothing wrong with my heart. That's what doctors always say: "There's probably nothing wrong . . . but just in case we're going to run a few tests."

"Probably nothing wrong" is the leading cause of health care in America today.

The Stress Test, like most medical procedures, was originally developed by the ex-Nazi researchers at the Institute of Punitive Medicine as a means of maintaining hospital discipline. If you're a hospital patient, and you start to become irritated because the food tastes like Purina Rat Chow and they charge you $2,316.17 every time you flush the toilet, and

you are foolish enough to complain about this, they'll say, "Sounds like we need to *run some tests* on you." And if you have the common sense that God gave gravel you will never open your mouth again. Because the way these tests work is, whatever part of your body they claim they want to look at, they insist upon entering you via some OTHER part. If you have, for example, an ankle problem, they'll say, "What we're going to do is insert this one-inch-diameter exploratory garden hose into your eye socket and run it the length of your body, so you *might experience some discomfort.*"

I won't even TELL you where they insert the hose if you have an eye problem.

So anyway, my doctor—his actual name is Dr. Hamburg, but to avoid a costly lawsuit I will refer to him here as "Dr. Frankfurt"—made the alarming discovery that there was probably nothing wrong with my heart, which is why Bette stuck a tube in my arm and sandpapered my chest and attached wires all over my skin and strapped a large electronic box to me so that I looked like a man being attacked by a crazed mutant home appliance.

I was close to passing out from the stress of all this, but I was thinking to myself, "Well, at least it's almost over, because there's nowhere else on my body for them to attach anything," when in walked Dr. Frankfurt, who ordered me to *run on a treadmill.* With a TUBE in my arm. I bet no medical person has ever even considered doing such a bizarre thing himself.

But Dr. Frankfurt made me do it. While I was running, a small man who had been lurking in the shadows rushed in without warning and put thallium into my arm tube. This made me feel VERY stressful because thallium is basically atomic radiation, and I distinctly remember a horror movie from the 1950s when a man—it might have been James Arness—became radioactive and started glowing like a gambling casino and acting antisocial to the point where he had to be subdued by several branches of the Armed Forces.

The next thing I knew I was in a wheelchair being rushed through the hospital halls with a terrified look on my face and a tube in my arm and radiation in my body, and I was thinking how only an hour earlier I felt fine, and now, thanks to Modern Medicine, people were looking at me in the same pitying way that they'd look at a recently run-over cat. And then I was wheeled into a department called "Nuclear Medicine," which are two words that do NOT go together at all, and they put me on a slab, and all the humans sprinted from the room, probably because of the radiation. Then a medical robot swooped down and examined my body very closely. It did not have a good bedside manner. It would peer at one spot for a while, and then go: "Whir." "Is that BAD?" I would ask it.

"Whir," it would say.

It turned out that there was nothing wrong with my heart. Just as we had suspected all along. But I'm actually glad that I went through the Thallium Stress Test. For one thing, I know I'm OK. For another thing, I no longer need a bedside lamp. I just read by the glow from my body.

Sports Nuts

Today, in our continuing series on How Guys Think, we explore the question: How come guys care so much about sports?

This is a tough one, because caring about sports is, let's face it, silly. I mean, suppose you have a friend who, for no apparent reason, suddenly becomes obsessed with the Amtrak Corporation. He babbles about Amtrak constantly, citing obscure railroad statistics from 1978; he puts Amtrak bumper stickers on his car; and when something bad happens to Amtrak, such as a train crashes and investigators find that the engineer was drinking and wearing a bunny suit, your friend becomes depressed for weeks. You'd think he was crazy, right? "Bob," you'd say to him, as a loving and caring friend, "you're a moron. The Amtrak Corporation has *nothing to do with you.*"

But if Bob is behaving exactly the same deranged way about, say, the Pittsburgh Penguins, it's considered normal guy behavior. He could name his child "Pittsburgh Penguin Johnson" and be considered only mildly eccentric. There is something wrong with this. And before you accuse me of being some kind of sherry-sipping ascot-wearing ballet-attending MacNeil-Lehrer Report-watching wussy, please note that I am a sports guy myself, having had a legendary athletic career consisting of nearly a third of the 1965 season on the track team at Pleasantville High School ("Where The Leaders Of Tomorrow Are Leaving Wads Of Gum On The Auditorium Seats Of Today"). I competed in the long jump, because it seemed to be the only event where afterward you didn't fall down and throw up. I probably would have become an Olympic-caliber long-jumper except that, through one of those "bad breaks" so common in sports, I turned out to have the raw leaping ability of a convenience store. I'd race down the runway and attempt to soar into the air, but instead of going up I'd be seized by powerful gravity rays and yanked *downward* and wind up with just my head sticking out of the dirt, serving as a convenient marker for the other jumpers to take off from.

So, OK, I was not Jim Thorpe, but I care as much about sports as the next guy. If you were to put me in the middle of a room, and in one corner was Albert Einstein, in another corner was Abraham Lincoln, in another corner was Plato, in another corner was William Shakespeare, and in another corner (this room is a pentagon) was a TV set showing a football game between teams that have no connection whatsoever with my life, such as the Green Bay Packers and the Indianapolis Colts, I would ignore the greatest minds in Western thought, gravitate toward the TV, and become far more concerned about the game than I am about my child's education. And *so would the other guys.* I guarantee it. Within minutes Plato would be pounding Lincoln on the shoulder and shouting in ancient Greek that the receiver did *not* have both feet in bounds.

Obviously, sports connect with something deeply rooted in the male psyche, dating back to prehistoric times, when guys survived by hunting and fighting, and they needed many of the skills exhibited by modern athletes—running, throwing, spitting, renegotiating their contracts, adjusting their private parts on nationwide television, etc. So that would explain how come guys like to *participate* in sports. But how come they care so much about games played by *other* guys? Does this also date back to prehistoric times? When the hunters were out hurling spears into mastodons, were there also prehistoric guys watching from the hills, drinking prehistoric beer, eating really bad prehistoric hot dogs, and shouting "We're No. 1!" but not understanding what it meant because this was before the development of mathematics?

There must have been, because there is no other explanation for such bizarre phenomena as:

- Sports-talk radio, where guys who have never sent get-well cards to their own mothers will express heartfelt, near-suicidal anguish over the hamstring problems of strangers.
- My editor, Gene, who can remember the complete starting lineups for the New York Yankee teams from 1960 through 1964, but who routinely makes telephone calls wherein, after he dials the phone, he forgets who he's calling, so when somebody answers, Gene has to ask (a) who it is, and (b) does this person happen to know the purpose of the call.
- Another guy in my office, John, who appears to be a normal middle-aged husband and father until you realize that he spends most of his waking hours managing a *pretend baseball team.*

This is true. He and some other guys have formed a league where they pay actual money to "draft" major-league players, and then they have their pretend teams play a whole pretend season, complete with trades, legalistic memorandums, and heated disputes over the rules. This is crazy, right? If these guys said they were managing herds of pretend caribou, the authorities would be squirting lithium down their throats with turkey basters, right? And yet we all act like it's *perfectly normal.* In fact, eavesdropping from my office, I find myself getting involved in John's discussions. That's how pathetic I am: I'm capable of caring about a pretend sports team that's not even my own pretend sports team.

So I don't know about the rest of you guys, but I'm thinking it's time I got some perspective in my life. First thing after the Super Bowl, I'm going to start paying more attention to the things that should matter to me, like my work, my friends, and above all my family, especially my little boy, Philadelphia Phillies Barry.

The Male Animal

Speaking on behalf of all the guys in the world except possibly Phil Donahue, I want to say that I am really ticked off about the results of this recent poll of women. You probably read about it. The Roper Organization asked 3,000 women the following question:

"Do you agree that the average man today is a lazy selfish opinionated egotistical sex-crazed tub of crud who never thinks about anybody but himself and refuses to help with child-rearing or housework and wants to go to bed with practically every woman he meets who is not legally his grandmother and tends to have the same annual output of natural gas as Montana?"

Eighty-seven percent of the women agreed with this. The other 13 percent noted that men also pick their noses at stoplights.

By scientifically analyzing these results, we can conclude that women do not appear to have a high

opinion of men. This is unfair. Oh, sure, men in the past have displayed certain unfortunate behavior patterns that tended to produce unhappy relationships, world wars, etc. But today's man is different. Today's man knows that he's supposed to be a sensitive and caring relationship partner, and he's making radical life-style changes such as sometimes remembering to remove the used tissue wads from his pockets before depositing his pants on the floor to be picked up by the Laundry Fairy.

As so here we men are, making this kind of extreme sacrifice, and WHAM, the Roper Organization hits us with the fact that women still think we're jerks. This really burns my briefs. I mean, I'd like you women to stop and think for a moment about what this world would be like without men. Think of the vast array of cultural and scientific achievements you'd have to do without, including:

1. Football.
2. Professional football.
3. Ear hair.
4. Betting on football.

The list just goes on and on. And let's talk about men's alleged obsession with sex. Do you women think that men are just animals? Do you really think that all they want to do is get you into bed? Wrong! A lot of guys, especially in bars, would be happy to get you into a phone booth! Or right there on the bar! ("Nobody will notice us," the guy will say, being suave. "They're watching 'Wheel of Fortune.' ")

But that doesn't mean ALL guys are like that. There are countless examples of guys who think about things beside sex. The guys on the U.S. Supreme Court, for example, think about important constitutional issues, as is shown by this transcript from recent court deliberations.

CHIEF JUSTICE WILLIAM H. REHNQUIST: Whoa! Get a load of the torts on THAT plaintiff!

ASSOCIATE JUSTICE BYRON R. WHITE: (Dies.)

And I am particularly outraged by the charge that guys never help out around the house. I happen to be a guy, and often, when my wife goes away, I assume Total Responsibility for the household, and my wife has such confidence in me that she will often wait for an entire half-hour before she calls:

MY WIFE: Is everything OK?
ME: Fine!
MY WIFE: Is Robert OK?
ME: Robert?
MY WIFE: Our child.
ME: Robert is here?

My wife likes to give me these helpful reminders from time to time because once she went away for several days, and when she got home, she determined that all Robert had eaten the entire time was chocolate Easter bunny heads. But other than that I am very strong in the homemaking department, the kind of guy who, if he gets Cheez Whiz on the sofa, will squirt some Windex on it without even having to be told.

So come on, women. Stop being so harsh on us guys, and start seeing past our macho hairy exteriors, into the sensitive, thoughtful, and—yes—vulnerable individuals that we are deep down inside. And while you're at it, fix us a sandwich.

Male Fixations

Most guys believe that they're supposed to know how to fix things. This is a responsibility that guys have historically taken upon themselves to compensate for the fact that they never clean the bathroom. A guy can walk into a bathroom containing a colony of commode fungus so advanced that it is registered to vote, but the guy would never dream of cleaning it, because he has to keep himself rested in case a Mechanical Emergency breaks out.

For example, let's say that one day his wife informs him that the commode has started making a loud groaning noise, like it's about to have a baby commode. This is when the guy swings into action. He strides in, removes the tank cover, peers down into the area that contains the mystery commode parts, and then, drawing on tens of thousands of years of guy mechanical understanding, announces that *there is nothing wrong with the commode.*

At least that's how I handle these things. I never actually fix anything. I blame this on tonsillitis. I had tonsillitis in the ninth grade, and I missed some school, and apparently on one of the days I missed, they herded the guys into the auditorium and explained to them about things like carburetors, valves, splines, gaskets, ratchets, grommets, "dado joints," etc. Because some guys actually seem to understand this stuff. One time in college my roommate, Rob, went into his room all alone with a Volvo transmission, opened his toolbox, disassembled the transmission to the point where he appeared to be working on *individual transmission molecules,* then put it all back together, and it *worked.* Whereas I would still be fumbling with the latch on the toolbox.

So I'm intimidated by mechanical guys. When we got our boat trailer, the salesman told me, one guy to another, that I should "re-pack" the "bearings" every so many miles. He said this as though all guys

come out of the womb with this instinctive ability to re-pack a bearing. So I nodded my head knowingly, as if to suggest that, sure, I generally re-pack a couple dozen bearings every morning before breakfast just to keep my testosterone level from raging completely out of control. The truth is that I've never been 100 percent sure what a bearing is. But I wasn't about to admit this, for fear that the salesman would laugh at me and give me a noogie.

The main technique I use for disguising my mechanical tonsillitis is to deny that there's ever anything wrong with anything. We'll be driving somewhere, and my wife, Beth, who does not feel that mechanical problems represent a threat to her manhood, will say, "Do you hear that grinding sound in the engine?" I'll cock my head for a second and make a sincere-looking frowny face, then say no, I don't hear any grinding sound. I'll say this even if I have to shout so Beth can hear me over the grinding sound; even if a hole has appeared in the hood and a large, important-looking engine part is sticking out and waving a sign that says HELP.

"That's the grommet bearing," I'll say. "It's supposed to do that."

Or, at home, Beth will say, "I think there's something wrong with the hall light switch." So I'll stride manfully into the hall, where volley-ball sized sparks are caroming off the bodies of recently electrocuted houseguests, and I'll say, "It seems to be working fine now!"

Actually, I think this goes beyond mechanics. I think guys have a natural tendency to act as though they're in control of the situation even when they're not. I bet that, seconds before the *Titanic* slipped beneath the waves, there was some guy still in his cabin, patiently explaining to his wife that it was *perfectly normal* for all the furniture to be sliding up the walls. And I bet there was a guy on the *Hindenburg* telling his wife that, oh, sure, you're going to get a certain amount of flames in a dirigible. Our federal leadership is basically a group of guys telling us, hey, *no problem* with this budget deficit thing, because what's happening is the fixed-based long-term sliding-scale differential appropriation forecast has this projected revenue growth equalization sprocket, see, which is connected via this Gramm-Rudman grommet oscillation module to . . .

The Web Badge of Courage

On my 41st birthday, a Sunday in July, I went out to face the spider. It had to happen. There comes a time in a man's life, when a man reaches a certain age (41), and he hears a voice—often this happens when he is lying on the couch reading about Norway in the Travel Section—and this voice says: "Happy Birthday. Do you think you could do something about the spider?" And a man knows, just as surely as he knows the importance of batting left-handed against a right-handed pitcher, that he must heed this voice, because it belongs to his wife, Beth, who, although she is a liberated and independent and tough Woman of Our Times, is deeply respectful of the natural division of responsibilities that has guided the human race for nearly 4 million years, under which it is always the woman who notices when you are running low on toilet paper, and it is always the man who faces the spider.

And so I called softly for my son, Robert. "Robert," I called, and within a matter of seconds he did not appear at my side, because he was in the family room watching TV commercials for breakfast cereals that are the same color and texture as Pez, but have less nutritional content. So I called louder.

"Robert," I said. "Fetch me the wooden stick that your pirate flag used to be attached to, and the Peter Pan 'creamy'-style peanut butter jar with the holes punched in the lid, for I am going to face the spider."

Upon hearing those words Robert came instantly, and he looked at me with a respect that I have not seen in his eyes for some time now, not since we got the Nintendo. The Nintendo is an electronic video game that is mindless and noncreative and stupid and hateful, and Robert is much better at it than I am. He is 7, and he can consistently rescue the princess, whereas I, a 41-year-old college gradu-

ate, cannot even get past the turtles. The worst part is the way Robert says, "Good try, Dad!" in a perfect imitation of the cheerfully condescending voice I used to use on him back when I could beat him at everything. I don't know where kids pick up this kind of behavior.

But there was respect in Robert's eyes as I strode out to face the spider. As well there should have been. Here in South Florida we have a special name for this kind of spider: We call it "a spider the size of Harold C. Crittenden Junior High School," although its technical Latin name is *Bernice*. Bernice had erected a humongous web right outside our front door, an ideal location because in July the South Florida atmosphere consists of 1 part oxygen and 247 parts mosquito, which meant Bernice had plenty to eat. Also on hand in the web was her husband, Bill, who, despite the fact that he was one-sixteenth her size, nevertheless played an important ecological role in the relationship, namely trying not to look like prey.

"I may be small," Bill would say, all day long, in spider language, "but I am certainly not prey! No sir! I am a spider! Yes! Just a regular, NON-prey . . ."

"Shut up," Bernice would say.

"Yes!" Bill would point out. They were a fun couple.

Nevertheless, I approached them cautiously, hoping any noise I made would be drowned out by the roar of the lawn growing. July is in what we South Floridians call the "Rainy Season" because it would depress us too much to come right out and call it the "Giant Armpit Season." When we read the stories about drought-stricken midwestern farmers who can't grow crops in their fields, we are forced to laugh with bitter irony, because down here we can, without trying, grow crops in our *laundry*.

And now I was up to the web. And now, with my son's eyes glued on me, I drew back the pirate-flag stick, and I struck.

"Hey!" said Bernice, in spider. *"HEY!!"*

"Don't hit me!" said Bill. "I'm prey!"

But it was Bernice I had my eye on. If I could poke her into the Peter Pan jar, all would be well. But if she turned and lunged for me, I would have no choice, as a man defending his family, but to drop everything and sprint off down the road, brushing wildly at myself and whimpering.

Fortunately, she went into the jar, and I got the lid on real quick, and for a while we watched her pace around in there and indicate via sweeping arm gestures what she was going to do to us when she got out.

"I'm gonna sting all of your eyeballs," she was saying. "I'm gonna lay 175 billion eggs in your *ears*. I'm gonna . . ."

This was fun, but eventually we decided it was

time to get rid of Bernice, following the standard procedure recommended by leading ecologists for the disposal of revenge-crazed spiders, namely: Release them on a drug dealer's lawn. Like many South Floridians, we have our house in a neighborhood that we are pretty sure is occupied by drug dealers, as indicated by subtle clues such as cars coming and going at all hours, bed sheets over the windows, a big sign stating, DRUGS FOR SALE HERE, etc. We decided this would make a fine new home for Bernice, so we drove casually by, and I real quick opened the jar and shook Bernice onto the lawn. She scuttled off angrily straight toward the house. "I'm gonna *fill your nasal passages with web,*" she was saying. "I'm gonna . . ."

But she was no longer our problem. We were already driving off, Robert and I, going shopping for a present for my 41st birthday. We went to Toys "Я" Us.

Confessions of a Weenie

Recently I've been reading horror novels at bedtime. I'm talking about those paperbacks with names like *The Brainsucker,* full of scenes like this:

"As Marge stepped through the doorway into the darkening mansion, she felt a sense of foreboding, caused, perhaps, by the moaning of the wind, or the creaking of the door, or possibly the Kentucky Fried Chicken bucket full of eyeballs."

Of course if Marge had the intelligence of paint, she'd stop right there. "Wait a minute," she'd say. "I'm getting the hell out of this novel." Then she'd leap off the page, sprint across my bedspread, and run into my son's bedroom to become a character in a safe book like *Horton Hears a Who.*

But Marge, in the hallowed horror-novel-character tradition, barges straight ahead, down gloomy corridors where she has to cut through the foreboding with a machete, despite the obvious fact that something hideous is about to happen, probably involving the forced evacuation of her skull cavity by a demonic being with the underworld Roto-rooter franchise. So I'm flinching as I turn each page, thinking, "What a moron this woman is!" and Marge is thinking: "Well, I may be a moron, but at least I'm not stupid enough to be *reading* this."

And of course Marge is right. I should know better than to read horror books, or watch horror movies, because—this is not easy for a 42-year-old male to admit—*I believe them.* I have always believed them. When I was a child, I was routinely terrified by horror movies, even the comically inept ones where, when Lon Chaney turned into a werewolf, you could actually see the makeup person's hand darting into the picture to attach more fake fur to his face.

When I was 17—this is a true anecdote—I had to explain to my father one Sunday morning that the

reason our car was missing was that the night before, I had taken my date to see *Psycho,* and afterward I had explained to her that it made more sense for her to drive me home, because of the strong possibility that otherwise I would be stabbed to death by Anthony Perkins.

For years after I saw *The Exorcist,* I felt this need to be around priests. Friends would say, "What do you want to do tonight?" And I'd say, "Let's take in a Mass!"

I'm still this way, even though I'm a grown-up parent, constantly reassuring my son about his irrational fears, telling him don't be silly, there aren't any vampires in the guest bathroom. Part of my brain—the rational part, the part that took the SAT tests—actually believes this, but a much more powerful part, the Fear Lobe, takes the possibility of bathroom vampires far more seriously than it takes, for example, the U.S. trade deficit.

And so late at night, when I finish my horror novel and take the dogs out into the yard, which is very dark, I am highly alert. My brain's SAT Sector, trying to be cool, is saying, "Ha ha! This is merely your yard!" But the Fear Lobe is saying: "Oh yes, this is exactly the kind of place that would attract The Brainsucker. For The Brainsucker, this is Walt Disney World."

And so I start sauntering back toward the house, trying to look as casual as possible considering that every few feet I suddenly whirl around to see if anything's behind me. Soon I am sauntering at upwards of 35 miles per hour, and the Fear Lobe is screaming "IT'S COMING!" and even the SAT Sector has soaked its mental armpits and now I'm openly sprinting through the darkness, almost to the house, and WHAT'S THAT NOISE BEHIND ME OH NO PLEASE AAAIIIEEEE WHUMP I am struck violently in the back by Earnest, our Toyota-sized main dog, who has located a cache of valuable dog poo and shrewdly elected to roll in it, and is now generously attempting to share the experience with me.

Thus the spell of horror is broken, and my SAT Sector reasserts control and has a good laugh at what a silly goose I was, and I walk calmly back inside and close the door, just seconds before the tentacle reaches it.

Blood, Sweat, and Beers

OK, this is it. the last day of the Red Cross blood drive at the *Miami Herald*. Either I am going to do it, or, for the umpteenth consecutive time, I am going to chicken out. All the smart money is on chicken out.

I am a world-class weenie when it comes to letting people stick needles into me. My subconscious mind firmly believes that if God had wanted us to have direct access to our bloodstreams, He would have equipped our skin with small, clearly marked doors. I've felt this way ever since a traumatic experience I had in Mrs. Hart's first-grade class at Wampus Elementary School in the 1950s. There I was, enjoying life and drawing unrecognizable pictures for my mom to put on the refrigerator, when suddenly—you never know when tragedy is going to strike—Mrs. Hart announced in a cheerful voice that somebody named "Dr. Salk" had discovered a "vaccine" for "polio." I had no idea what any of this meant. All I knew was that one minute I was having a happy childhood, and the next minute they were lining us all up in alphabetical order, with You Know Who in front, marching us to the cafeteria, where we encountered a man—I assumed this was Dr. Salk—holding a needle that appeared to be the size of a harpoon.

"You'll hardly feel it!" said Mrs. Hart, this being the last time I ever trusted a grown-up.

And it got worse. It turned out that you had to get vaccinated several times, plus there was talk that you had to get a "booster shot," which, according to reliable reports circulating around Wampus Elementary, turned your entire arm purple and sometimes made it actually *fall off*. I realize now that Dr. Salk was a great scientist, but at the time I viewed him as a monstrously evil being, scheming in his laboratory, dreaming up newer, more horrible vaccination procedures ("I've GOT it! We'll stick the needle into their EYEBALLS HAHAHAHAHA") and then traveling around the nation, like some kind of reverse vampire, injecting things into innocent victims selected by alphabetical order.

And when we talk about fiendish plots to jab large needles into small children, we certainly have to mention the huge and powerful Tetanus Shot Corporation, which employed undercover agents who were constantly sneaking into my doctor's office, getting hold of my medical file, and altering the date of my last tetanus shot. The result was that whenever I cut myself semi-seriously, which was often, Dr. Cohn would look at my file and say to my mother: "Well, he's due for a tetanus shot."

"But I had one LAST WEEK!" I'd shriek. They never believed me. They were grown-ups, so they believed the stupid file, and sales continued to boom at the Tetanus Shot Corporation.

Of course I am no longer a little boy. I'm a grown-up now, and I'm aware of the medical benefits of inoculations, blood tests, etc. I'm also aware that the actual physical discomfort caused by these procedures is minor. So I no longer shriek and cry and run away and have to be captured and held down by two or more burly nurses. What I do now is faint. Yes. Even if it's just one of those procedures where they prick your finger just a teensy bit and take barely enough blood for a mosquito hors d'oeuvre.

"I'm going to faint," I always tell them.

"Ha ha!" they always say. "You humor columnists are certainly . . ."

"Thud," I always say.

One time—this is true—I had to sit down in a shopping mall and put my head between my knees because I had walked too close to the ear-piercing booth.

So I have never given blood. But I feel guilty about this, because more than once, people I love have needed blood badly, and somebody, not me, was there to give it. And so now I am forcing myself to walk down the hall to the blood drive room at the *Miami Herald*. And now one of the efficient Red Cross ladies is taking down my medical history.

"Name?" she asks.

"I'm going to faint," I say.

"Ha ha!" she says.

And now I'm sitting down on some kind of medical beach chair, and a Red Cross lady is coming over with . . . with this *bag*. Which I realize she intends to fill with *my blood*. I am wondering if, since this is my first time, I should ask for a smaller bag. Also I am wondering: What if she forgets I'm here? What if she goes out for coffee, and meanwhile my bag is overflowing and dripping down into the Classified Advertising Department? What if . . .

Too late. She has my arm, and she's, oh no, she is, oh nooooooo

Hey! Look up there, in the sky! It's Red Cross ladies! Several of them! They're reaching down! Their arms are thousands of feet long! They're putting cold things on my head!

"It's over," one of them is saying. "You did fine."

I'd ask her to marry me, except that (a) I'm already married and (b) I'd be too weak to lift her veil. But other than that I feel great. Elated, even. I have a Band-Aid on my arm, a Beige Badge of Courage. And somewhere out there is a bag of my blood, ready to help a sick or injured person become his or her same old self again, except that he or she might develop a sudden, unexplained fondness for beer.

Not that you asked, but the Red Cross number for information about giving blood is 1-800-GIVE LIFE.

An Offer They Can't Refuse

Recently I received an exciting offer in the mail from my credit-card company. Usually their offers involve merchandise that no actual human would ever need.

"Dear Mr. Dave Barry," they say. "How many times have you asked yourself: 'Why can't I cook shish ke-bab AND enjoy recorded music?' Well, Mr. Dave Barry, because you are a valued customer who has consistently demonstrated, by paying us three million percent interest, that you have the financial astuteness of a lint ball, we are making available to you a Special Opportunity to purchase this deluxe combination gas barbecue grill and CD player."

But this recent offer was even better. This was an offer to sell me *my own credit rating*. Yes. One of the great benefits of living in America is that, regardless of your race or religion or hygiene habits, you are entitled to have a credit rating maintained by large corporations with powerful computers that know *everything about you*. For example, let's say that this morning you deposited your paycheck at the bank, made a phone call, wrote a check for your electric bill, and charged some gasoline on your credit card. By this afternoon, thanks to high-speed laser fiber-optic data transmission, the computers will know *every sexual fantasy you had* while you were doing these things. And don't think they keep it to themselves, either. They are as human as the next person. They go to computer parties, they have a few too many diskettes, and the next thing you know they're revealing your intimate secrets at the rate of four billion per second.

That's why I was so excited about this offer from my credit-card company to sell me the TRW CREDENTIALS service. TRW is a large company that collects credit information about people and sells it. According to the TRW CREDENTIALS offer, if I give them $20 a year, they'll let me see my information.

The offer states: "Financial experts recommend that you carefully review your credit report *twice a year* to check its information and make certain that it is accurate."

In other words—correct me if I am wrong here—they're telling me that I should give them $20 a year so I can look at the information ABOUT ME that they collected WITHOUT MY PERMISSION and have been selling for years to GOD ALONE KNOWS WHO so I can see if it's INCORRECT.

Which it very well could be. Because even with computers, things sometimes go wrong. I know you find this hard to believe, inasmuch as we live in such a competent nation, a nation capable of producing technological wonders such as the Hubble Orbiting Space Telescope, the only orbiting telescope in the universe equipped with dark glasses and a cane. But sometimes mistakes do get made, and they could affect your credit.

For example, just recently we got a phone call at home, at night, from a woman from a collection agency. She said we'd be in big trouble if we didn't turn over four cable-TV boxes, which she said we had failed to return to the cable company when we moved a year ago. I explained that, (1) it was only two boxes, and (2) we had made three appointments with the cable company to come get them, but nobody ever showed up, and (3) we would love to get rid of them, and (4) maybe SHE could get the cable company to come get them. The woman said, basically, that it was too late for that, because this matter had been turned over to *a collection agency,* which is apparently several levels above the U.S. Supreme Court, and we had better hand over four cable boxes or this would go on our Permanent Credit Record.

So I called up the cable company, and joined the millions of Americans on hold, waiting to talk to one of the nation's estimated four cable-company service representatives, two of whom are on break. Future generations, when they look at formal family portraits from this era, will say, "There's Aunt Martha, who was a teacher, and the man holding the phone receiver to his ear is Uncle Bob, who was on hold to the cable company."

Finally, miraculously, I got through, and even more miraculously, they came out and got our boxes. And I was feeling very good about America until the collection-agency woman called again, at night, to inform me that we'd be in big trouble if we didn't turn over the boxes. All four of them.

So I don't know what our credit record says. I wouldn't be surprised if it holds us largely to blame for the savings-and-loan scandal. So I'm definitely interested in the TRW CREDENTIALS offer.

However, I don't like to do business with an outfit unless I know something about it. So I've decided to develop a file on TRW. I'd certainly appreciate anything you can contribute. But I don't want any wild speculative unfounded rumors, such as:

- TRW is the world's largest distributor of hard-core pornography.
- TRW has destroyed two-thirds of the Earth's ozone layer.
- TRW is a satanic vampire cult headed by the love child of Jim Bakker and Leona Helmsley.

There is no need to run the risk that absurd statements such as these might get into print. In fact, it would probably be a wise idea for TRW to examine my file, from time to time, just to make sure *nothing inaccurate* appeared in there.

I'm sure we can work something out.

The Roll of the Humorist

If you're looking for a sport that offers both of the Surgeon General's Two Recommended Key Elements of Athletic Activity, namely (1) rental shoes and (2) beer, then you definitely want to take up bowling.

I love to bowl. I even belong to a bowling team, the Pin Worms. How good are we? I don't wish to brag, but we happen to be ranked, in the World Bowling Association standings, under the heading "Severely Impaired." Modern science has been baffled in its efforts to predict what will happen to a given ball that has been released by a Pin Worm. The Strategic Air Command routinely tracks our bowling balls on radar in case one of them threatens a major population center and has to be destroyed with missiles.

But the thing is, we have fun. That's what I like about bowling: You can have fun even if you stink, unlike in, say, tennis. Every decade or so I attempt to play tennis, and it always consists of 37 seconds of actually hitting the ball, and two hours of yelling "Where did the ball go?" "Over that condominium!" etc. Whereas with bowling, once you let go of the ball, it's no longer your legal responsibility. They have these wonderful machines that find it for you and send it right back. Some of these machines can also keep score for you. In the Bowling Alley of Tomorrow, there will even be machines that wear rental shoes and throw the ball for you. Your sole function will be to drink beer.

Besides convenience, bowling offers drama. I recently witnessed an extremely dramatic shot by a young person named Madeline, age 3, who is cute as a button but much smaller. We were in the 10th frame, and Madeline had frankly not had a good game in the sense of knocking down any of the pins or even getting the ball to go all the way to the end of the lane without stopping. So on her last turn, she

got up there, and her daddy put the ball down in front of her, and she pushed it with both hands. Nothing appeared to happen, but if you examined the ball with sensitive scientific instruments, you could determine that it was actually rolling. We all watched it anxiously. Time passed. The ball kept rolling. Neighboring bowlers stopped to watch. The ball kept rolling. Spectators started drifting in off the street. TV news crews arrived. A half dozen Communist governments fell. Still Madeline's ball kept rolling. Finally, incredibly, it reached the pins and, in the world's first live slow-motion replay, *knocked them all down.* Of course by then Madeline had children of her own, but it was still very exciting.

For real bowling excitement, however, you can't beat Ponch, the bowling dog. I'm not making Ponch up; he holds the rank of German shepherd in the Miami Police Department, and he bowls in charity tournaments. He uses a special ramp built by his partner, K-9 Officer Bill Martin. Bill puts the ball on the ramp, then Ponch jumps up and knocks the ball down the ramp with his teeth. It looks very painful, but Ponch loves it. He loves it so much that as soon as the ball starts rolling, he wants to get it back, so he starts sprinting down the lane after it, barking, his feet flailing wildly around, cartoon-style, on the slick wood (this is a violation of the rules, but nobody is brave enough to tell Ponch).

When Ponch is about halfway down the lane, he suddenly sees his ball disappear into the machinery, so he whirls around and flails his way back to the ball-return tunnel, where he sticks his head *down into the hole,* barking furiously, knowing that his ball is in there somewhere, demanding that it be returned *immediately,* and then suddenly WHAM there it is, hitting Ponch directly in the face at approximately 40 miles per hour, and *he could not be happier.* He is overjoyed to see his ball again, because that means Officer Bill's going to put it on the ramp and Ponch can hit it with his teeth again! Hurrah!

Not only is Ponch a lot of fun to watch, but he's also very naive about scoring, so you can cheat. "Sorry, Ponch," you can say, "I scored 5,490 in that last game, so you owe me a million dollars." He'll just wag his tail. Money means nothing to him. But touch his ball and he'll rip out your throat.

Full-Bore Book Tour

I didn't lose my luggage until Day 12 of the Book Promotion Tour From Hell. By then I was glad to get rid of it. I'd been dragging it to every North American city large enough to have roads, appearing on thousands of radio talk shows, all named "Speaking About Talking," for the purpose of pretending to be enthusiastic about my book, although after about the fifth day I usually just staggered into the radio station, put my head down on the host's lap, and went to sleep. Most hosts are accustomed to interviewing unconscious book-tour victims, so they'd just plunge ahead. "Our guest today on 'Speaking About Talking,' " they'd say, "smells like the bottom of a homeless person's shopping bag."

This was true. The reason was that, no matter how many days I'm on the road, I insist on taking only one small carry-on suitcase so as to prevent my luggage from falling into the hands of the Baggage People, who would pounce upon it like those grief-stricken Iranian mourners who nearly reduced the late Mr. Ayatollah Khomeini to Corpse McNuggets. So my garments and toiletry articles spend their days compressed into an extremely dense carry-on wad in which they are able to freely exchange grime, mayonnaise stains, B.O. vapors, etc., the result being that after several days my "clean" shirts look like giant community handkerchiefs and my Tartar Control toothpaste tastes like sock dirt. Eventually my luggage undergoes a process known to physicists and frequent fliers as "suitcase fusion," wherein the contents all unite into one writhing, festering, pulsating blob of laundry that, when I get to the hotel room, climbs angrily out of the suitcase by itself and crawls over to the TV to watch in-room pornographic movies. This worries me, because the movie goes on my computerized hotel bill, and I'm afraid that when I check out, the clerk will say, in a loud and perky voice: "Mr. Barry, we certainly hope you enjoyed your stay here, especially your private in-room viewing of *Return to Planet Nipple.*"

Actually I don't have time to watch movies, because I have to forage for food. The split-second schedule of the Book Promotion Tour From Hell calls for me to arrive at the hotel five minutes after room service closes, so I usually enjoy a hearty and nourishing meal from the "mini-bar," which is a little box provided as a service to hotel guests by the American Cholesterol Growers Association, featuring foodlike items that are perfect for the busy traveler who figures he's going to die soon anyway, such as Honey-Roasted Pork Parts.

After dinner it's time to crawl into bed, turn out the lights, and listen to the Subtle But Annoying Air-Conditioning Rattle, which is required by law to be in all hotel rooms as a safety precaution against the danger that a guest might carelessly fall asleep. You notice that the bellperson never tells you about this. The bellperson gives you a lengthy orientation speech full of information that you have known since childhood, such as that you operate the TV by turning it on, but he never says, "Incidentally, the only way to stop the annoying rattle is to jam a pair of Jockey shorts into that air register up there." No, part of the fun of hotel life is that you get to solve this puzzle for yourself, which I usually do at 1:30 A.M., just in time for the start of the Sudden Violent Outburst of Hallway Laughter Tournament, in which teams of large hearing-impaired men gather directly outside my door to inhale nitrous oxide and see who can laugh loud enough to dislodge my shorts from the air register. In less time than it took to form the Hawaiian Islands the night has flown by and it's 5:42 A.M., time for the Housekeeping Person, secure in the knowledge that I cannot pack a gun in my carry-on luggage, to knock on my door, just above the sign that says PLEASE DO NOT DISTURB in 127 languages, and inform me helpfully that she'll come back later. But I usually get up anyway, because the sooner I check out, the sooner I can appear on a radio talk show and get some sleep.

Sometimes I also go on TV, which is how I lost my luggage. What happened was, a TV crew was following me around, doing a story about a Typical Day on a book tour. They put a wireless microphone on me so they could record me making typical remarks, such as: "Is this recording me in the bathroom?" And: "I'm wearing a wireless microphone." I made this last typical remark to a concerned security person after I set off the alarm at the Minneapolis–St. Paul airport. So he started poking around under my shirt, bravely risking Death by Armpit Fumes, and while this was going on some other unfortunate air traveler mistakenly walked off with my suitcase. I hate to think what happened to this person. My

guess is that at some point he foolishly opened my suitcase and a tentacle of my laundry came snaking out and dragged him back inside.

The airline people eventually gave me back my suitcase, but now I'm afraid to open it, because this person is probably still in there, being genetically combined with my Prell shampoo. So if you're missing a friend or loved one who was last seen in the Minneapolis–St. Paul airport, I've got him, and I'll be glad to return him when I come to your town, which will be any day now on the Book Tour From Hell. You'll smell me coming.

Coffee? Tea? Weasel Spit?

So I was getting on a plane in Seattle, and I was feeling a touch nervous because that very morning a plane was forced to make an emergency landing at that very airport after a window blew out at 14,000 feet and a passenger almost got sucked out of the plane headfirst. This is the kind of thing that the flight attendants never mention during the Preflight Safety Demonstration, although maybe they should. I bet they could put on a very impressive demonstration using an industrial vacuum cleaner and a Barbie doll, and we passengers would NEVER take our seat belts off, even when the plane landed. We'd walk out into the terminal with our seats still strapped to our backs.

Anyway, the good news is that the passenger in Seattle was wearing his seat belt, and the other passengers were able to pull him back inside, and he's expected to make a complete recovery except for no longer having a head. This will definitely limit his ability to enjoy future in-flight meals ("Would you like a dense omelet-like substance, sir? Just nod your stump.").

Ha ha! I am just joshing of course. The man retained all his major body parts. But just the same I don't like to hear this type of story, because I usually take a window seat, because I want to know if a wing falls off. The pilot would never mention this. It is a violation of Federal Aviation Administration regulations for the pilot to ever tell you anything except that you are experiencing "a little turbulence." You frequent fliers know what I'm talking about. You're flying along at 500 miles an hour, 7 miles up, and suddenly there's an enormous shuddering WHUMP. Obviously the plane has struck something at least the size of a Winnebago motor home—in fact sometimes you can actually see Winnebago parts flashing past your window—but the pilot, trying to sound bored, announces that you have experienced "a little turbulence." Meanwhile you just know that up in the cockpit they're hastily deploying their Emergency Inflatable Religious Shrine.

Here's what bothers me. You know how, during the Preflight Safety Demonstration, they tell you that in the event of an emergency, oxygen masks will pop out of the ceiling? My question is: *Who wants oxygen?* If I'm going to be in an emergency seven miles up, I want *nitrous oxide,* followed immediately by Emergency Intravenous Beverage Cart Service, so that I and my fellow passengers can be as relaxed as possible. ("Wow! Those are some beautiful engine flames!")

Anyway, nothing terrible happened on my flight, which was unfortunate, because there was a high school marching band on board. My advice to airline passengers is: Always request a non-marching-band flight. Oh, I'm sure that these were wonderful teenage kids on an individual basis, but when you get 60 of them together in a confined area, they reach Critical Adolescent Mass, with huge waves of runaway hormones sloshing up and down the aisle, knocking over the flight attendants and causing the older passengers to experience sudden puberty symptoms (the pilot's voice went up several octaves when he tried to say "turbulence").

Mealtime was the worst. The entree was Beef Stroganoff Airline-Style, a hearty dish featuring chunks of yellowish meatlike byproducts that apparently have been pre-chewed for your convenience by weasels. I was desperately hungry, so I was actually going to attempt to eat mine, when one of the male band members seated near me, in the age-old adolescent tradition of Impressing Girls Through Grossness, launched into an anecdote about an earlier inflight meal:

". . . so she was eating chocolate all day, right? And she gets on the plane and they serve her the meal, right? And she looks at it, and she goes, like, RALPH all over her tray, and it's like BROWN and it's getting ALL OVER her TRAY and onto the FLOOR, so she like stands up and she goes RALPH all over the people in front of her and it's like running down their HAIR and . . ."

This anecdote didn't bother the band girls at all.

"Ewwwwww," they said, chewing happily. Whereas I lost my appetite altogether. I just sat there, a frequent flier looking at his Vaguely Beeflike Stroganoff and wondering how come airline windows never suck people out then you really need them to.

I'm Dave. Fly Me.

I'm going to start my own airline. Hey, why not? This is America, right? *Anybody* can have an airline. They even let Donald Trump have one, which he immediately renamed after himself, as is his usual classy practice despite the fact that "Trump" sounds like the noise emitted by livestock with gastric disorders ("Stand back, Earl! That cow's starting to Trump!").

Well if he can do it, I can do it. My airline will be called: "Air Dave." All the planes in the Air Dave fleet will utilize state-of-the-art U.S. Defense Department technology, thus rendering them—this is the key selling point—invisible to radar. That's right: I'm talking about a *stealth airline.*

Think about it. If you're a frequent flier, you know that the big problem with commercial aviation today is that the planes can be easily detected by Air Traffic Control, which is run by severely overstressed people sitting in gloomy rooms drinking coffee from

Styrofoam cups and staring at little radar-screen dots, each one representing several hundred carefree people drinking Bloody Marys at 35,000 feet. Naturally the air-traffic controllers become resentful, which is why they routinely order your Boston-to-Pittsburgh flight to circle Mexico City until the captain reports that the entire passenger sector is experiencing Barf Bag Overload.

They won't be able to do that stuff to Air Dave. They won't even be aware that an Air Dave flight is in the vicinity until it screams past the control tower at Mach 2, clearly displaying its laser-guided air-to-tower missiles, and requests permission to land *immediately.*

Air Dave planes will not park at a gate. Air Dave planes will taxi directly to the rental-car counter.

The official Air Dave spokesperson will be Sean Penn.

There will be no mutant in-flight "food" served on Air Dave. At mealtime, the pilot will simply land —on an interstate, if necessary—and take everybody to a decent restaurant.

Air Dave will do everything possible to live up to its motto: "Hey, You Only Go Around Once." There will be no in-flight movies. There will be *live bands.* Every flight will feature a complimentary Petting Zoo Cart. Air Dave will also boast the aviation industry's finest inflight pranks. For example, just after takeoff the door to the cockpit might "accidentally" swing open, revealing to the passengers that the sole occupant up there, cheerfully sniffing the altimeter, is a Labrador retriever named "Boomer."

All Air Dave planes will have skywriting capability.

Air Dave pilots will be chosen strictly on the basis of how entertaining their names sound over the public-address system, as in "First Officer LaGrange Weevil" or (ideally) "Captain Deltoid P. Hamsterlicker." Pilots will be encouraged to share their thoughts and feelings with the passengers via regular announcements such as: "What the heck does THIS thing do?" and "Uh-oh!"

In the event of an emergency, a ceiling panel will open up over each seat and out will pop: Tony Perkins.

I've given a lot of thought to the flight attendants. My original idea was to use mimes, who would go around *pretending* to serve beverages, etc. But then I got to thinking about an opinion voiced a few months back by Al Neuharth, the brain cell behind *USA Today* ("The Nation's Weather Map"). You may remember this: Mr. Neuharth wrote a column in which he was highly critical of today's flight attendants, whom he described as "aging women" and "flighty young men." And quite frankly I think he has a point, which is why all the flight attendants on Air Dave will be hired on the basis of looking as much as possible like the ultimate human physical specimen: Al Neuharth. Assuming we can find anybody that short.

The Preflight Safety Lecture on Air Dave will consist of five minutes of intensive harmonica instruction. Passengers will also be notified that under Federal Aviation Administration regulations, anyone requesting a "light" beer must be ejected over Utah.

Air Dave pilots will have standing orders to moon the Concorde.

So that's the Air Dave Master Plan. On behalf of Captain Hamsterlicker and the entire crew of Neuharths, let me say that it's been a real pleasure having you read the column today. And remember: Under the Air Dave Frequent Flier program, if you log just 25,000 miles, *we'll let you off the plane.*

READER ALERT

Dave Barry for President

In this historic column I became the first humor columnist that I know of to openly declare his candidacy for the presidency in 1992. The public responded with a massive outpouring of support conservatively estimated at seven or eight letters, only a few of which directly threatened my life. A couple of people actually sent money in denominations as high as one dollar; as a token of my gratitude, I plan to nominate these people to the U.S. Supreme Court. I'll nominate them even if the court has no vacancies. That's the kind of "people president" I plan to be. One of my mottoes is: "Dave Barry: He'll Award A High Federal Office To Virtually Any Dirtbag Who Gives Him Money." Another one is: "Dave Barry: He'll Keep Dan Quayle." This is to ensure my personal security.

We Will Barry You

I know what's bothering you, as a concerned American. What's bothering you is that it's 1991 already, and nobody is running for president. It's eerie. At this time four years ago Iowa was already infested with presidential timbers such as Bruce Babbitt and Pierre S. "Pete" du Pont IV Esquire, Inc. The average Iowa farmer could not take a step without bumping into several leading presidential contenders demonstrating their concern for agriculture by lifting small pigs. And yet today, four years later, nobody is actively campaigning out there. (Not that the pigs are complaining.)

Of course George Bush has been busy, what with the Persian Gulf, the economy, bonefishing, etc. And there is speculation about Mario Cuomo running. But there has always been speculation about Mario Cuomo running. A large portion of the Rosetta stone is devoted to ancient Egyptian speculation about Mario Cuomo running. You also hear talk about Sen. Albert Gore, but the U.S. Constitution clearly states in Article III, Section 4, Row 8, Seat 5, that the president cannot be somebody named "Albert."

"Arnold, maybe," states the Constitution. "But not Albert."

Another possible candidate, Sen. Bill Bradley, possesses the one quality that thoughtful American voters value above all in a leader: height. Unfortunately, Senator Bradley also has, with all due respect, the charisma of gravel. Hospitals routinely use tapes of his speeches to sedate patients for surgery. Rep. "Dick" Gephardt has no eyebrows and is, in the words of a recent *New York Times* editorial, "probably an alien being."

Clearly, the nation has a Leadership Vacuum. Well, where I come from, we have a saying: "If you're not going to grab the bull by the horns while the iron is in the fire, then get off the pot." (There are a lot of

chemicals in the water where I come from.) And that is why I am announcing today that I am running for President of the United States.

(Wild sustained applause.)

Thank you. But before I accept your support and your large cash contributions, I want you to know where I stand on the issues. Basically, as I see it, there are two major issues facing this nation: Domestic and Foreign. Following are my positions on these issues as of 9:30 this morning.

DOMESTIC AFFAIRS: I would eliminate all giant federal departments—Transportation, Commerce, Interior, Exterior, etc.—and replace them with a single entity, called the Department of Louise. This would consist of a woman named Louise, selected on the basis of being a regular taxpaying individual with children and occasional car trouble and zero experience in government. The Department of Louise would have total veto power over everything. Before government officials could spend any money, they'd have to explain the reason to Louise and get her approval.

"Louise," they'd say, "We want to take several billion dollars away from the taxpayers and build a giant contraption in Texas so we can cause tiny invisible particles to whiz around and smash into each other and break into even tinier particles."

And Louise would say: "No."

Or the officials would say: "Louise, we want to use a half million taxpayer dollars to restore the childhood home of Lawrence Welk."

And Louise would say: "No."

Or the officials would say: "Louise, we'd like to give the Syrians a couple million dollars to reward them for going almost a week without harboring a terrorist."

And Louise would say: "No."

Or the officials might say: "Louise, we want to . . ."

And Louise would say: "No."

All of these decisions would have to be made before 5:30 P.M., because Louise would be very strict about picking up her kids at day care.

FOREIGN AFFAIRS: These would be handled via another new entity called The Department of A Couple of Guys Named Victor. The idea here would be to prevent situations such as the Panama invasion, where we send in the army to get Manuel Noriega, and a whole lot of innocent people get hurt, but NOT Manuel Noriega. He gets lawyers and fax machines and a Fair Trial that will probably not take place during the current century.

The Department of A Couple of Guys Named Victor would not handle things this way. I'd just tell them, "Victors, I have this feeling that something unfortunate might happen to Manuel Noriega, you know what I mean?" And, mysteriously, something would.

Or, instead of sending hundreds of thousands of our people to fight hundreds of thousands of Iraqis all because of one scuzzball, I'd say: "Victors, it would not depress me to hear that Saddam Hussein had some kind of unfortunately fatal accident in the shower."

I realize there will be critics of this program. "What if he doesn't take showers?" they will say. But these are mere technical details. The important thing is that I have a platform, and next week I'm going to Iowa—really—as the first declared candidate, and if you want to get on the bandwagon, now is the time, because there is a lot of important work to be done, such as selecting the band for the Victory Party. Right now I am leaning toward Little Richard.

Also, I need to locate a small pig.

Afterword

(NOTE TO PEOPLE WHO HAVE ACTUALLY READ THIS BOOK:
Please disregard the following section. It's intended purely as a sales device to entice people at bookstores who decide whether or not to buy a book by flipping directly to the end to see how it comes out.)

Lance looked at Laura, and there was lust in his eyes, because he knew, from the 173 sex scenes that took place in this action-packed novel, that she was a woman of major sexual appetites, not to mention hooters the size of Lincoln, Nebraska.

"Oh, Lance," she said. "We have been through so much in this steamy, action-packed novel, which is a real bargain at the suggested retail hardcover price of only $15.95, higher in Canada."

"You're not kidding," remarked Lance. "It would be a steal even without the section that explains in simple, easy-to-understand terms how anybody who has the brain-wave activity of a carrot can make up to $50,000 a month in his or her spare time without doing anything remotely productive!"

"Not to mention the chapter explaining the Amazing Surgeon General's Diet Plan that enables a person to lose as many as 17 pounds per hour without hunger or even conscious awareness!" laughed Laura.

"Buy this book right now!" they chorused. "Mrs. L. Puttee of Big Stoat, Ark., bought this book, and the next day she won four billion dollars in the lottery! Myron Fennel of Syracuse, N.Y., failed to buy this book, and the next day his head was sliced off by a helicopter rotor and landed on the roof of a Holiday Inn four miles distant!"

Your eyes are getting heavy. You are getting sleepy, very, very sleepy. You are walking up to the bookstore clerk. You are taking out your wallet. We take all major credit cards. Thank you.

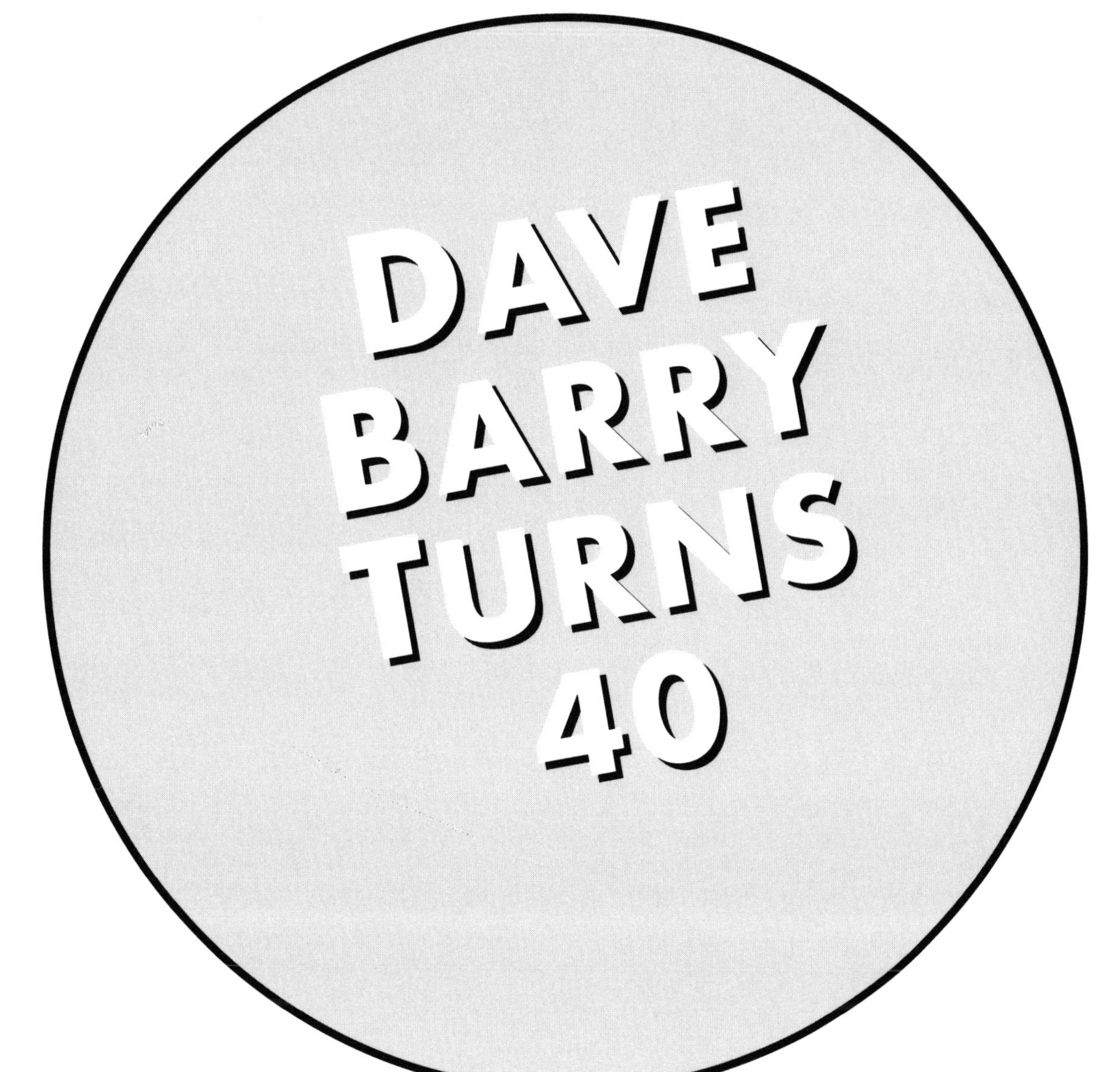
DAVE
BARRY
TURNS
40

For Dan Quayle,
who proved to my generation that,
frankly, anybody can make it

Contents

Introduction

Well, it's finally happening. I'm talking about the long-predicted Aging Process. I see many signs of it in my own life. For example, I have become tremendously concerned about my gums. There was a time when I could go for *decades* without thinking about my gums, but recently they have come to loom far larger in my mind than the Greenhouse Effect.

Also, young people I meet keep using the word "Mister," causing me to whirl around and look behind me, expecting to see somebody with whom I associate this title, such as the Pope or Walter Cronkite, only to realize that these young people are talking to *me*.

Also, if I attempt to throw a softball without carefully warming up, I have to wait until approximately the next presidential administration before I can attempt to do this again.

Also, I have long, animated conversations with my friends—friends with whom I used to ingest banned substances and swim naked—on the importance of dietary fiber.

Also, I find myself asking my son, in a solemn parental voice, the same profoundly stupid old-fogey questions that my parents used to ask me, such as: "Do you want to poke somebody's *eye* out?"

Also—this is most terrifying—I sometimes catch myself humming along to elevator music.

Of course I'm not alone. Growing older is a Major Lifestyle Trend, potentially even bigger than cable television. Millions of us, the entire legendary Baby Boom herd of Mouseketeer-watching, Hula-Hoop-spinning, Beatles-admiring, hair-growing, pot-smoking, funky-chicken-dancing, lovemaking, résumé-writing, career-pursuing, insurance-buying, fitness-obsessing, Lamaze-class-taking, breast-feeding, data-processing, mortgage-paying, Parents'-Night-attending, business-card-exchanging, compact-disc-owning, tooth-flossing individuals, are lunging toward:

→ MIDDLE AGE ←

Yes. Say it out loud, Boomers: We are MIDDLE-AGED. The time has come for us to stop identifying with Wally and The Beav; we are now a *lot* closer to Ward and June. *Somebody* has to be the grownups, and now it's our turn.

The problem is, I'm not sure we're ready. I've been hanging around with people roughly my own age for the bulk of my life, and I frankly do not feel that, as a group, we have acquired the wisdom and maturity needed to run the world, or even necessarily power tools. Many of us, I'm convinced, only *look* like grownups.

For example, I work for a newspaper Sunday magazine whose staff consists mostly of people about my age. If you happened to visit us briefly from the outside world, we'd strike you as being regular middle-aged guys with ties and desks and families and various degrees of hair loss. "Huh!" you'd say. "This is a group of adults charged with putting out a magazine under constant deadline pressure! They must be very responsible!" Then you'd leave, and we'd resume playing chairball, a game we invented one day in the conference room while attempting to hold a conference, in which the players scuttle violently around on rolling chairs, trying to throw a foam-rubber ball through a hoop up on the wall.

I don't mean to suggest that all we do, at the office, is play chairball. Sometimes we throw the Frisbee. Sometimes we practice our juggling. Sometimes we even put out the magazine, but you would never conclude, if you secretly observed us for several weeks, that this was anywhere near our highest priority.

And I don't think it's just me and my co-workers who do stuff like this. I think the entire Baby Boom generation is having trouble letting go of the idea that it represents The Nation's Youth and has an inalienable right to be wild and carefree. The whole Iran-contra scandal, in my opinion, basically boiled down to some fortyish guys in the White House basement playing an international top-secret multimillion-dollar version of chairball.

This is why I'm alarmed at the prospect of somebody my age getting into the Oval Office. Because I know that if *I* got in there, I'd probably be okay for the first few days, but then I'd do something to amuse myself, such as order the Marines to invade Cleveland, or issue a proclamation honoring Nasal Discharge Week, or leave a prank message on the Hot Phone answering machine ("Thanks for calling the White House. We can't recall our bombers right now, but if you leave your name and the time you called . . .").

But the alarming truth is, people my age *are* taking over the government, along with almost everything else. And what is even more terrifying, I'm seeing more and more important jobs being done by people who are even *younger* than I am. The scariest example is doctors. If you wake up from a terrible accident to find yourself strapped down on your back in an operating room awaiting emergency surgery, and a person walks in who is about to open you up with a sharp implement and root around among your personal organs, you want this person to look as much as possible like Robert Young, right? Well, today the odds are that you're going to look up and see Sean Penn.

And let's talk about airline pilots. I have long felt that if I'm going to risk my life and valuable carry-on belongings in a profoundly heavy machine going absurdly fast way the hell up in the air over places such as Arkansas, where I don't even know anybody, then I want whoever is operating this machine to be *much* older and more mature than I. But now I routinely get on planes where the entire flight crew looks like it's raising money for its Class Trip. I am very nervous on these flights. I want the crew to leave the cockpit door open so I can make sure they're not using the navigational computer to play Death Blasters from Planet Doom.

I'm not suggesting that anything can be done about this trend. I mean, we can't pass a law requiring, for example, that airline pilots always have to be older than we are. That could become a real problem once we started reaching, say, our eighties ("This is your captain, and my name is, um . . . it's . . . my name is right on the tip of my tongue . . .").

No, the only solution is for us to face up to the fact that we are no longer the Hope for the Future. The Hope for the Future now consists of the kids who like to shave their heads and ride skateboards off the tops of buildings. We Baby Boomers are the Hope for Right Now, and we're going to have to accept it.

Which is why I wrote this book. My goal is to explore all the ramifications—physiological, emotional, and social—of turning 40, in hopes that, by improving our understanding and awareness of the true significance of this challenging and extremely important new phase in our lives, we will acquire, as countless generations have acquired before us, the wisdom, vision, and maturity we need to assume our rightful responsibilities and obligations as the moral, intellectual, political, and spiritual leaders—and, yes, caretakers—of this increasingly fragile planet.

Then let's drink a bunch of beer and set off fireworks.

Are You a Grownup Yet? A Scientific Quiz

This quiz is designed to help you get a handle on how far you have progressed toward becoming a grownup, as measured by the Standardized Psychological Maturity Scale, which assesses your maturity level on a scale of zero (Very Immature) to ten (Legally Dead). Answer the questions below as honestly as you can, bearing in mind that there are no "right" or "wrong" answers. Our goal, in this exercise, is not to judge you according to someone else's arbitrary system of values. Our goal is to waste time.

1. If another driver cuts you off in traffic, you will:
   a. Keep your temper firmly in check, because nobody wins when you "play games" with Traffic Safety.
   b. Honk your horn in an irritated fashion and possibly even make a famous hand gesture.
   c. Dedicate yourself totally to gaining automotive revenge—no matter what the risk to property or human life—by *cutting the other driver off,* even if this means drastically altering your plans and, if necessary, following him to Mexico.

2. When you participate in a friendly, informal, meaningless pickup game such as volleyball or softball, you play at an intensity level that would be appropriate for:
   a. A friendly, informal, meaningless pickup game.
   b. The Olympic finals.
   c. Iwo Jima.

3. You generally leave parties:
   a. Well before all the other guests have left.
   b. When there are only one or two other guests remaining.
   c. At gunpoint.

4. What do you do when the song "Jumpin' Jack

Flash," by the Rolling Stones, comes on your car radio?

a. You turn it off and call the office on your car phone to see if any of your business associates have tried to reach you on *their* car phones.

b. You change to a "mellow rock" station oriented toward sensitive songs such as "Feelin' Groovy" from Simon and Garfunkel's early years ("The Weenie Period"), played by disc jockeys who are so low-key that they take Quaaludes to *wake up*.

c. You crank the radio volume all the way up and do the Car Dance, wherein you bounce your butt rhythmically on the seat, and you sing along with Mick Jagger using the cigarette lighter as a microphone while gradually pressing down harder and harder on the accelerator, so that when you get to the part where you and Mick sing that "Jumpin' Jack Flash is a GAS GAS GAS," you are going at least eighty-five miles per hour, even inside your garage.

5. If it were entirely up to you to feed yourself, your diet would consist of:

a. Fruits, vegetables, and low-cholesterol protein sources.

b. Fried foods and frozen dinners.

c. Milk Duds.

6. In conversations with your co-workers, how do you refer to your boss?

a. "Mr. Druckerman."

b. "Ted."

c. "The Human Hemorrhoid."

7. If you have any money left after you take care of basic living expenses, you put it into:

a. A diversified investment portfolio with emphasis on proven equities offering secure long-term growth potential.

b. Paying off your Visa bill.

c. Skee-ball.

8. You are in a very important, very serious corporate meeting attended by major, high-level officers. During a momentary silence, one of the participants—the chief executive officer of a firm that your company desperately wants to win as a client—emits a brief but fabric-rendingly-loud burst of flatulence. What do you do?

a. Act as though absolutely nothing has happened.

b. Titter involuntarily, but quickly regain your composure.

c. Lunge for the 179-page market survey report in front of you and hide your face behind it and make a desperate but clearly hopeless effort to remain silent while your body vibrates with pent-up laughter that finally erupts with a violent, wet gasping noise like several dozen whales surfacing simultaneously, accompanied by a rivulet of fast-moving drool trickling out from under the report and making its away across the conference table and finally dribbling into the lap of the potential client's attorney, at which point you emerge from behind the report and attempt to apologize to seventeen stony, staring corporate faces, who unfortunately serve only to remind you of the awesome, nearly life-threatening *humor* of the situation, so that all you can say to them—to the people who hold your professional future in their hands—is, quote, "WHOOOOO," after which you pull your head, turtle-like, back into the report, and the only noise in the conference room, aside from the labored, gurgling gasps that you continue to emit, is the sound of the potential client picking up his briefcase and marching grimly and permanently from the room.

9. Your taste in the performing arts runs toward:
a. Ballet, opera, classical music.
b. Television, movies, pop concerts.
c. Booger jokes.

10. If you had just acquired a puppy, your highest priority, in terms of discipline, would be training it to:
a. Heel.
b. Roll over.
c. Pee on the Amway distributor.

How to Score First off, you have to make the woman believe that you really *care* about her as a person, and then you . . .

Whoops! Sorry! Wrong kind of scoring! To score yourself on the maturity quiz, give yourself one point for each "A" answer, half a point for each "B" answer, and zero points for each "C" answer, then total up your points. If you actually take the trouble to *do* this, you are a fairly mature person. A lot of us are already reading the next chapter.

CHAPTER TWO

Your Disintegrating Body

One of the more traumatic aspects of reaching age 40 is the realization that you no longer have the same body you had when you were 21. I know *I* don't. Sometimes when I take a shower I look down at my body and I want to scream: "Hey, THIS isn't my body! THIS body belongs to Willard Scott!"

But this is perfectly natural. Screaming in the shower, I mean. Reaching age 40, however, is NOT natural. I base this statement on extensive scientific documentation in the form of a newspaper article I vaguely remember reading once, which stated that the life expectancy for human beings in the wild is about 35 years. Think about what that means. It means that if you were in the wild, even in the non-smoking section, by now you'd be Worm Chow. So we can clearly see that going past age 40 is basically an affront to Nature, with Exhibit A being the Gabor sisters.

Nevertheless, we *are* living longer. Thanks to modern medical advances such as antibiotics, nasal spray, and Diet Coke, it has become quite routine for people in the civilized world to pass the age of 40, sometimes more than once. As a person reaching this milestone, you need to take the time to learn about the biological changes that are taking place within your body, so that you will be better able to understand and cope with the inevitable and completely natural elements of the aging process—the minor aches, pains, dental problems, intestinal malfunctions, muscle deterioration, emotional instability, memory lapses, hearing and vision loss, impotence, seizures, growths, prostate problems, greatly reduced limb function, massive coronary failure, death, and, of course, painful hemorrhoidal swelling—that make up this exciting adventure we call "middle age."

My goal, in this chapter, is to explore these topics in as much detail as possible without doing any actual research, in the hopes that when I am done, you will have the knowledge you need to develop healthier lifestyle habits. For example, right now you may be the kind of person who goes to a restaurant and, without thinking, orders a great big juicy steak. My hope is that, after reading this chapter and becoming aware of the dangers of ingesting high-cholesterol foods, you will also order a martini the size of Lake Huron. Remember the words of the wise old Health Proverb: "A person who observes the rules of proper nutrition is a person who should never be placed in charge of a barbecue."

But enough inspiration. It's time to put on our protective eyewear and take a detailed, probing look inside your increasingly Spam-like body, starting with a factual overview of:

The Aging Process

Why do we get older? Why do our bodies wear out? Why can't we just go on and on and on, accumulating a potentially infinite number of Frequent Flier mileage points? These are the kinds of questions that philosophers have been asking ever since they realized that being a philosopher did not involve any heavy lifting.

And yet the answer is really very simple: Our bodies are mechanical devices, and like all mechanical devices, they break down. Some devices, such as battery-operated toys costing $39.95, break down almost instantly upon exposure to the Earth's atmosphere. Other devices, such as stereo systems owned by your next-door neighbors' 13-year-old son who likes to listen to bands with names like "Nerve Damage" at a volume capable of disintegrating limestone, will continue to function perfectly for many years, even if you hit them with an ax. But the fundamental law of physics is that sooner or later every mechanism ceases to function for one reason or another, and it is never covered under the warranty.

As we know from slicing up dead worms in Biology Lab, the "parts" that make up this miraculous "mechanism" that we call the human body are called "cells"—billions and billions (even more, in the case of Marlon Brando) of organisms so tiny that we cannot see or hear them unless we have been using illegal narcotics. When you are very young, each of your cells, based on its individual personality and aptitude, selects an area of specialization, such as the thigh, in which to pursue its career. As you grow, the cell multiplies, and it teaches its offspring to be thigh cells also, showing them the various "tricks of the trade." Thus the proud thigh-cell tradition is handed down from generation to generation, so that by the time you're a teenager, you have an extremely competent, efficient, and hard-working colony down there, providing you with thighs so sleek and taut that they look great even when encased in Spandex garments that would be a snug fit on a Bic pen. But as your body approaches middle age, this cellular discipline starts to break down. The newer cells—you know how it is with the young—start to challenge the conventional values of their elders. "What's so great about sleek and taut?" is what these newer cells would say, if they had mouths, which thank God they do not. They become listless and bored, and many of them, looking for "kicks," turn to cellulite. Your bodily tissue begins to deteriorate, gradually becoming saggier and lumpier, until one day you glance in the mirror and realize, to your horror, that you look as though for some reason you are attempting to smuggle out of the country an entire driveway's worth of gravel concealed inside your upper legs.

RUN FOR IT!! THE BABY BOOMERS ARE GETTING HOT FLASHES!!

And this very same process is going on *all over your body*.

Is there something you can do about it? You're darned right there is! You *can* fight back. Mister Old Age is not going to get *you*, by golly! All you need is a little determination—a willingness to get out of that reclining lounge chair, climb into that sweatsuit, lace on those running shoes, stride out that front door, and *hurl yourself in front of that municipal bus*.

No, wait. Sorry. For a moment there I got carried away by the bleakness of it all. Forget what I said. Really. There is absolutely no need to become suicidally depressed about the fact that every organ in your body is headed straight down the biological toilet. There really *are* things that you can do to keep your body looking healthy and youthful for years to come. But before I discuss these things, I want you to answer the following questions honestly: Are you willing to make the hard sacrifices needed to be *really* healthy? Are you willing to commit yourself *totally* to a program of regular exercise, close medical supervision, and the elimination of all caffeine, alcohol, and rich foods, to be replaced by a strict diet of nutrition-rich, kelp-like plant growths so unappetizing that they will make you actually lust for tofu? Or are you the kind of shallow, irresponsible person who wants a purely cosmetic change, a "quick and dirty" surface gloss that may make you *look* young and healthy, but actually has no long-term value? Me too.

Liposuction

A few people—and I see no reason why we should not beat them to death with sticks—manage to reach middle age with lean, slender bodies. But most of us, by the time we turn 40, contain large sectors of fatty tissue, living memorials to every high-calorie item we have ever consumed—every brownie, ice cream cone, Milky Way, Chuckle, Eskimo Pie, Sno-Ball, and Twinkie. Every jelly bean, Frosted Flake, and potato chip. *Every single M&M.* It's all still there. Your body is convinced that you're going to need it someday, that the only thing standing between you and starvation will be the stored fat from a Ring Ding you ate in second grade.

This is stupid, of course. Now that we have refrigerators, there is no longer any need to use the human buttock as a food-storage device. But try getting this message through to your body. Try leaning back over your shoulder and shouting at your buttocks: "HEY BACK THERE! STOP STORING FAT!" See if you get anywhere. If you do, let me know. I'll try anything that does not require actually eating less.

In fact, many of us are willing to consider extreme measures to become slimmer. I bet that more than once, when nobody was around, you've grabbed a handful of your fat and wished something truly ridiculous, something like: "I wish some doctor would just stick a tube into my body and turn on a pump and *suck this fat right out*." Ha ha! You crazy nut! What a wacky idea! Do you honestly think, with all the serious medical problems confronting the human race, that a physician—a person who has gone through long, grueling years of medical training in order to acquire vital healing skills that could be used to make a real difference in the lives of suffering people—do you honestly think that such a person would use this precious ability to suck bacon cheeseburgers out of your thighs?

Well, certainly not for *free*. No sir, it could run you more than a thousand buckeroos per thigh. This is not because the liposuction procedure itself is difficult. The procedure itself could be performed flawlessly by anyone who has completed the basic training course at Roto-Rooter. What makes it expensive is the problem of *what to do with your fat.* Think about it. You know from personal experience that your fat is the most malevolent, indestructible substance on the planet. There is no way to kill it. You've tried starving it, stretching it, cursing at it, pummeling it, and squeezing it into foundation garments, yet nothing has had the slightest effect. So it is very tough, and it is also going to be *very angry* that it has been unceremoniously sucked out of your body. The liposuction clinic cannot simply throw this dangerous substance into the garbage can. It would escape and follow you home. Even if you moved across the country and got a whole new identity, your fat would *track you down,* and one day when you least expected it, probably at a swimming pool, it would pounce upon you and bloat your butt up to the size of a postal facility.

For this reason, every liposuction clinic is required to maintain, at great expense, a Maximum Security Fat Prison where the contents removed from patients are incarcerated under twenty-four-hour armed guard. Unfortunately, as liposuction becomes increasingly popular, these facilities have become more and more overcrowded, and unless something is done soon, we are going to see a tragic incident wherein a medical professional building is rocked by the unmistakable sound ("Splooosh") of high-pressure liposuction by-products exploding through steel doors, followed by the dreaded, revenge-seeking Wall of Fat surging down once-quiet suburban streets and engulfing innocent civilians. But other than that, there are few side effects.

Another very popular form of anti-aging cosmetic surgery is, of course:

The Facelift

This is the procedure wherein the plastic surgeon perks up your face by standing behind you, pulling your skin back on both sides of your head until the front is nice and tight, and then attaching the flaps of excess skin to the back of your head with a staple gun. Sure it stings, but the visual effect is stunning, as you are miraculously transformed from a person with bags and wrinkles into a person whose eyes appear to be just slightly too far apart. In fact, if you get repeated facelifts, your eyes will gradually migrate around to the side of your head, carplike, and you will experience a real bonus in the peripheral-vision department.

But the above are only two of the many cosmetic-surgery possibilities. Great strides forward are being made in this exciting field as the medical community becomes increasingly aware of the benefits, both psychological and physical, of getting rich. One popular new technique is called lipografting, or "fat recycling," wherein fat cells are removed from one part of your body that is too large, such as your buttocks, and injected into an area where you wish to have added fullness, such as your lips; people will then be literally kissing your ass.

Ha ha! That was just a small example of lipografting humor, to give you a sense of the happy, upbeat spirit that pervades this fast-growing field. And the best is yet to come. Someday, within your lifetime, it may be possible for a plastic surgeon to attach a tube to you and, using a very powerful pump, slurp up *your entire body* and replace it with that of a scientifically selected teenager. Of course this would raise serious ethical questions, such as how many exemptions you could claim on your income tax. But I am confident that we will one day be able to solve problems like this, which is a lot more than I can say for the problem of:

Male Pattern Baldness

Let me begin this very sensitive discussion by stating that I see *nothing funny* about baldness. The fact that I, personally, have reached age 42 without any significant hair loss does NOT mean that I have the right to make insensitive remarks about those of you whose heads are turning into Mosquito Landing Zones.

Actually, massive hair loss is not the tragedy that many men make it out to be. There are countless examples of men who actually look *better* without hair. The late Yul Brynner springs immediately to mind. Also there was what's-his-name, the guy who was in *The Magnificent Seven.* No, wait, that was also the late Yul Brynner. Hmmmmm.

Well, I'm certain that there are many examples of non-deceased men who look better bald, but quite frankly I cannot afford to spend the next decade trying to think of their names. The point is that going bald is a *perfectly natural* part of the aging process, like having all your teeth rot and fall out, and there is no reason to be self-conscious about it and assume that your co-workers are always staring at the top of your head and snickering behind your back. Sometimes they actually laugh out loud.

No! I'm just kidding! Really, I'm sure everybody is getting used to your head. However, if you're really bothered by your hair loss, there *are* various techniques that you can employ to combat it. And although these techniques vary greatly in cost and degree of medical risk, each of them, if used correctly, can enable the man who's getting a little "thin on top" to turn himself into a man who looks "silly."

The method preferred by most balding men for making themselves look silly is called the "comb-over," which is when the man grows the hair on one side of his head very long and combs it across the bald area, creating an effect that looks very realistic and natural to observers who have been blind since birth. To everyone else, it looks like hair being combed over a bald area, which is usually clearly visible through the hair strands, so that from the top, the head looks like an egg in the grasp of a large tropical spider. Comb-over users with large balding areas have to get the hair from far down on the sides of their heads, which means they must part their hair comically low, sometimes around the ear. You will see men who are basically trying to cover their entire skulls with one gigantic Sideburn From Hell. It's definitely an "eye-catching" look, men! Trust me!

Another option, of course, is to wear a hairpiece. Famous actor and stud muffin Burt Reynolds wears one, and he looks terrific; there's no reason why you can't do the same thing.

Of course, when I say "do the same thing," I mean: "Wear Burt Reynolds's hairpiece." This is definitely your best bet, because Burt spends as much money for his hairpiece as most people spend on their dream retirement homes. A hairpiece that costs any less—the kind *you* could afford, for example—is inevitably going to make you look as though you have for some reason decided to glue a road-kill to your scalp. Which is not entirely a bad thing. Ludicrously obvious hairpieces serve as an important source of harmless entertainment for society in general. My wife and I and another couple were once entertained for an entire seven-hour plane flight by two men, traveling together, who were both wearing toupees that would have been detectable from outside the solar system. Apparently they were on their way to the international convention of the Bad Hairpiece Club. We made numerous unnecessary trips to the lavatory so that we could view these men from various angles at close range. It was such fun that we felt like applauding them as they got off the plane. We wanted to find out if they were available for weddings, bar mitzvahs, etc. So there you have one true-life example of how a hairpiece can really change the way people look at you. Kind of sideways, is how we did it.

A more extreme option for balding men is to have "plugs" of hair removed from somewhere else on your body and transplanted to your head, where they take root and, over the course of time, come to look like plugs of hair transplanted from somewhere else. And here's an exciting piece of news: There is now a miraculous new product, available by prescription, that can actually *reverse* a certain specific type of male-pattern baldness that, needless to say, is not the same as yours!

So the bottom line, guys, is that there are many positive avenues for you to pursue. My only advice would be, don't become obsessive about your baldness. It's really no big deal. And there's no reason for you to be jealous of guys like me, guys with more hair than they know what to do with, guys who can run their hands through their hair and feel the luxurious . . . Hey, what's this? What's this little empty patch? HEY, WAIT A MINUTE!!

Teeth

What teeth? That is the question. Oh sure, it *looks* like you have teeth, but in fact the dental profession, working gradually so you would not notice, has over the years ground large sectors of your natural teeth into powder, which you then obligingly spit down the little dental toilet. Your mouth is now a whole menagerie of toothlike objects and dental contraptions installed at various times dating back to the Eisenhower administration, a house of dental cards that you know could collapse if you made one wrong bite. Dental tragedies are common among middle-aged people. They'll stop in mid-chew and start thrusting their tongues around, seeking to assess the severity of the damage, knowing that they'll have to make an emergency visit to the dentist, who will, in accordance with the Dental Professionals' Code of Conduct, explain that the only thing to do is grind still *more* sectors of natural tooth into powder and install *more* contraptions that are, judging from the price, made of plutonium. Or maybe the dentist, if he is feeling hostile, will decide to do a "root canal," so called because he uses a special dental backhoe to create a trench in your gum tissue large enough for barge traffic.

This wasn't supposed to happen to us. We were the generation that had Fluoride the Wonder Ingredient in our water supply. We were the generation that was taught the importance of brushing after every meal and getting regular checkups and shrieking, "Look, Mom! No cavities!" We watched Ipana toothpaste commercials starring Bucky Beaver. We watched Colgate commercials where the little smiling tooth knocked out Mister Tooth Decay. We watched Gleem commercials where the baseball player threw a ball at the announcer, but it bounced right off the Invisible Protective Shield made from "Gardol," a substance that could also, as I recall, deflect *machine-gun bullets,* in case somebody ever fired some at your teeth.

So for years we brushed and brushed, and then one day the dental profession announced that, sorry,

MACNELLY

there had been a mistake. The problem was not Mister Tooth Decay: the problem was Mister Tartar and his evil sidekick Mister Plaque, and it didn't matter *how* much we brushed, because now we all had gum disease, the only treatment for which is to (surprise!) grind additional teeth into powder.

So now many of us have taken up flossing, wherein each night we savagely assault our own gum tissue and stagger off to bed with blood dribbling from our mouths, looking like losing boxers. But we know we're only fooling ourselves. We know that in a few years the dental profession will announce that, sorry, the real problem is not tartar or plaque: The *real* problem is something called "mouth scunge," and the only way to kill it is to heat your teeth to 1,700 degrees with a special home dental laser device after every meal. And even if you do that, it will probably be necessary to locate, via microscope, any of your remaining natural teeth and grind them into powder. In fact, as our life spans increase, the dental professional will eventually run out of teeth, and will have to start grinding away at our skulls. By the year 2010, the average person of your age who has received regular professional dental care will have a head the size of a walnut.

Okay, you can rinse now.

Eyes

If you're like most people, as you enter your forties you'll start to become "farsighted," which simply means that you won't be able to read any document located within your immediate Zip Code. The solution is to wear "bifocals," which are a special kind of eyeglasses that somehow make the world look *different,* but not any *clearer.* The best angle for looking through bifocals is when you lean way back and look through the lens bottoms, thus affording the public a spectacular panoramic view of your nasal passages; although a lot of people also get good results by wearing their bifocals up on their foreheads, thus allowing the light rays to bypass the eyeballs altogether and penetrate the brain directly.

Final Piece of Health Advice for People Turning 40

You should definitely schedule a thorough medical checkup. Notice I say "schedule." I do not advise that you actually *submit* to a thorough medical checkup, because when you reach age 40 the medical profession suddenly develops an intense interest in a bodily region that I will not name here except to say that the procedure for examining it is so humiliating that even if the doctor says you're perfectly healthy, you will probably want to kill yourself.

Also, you should learn to recognize the various warning signs of heart attack, such as that you feel sharp chest pains or dizziness, or certain familiar printed words suddenly start to appear difoonable and remulatious weedle volcrantitude understand them. That is definitely the time to get help.

CHAPTER THREE

Beauty Tips for the More Mature Gal (Or, Don't Discard Those Grocery Bags!)

One of the wonderful things about being a woman reaching middle age in the 1990s is that, having grown up during the era of women's liberation, you do not foolishly allow yourself to be constrained by mindless outdated sexist stereotypical notions of what "beauty" is. Right, women? *You* don't feel insecure about growing older! If you glance in the mirror and happen to notice that you've developed crow's-feet formations the size of the Mekong River Delta, you just laugh gaily and say, "Thank goodness I do not foolishly allow myself to be constrained by mindless outdated sexist stereotypical notions of waaaaaaaaAAAAAAAHHHH (sob) (choke) (sound of wrists being slit)." Because let's not kid ourselves: Modern women are no more free from stereotypical notions about beauty than modern men are free from the primal male belief that if you let another male cut in front of you in traffic, this is proof that he has a larger penis.

So let's be realistic: You still want to look good. This is not to say that you assign the same priority to mere physical appearance as to being an independent, fulfilled person. No, you assign a much *higher* priority to mere physical appearance on some occasions, such as when you're at the beach, idly pummeling your cellulite and wondering whether your varicose veins, if stretched end to end, would reach Japan, and suddenly you notice that your husband, who has been pretending to read page 13,462 of James Michener's recent blockbuster epic novel *Cleveland,* is in fact ogling a 19-year-old Barbie-shaped woman wearing a bathing suit the size of a hospital identification bracelet.

In situations like this it's quite natural for you to feel insecure, to wonder if your husband secretly wishes that *you* had the body of a 19-year-old. Trust me, this is not the case: He secretly wishes you had the body of a *16*-year-old. The slimeball. I mean, exactly how does he think you got your current set of hips? You got them from *bearing his children,* that's how. You got them from undergoing pregnancies that lasted, according to your calculations, for as long as six years apiece, during which you were forced to bloat up like Rhonda Rhinoceros through no fault of your own because your body was seized by irresistible eons-old hormonal instincts that compelled you to stop at the Dunkin' Donuts so often that they finally gave you a reserved parking space, and all so that *your husband's unborn children* would be supplied with their necessary daily nutritional input of Bavarian cream.

And, okay, even since the birth of your children, you have, on occasion, been guilty of snacking. Why? Because you were *stuck in the damned kitchen,* that's why. Because all of the grand claims your husband made, back when you were dating, about how you two were going to be Equal Housework Partners, turned out to mean in actual practice that he occasionally, with great fanfare, refills the ice-cube tray. In fourteen years of marriage he has prepared approximately four meals, at least three of which involved peanut butter, the result being that you have spent thousands of hours preparing food for the family, a job that requires you, for strictly altruistic reasons, to taste the soup and the spaghetti sauce and, yes, sometimes as much as three-quarters of the uncooked chocolate-chip-cookie dough.

And so now here you are, at the beach, stuck in a body that looks somehow alien to you, a body that seems so large that you're afraid to go swimming for fear that the Coast Guard will attempt to board you, and this is at least partly the fault of your husband, who promised to stick by you in thickness as well as health and who has not maintained his *own* body in exactly Olympic-diver condition, and the son of a bitch has the *nerve* to sit *right next* to you and stare at this *bimbo* so hard that his eyeballs have actually left their sockets and are crawling, crablike, across the sand.

Not that you are bitter.

Oh, sure, the women's magazines keep saying that it's no longer important to look young, that maturity is "in." But they never use normal mature women to illustrate this point. They use women such as Sophia Loren, an obvious genetic mutation who will continue to have the skin of a child long after the Earth has crashed into the sun. Or they use Jane Fonda, who is so obsessed with remaining inhumanly taut by working out ninety-two hours a day that it took her more than a decade to notice that she was married to a dweeb. Or they use *Cher,* for God's sake, a woman who has had so much cosmetic surgery that, for ease of maintenance, many of her body parts are attached with Velcro.

So we have to face up to the fact that there is still a flagrant double standard, wherein porky gray men like Raymond Burr are considered physically attractive, whereas women are considered over the hill moments after they reach puberty. Of course you already know this, which is why, like most middle-aged women, you're probably determined to battle the aging process unto death and beyond if necessary. Fortunately, thanks to the selfless, caring people who make up the cosmetics industry, it is now possible for you to remain surprisingly youthful-looking for at least a little longer, with no more of a daily investment in time and money than would be required to build a working steam locomotive by hand. The key, of course, is:

Proper Skin Care

Your skin's number one enemy is Mister Sun, whom we used to think of as a friend. Remember? Remember when you used to lie on the beach practically naked at high noon and shout, "Take my body, Mister Sun!" I bet you even used an aluminum-foil reflector so you could catch *extra* sun rays and aim them at your flesh while you rolled around like a frankfurter on a grill to make sure your entire body was cooked until Well Done.

Of course we now realize, thanks to advances in scientific knowledge, that you were a moron. In terms of responsible skin care, you might just as well have been scrubbing yourself with Brillo pads drenched in battery acid. Because all that time, Mister Sun was bombarding you with tiny vicious invisible rays called "ultraviolets" that are slowly heating up the Earth to the point where they may ultimately destroy all life on the planet. And what is worse, they cause *dry skin.*

Even as you read these words, scientists from many nations are working feverishly to develop some practical solution to this problem, such as launching a giant orbiting plastic squeeze tube that would squirt humongous gobs of Clinique number 74 sun block all over the planet. But for now it's up to you, the individual aging woman, to deal with the problem yourself.

Step One is never go out in the daylight. Your role model here is the vampire community, whose members keep their skin attractively smooth and waxy for thousands of years. I am not suggesting here that you should live in some dank castle, sleeping in a coffin by day and venturing forth at night to drink human blood; top dermatologists agree that there's no reason why you can't keep your coffin in your current home. The important thing is that you *stay out of the sun.* You shouldn't even look at the sun on *television,* or stand in a room with bright wallpaper, or hum "Here Comes the Sun," unless you're wearing a layer of UV-blocking cream thick enough to conceal a set of car keys in.

But even if you take these precautions, your skin is eventually going to deteriorate. When you're young, your skin contains many natural fluids that make it smooth and supple, but as you age, Mother Nature, who is, let's face it, a heartless bitch, takes these fluids away from you and gives them to undeserving teenagers. This means that unless you wish to wind up with skin so dry and pebbly that the mere sight of you causes lizards to become sexually aroused, you will need to purchase vast amounts of good-quality cosmetic skin-care products. And when I say "good quality," I of course mean "costing more per one-ounce tube than a semester at Yale." You will need products designed specifically for each sector of your face, including forehead, chin, cheeks, upper lip, lower lip, left eye, right eye, upper nose, middle nose, sub-nostril zone, and wattles.

Cosmetic-industry scientists tell us that, within our lifetimes, there will be a separate skin-care product for *each individual pore,* so that you'll need to add a gymnasium-sized Skin-Care Product Storage Facility to your home, and in order to be ready to leave for work at eight A.M. you'll have to start working on your face by six P.M. the previous day. And even *that* may not be enough to keep your skin moist. You may also want to undergo a recently developed surgical procedure wherein doctors implant a miniature sprinkler system—patterned after the ones used for lawns—right in your face, with tiny sensors that cause it to spray water on your skin when they detect dryness. Of course there are still some wrinkles to be ironed out of this system, as was shown in a recent tragedy wherein a facial sprinkler installed in Mrs. Phyllis Schlafly was triggered by a restaurant candle and, before it could be brought under control, spewed out more than seventeen gallons of water, thus destroying a salad valued at nearly forty dollars. But such is the price of progress.

Weight Control

Have you noticed that some women just don't seem to gain weight, no matter what they eat? You'll be in a restaurant, eating a Diet Plate consisting of four tunafish molecules garnished with low-sodium parsley, and you can nevertheless actually *feel* yourself gaining weight. Meanwhile at the next table is a woman wearing a size zero dress, wolfing down a chocolate cake that had to be delivered to her table via forklift. How does she get away with it? Where does she put the calories?

The answer is: *into your body*. Yes! If you look into her purse, you'll find that she, like many modern weight-conscious women, is carrying an electronic device called a Calorie Transmaterializer, which transforms the food entering her body into invisible rays and shoots them into the body of whoever is sitting nearby. If you are so unfortunate as to be sitting near *several* hungry women with Calorie Transmaterializers, you could easily explode before they get past their appetizers. If I were you, I'd get one of these handy devices *soon*.

CHAPTER FOUR

The Midlife (Yawn) Marriage

I believe it was Shakespeare, or possibly Howard Cosell, who first observed that marriage is very much like a birthday candle, in that "the flames of passion burn brightest when the wick of intimacy is first ignited by the disposable butane lighter of physical attraction, but sooner or later the heat of familiarity causes the wax of boredom to drip all over the vanilla frosting of novelty and the shredded coconut of romance."

I could not have phrased it better myself. There can be no doubt that the institution of marriage is in serious trouble in our society, to the point where we have to wonder whether it can even survive. Take a look at these alarming statistics:

- In the past decade, at least five U.S. military personnel have been killed by toppling vending machines onto themselves.
- The female pinworm lays an average of *11,000* eggs.

And I'm sure we would be even more alarmed if we had some way of knowing the percentage of marriages that end in divorce. I bet it's very high, because you rarely see couples who have been married for a long time. Nowadays, when two people manage to reach their fiftieth wedding anniversary, it's considered a news event at least as important as the U.S. trade deficit. You'll see newspaper stories with charming photographs of the couple holding hands, and heartwarming quotes about how, after all those years, they still by gosh have the hots for each other. How do they do it? What's their "secret recipe" for keeping the romance and spontaneity in their relationship after all those decades?

The answer is: senility. These people barely recognize each other. Every morning they wake up and look at each other, and they think, "Who the heck is *this*?" Novelty, that's what they have going for them. A feeling of "something different." Oh sure, you run a certain risk when you reach this level of obliviousness. If you attempt to go to the post office, there's always a chance that you'll wander off and wind up in Brazil. But that's a small price to pay for lasting romance.

Chances are, however, that you're all *too* familiar with your spouse. Chances are you feel as though you've been involved with this person since at least the Paleolithic period. You're so familiar with each other's thought processes that your "conversations" make you sound as though your brains have been surgically replaced by Random Phrase Generators:

YOU: I was thinking we . . .
YOUR SPOUSE: No, because of the . . .
YOU: Oh, right, the . . .
YOUR SPOUSE: From Cleveland.
YOU: With the, with the . . .
YOUR SPOUST: Pit bull because of the . . .
YOU: Trash compactor.
YOUR SPOUSE: Right.

After a decade or so of marriage, you know *everything* about your spouse, every habit and opinion and twitch and tic and minor skin growth. You could write a seventeen-pound book solely about the way your spouse *eats*. This kind of intimate knowledge can be very handy in certain situations—such as when you're on a TV quiz show where the object is to identify your spouse from the sound of his or her chewing—but it tends to lower the passion level of a relationship.

Imagine, for example, a man and a woman who have been married for a dozen years. And imagine that the woman feels that their relationship has perhaps gone just a bit stale, as evidenced by the fact that since 1984 their most intimate moment together was the warm embrace they shared when they found out that their homeowners' insurance covered the unexplained explosion in their septic tank.

So let's say that one day the woman decides she is going to by God inject a spark of renewed passion into the marriage, so on her lunch hour she goes to the Frederick's of Hollywood at the mall and purchases an explicit lingerie outfit so sheer that you could read an appliance warranty through it in an unlit closet. And that night, after the children have been tucked into bed, she puts it on, and when her husband comes into the bedroom, all ready to indulge in his usual highly sensuous nighttime routine of watching the news while flossing his teeth, she is waiting for him, wearing nothing but her sexy new outfit and a sultry expression.

As he gazes upon her, standing there in her most provocative pose, he feels a sudden, unexpected stirring of excitement, stemming from the realization that *she has charged this outfit on their Visa card.* Yes, he can even see the charge slip lying on the dresser. Forty-seven dollars! My God! Here they are already *very* close to their credit limit, thanks to her incomprehensible (to him) decision to buy a brand-new clothes dryer despite the fact that he was perfectly capable of fixing the old one—he had told her this *at least* a hundred times—and now here she has spent *forty-seven dollars* on a garment that is approximately the size of a sandwich bag. This is what he is thinking as he gazes upon her, and she can tell immediately that he is not overwhelmed with lust because he is scratching himself absentmindedly in the groin region, a habit that just drives her *crazy* sometimes, especially when he has promised that he was going to do something useful, such as fix the damn clothes dryer, and instead he spends the day sprawled on the Barcalounger, watching some idiotic televised golf match and rooting around in his underwear with both hands as though he thought the Hope diamond was concealed down there.

But she is *determined* that they're going to have a romantic interlude, and so, licking her lips lasciviously, she steps toward him; and he, finally realizing —sensitive human that he is—that this would not be the ideal moment to raise the topic of household finances, steps toward her; and they draw each other close; and as their lips meet, a new feeling comes over both of them, an urgent, insistent feeling; and it is of course the feeling of their seven-year-old daughter tugging on them to inform them that their five-year-old son is throwing up on the dog.

So we can see that it is not easy to maintain a high Romance Quotient in a relationship over long periods of time. Even Romeo, if he had spent enough time under the balcony gazing up worshipfully at Juliet, would eventually have noticed her protruding nostril hairs.

The question is, what can you do about this? By "this," of course, I mean "protruding nostril hairs." Tweezers are *not* the solution, take it from me. Another important question is: How can you keep your marriage from going stale? Fortunately, there are some effective techniques you can use—reliable, time-tested techniques that I will discuss in detail just as soon as I think them up. While I'm doing that, it would be a good idea for you to take the following:

Scientific Quiz for Determining How Bad Your Marriage Is

1. What do you and your spouse have in common?
- **a.** We have essentially the same moral values, political views, and aesthetic judgments.
- **b.** We both like Chinese food.
- **c.** We are both protein-based life-forms.

2. You are most likely to share your true feelings with your spouse when you are feeling:
- **a.** Love.
- **b.** Anger.
- **c.** Sodium pentathol.

3. When you have a serious conversation with your spouse, the topic is most likely to be:
- **a.** Your relationship, and how you can make it better.
- **b.** Your children, and how you should rear them.
- **c.** Your remote control, and who gets to hold it.

4. In the special, most secret, most private moments that you and your spouse share together, you call each other:
- **a.** "Darling."
- **b.** "Lust Machine."
- **c.** Long distance.

5. When you and your spouse disagree, you generally try to resolve your differences via:
- **a.** Discussion.
- **b.** Argument.
- **c.** Assault rifle.

6. How would you describe your sex life?
- **a.** Fantastic.
- **b.** Excellent.
- **c.** Superb.

7. No, I mean your sex life with *each other.*
- **a.** Oh.
- **b.** Our *what?*
- **c.** With *each other?*

8. Men: What did you buy your wife on her last birthday?

- a. Nice jewelry.
- b. A new coffeemaker.
- c. Bait.

9. Women: What do you usually wear to bed?
- a. A silky negligée, makeup, and several strategic dabs of Calvin Klein's "Night Moan" cologne.
- b. A cotton nightgown, a hair net, and a small yet distinctive chin smear of Crest "Tartar Control" toothpaste.
- c. A nightgown made of tent-grade flannel; a pair of official National Hockey League Wayne Gretzky Model knee socks; a sufficient number of hair curlers (in the ever-popular, highly seductive Bazooka Bubble Gum Pink) to meet the plastic needs of Western Europe for a decade; and of course "skin moisturizer" that has the same erotic appeal as industrial pump lubricant and has been applied to your face thickly enough to trap small woodland creatures.

10. If you could change just one thing about your spouse, that thing would be his or her:
- a. Tendency to snore.
- b. Physical appearance.
- c. Identity.

How to Score The correct scoring procedure is to give yourself a certain number of points for each answer, although quite frankly I think that a person in your particular marital situation ought to spend less time fooling around with some idiot quiz and more time lining up a good attorney. Or, if you're a real dreamer, you could always try:

Putting the "Spark" Back Into Your Marriage

Your best bet here is to leave the kids with your parents and take a second honeymoon, although under no circumstances should the man (see chapter 2, "Your Disintegrating Body") attempt to carry the woman across the threshold unless your idea of an intimate evening involves paramedics. But other than that, a second honeymoon is a terrific idea—a chance for the two of you to spend some time alone, away from the numbing grind of your daily domestic routine, with nothing to distract you from days of pleasure and nights of passion except possibly the phone call from your mother asking if there is a particular pediatric surgeon you generally go to, or should she just pick one on her own. Which brings us to our next chapter, on children as a leading cause of old age.

CHAPTER FIVE

The (Rapidly) Aging Parent

If you're like most members of the Baby Boom generation, you decided somewhere along the line, probably after about four margaritas, to have children. This was inevitable. Mother Nature, in her infinite wisdom, has instilled within each of us a powerful biological instinct to reproduce; this is her way of assuring that the human race, come what may, will never have any disposable income.

Of course, there's more to parenthood than mere biology. Parenthood is also an opportunity for each of us to advance the cause of civilization by passing along to the next generation—as our parents passed along to us—the cherished values and ideals, developed over thousands of years, that define what the human race truly stands for, namely:

- "Don't spit."
- "How do you *know* you hate asparagus when you haven't even *tried* it?"
- "No, you are NOT going to get a snake."
- "I said DON'T SPIT!"
- "Well, how do *you* suppose your underpants got into the microwave? Do you suppose they just crawled in there *by themselves?*"
- "All right then, but it's going to be YOUR snake, and I expect YOU to take care of it."
- "If you spit on your sister ONE MORE TIME, there is going to be NO MORE TELEVISION until THANKSGIVING and I MEAN IT!!"
- "Yes I KNOW Daddy called Mr. Stimson a dickhead, but that does NOT mean that YOU may call Mr. Stimson a dickhead."
- "NO, YOU ARE *NOT* GOING TO GET A DOG, NOT AFTER WHAT HAPPENED TO THE SNAKE."

And so on. Yes, parenthood can be difficult, but it also has its rewards. In the end, there's no substitute for the sense of satisfaction that comes from

LOVE
MACNELLY

watching as your children, under your steady guiding hand, develop from tiny, helpless Frequent Barfer modules into full-grown, self-reliant young adults fully capable of crashing your car into a day-care center.

Of course, we must remember that growth is not a "one-way street." As our children grow, so must we grow to meet their changing emotional, intellectual, and designer-footwear needs. In this chapter we'll examine some of the challenges that we face as parental units entering middle age, a time when we are coming to the somber realization that we will not always be there to guide and direct our children, which is just as well, because this is also a time when our children are coming to the conclusion that we are unbelievable dorks.

One big reason for this, of course, is our taste in music. I'm assuming that you're like most of us Boomers in the sense that, musically, you have always considered yourself to be a Major Hipster. Why not? Hey, we were frontline troops in the Rock 'n' Roll Revolution, right? Damn straight! We were Born to Boogie. We grew up dancing the Twist, the Mashed Potato, the Boogaloo, the Jerk, the Watusi, the Pony, the Alligator, the Clam, and the Vicious Bloodsucking Insect. We knew the dirty words to "Louie Louie," including the ones that did not actually exist. We knew the Beach Boys when they could sing and Elvis when he was alive the *first* time. We knew the Beatles and the Stones when they were actual bands as opposed to multinational corporations. We were *there* during the legendary sixties, with visions and insights and lava lamps and black lights and sitar music and really *dynamite* home-grown weed that would get you high in only 178 tokes. We lit candles and sat around listening to John Lennon sing, with genuine passion in his voice, about how he was the egg man, and *they* were the egg men, and *he* was also the walrus, and by God we knew *exactly what he meant.* That was the level of hipness that we attained, in My Generation. Oh sure, people tried to put us down, just because we got around. Our parents would come into our bedroom, where we were listening to the opening guitar lick of "Purple Haze" with the stereo cranked up loud enough to be audible on Mars (which is where Jimi Hendrix originated) and they'd hold their hands over their ears and make a face as though they were passing a kidney stone the size of a volleyball and they'd shout: "You call that *music?* That sounds like somebody strangling a *cat.*" Our parents' idea of swinging music was Frank Sinatra snapping his fingers in front of sixty-seven guys who looked like your dentist playing the trombone. Our parents danced *holding hands,* for God's sake. They did the "fox trot," which was invented by the Phoenicians. They were totally Out Of It, our parents. Hopeless. They were so square they thought that people, other than Maynard G. Krebs, actually *used* words like "square." As Bob Dylan, who was so hip that sometimes even *he* didn't understand what he meant, put it: "Something is happening here, and you don't know what it is, do you, Mr. Jones?" That was our parents: Mr. and Mrs. Jones. But not us. We *defined* hip. We set all kinds of world hipness records, and we were sure they'd never be broken.

Then came the seventies, and the major new musical trends were (1) disco, which consisted of one single song approximately 14,000 minutes long; and (2) heavy metal, which consisted of skinny, hostile, pockmarked men wearing outfits that looked as though they had smeared toxic waste on their bodies, playing what sounded like amplified jackhammers and shrieking unintelligibly at auditoriums full of whooping, sweating, hyperactive, boot-wearing, tattooed people who indicated their approval by giving each other head injuries with chairs. We old-time rock 'n' rollers looked at this scene, and we said, "Nah." We were sure it would pass. So we played our Buffalo Springfield albums and our Motown dance tapes, and we waited for the day when good music, *hip* music, would become popular again.

By the eighties, a lot of radio stations, realizing the size of the market out there, had started playing sixties music again. They called it "classic rock," because they knew we'd be upset if they came right out and called it what it is, namely "middle-aged-person nostalgia music." It's a very popular format now. You drive through a major urban area and push the "scan" button on your car radio, and you'll probably hear a dozen "classic rock" stations, ten of which will be playing "Doo-wah diddy diddy." (The other two will be playing *commercials* featuring "Doo-wah diddy diddy.") We hear "classic rock" being played constantly in elevators, department stores, offices, churches, operating rooms, the space shuttle, etc. Almost every sixties group with at least one remaining non-dead member has reunited and bought new dentures and gone on tour, sometimes using special guitars equipped with walkers.

And so, because we represent the world's largest consumer horde, we get to hear Our Music all the time. We're wrapped in a snug, warm cocoon of sixtiesness, and we actually think that we're still With It. Whereas in fact we are nowhere near It. The light leaving from It right now will not reach us for several years. I've become intensely aware of this through my son, who, despite constant exposure to my taste in music, does NOT choose to listen to "classic rock." When he's in control of the radio, he tunes it to a different kind of music, a new kind of music, a *now* kind of music that can only be described—and I do not mean to be making any value judgments here—as "stupid."

If you have kids, you probably know the music I mean. It sounds as though an evil scientist had gone into his laboratory and, for some insane reason, *combined disco with heavy metal.* It has no melody and hardly any words; it consists almost entirely of bass notes registering 7.4 on the Richter scale. It's music to slaughter cattle by. It's the kind of music you hear emanating from refrigerator-sized boom boxes and black 1974 Camaros that have windows tinted so dark you could safely view a solar eclipse through them and sound systems so powerful that with every beat the sides of the car actually bulge outward, like in a Warner Brothers cartoon, such that you can't imagine how any form of life could survive in there. If you're unfamiliar with this kind of music, hold this page right up close to your ear for a second and I'll play a sample for you:

BOOM boom BOOM boom BOOM boom BOOM!
BOOM boom BOOM boom BOOM boom BOOM!
BOOM boom BOOM boom BOOM boom BOOM!
BOOM boom BOOM boom BOOM boom BOOM!
(repeat chorus)

Isn't that *awful?* That's what my son likes to listen to. This leads to conflict when we're in the car. He'll push the radio button for BOOM boom BOOM etc., and then I, in a loving parental effort to guide him toward a more sophisticated and meaningful cultural experience, will thoughtfully swat his hand aside and push the button for Doo-wah diddy diddy. Then he'll lean back in his seat and look at me with exactly the same disgusted look that I aimed at my parents thirty years ago when they made me take my Buddy Holly 45s off of our RCA phonograph so they could play Rosemary Clooney.

And I think: Something is happening here, and I don't know what it is. And neither does Bob Dylan.

Another area in which my son makes me feel

old is fashion. Especially hair fashion. I've always considered myself to be extremely liberal when it came to hair, because I remember how much I hated the hair hassles I went through back in the sixties when I had long hair. I'd be walking past a clot of geezers who were sitting in front of a volunteer fire department, hoping somebody's house would catch fire so they could watch the trucks pull out, and one of them would invariably look at me and say, in a tone of voice suggesting that this was the cleverest and most original remark ever thought up by anybody with the possible exception of Mark Twain, "Hey, is that a BOY or a GIRL??" This awesome display of wit never failed to absolutely slay the other geezers, who'd laugh themselves into various stages of coronary seizure ("har har har har hack hack hack hack hawk hawk HAWK SPIT"), and I, being a Flower Child Peace Person in the Summer of Love, would give them the finger. But I would also vow to myself that no matter how old I got, I would never, ever, hassle anybody about his haircut.

Of course, back then there was no such thing as "punk."

So anyway, for the first few years after my son was born, things were fairly frictionless on the haircut front. My son favored the Dwight Eisenhower style so popular with babies, consisting of approximately eight wisps of hair occasionally festooned with creamed spinach. When he grew real hair, I'd take him to the barbershop and request that he be given a regular haircut, defined as "a haircut exactly like mine."

Then one day, when he was six, he came home from school, which is where they pick this stuff up, and announced that he wanted a punk haircut. Remembering my experiences in the sixties, I sat him down and thoughtfully explained to him that although I, personally, did not care for the punk style of haircut, the real issue here was personal freedom of choice, and since it was, after all, his hair, then by gosh if he really, really wanted to, he could get a punk haircut just as soon as I had been dead and buried for a minimum of forty-five years.

I thought that this honest sharing of feelings had settled the matter, so you can imagine my surprise when, about a week later, my son went to the mall with my wife, whom I will never fully trust again, and came home looking like Sid Vicious. His hair was very short around the sides except for a little tail going down the back of his neck, as though the barber had suddenly remembered an important appointment and had to rush off without finishing my son. The hair on the top was smeared with what appeared to be transmission fluid and sticking up in spikes, which made it look like a marine creature striking a defensive posture.

I really, really hate this haircut, and, needless to say, my son really, really loves it. He is constantly checking himself out in the mirror and performing routine spike maintenance. I'll say: "It's time for your bedtime story!" And he'll say: "Not now! I'm gelling my hair!"

And of course it's just going to get worse. I'm constantly being assured of this by the parents of teenagers. "You think his *haircut* is bad?" they say. "Wait until he wants an earring." Which of course he will. In fact he'll probably want an earring in his *nose,* as part of his ongoing, totally instinctive campaign to make me feel like a fossilized fud.

I'll tell you what would *really* age me fast: if I had a teenaged daughter. I don't think I could handle that. Because that would mean that teenaged boys would be coming around to my house. "Hi, Mr. Barry!" they'd say, with their cheerful, innocent young voices. "We're here to have sex with your daughter!"

No, of course they wouldn't come out and *say* that, but I know that's what they'd be *thinking*, because I was a teenaged boy once, and I was basically a walking hormone storm. I'm sure modern boys are no different. So if I had a teenaged daughter, and a boy came to my house, after somehow picking his way through the land mines in the lawn, I'd probably lunge through the screen door and strangle him right there ("Hi, Mr. Barry! Is Jennifer heAAAAAAWWWWK").

You think I'm exaggerating, but I have male friends whose daughters are approaching puberty at speeds upwards of 700 miles per hour, and when you say the word "dating," my friends get a look in their eyes that makes Charles Manson look like Captain Kangaroo. So in some ways I'm relieved that I don't have daughters, although in other ways I envy people with daughters, because little girls tend to be thoughtful, whereas little boys tend to be—and I say this as a loving father who would not trade his son for anything in the world—jerks.

I used to think this was society's fault. This was back in the idealistic sixties and seventies, when we Boomers had many excellent child-rearing theories and no actual children. Remember those days? Remember when we truly believed that if society treated boys and girls exactly the same, then they wouldn't be bound by sexual stereotypes, and the boys could grow up to be sensitive and the girls could grow up to be linebackers? Ha ha! Boy, were we ever idealistic! By which I mean "stupid." Because when we look at actual children, no matter how they are raised, we notice immediately that little girls are in fact smaller versions of real human beings, whereas little boys are Pod People from the Planet Destructo. I don't think society has anything to do with this. I think that if you had two desert islands, and you put girl babies on one island and boy babies on another island, and they somehow were able to survive with no help from adult society, eventually the girls would cooperate in collecting pieces of driftwood and using them to build shelters, whereas the boys would pretend that driftwood pieces were guns. (Yes, I realize they'd have no way of knowing what guns were. This would not stop them.) Not only that, but even if the island had 176,000 pieces of driftwood on it, the boys would all end up violently arguing over *one* of them.

I base my opinions on several years of working in an office located in a house with a large transient little-boy population. Individually they're okay, but if two of them get together, their combined total IQ is immediately halved, and if a third boy comes along it's halved *again*, and so on, so that if you have, say, six of them, you're talking about the destructive force of a tank commanded by the brainpower of a Labrador retriever. They communicate with each other by slamming doors. They have the attention span of gnats. "STOP SLAMMING THE DOORS!" I'll yell at them. "Okay!" they'll reply (SLAM). They are so busy running around and arguing and breaking things and strewing random objects over every square inch of floor that they barely have time to pee, and they *definitely* don't have time to aim. They just race into the bathroom, let loose in any old random direction, and then race out again, because by God there are doors to be slammed.

Not that I'm complaining. For reasons I can't explain, I really like being a parent. It's just that there's a lot more *to* it than I expected. Take school projects. A school project is a kind of activity designed by educators to provide our children with valuable learning experiences that they would carry with them for the rest of their lives if they were capable of remembering anything for longer than three-tenths of a second, which unfortunately they are not. At least my son isn't. If I want to make sure he has his shoes on by Monday morning, I have to start reminding him no later than Saturday afternoon.

"Robert," I'll say, while he is engaged in some vital activity such as pouring PurpleSaurus Rex flavor Kool-Aid on the patio to form a Liquefied Sugar Theme Park for ants, "I want you to put on your shoes *right now*."

"Okay," he'll say, with total sincerity. Meanwhile, inside his skull, a small but powerful organ found in children and known to medical science as the Instruction Diverter has taken my words as they entered his left ear and, before they could begin to penetrate his brain, ejected them out his right ear at nearly the speed of light. He continues to stare at the ants.

"What did I just ask you?" I'll ask.

"What?" he'll answer. He has *no idea* what we're talking about. At that very moment my instructions are whizzing past the asteroid belt.

"I WANT YOU TO PUT YOUR SHOES ON RIGHT NOW!" I'll say.

"Okay!" he'll say, irritated that I'm yelling at him for absolutely no reason. If I squint, I can actually see my words shooting out his ear as he continues to stare at the ants, who are scurrying around putting on tiny ant shoes because even *they* have a better ability to retain instructions than Robert.

Of course, my son is perfectly normal. (Right? RIGHT??) A lot of children have trouble remembering instructions, which is why we parents often find out about school projects at the very last minute, usually from other parents. "Didn't you hear?" they'll say. "Each child is supposed to come in tomorrow with a model medieval village made entirely from typewriter parts."

School projects generally contain an element of inexplicable weirdness. I think this is a form of revenge on the part of the teachers, getting even with us parents for spending our day in adult company while they're stuck in crowded rooms trying to get our children to stop writing their 5's backward. I bet they have fun at teachers' meetings, thinking up projects to inflict on us. ("I've got it! We have them make a cement volcano that erupts real ketchup!" "No, we had them do that last year.")

Whatever they come up with, we do it, because we want our children to succeed in school so they'll eventually graduate and we won't have to do projects anymore. Science Fair projects are the worst. Parents go completely insane at Science Fair time, which is why you see second-graders showing up with small fusion reactors that they allegedly made themselves. I know a woman named Janice who became so deranged by an approaching Science Fair that she actually spat in her daughters' Knox unflavored gelatin. I'm not making this up. Her two daughters were doing projects that were supposed to demonstrate how common household molds would grow in little containers of gelatin, and so naturally the mold refused to grow. Isn't that just like mold? When you DON'T want it to grow, such as when company is coming, it flourishes, especially around the base of the toilet. Whereas when you really WANT it to grow, when you have gone to the supermarket and purchased FOOD for it, it does nothing. Mold is scum.

So anyway, the Science Fair was approaching, and Janice's daughters were getting more and more upset, and finally, late one night when they were asleep, Janice spat in their gelatin. The mold grew like crazy, thereby demonstrating the important scientific principle that school projects can cause normal adults to lose all contact with reality.

This is why one year, the night before my son's

project was due, my wife and I got into an emotional kitchen argument over buoyancy. Buoyancy had never before played much of a role in our relationship, but it was the subject of Robert's project, and he and I had spent the afternoon driving frantically from store to store trying to locate the items we needed, including cork and plastic bottles and a special kind of foam board that your child absolutely HAS to have for his project backdrop or you will be arrested for child abuse.

So by nightfall I was *heavily* involved in buoyancy, and you can imagine how I felt when my wife looked at the project—which showed scientifically how come corks float and rocks sink—and she said she didn't understand it. She said she thought corks floated because they were light and rocks sank because they were heavy. This is also what I always thought, but I wasn't about to admit it, not after the work I'd put into this project. So I told her that she was crazy, and that anybody who knows anything about science knows that corks float because of buoyancy, which is related to displacement, which is caused by plastic bottles. I admit I was bluffing, but I was damned if I was going to let anybody attack my Science Fair project. Robert, meanwhile, had wandered off. Children have too much sense to become overly involved in their educations.

What scares me most about parenting is that I'm really just starting out. There are plenty of scary parts that I haven't even gotten to yet. Driving, for example. In most states you can get a driver's license when you're 16 years old, which made a lot of sense to me when I was 16 years old but now seems insane. I mean, my son is 9, which means that most states consider him to be more than halfway old enough to drive, and we are talking about a person who still sleeps on *Return of the Jedi* sheets. So I am definitely in favor of raising the minimum driving age. In fact, I think it should be raised every year, to keep my son from ever reaching it. I think that when my son is 58 years old and comes to visit me in the Old Persons' Home, he should arrive via skateboard.

And then there are the money worries. You need a lot of money to raise a modern child. Hair gel alone will run you thousands of dollars. And let's not forget Mr. Orthodontist, with his private jet and his villa in Switzerland. He is sure to notice that your child's teeth have come in backwards, or some other terrible problem that can only be corrected via an orthodontic project comparable in scope to the interstate highway system, only more expensive. This will of course prevent you from saving any money to put your child through college, which, as you know from reading numerous alarming articles, will be so expensive by the time your child is old enough that the only way you'll be able to afford it will be by selling your body parts—a kidney for freshman year, a section of liver for sophomore year, maybe an eyeball for that all-important junior year abroad, etc. God help you if your children decide to go to graduate school. You'll wind up being carried to the commencement exercises in a cigar box.

But it will be worth the sacrifice, knowing that you've done all you can to prepare your children to go out and make their way, on their own, in the Real World. Although they'll probably decide it's easier to just move back in with you.

CHAPTER SIX

Planning Your Male Midlife Crisis

The past twenty years have seen tremendous advances in our understanding of these mysterious creatures called men—what motivates them; what kinds of complex and subtle emotions they're really experiencing underneath their brusque "macho" exteriors; and why they are all basically slime-sucking toads. Most of this understanding has been supplied by popular psychologists, dedicated men and women who—despite the very real risk that they will have to appear on the Oprah Winfrey Show—are constantly churning out insightful groundbreaking books with titles like:

- Men Who Hate Women
- Men Who Claim Not to Hate Women But Trust Me They Are Lying
- Men Who Okay, Maybe They Don't Hate ALL Women, But They Definitely Cannot Stand YOU

And so on. Reading between the lines, we can see that men do not have a terrific reputation for being dependable, lifelong partners in a relationship. In this chapter we will put on our pith helmets and begin to explore a major reason for this—namely, the midlife crisis. This is a phase that all men are required, by federal law, to go through, as part of the Official Popular-Psychology Schedule of:

Male Lifestyle Phases

AGE	PHASE	INTERESTS
0–2	Infancy	Pooping
3–9	Innocence	Guns
10–13	Awareness	Sex
14–20	Emancipation	Sex
21–29	Empowerment	Sex
30–39	Attainment	Sex
40–65	MIDLIFE CRISIS OCCURS HERE	
66–Death	Contemplation	Pooping

We can see from this scientific chart that if you're a male who has reached age 40, you should be preparing for this exciting lifestyle phase.

What is a Male Midlife Crisis?

Basically, it's when a man, reaching his middle years, takes stock of his life and decides that *it isn't enough* —that although he has a loving wife, nice kids, a decent job, and many caring friends, he feels that he is trapped—that there is still *something more he must do,* something that we will call, for want of a better term, "making a fool of himself."

The first thing you have to understand is that this is perfectly natural. The midlife crisis occurs in virtually all males, including members of the animal kingdom. A good example is the caterpillar. He will spend a large part of his life on a predictable career path, engaging in traditional caterpillar activities such as crawling around and munching on the leaves of expensive ornamental shrubbery, and then one day, out of the blue, he'll say to his wife, "Dammit, Louise, I'm *sick* of shrubbery." She does not understand him, of course. Partly this is because she has a brain the size of an electron, but mostly it is because he seems like a complete stranger to her, a different insect altogether. Soon he has left her to live in his own cocoon, from which he eventually emerges with a whole new youthful "look"—wings, bright colors, gold jewelry, etc. As he soars into the sky, feeling fulfilled and exhilarated, free at last from the restrictive routines of his humdrum former life, Louise watches him from far below. She feels conflicting emotions: sorrow, for she knows that she has lost her mate forever; but also a strange kind of joy, for she also knows, as she watches his multihued wings flashing in the glorious golden-red glow of the sinking sun, that he is about to be eaten by a bat.

Fortunately, this rarely happens to human males. Unfortunately, what happens to human males is worse. There is virtually no end to the humiliating activities (see chapter 2, on "hair transplants") that a man will engage in while in the throes of a midlife crisis. He will destroy a successful practice as a certified public accountant to pursue a career in Roller Derby. He will start wearing enormous pleated pants and designer fragrances ("Ralph Lauren's Musque de Stud Hombre: For the Man Who Wants a Woman Who Wants a Man Who Smells Vaguely Like a Horse"). He will encase his pale, porky body in tank tops and a "pouch"-style swimsuit the size of a gum wrapper. He will buy a boat shaped like a marital aid. He will abandon his attractive and intelligent wife to live with a 19-year-old aerobics instructor who once spent an *entire summer* reading a single *Glamour* magazine article entitled "Ten Tips for Terrific Toenails."

And if this is a particularly severe case of the male midlife crisis, if this male has no idea whatsoever how pathetic he looks, if he has lost all touch with reality, he will run for President of the United States. This is why every fourth year, just before the caucuses, Iowa becomes positively infested with obscure, uninspiring, middle-aged political figures, racing around the state with an air of great urgency and self-importance, issuing "position papers," lunging out of shadows to shake the hands of startled Iowans, demonstrating their concern for agriculture by frowning thoughtfully at pigs, etc. You see this on the evening news, and your reaction, as an informed voter, is: "What is *possessing* these dorks?" I mean, it is not as though they are responding to some massive groundswell of popular support. It is not as though large crowds of voters showed up at their homes and shrieked, "Hey, Congressperson! Please go to Iowa and reveal the key elements of your four-point tax-incentive plan for revitalizing heavy industry!" No, these tragically misguided men are acting on their own, trying to deny their own humdrum mediocrity, seeking desperately to inject some drama into their lives, and we could view the whole thing as harmless entertainment were it not for the fact that one of them invariably winds up becoming the leader of the Free World.

I'm going to assume that you're not a member of Congress, and that you therefore have a certain minimum amount of dignity. Nevertheless, you will eventually experience a midlife crisis, and if you're not careful, it could destroy everything you've worked so hard to build over the years. This is why it is so important that you recognize the problems that arise during this critical phase, and develop a practical, thoughtful strategy for dealing with them. This chapter will not help at all.

What Triggers the Midlife Crisis

Generally the midlife crisis is triggered when a male realizes one day at about 2:30 P.M. that he has apparently, for some reason, devoted his entire life to doing something he hates. Let's say he's a lawyer. He did not just become a lawyer overnight. He worked *hard* to become a lawyer. He made enormous sacrifices, such as drinking domestic beer, so that he could afford to go to law school. He studied for thousands of hours, sweated out the law boards, groveled to get into a firm, licked a lot of shoes to make partner, and now, finally, he has made it. And then one afternoon, while writing yet another deadly dull formal letter to a client, a letter filled with standardized, prefabricated phrases such as "please be advised" and "with reference to the aforementioned subject matter," he rereads what he has just written, and it says, "Please be advised to stick the aforementioned subject matter into your personal orifice." He may not be a trained psychologist, but he recognizes latent hostility when he sees it. And so he starts to think. And the more he thinks, the more he realizes that he hates *everything about* being a lawyer. He hates his clients. He (needless to say) hates other lawyers. He hates the way every time he tells people what he does for a living, they react as though he had said "Nazi medical researcher." He hates his office. He hates Latin phrases. He hates his *briefcase*. He hates it all, just hates it hates it hates it, and finally he decides that he really wants to have a *completely different* job, something fun, something carefree, something like . . . hang-gliding instructor. Yes! That's it! He tried hang-gliding once, on vacation, and he loved it!

Meanwhile, somewhere out there is a middle-aged hang-gliding instructor who has just discovered that he hates *his* life. He hates not making enough money to own a nice car. He hates sudden downdrafts. He hates having to be nice to vacationing lawyers. What he really wants is a better-paying job that enables him to do something truly *useful* with his life. Yes, the more he thinks about it, the more he wishes that he had become . . . a doctor.

Of course, if he did a little research, he'd find that most doctors hate the medical profession. They hate getting sued. They hate the way everybody assumes that they're rich (they *are* rich, of course; they just hate the way everybody *assumes* it). They hate their beepers. They hate peering into other people's personal orifices. They wish they had a career with less responsibility and fewer restrictions, a *fun* career that permitted them to drink heavily on the job and squander entire afternoons seeing how loud they could burp. In other words, they wish they were: humor writers.

My point is that there's no reason for you to feel depressed about being trapped in Career Hell, because so is everybody else. Doesn't that make you feel better? No? Hey, look, at least *you* can put this book down and go watch TV if you feel like it. *I* have to sit here and finish this stupid chapter so I can meet my stupid deadline. You think it's easy, being a humor writer? You think it's *fun,* sitting here all day in my underwear, trying to think up new material? *You* try it sometime! You'd hate it! Especially my underwear! You'd soon see why I've reached the point where I'd give anything to have a job in which I could wear a nice suit and write in standardized, prefabricated phrases. As soon as I finish the aforementioned chapter, I'm applying to law school.

Is there any proven method for coping with a midlife career crisis? If you put that question to a group of leading psychologists, they wouldn't bother to answer you. They're *sick* of dealing with your pathetic little problems. They want to be test pilots. So I'll just tell you the answer: Yes, there *is* a proven method for coping with the male midlife crisis; a method that enables you to have the stability and security of a conventional lifestyle PLUS an element of adventure and excitement; a method that has been employed for years with great success by thoughtful, sophisticated male role models such as Batman. That's right: I'm talking about having a *secret identity*. No doubt you have often asked yourself, "Why *does* Batman have a secret identity? Why doesn't he just come out and announce that he is Bruce Wayne, wealthy millionaire, so that the police chief could simply call him up when there was trouble, instead of shining that idiot Bat Signal into the sky? I mean, what if Bruce Wayne doesn't happen to be *looking* when the Bat Signal is turned on? What if he's in the bathroom? Or doesn't he ever *go* to the bathroom? Is that why he's always sort of grimacing? Is that why he . . ."

All RIGHT. Shut UP. The point is that Bruce Wayne doesn't need a secret identity for any crime-fighting reason; he needs it because he's supposed to be a grown man, and his wealthy millionaire friends would laugh at him if they found out that he was wearing tights and driving around in a Batmobile chasing after the Joker (who, when he's not wearing *his* secret-identity disguise, is a gynecologist).

OVER 40
MACNELLY

What a Woman Can Do When Her Husband is Having His Midlife Crisis

If your husband is exhibiting signs of a midlife crisis, at first you should try to humor him. If he wants to buy a ludicrously impractical sports car, tell him you think it's a terrific idea. If he wants to wear "younger" clothes, help him pick them out. If he wants to start seeing other women, shoot him in the head.

CHAPTER SEVEN

Sex After 40 (Or, Sex? After 40?)

I realize that sex is a delicate subject, so please be assured that in this chapter I intend to discuss it in a mature and tasteful manner devoid of such expressions as "getting a boner." But we definitely need to take a long, hard, penetrating look at sexuality, because, as we find ourselves plunging deeper and deeper into middle age, it becomes increasingly important that we have the knowledge we need to maintain a firm intellectual grasp on our private parts, so we can avoid becoming victimized by:

Common Myths About Sex and Aging

The biggest myth, as measured by square footage, is that as you grow older, you gradually lose your interest in sex. This myth probably got started because younger people seem to want to have sex with each other at every available opportunity including traffic lights, whereas older people are more likely to reserve their sexual activities for special occasions such as the installation of a new Pope.

But does this mean that, as an aging person, you're no longer capable of feeling the lust that you felt as an 18-year-old? Not at all! You're attracted just as strongly as you ever were toward 18-year-olds! The problem is that everybody your *own* age seems repulsive.

This is the fault of the advertising industry, which goes out of its way to make aging appear to be as attractive a process as death by maggot. When the advertising industry wants to convey the concept of glamour, it fills its commercials with beautiful young people who have Ph.D.'s in bodily tautness, writhing sensuously around the product as though it's making them so excited that at any moment they're going to have sex with each other, or possibly even the product. Whereas when you see older people in advertisements, they're usually having demeaning conversations with relentlessly cheerful pharmacists:

PHARMACIST: Hi, Mr. Hopkins! You're looking even more wretched than usual today!
OLDER PERSON: Yes, Bob, it's this darned swollen hemorrhoidal tissue.
PHARMACIST: Could you say that louder, Mr. Hopkins? I'm not sure that everybody in the entire store could hear you!
OLDER PERSON: I SAID IT'S THIS DARNED SWOLLEN HEMORRHOIDAL TISSUE.
PHARMACIST (brightening): I see!
OLDER PERSON: It feels like I'm sitting on a grapefruit.
GATHERING AUDIENCE OF INTERESTED SHOPPERS: Yuck.
PHARMACIST: Don't worry, Mr. Hopkins! Because we have a product here that . . .
OLDER PERSON: Also I have horrible arthritis pain.
PHARMACIST: Well, that's no problem either! Because this product contains an amazing new ingredient called . . .
OLDER PERSON: Also my dentures are encrusted with brownish gunk and frequently fall out in public restaurants.
VOICE FROM CROWD: Stone him!
OTHERS: Yes! Stone him!

So we see that the image of aging created by advertising is not entirely glamorous. So naturally, as we grow older, we tend to assume that we should become less active sexually. In fact, however, there is no biological reason for this assumption. This was proved in a famous experiment wherein biologists placed laboratory rats in cages and allowed them to age for several years, during which they (the biologists) made the following observations:

1. The rats displayed no interest in sex. The rats displayed an interest only in pooping and looking nervous, even when the biologists read letters aloud to them from the "Penthouse Forum."
2. The biologists, on the other hand, regularly became horny, especially during the Christmas party.

So there's no reason for us to feel that getting older should stop us from having sex. Our role model in this area should be such biblical stud muffins as Job, who, if I remember my Sunday school lessons correctly, remained sexually active for several hundred years. Of course I vaguely recall that at one point in the story, all of Job's cattle and relatives died and he got boils all over his body, which should serve as a reminder to all of us, no matter what our age, of the importance of practicing safe sex.

With that in mind, there's no reason why we can't continue to lead sexually fulfilling lives well into our Golden Years, as millions of older people have done before us—including, for all we know, your own parents. Yes! It's possible! Your parents having sex! I realize that this is difficult to accept. Most of us have trouble believing that our parents *ever* had sex, even when they conceived us. Deep down inside, we believe that our mothers got pregnant because of fallout from atomic testing during the Truman administration.

But the truth is that our parents were probably engaging in sex, and some of them still do, and we can, too. Physiologically, there is absolutely nothing to prevent us from remaining sexually active into our sixties and seventies and even eighties, except of course the possibility that Doing It will cause sudden death. This has been known to happen. In the interest of common decency I am not going to name any names, but this is apparently what happened to a billionaire who was Vice-President of the United States under Gerald Ford and whose name rhymes with "Pelson Pockefeller." He was allegedly working late one night on a book with a "research assistant," and all of a sudden, probably right in the middle of an important footnote, bang, so to speak, old Pelson was *gone*.

But this is unlikely to happen to you. For one thing, you don't even *have* a research assistant. Nevertheless, it's important that when you engage in sex during your middle and older years, you follow the:

U.S. Surgeon General's Recommendations for Older People Having Sex

1. Use only low-sodium margarine.
2. No whips, chains, or appliances requiring more than 200 watts.
3. No poultry.
4. No playing "Mister Johnson Goes to the Circus."

If you bear these commonsense rules in mind, there's no reason why you can't enjoy a vigorous and satisfying sex life, unless of course you happen to be a guy, in which case there's a good chance that at some point you'll have an experience wherein your partner is all ready to have sex, and you *want* to have sex, but no matter how hard you try, you can't seem to get any crisp in your cucumber (or, if you prefer strict medical terminology, any pop in your pickle). If this happens to you more than once, you may start wondering if maybe, just possibly:

You Are Impotent!

If this happens, the important thing is not to dwell on the idea that

You Are Impotent!

Because the odds are that the whole thing is purely psychological. The odds are that your organs are just fine, but for some reason your subconscious is telling you that

You Are Impotent!

over and over and over again, like a broken record, hammering home the message that

You Are Impotent!

until finally you start to *believe* it. Psychiatrists agree that if this happens, the best thing for you to do is

You Are Impotent!

No! Shut up! Stop! Psychiatrists say the best

You Are Impotent!

I'm sorry, but it's no use. I can't finish this paragraph.

Ha ha! Just a little impotency humor there. Really, there's really no reason to worry about this, because even if it turns out that

You Really *Are* Impotent!

there are all kinds of medical things they can do to you now involving surgical implants and valves and switches and remote-control devices, so that you'll be able to get an erection not only when you wish to have sex, but also whenever anybody within a mile of you operates a microwave oven. Which may not sound so terrific, but at least we guys don't have to go through:

The Change

This is the stage that a woman goes through when her body, through a complex biological process, senses that the woman has reached the stage in her life where her furniture is much too nice for her to have a baby barfing on it. So the body stops producing estrogen, which is the hormone that causes certain distinct female characteristics such as ovulation and the ability not to watch football. This bodily change is called "menopause," from the ancient Greek words *meno* (meaning "your skin sometimes gets so hot") and *pause* (meaning "that it melts Tupperware"). Also some women tend to become emotional and easily irritated by minor things that never used to bother them, such as when their husbands leave a partly used meatloaf sandwich in bed, as though the Meatloaf Sandwich Fairy were going to come along and pick it up for him.

The traditional way to cope with menopause is to ask your physician to prescribe costly pharmaceuticals, but of course these can cause harmful side effects. The pharmaceuticals industry Code of Ethics does not allow the production of any product unless merely pronouncing its chemical name in front of laboratory rats causes at least a third of them to die. So more and more, health experts are recommending a "holistic" approach, in which you develop a deeper understanding of the natural process that your body is going through, and then, with this newfound knowledge as your guide, you stick the meatloaf sandwich into the breast pocket of your husband's best suit.

CHAPTER EIGHT

Time Management (Tip: Read This Chapter Very Quickly)

Remember when you were a kid, and it seemed as though there was too *much* time? I can remember, at around age 9, having so much spare time, especially during the summer, that I could afford to spend entire *days* on activities such as coloring my entire stomach blue with a ballpoint pen, or breaking the world's record for Highest Pile of Cheerios Stuck Together with Peanut Butter, or conducting a scientific experiment to see exactly how many candles the dog would eat before it started walking funny.

Well, those innocent days are long gone. Today, as grownups, we're all so busy rushing madly around trying to meet the demands of families, friends, careers, homes, etc., that we barely have time for personal hygiene, which many people now are forced to perform in the car. Especially women. Most women manage to arrive at work looking terrific, but a lot of them got into their cars looking like Oonga, She-Walrus of the North. Driving to work on I-95 in Miami, I have seen women styling their hair, putting on makeup, sometimes even sticking their arms out the windows on both sides of the car to be worked on by professional manicurists riding motorcycles. Of course, this requires them to take their hands off the wheel, but in Miami (Official Driving Motto: "Death Before Yielding") this actually gives them an advantage.

Male drivers, of course, generally don't engage in such automotive beauty regimens. Males like to save their precious car time for picking their noses. For some reason, males think that car windows have one-way glass, so when they stop at a red light, even with cars all around them, they'll start rooting around their nostrils as though they have a gold brick in there. This is why truly classy individuals such as Donald Trump have those dark-tinted windows on their limousines. (Not that I'm suggesting here that Donald Trump picks his nose. That's why he has a *staff,* for God's sake.)

My point is that the older you get, the less you can afford to fritter away your valuable time on wasteful and stupid activities such as reading either of the two preceding paragraphs. You need to learn some proven time-management techniques, which we'll get to after we kill a few more minutes here with:

A Brief and Highly Inaccurate History of Time

Aside from Velcro, time is the most mysterious substance in the universe. You can't see it or touch it, yet a plumber can charge you upwards of seventy-five dollars per hour for it, *without necessarily fixing anything.*

Human beings first became aware of time during the era of the ancient Egyptians, who, while getting ready to build the Pyramids, invented the fundamental time unit, which is still in regular use today: the weekend. "We'll build those pyramids first thing after the weekend," the Egyptians were fond of saying, although of course when the weekend ended, they'd immediately start another one because it was the only unit they had. This was the Golden Age, and it was marked by the invention of beer.

The Golden Age ended tragically with the discovery of Wednesday, which led to the modern calendar featuring Friday, Tuesday, Pork Awareness Month, etc. This was followed by three major time advances:

- *Sometime,* which is a scientific unit of measurement meaning "in approximately 43 hillion jillion years," as in "Let's have lunch sometime!"
- *Daylight Savings Time,* which originated as a prank played by government employees who wanted to see if they could get an entire nation to change all its clocks twice a year without having the faintest idea why.
- *Military Time,* which is when you say things like "1400 hours." This is very useful for making brisk and efficient military statements, as in: "It took the squadron 1400 hours to deploy the $4.2-million Mobile Laser-Enhanced Tactical Field Latrine, and it still flushes backward."

Today, more and more households are operating on Blink Time. This is when a power outage causes all the digital clocks in all of your appliances to blink "00:00," sometimes for months, because you can't figure out how to make them stop because the owner's manuals are totally unintelligible because all the actual instructions have been replaced by pages upon pages of lawyer-excreted statements beginning with the word WARNING. We've been on Blink Time in our household for as long as I can remember, and I've adjusted to it pretty well. I'm always looking at the microwave oven and saying, "Huh! It's 00:00 already! Time for a beer!" This is only one of the ways that I use time management to keep my life "on track," and you can, too, by following these:

Proven Time-Management Techniques

When we talk about people who knew how to manage their time, the name that immediately springs to our lips, sometimes chipping our teeth, is Leonardo ("Leon the Vinci") da Vinci, a man who not only painted the famous *Mona Lisa,* but also, over the course of an incredibly prolific career, wrote Dante's

Inferno and invented the Sony Walkman, not to mention accomplishing countless other accomplishments that would really amaze you if I had time to look them up.

How was Leonardo able to accomplish all this? His "secret" was actually the same basic, simple time-management technique that was also used by Alexander the Great, Benjamin Franklin, Thomas Jefferson, and many others who were famous for their productivity: *He never talked on the telephone.* "Tell them I'm in a meeting," he always used to say to his secretary (who, fortunately, spoke English). Because Leonardo knew that nothing on earth wastes time like a telephone.

This is a problem dating back to the very first telephone call, which, as you remember from elementary school, occurred when Alexander Graham Bell needed his assistant, Watson, so he invented the telephone and called him up. But what you *didn't* learn in school was that *Watson wasn't there.* He was out working on a case with Sherlock Holmes, so Bell had to invent the first telephone message slip and leave it on Watson's desk and sit around for hours, waiting for a return call, until finally he ducked out for a sandwich, which is of course when Watson called back, and they ended up leaving messages back and forth for weeks, and when they finally *did* get in touch with each other they felt obligated to exchange pleasantries, talk about sports, and tell jokes for fifteen minutes, during which they were repeatedly interrupted by loud, irritating clicks caused by Nazi scientists who at that time were perfecting the popular "call waiting" feature. By the time Bell and Watson finally got to the actual purpose of their conversation, neither one had the vaguest recollection of what it was.

That's what the telephone does: sucks the time right out of your life. You see these people driving around, talking on their car telephones, and you think, "Gosh, that must be *efficient,* having a car phone." What you don't realize is that some of these people have been stuck in those cars, glued to the damned phone, for *months,* surviving on drive-thru food and peeing in the ashtray. You want to go the *opposite* direction. You want to *dephone* your life to the maximum extent possible. The key is to remember this Efficiency Rule:

> *Never use the telephone to actually talk to people. Use it only to return their messages, comparable to the way a tennis player returns a serve.*

"Here, take your damned message back," is the concept you are trying to convey. This is why it's very important that you call people back only when you're fairly sure they won't be there, such as lunchtime or Thanksgiving. Even then, you have to be alert in case you're dealing with a slippery customer who's actually *there:*

YOU: Hello, I'm returning Mr. Leonard Prongmaker's call.

PERSON ON THE OTHER END: This is Leonard Prongmaker.

YOU: Okay, then, I'll try again another time. (Hang up briskly.)

You can also cut down drastically on incoming messages by unplugging your answering machine. (If you don't have one, you should buy one, *then* unplug it.)

Another excellent tip for saving time in the business environment is: never attend a meeting. Meetings are an addictive, highly self-indulgent activity that corporations and other large organizations habitually engage in only because they cannot actually masturbate. Nothing productive has ever happened in a meeting. If Noah had formed an Ark

Construction Task Force, it would still be arguing over the ideal number of cubits. The federal government is basically one enormous, ongoing Meeting From Hell. Meetings are so inefficient that many major corporations are now staffing them entirely with temporary employees who are specially trained in what to do at meetings, namely not snore out loud. This frees the regular employees to get on with the vital work of attempting to return phone messages.

You can also save time by making your domestic routines more efficient. My son, for example, never turns off lights or closes the refrigerator door, thus saving several valuable nanoseconds per year. My wife and I avoid those long, time-consuming trips to the supermarket by buying our food in small quantities over the course of thirty to forty trips per week to convenience stores with names like the Way-Mor Expensive Food 'n' Microbe Mart. We even save time with our two dogs by frequently addressing them both by the same name ("NO!").

Using proven time-management techniques like these, I have transformed myself into a regular productivity machine, operating with the smooth precision of a fine Swiss watch that has been run over repeatedly by a coal train. The key to my efficiency is my daily schedule, a miracle of smart planning and split-second timing:

Daily Schedule

6:00 A.M.—Alarm goes off.

6:10, 6:20, 6:30, 6:40, 6:50 A.M.—Alarm goes off.

7:00 A.M.—Wake up and mentally review Plan of Action for accomplishing Today's Target Tasks.

7:10 A.M.—Alarm goes off.

7:11 A.M.—Open bedroom door and greet dogs. (NOTE: I always allow at least ten minutes for this, because dogs have the same IQ as artichokes, and thus when they see me close the door at night—even though they've seen me do this approximately 1,300 times—they are certain they'll never see me again, and consequently they give me an insanely joyful welcome comparable to the one given to the Allied forces when they liberated Paris, the difference being that the Parisians were slightly less likely, in their enthusiasm, to pee on your feet.)

7:21 A.M.—Wake up child.

7:25 A.M.—Commence bathroom activities, including intense 12-minute inspection and tentative probing of impending nose zit.

7:45 A.M.—Wake up child.

7:48 A.M.—Prepare breakfast of modern, easy-to-prepare, nutrition-free food substances, such as Waffles In A Can.

7:50 A.M.—Wake up child.

8:00 A.M.—Read newspaper. Save time by skipping stories whose headlines contain any of the following words: NATO, ECONOMY, DOLLAR, MIDEAST, ENVIRONMENT, FEDERAL, OZONE, ASIA, PRESIDENT, CONGRESS, NUCLEAR, and CANCER. If running late, go directly to comics.

8:03 A.M.—Wake up child.

8:06 A.M.—Feed child quick breakfast consisting of cereal advertised on Saturday-morning television cartoon shows, such as Sug-a-Rama with Lumps o' Honey ("The Cereal That Makes Your Attention Span Even Shorter").

8:12 A.M.—Rush to car and drive child to school, learning en route that child's Science Fair project, which child has never mentioned, is due that morning.

8:23 A.M.—Arrive at school with completed Science

Fair project, entitled "Objects Found in 1984 Jeep Ashtray."

8:25 A.M.—Drive to office, turning "dead time" in car to productive use by examining nose zit in rearview mirror and making helpful corrective gestures at other drivers.

9:07 A.M.—Arrive at office and immediately plunge into the hectic but invigorating task of getting coffee.

9:14 A.M.—Meet with co-workers to review issues left unresolved from previous day concerning pathetic state of Miami Dolphin defense.

9:37 A.M.—Coffee.

9:43 A.M.—Receive phone call from school official wondering how come child is not wearing shoes.

9:49 A.M.—Turn on word processor in preparation for day's highest-priority Target Task, writing humor column due several days earlier.

9:51 A.M.—Coffee.

10:20 A.M.—Stop in office of colleague for briefing concerning the story about the Polish airliner that crashed in a cemetery. (NOTE: They recovered 11,000 bodies.)

10:56 A.M.—Lunch.

11:27 A.M.—Back to work on humor column. Develop strong opening phrase: "One thing that has always struck me as very funny is . . ." Sink back in chair in exhaustion due to creative effort.

11:34 A.M.—Lunch.

12:22 P.M.—Review Polish airliner story with various colleagues.

1:34 P.M.—Revise opening phrase to read: "A very funny thing, and one that lends itself quite naturally to being the topic of a humor column, is . . ."

2:05 P.M.—Lunch.

2:42 P.M.—Come up with very strong new opening phrase: "If you're going to write a funny column, probably the easiest topic you could pick is . . ."

3:32 P.M.—Coffee.

3:51 P.M.—Nose zit update.

4:23 P.M.—Brief additional colleagues on Polish airliner matter.

4:47 P.M.—Lunch.

5:08 P.M.—Make final revisions to opening column phrase ("A humor-column topic so obvious that it practically writes itself is . . .").

5:27 P.M.—Explain to editor that only minor "fine-tuning" remains and column will definitely be finished by next day or following summer at latest.

6:39 P.M.—Arrive home to insanely joyful greeting from dogs, who, believing themselves abandoned forever, spent entire day throwing up in despair.

7:22 P.M.—Finish cleanup and commence quiet, intimate, romantic microwave pizza dinner with spouse.

7:23 P.M.—Receive phone call from school official with talent for sarcasm, inquiring about any possible plans in near future to pick up child.

7:52 P.M.—Return home with child to discover that dogs, grief-stricken over most recent departure, have managed to get pizza smears as high as seven feet up on living-room walls.

8:51 P.M.—Enjoy wholesome fast-food family dinner at Cholesterol Castle.

9:47 P.M.—Return home and enjoy emotional dog reunion resulting in several hairline fractures.

10:23 P.M.—Put child to bed and experience touching parental moment when, just as he is falling asleep, child remembers that on following day he is supposed to come to school in authentic costume of Yap islander.

10:32 P.M.—Nose zit update.

10:47 P.M.—Lunch.
11:00 P.M.—Turn on late news.
11:01 P.M.—Turn off late news when announcer uses word "nuclear."
11:02 P.M.—Sex life.
11:03 P.M.—Think about Target Tasks for tomorrow. Lots to do. Got column to write. Got developing nose zit. Got dogs to kill. Better set alarm for 6:00 A.M. sharp.

Of course, not every day goes as smoothly as this. Some days, despite my organizational efforts, unforeseen problems arise. Just today, for example, a couple of things came up at the last minute, and I never did get around to figuring out

NOTE: FIRST THING TOMORROW, THINK OF A CLEVER ENDING FOR THIS CHAPTER.

CHAPTER NINE

Wise Financial Planning for Irresponsible Scum Such as Yourself

To understand the importance of financial planning for your retirement years, let's consider the famous true Aesop's fable about the grasshopper and the ant.

It seems that many years ago, there lived a lazy grasshopper and a hardworking ant. All summer long, while the ant was busily networking with other ants and gathering food, the grasshopper sat around drinking vodka gimlets and watching "General Hospital." When winter came, the grasshopper had nothing to eat, while the ant was snug and warm in his cozy little house filled with putrefying chunks of road-kill raccoon. Finally the grasshopper, starving, came to the ant's door and said, "Can I have some food?" And the ant said: "Well, I suppose GAACCKK," and they were both crushed by rocks dropped on them by Boy Scouts on a nature walk. This was a very poor financial decision, when you think how much money these boys could have gotten for a pair of talking insects.

As a person in your forties, you definitely want to avoid this kind of foolish financial decision, because the odds are that you'll be earning a paycheck for only about twenty more years, and even less if your employer realizes how often you use the Xerox machine for personal documents. This means that your future standard of living depends on the investments you make *today* (Wednesday). If you fail to plan ahead, you could well spend your retirement years eating dumpster food and living under a highway overpass. Whereas if you heed the advice outlined in this chapter, you'll be able to spend your "golden years" in a modern, state-of-the-art appliance carton. The choice is yours!

And let's not forget about financing your children's future educational needs. As you are no doubt aware, tuition costs have skyrocketed in recent years and are currently running as high as $15,000, sometimes even $20,000, per semester. And that's for nursery school. College is even worse. And yet, as a concerned parent, you want to make sure that your child does receive the benefits of a college education, to acquire the vital knowledge and skills that *you* acquired in college, such as how to take notes while sleeping, or drink bourbon through your nose. Yes, you want your child to have these advantages, but how can you afford it? Experts predict that by the year 2000 you'll have to pay $178 million just to put your child through a *bad* college, a college with a team nickname like "The Fighting Room Fresheners." Where are you going to get that kind of money? The only logical solution is to *rob college treasurers at gunpoint.*

No! Sorry! What I meant to say was that the only logical solution is to get yourself on a sensible investment program. Of course, I can't give you any specific investment advice without having detailed knowledge of your current financial situation. So let's start off by taking a close look at your investment portfolio. Let's see here . . . Hey! Wait a minute! *This* isn't an investment portfolio! This is your fifth-grade science project, entitled "How Worms Eat." Ha ha! Nice try, but you might as well admit it —you don't even *have* an investment portfolio. You've spent virtually all the money you've ever earned on basic necessities of life such as mortgages, car payments, pediatricians, plumbing, rental movies, take-out Chinese food, thousands of toys and accessories (sold separately), and untold millions of AA batteries (not included). You have nothing to show for all the money you've earned over the past twenty years except a heavily mortgaged house; a car that you owe twenty-seven more payments on, even though it's already showing symptoms of Fatal Transmission Disease; numerous malfunctioning appliances; huge mounds of books you never read, records you never listen to, clothes you never wear, and membership cards to health clubs you never go to; and—somewhere in the depths of your refrigerator—a year-old carton half-filled with a substance that may once have been mu-shu pork. Currently your major tangible financial asset is a coffee can containing seventeen pounds of loose change, much of it Canadian.

So your financial situation is a mess. Okay, fine. The important thing is—*don't be discouraged.* There's no reason to get down on yourself, just because you've been an unbelievable jerk. The important thing is to get yourself straightened out *now,* with Step One being to track your "cash flow" to determine where your money comes from, where it goes, whether it's having an affair, etc. Odds are you'll find out that you have what economists call:

THE NORMAL HUMAN CASH FLOW
(With Key Terms in Boldface)

Money comes from the **bank,** *which puts it in the* **automatic** *teller, from which it flows into your* **wallet,** *at which point* **UFO Rays from Space** *cause all the money to* **disappear** *so* **mysteriously** *that you often remark upon it to your* **spouse,** *as in: "I don't understand it! I had forty-seven dollars in my wallet this morning and all I bought was* **gas** *and some* **guacamole dip** *and now it [meaning the money] [also the guacamole dip] is all* **gone!**" *So you go back to the* **automatic bank teller** *to see if there's any* **more money,** *which there probably is* **not** *because your last* **credit-card statement** *showed that you had gone way over your* **credit limit** *due to* **several dozen ludicrously unnecessary purchases** *that you apparently made while* *under the influence of* **powerful narcotics,** *such as the purchase totaling* **$168.92** *from a place called* **Spatula World,** *the result being that you had to write a* **fairly massive check** *to the* **Visa Corporation,** *which is hooked up somehow with the* **bank,** *and which you hope will get your money and put some of it back in the* **automatic teller** *soon so you can get it back* **out** *again because you already need more* **gas.**

Of course, your individual mileage may vary. But we can see from this analysis that the only way you'll be able to save for your retirement years will be if you put yourself on a regular savings plan wherein the first thing you do whenever you get some money is to take a certain amount away from yourself, by force if necessary, and put it to work for you by means of a simple investment strategy. The simplest strategy I know of is the one we use in our household, which we call:

The Wealth-Through-Sickness Investment Program

Here's how it works:

1. Every week, rain or shine, one or more of us gets sick and we go to the doctor's office and pay varying amounts of money in exchange for finding out that we are sick.
2. Every six or eight months, whichever comes later, I sit down at the kitchen table with huge piles of medical receipts and attempt to fill out my medical insurance claim forms, which, in the honored tradition of forms, have apparently been designed by people with severe disorders of the attention span. The questions go like this:
   1. What is your name?
   2. What is the patient's name?
   3. Are you the same as the patient? (If "no," then who is?)
   4. What was your name again?
3. Several weeks later, the insurance company mails us a check and an explanation written in extremely clear language, although unfortunately not English ("This amount reflects your total coverage exposure MINUS your accrued deductible TIMES your applicable exemptions PLUS your windfall profits tax DIVIDED BY the cosine of your . . ." etc.). Sometimes we get back as much as 70 percent of our money (called the "rate of return," or "Fanny Mae"), which we then wisely reinvest in doctors' fees, unless we're running low on beer.

The advantage of the Wealth-Through-Sickness Investment Program is that it's virtually automatic. The disadvantage is that the only person who becomes wealthy is the doctor. You, on the other hand, gradually become poorer, and probably also fatter, depending on your beer consumption. So if you're looking to actually *increase* the amount of money you have, my advice would be to get yourself into a sound, stable, diversified, long-term investment program of betting on dog races. Unless, of course, you're more of a risk-taker, in which case you could put your money into a savings-and-loan institution, which is kind of like a bank except it has boards on the windows. Or, if you're a *real* gambler, you might want to consider investing in:

The Stock Market

The way this works is, you find yourself a reputable stockbroker (defined as "a stockbroker who has not been indicted yet"), and you give him some money. He keeps some for himself and uses the rest to buy you a stock that he got a Hot Tip on and Recommends Highly, although of course he keeps his own personal money in a mayonnaise jar. Next you spend a lot of time trying to keep track of your stock by frowning at the newspaper financial listings, which look like this:

	UP	ODDS	RBI	VCR	LOW TIDE	EAST
Gmrh	34	4-3	23	$349	3:43	One Spade
Sodm	12	8-1	8(e)	45% off	IRT #2	No Trumps

You also spend a lot of time listening to radio and TV "financial analysts" who clearly have no idea what the stock market is going to do next, but are absolutely brilliant at coming up with creative explanations as to why it did whatever it just did. ("Stocks were off sharply today in response to rumors that the July unemployment figures have been eaten by goats.") Eventually you start to notice that your "can't-miss" stock is not performing up to expectations, as evidenced by the fact that the newspaper is now listing it on the comics page. Finally you tell your broker to sell it, which he does, taking another chunk of the proceeds for himself and paying the balance to you out of one of those bus-driver-style change dispensers. Then he's off to the golf course, to pick up some more Hot Tips for you.

Aside from providing your stockbroker with a steady income, another important objective of your long-term investment strategy is to feel a constant nagging guilt about:

Life Insurance

How do you know whether you have enough life insurance? How can you be sure that if, God forbid, something terrible were to happen to you, your loved ones would be able to continue squandering money in the manner to which they have become accustomed? I put this question to the Life Insurance Institute, which provided this:

Helpful Self-Test Questionnaire to see if You Have Enough Life Insurance (Sponsored by the Life Insurance Institute)

1. How much insurance do you have?
2. You need more.
3. We'll send somebody over right now.

Of course, no discussion of your financial future would be complete without some mention of the terrific retirement program dreamed up by the federal government, which is the same shrewd financially savvy outfit that gave us the $600 military toilet seat. I refer, of course, to:

Social Security

The way this works is: the government takes an ever-larger chunk of money out of your paycheck and gives it to retired people, even the ones who already have a whole lot more money than you do and use their social security checks exclusively to purchase sun hats for their racehorses. But you continue to pay, because you're a generous, caring person who does not wish to be thrown into jail. Also you figure that someday *you'll* retire, and you'll get back all the money you paid in. The flaw in this reasoning is that when our whole humongously oversized generation retires, there's going to be virtually no work force left to support us. The government will be trying to suck billions of dollars every week out of an estimated fifty-three teenage Burger King employees. It's not going to work. The whole social security system is going to come crashing down, and you're not going to get a nickel, which is okay because there won't be anything to buy anyway, once the Greenhouse Effect causes the polar ice caps to melt to the point where the shopping malls are patronized mainly by jellyfish, assuming that all life on the planet hasn't already been wiped out by toxic waste or nuclear war, which could of course break out at any moment, which is why I can't stress enough the importance of getting started *today* on your long-term financial planning. Me, I'm going to order some Chinese food.

Politics After 40: You Don't Need a Weatherman to Know That Harsh Sunlight Can Harm Your BMW's Finish

You hardly ever see radical activists anymore. The last time I saw any up close was at the 1988 Democratic convention in Atlanta, the one where the Democrats nominated Michael "The Human Quaalude" Dukakis. The Democrats had thoughtfully set up a Designated Protest Area right next to the convention hall. (This was in stark contrast to the Republicans, who held *their* convention right next to—this is true—a shopping center.)

The Democrats' Designated Protest Area featured a powerful public-address system and a stage where, according to the official protest schedule, various groups or individuals would get up and make long, impassioned speeches for or against endangered crustaceans or transvestite canoeists' rights or whatever, their voices booming out from the huge speakers and thundering across a listening throng averaging maybe nine people, seven of whom were waiting for their turn to protest.

The protesters who showed up most often, sometimes interrupting other people's protests, were a group of left-wing radical activists. They were mostly kids in their teens or early twenties. Fashion-wise, they favored a sportswear look that I would call "Pretend Guerrilla," sometimes including bandannas pulled up over their faces, thus enabling them to blend into the downtown Atlanta environment as unobtrusively as water buffalo at a formal wedding. They communicated almost exclusively by shouting slogans, and their philosophy boiled down to two basic points:

1. They represented The People.
2. They hated people.

At least that's the way it seemed, because they were always in a spittle-emitting rage, loudly accusing everybody they encountered—police, other protesters, media people, spectators, trash cans, squirrels—of being mother-f-wording CIA fascists. They used this expression reflexively, the way supermarket cashiers use "Have a nice day."

Needless to say, the radicals were very persuasive. After a few minutes of listening to them shout in your face, you were ready to march down to the CIA Recruitment Center and sign up. At least I was, and this bothered me somewhat. Because, like almost everybody in my generation except Julie Nixon and David Eisenhower, I used to be a left-wing, anti-establishment, protest-oriented, march-on-Washington type of individual. Once, back in college, I even participated in a hunger strike to end the Vietnam War. By not eating, I was supposedly enabling myself to focus my consciousness on peace. What actually happened was that I became absolutely obsessed with cheeseburgers, although if I really, really forced myself to concentrate on the tragedy in Southeast Asia, I could also visualize french fries. I kept this up for several days, but failed to have much of an impact on Washington. At no point, as far as I know, did a White House aide burst into the Oval Office and shout with alarm, "Some students at Haverford College have been refusing to eat for several days!" followed by Lyndon Johnson saying, "Mah God! Ah got to change mah foreign policy!"

But the point is, at least I was *trying,* in my own naïve and painfully earnest way, to do what I thought was the right thing. Whereas these days I never seem to get involved in causes. The last time I remember protesting anything with any real passion was when I was at a professional basketball game and the arena management decided to stop selling beer in the fourth quarter.

Of course, some would argue that, hey, the war is over, so there aren't any causes to get involved in anymore. Which is of course ridiculous. There are all *kinds* of causes to be alarmed about. For example, there's the Greenhouse Effect, which is one of the more recent in a series of alarming worldwide homicidal trends to be discovered by those busy beavers, the scientists. They've found that the Earth is slowly being turned into a vast greenhouse, so that by the year 2010—unless something is done—the entire human race will be crushed beneath a humongous tomato.

Or something along those lines. I confess that I haven't been following the Greenhouse Effect all that closely. Whenever I'm reading the newspaper and I come to the words "Greenhouse Effect," I continue reading, but I squinch my eyes up real tight so that the words become a meaningless blur. I originally developed this technique for watching suspense movies, in which the characters wander around inside a house with menacing background music and nothing happens and nothing happens and nothing happens and nothing happens and *my God it plucked her eyeballs out like a pair of grapes.*

I'm not saying that the Greenhouse Effect is not extremely important. Hey, I live in Miami, and if the polar ice caps start melting, I stand a good chance of waking up one morning and finding myself festooned with kelp. It's just that, what with working and paying bills and transporting my son to and from the pediatrician and trying to teach the dog not to throw up on the only nice rug in the entire house, I just don't seem to have enough room in my brain for the Greenhouse Effect and all the other problems I know I should be concerned about, such as drugs and AIDS and Lebanon and pollution and cholesterol and caffeine and cancer and Japanese investors buying the Lincoln Memorial and nuclear war and dirty rock lyrics and this new barbecue grill we got. Our old grill rusted out. It was your basic model, the kind where you put your charcoal in, you lit it, you noticed about an hour later that the charcoal had gone out, and you ordered a pizza. It gave us many years of good service.

Our new grill was purchased by my wife, Beth, who would be a natural in the field of military procurement because whatever she's buying, she always gets the most fangled one they sell. She came home with a grill approximately the size of a nuclear submarine but more complicated, featuring knobs, valves, switches, auto-ignite, a fold-down side table, "flavor bars," a side burner, an electric rotisserie, and much more. This grill squats out on the patio, the lord of all it surveys. For weeks I was afraid to go near it. Finally I decided, hey, it's just a grill, so I got out the owner's manual, which is twenty-eight pages long. Here's what it says:

CAUTION! (five times)
DANGER! (six times)
WARNING! (thirty-eight times)

These are true statistics. So we are talking about a total of forty-nine scary things to remember just about a barbecue grill, and, frankly, I do not feel up to it. The only warning I even started to read was on page 3, which begins, I swear, with the words:

WARNING!!!!!
SPIDER AND INSECT ALERT

This is followed by the statement: "Your Genesis Gas Barbecue as well as any outdoor gas appliance is a target for spiders and insects." Needless to say, I stopped reading right there, because the very thought of insects targeting my grill (For what? Theft?) makes me want to get into the fetal position.

My point is that whereas I once felt totally confident of my ability to shape the destiny of the nation and, yes, the world, I now have grave doubts about my ability to cope with a patio appliance. Aside from giving my Fair Share to the United Fund, I have pretty much withdrawn from causes, and so, apparently, have many other members of my generation, except perhaps for David and Julie Nixon Eisenhower, who, being 180 degrees out of sync, are probably living in a geodesic dome somewhere, smoking hashish by the kilogram and making plans to blow up the Pentagon.

Sometimes I think I'd like to get more involved politically, but I get depressed when I look at the two major name-brand political parties. Both of them seem to be dominated by the kind of aggressively annoying individuals who always came in third for sophomore class president. Which is not to say that there are no differences between the parties. The Democrats seem to be basically nicer people, but they have demonstrated time and again that they have the management skills of celery. They're the kind of people who'd stop to help you change a flat, but would somehow manage to set your car on fire. I would be reluctant to entrust them with a Cuisinart, let alone the economy. The Republicans, on the other hand, would know how to fix your tire, but they wouldn't bother to stop because they'd want to be on time for Ugly Pants Night at the country club. Also, the Republicans have a high Beady-Eyed Self-Righteous Scary Borderline Loon Quotient, as evidenced by Phyllis Schlafly, Pat Robertson, the entire state of Utah, etc.

But the biggest problem I have with both major political parties is that they seem to be competing in some kind of giant national scavenger hunt every four years to see who can find the biggest goober to run for President. I was hoping that things would improve when my generation took over—when somebody my age, representing the best that my generation had to offer, morally and intellectually, got nominated to a national ticket. When this finally happened, of course, the nod went to "Dan" Quayle, a man whose concept of visionary leadership is steering his own golf cart, a man who—and I mean no disrespect when I say this—would not stand out, intellectually, in a vat of plankton.

I can hear you saying: "Oh yeah, Mr. Smartass? Well, what kind of leader would *you* be?" The answer is, I'd be a terrible leader. I'd be such an inadequate leader that within a matter of days the United States would rank significantly below Belize as a world power. But at least I'd try to be an *interesting* leader. I wouldn't be one more pseudo-somber, blue-suited, red-tied, wingtip-shoed weenie, frowning at the issues with sincerely feigned concern. I'd try to truly represent my generation, the rock-'n'-roll generation that had the idealism and courage to defy the Establishment, stand up for what it believed in, march in the streets and go to Woodstock and sleep in the rain and become infested with body lice. If I were the President, I'd bring some *life* to the White House. The theme of my administration would be summarized by the catchy and inspirational phrase: "Hey, The Government Is Beyond Human Control, So Let's at Least Have Some Fun with It." Here are some of the specific programs I would implement:

- I would invite George Thorogood and the Delaware Destroyers to perform at the White House. Not just once. *Every night.* They would *live* there. Congress would constantly be passing Joint Resolutions urging the Executive Branch to keep the volume down.
- Whenever I entered the room for a formal dinner, the band would play the 1963 Angels' hit, "My Boyfriend's Back."
- I would propose that the government launch a $17-billion War on Light Beer.
- I would have a Labrador retriever, wearing a small earphone, sit in on all Cabinet meetings.
- I would request a summit meeting with the Soviet Premier, at which I would make a dramatic three-hour presentation, using flip-charts, of the benefits of becoming an Amway distributor.
- One of my highest priorities would be to have helium declared the National Element.
- I would awaken key congressional leaders at 2:30 one morning and summon them to the White House Situation Room for an urgent meeting, at which, after swearing them to secrecy, I would show them a top-secret spy-satellite photograph revealing that China is shaped vaguely like an eggplant.
- The cornerstone of my foreign policy would be playing pranks on France.
- Wherever I went, there would be a burly Secret Service man just a few feet away, and on his wrist would be a handcuff, which would be attached to a steel chain, which would be attached to a locked steel carrying case, and inside that case would be: an Etch-a-Sketch.

How to Tell if You're Turning Into a Republican

It's very common for people reaching middle age to turn into Republicans. It can happen overnight. You go to bed as your regular old T-shirt-wearing self, and you wake up the next morning with Ralph Lauren clothing and friends named Muffy. Here are some other signs to watch for:

- You find yourself judging political candidates solely on the basis of whether or not they'd raise your taxes. "Well," you say, "he *was* convicted in those machete slayings, but at least he won't raise my taxes."

- You assign a lower priority to ending world hunger than to finding a cleaning lady.
- You start clapping wrong to music.

The last item above is something I've noticed about Republicans at their conventions. The band will start playing something vaguely upbeat—a real GOP rocker such as "Bad, Bad LeRoy Brown"—and the delegates will decide to get funky and clap along, and it immediately becomes clear that they all suffer from a tragic Rhythm Deficiency, possibly caused by years of dancing the bunny hop to bands with names like "Leon Wudge and His Sounds of Clinical Depression." To determine whether Republican Rhythm Impairment Syndrome is afflicting you, you should take the Ray Charles Clapping Test. All you do is hum the song "Hit the Road, Jack" and clap along. A rhythmically normal person will clap as follows:

"Hit the road, (CLAP) Jack (CLAP)."

Whereas a Republican will clap this way:

"Hit the (CLAP), (CLAP)."

(By the way, if you don't even *know* the song "Hit the Road, Jack," then not only are you a Republican, but you might even be Cabinet material.)

I'll tell you what's weird. Not only is our generation turning into Republicans, but we also have a whole generation coming after us who are *starting out* as Republicans. With the exception of the few dozen spittle-emitting radicals I saw in Atlanta, the younger generations today are already so conservative they make William F. Buckley, Jr., look like Ho Chi Minh. What I'm wondering is, what will they be like when they're our age? Will they, too, change their political philosophy? Will millions of young urban professionals turn 40 and all of a sudden start turning into left-wing, antiestablishment hippies, smoking pot on the racquetball court, putting Che Guevera posters up in the conference room, and pasting flower decals all over their cellular telephones? It is an exciting time to look forward to. I plan to be dead.

CHAPTER ELEVEN

Sports for the Over-40 Person (Or, God Had a Reason for Creating the Barcalounger)

In the Pantheon of Sports Heroes (which is located next to the Skeet-Shooting Hall of Fame), you'll find the names of many legendary athletes who remained active in sports well after they turned 40—Babe Ruth, Jack Dempsey, Picasso, Secretariat—the list goes on and on.

What do these great competitors have in common? Right. They're all dead. So you see how important it is for you to slow down as you get older, to abandon the active sports you enjoyed so much in your youth—basketball, tennis, racquetball, drinking a quart of Jim Beam and leaping naked into the motel pool from the eighth-floor balcony, etc. It's time for you to start "acting your age" by getting involved in the kinds of sports activities that are more appropriate for mature, responsible adults, such as:

Shrieking at Little Leaguers

To participate in this highly popular sport, all you need to do is get a small child who would be infinitely happier just staying home and playing in the dirt, and put a uniform on this child and make him stand for hours out on a field with other reluctant children who are no more capable of hitting or catching or accurately throwing a baseball than they are of performing neurosurgery. Then you and the other grownups stand around the perimeter and leap up and down and shriek at these children as though the fate of the human race depended on their actions.

The object of the game is to activate your child if the ball goes near him, similar to the way you use levers to activate the little men in table-hockey games. Your child will be standing out in right field, picking his nose, staring into space, totally oblivious to the game, and the ball will come rolling his way, and your job is to leap violently up and down and shriek, "GET THE BALL! GET THE *BALL!!*" repeatedly for several minutes until your child finally is aroused from his reverie long enough to glance down and discover, to his amazement, the ball. The ball! Of all things! Right here in the middle of a Little League game! While your child is staring at the ball curiously, as if examining a large and unusual tropical insect, you switch to yelling: "THROW THE BALL! THROW THE BALL! THROWTHEBALL THROWTHEBALL THROWTHEBALL THROWTHEBALL THROWTHEBALL THROWTHEBALL! *THROW* THE BALL, DAMMIT!!" After several minutes of this an idea will start to form somewhere deep inside your child's brain: *Perhaps I should throw the ball.* Yes! It's crazy, but it just might work!

And so, seconds before you go into cardiac arrest on the sidelines, your child will pick up the ball and hurl it, Little League-style, in a totally random direction, then resume picking his nose and staring off into space. As you collapse, exhausted, the ball will roll in the general direction of some *other* child, whose poor unfortunate parent must then try to activate *him.* Meanwhile, the *other* team's parents will be shrieking at *their* children to run around the bases in the correct direction. It is not uncommon for 150 runs to score on one Little League play. A single game can go on for weeks.

I get to engage in a lot of sideline-shrieking, because tragically we have very nice weather down here in South Florida, which means that while most of the nation enjoys the luxury of being paralyzed by slush, we subtropical parents are trapped in Year-Round Youth Sports Hell. The reason we have a high crime rate is that many parents are so busy providing transportation that they have to quit their jobs and support their families by robbing convenience stores on their way to practices, games, lessons, etc.

But at least our children are becoming well rounded. That's what I tell myself while I shriek at my son, who is out there in left field, watching commercial aircraft fly overhead while the ball rolls cheerfully past him and seven runners score. I tell myself that if my son were not out there participating in sports, he would not be learning one of life's most important lessons, namely: "It doesn't matter whether you win or lose, because you are definitely going to lose."

My son's teams lose a lot. This is because he is a Barry. We Barrys have a tradition of terrible sports luck dating back to my father, whose entire high-school football career—this is true—consisted of a single play, which was blocking a punt with his nose. As a child, I played on an unbroken succession of losing baseball teams, although "played" is probably too strong a term. My primary role was to sit on the bench, emitting invisible but potent Loser Rays and joining with the other zero-motor-control bench-sitters in thinking up hilarious and highly creative insults to hurl at members of the other team. Let's say the opposing batter was named Frank. We'd yell: "Hey, FRANK! What's your last name? *FURTER?*" Then we'd laugh so hard that we'd fall backward off the bench while Frank hit a triple, scoring twelve runs.

My son is a much better player than I was, but he's still a Barry, and consequently his teams generally lose. He was on one Little League team, the Red Sox, that lost at least 45,000 games in a span of maybe four months. Teams were coming from as far away as Guam to play the Red Sox. All of these teams complied with the First Law of Little League Physics, which states: "The other team always has much larger kids." You parents may have noticed that your child's team always consists of normal-sized, even puny, children, while the other team is always sponsored by Earl's House of Steroids.

So the Red Sox were constantly playing against huge, mutant 9-year-olds who had more bodily hair than I do and drove themselves to the game, and we were getting creamed. I served as a part-time first-base coach, and I spent a lot of time analyzing our technique, trying to pinpoint exactly what it was that we were doing wrong, and as best as I could figure it, our problem was that—follow me closely here—*we never scored any runs.* Ever.

There was a good reason for this: The boys were not idiots. They did not wish to be struck by the ball. When they were batting, they looked perfect—good stance, fierce glare at the pitcher, professional-style batting glove, etc.—until the pitcher would actually pitch, at which point, no matter where the ball was going, the Red Sox batters would twitch their bodies violently backward like startled squids, the difference being that a squid would have a better chance of hitting the baseball because it keeps its eyes open.

Frankly, I didn't blame the boys. This was exactly the hitting technique that I used in Little League on those rare occasions when I got to play. But as a first-base coach I had a whole new perspective on the game, namely the perspective of a person who never had to get up to bat. So my job was to yell foolish advice to the batters. "Don't back up!" I'd yell. "He's not gonna hit you!" Every now and then a Red Sock, ignoring his common sense, would take me seriously and fail to leap backward, and of course when this happened the hormonally unbalanced, 275-pound pitcher always fired the ball directly into the batter's body. Then my job was to rush up and console the batter by telling him, "Legally, you cannot be forced to play organized baseball."

I'm just kidding, of course. Far be it from me to bring down the republic. What I'd say was, "Rub it off! Attaboy! Okay!" And the boy, having learned the important life lesson that adults frequently spout gibberish, would sniffle his way down to first base, while our next batter was silently resolving to be in a different area code by the time the ball reached home plate.

Speaking of coaching, this is an excellent way for the sports-oriented person to avoid the physical risks of actually participating physically in the sport, and yet still have the opportunity to experience the emotion and excitement of sudden heart failure. I coached my son's soccer team, the Phantoms, for one game. This was pretty ridiculous, because the only soccer rules I remembered, from junior high school, were:

1. You're allowed to hit the ball with your head.
2. But it hurts.

The way I was selected as coach was that the regular coach, Rick, was on vacation for two weeks, and the other parents decided that I was best qualified to be the substitute coach on account of I wasn't there when they decided this.

The Phantoms, needless to say, were a struggling team. In addition to being cursed by the Barry luck, they had been decimated by birthday parties, and they were not having a banner year in the sense of winning games or even necessarily getting the ball down the field far enough so the opposing goalkeeper had to stop picking his ear.

So I was concerned about being the coach. I had, of course, attended many soccer games over the years, but all I ever did was stand around with the other parents, randomly yelling, "KICK IT!" After I was elected substitute coach, I did attend a team practice in hopes of learning some strategy, but unfortunately this was the practice at which the Official

Team Photograph was taken, which was very time-consuming because every time the photographer got the team posed, several players would be attacked by ants. Down here in South Florida we have highly aggressive ants, ants that draw no distinction between a cashew nut and a human being. You turn your back on them, and next thing you know, you hear this rhythmic ant work chant and your child is being dragged underground.

So the Phantoms spent most of the practice swatting at their legs and moving, gypsy-like, around the field, looking for an ant-free location, and the only thing they really practiced was getting into team-photograph formation. I did speak briefly with Rick, who gave me the following coaching pointers:

1. The game starts at 1:30.

He also gave me a coach-style clipboard and some official league literature on Soccer Theory, which I attempted to read about an hour before game time. Unfortunately, it was not designed to be read by desperate, unprepared fathers. It was designed to be read by unusually smart nuclear physicists. It starts out with these handy definitions:

a. Principles of Play: the rules of action (guidelines) that support the basic objectives of soccer.
b. Tactics: the means by which the principles or rules are executed.
c. Strategy: which tactics are to be used, the arrangement of . . .

And so on. I read these words several times, gradually becoming convinced that they'd make equal sense to me in any order. They could say: "Strategy: the tactics by which the rules (principles) support the execution." Or, "Principles: the strategic (tactical) arrangement of executives wearing supporters."

So you can imagine how well prepared I felt when I arrived at the soccer field. The Phantoms gathered around me, awaiting leadership. Nearby, our opponents, looking like the Brazilian national team, only larger, were running through some snappy pre-game drills. The Phantoms looked at them, then looked at me expectantly. My brain, working feverishly under pressure, began to form a shrewd coaching concept, a tactic by which we might be able to execute the guidelines of our strategy.

"Okay!" I announced. "Let's run some pre-game drills!"

The Phantoms, showing rare unity of purpose, responded immediately. "We don't have a ball," they pointed out. There was nothing about this in the coaching materials.

Next it was time for the Pre-game Talk. "Okay, Phantoms!" I shouted. "Gather 'round! Listen up!"

The Phantoms gathered 'round. They listened up. Suddenly it occurred to me that I had nothing whatsoever to tell them.

"Okay!" I said. "Let's go!"

The game itself is a blur in my memory. My strategy—yelling "KICK IT!"—did not seem to be effective. The other team, which at times appeared to be playing with as many as four balls, was scoring on us regularly. We were not scoring at all. We were having trouble just executing the play where you run without falling down. As the situation deteriorated, I approached some of the other fathers on the sidelines. "What do you think we should do?" I asked. They did not hesitate.

"We should go to a bar," they said.

In the third quarter I changed my strategy from

yelling "KICK IT!" to yelling "WAY TO GO!" This had no effect on anything, but I felt better. Finally the game ended, and I attempted to console the Phantoms over their heartbreaking loss. But they were beyond consolation. They were already into racing around, pouring Gatorade on each other. I'm sure they'll eventually overcome the trauma of this loss. Whereas I will probably never again be able to look at a clipboard without whimpering.

Probably the fastest-growing sport for the over-40 person is one that combines the advantages of a good cardiovascular workout with the advantages of looking like you have a bizarre disorder of the central nervous system. I refer to:

Walking Like a Dork

Walking like a dork has become very popular among older people who used to jog for their health but could no longer afford the orthopedic surgery. The object of dork-walking is to make a simple, everyday act performed by millions of people every day, namely walking, look as complex and strenuous as Olympic pole-vaulting. To do this, you need to wear a special outfit, including high-tech, color-coordinated shorts and sweatclothes and headbands and wristbands and a visor and a Sony Walkperson tape player and little useless weights for your hands and special dork-walking shoes that cost as much per pair as round-trip airfare to London.

But the most important thing is your walking technique. You have to make your arms and legs as stiff as possible and swing them violently forward and back in an awkward, vaguely Richard Nixon-like manner. It helps a lot to have an enormous butt, waving around back there like the Fiji blimp in a tornado. You'll know you're doing it right when passing motorists laugh so hard that they drive into trees.

But as you age, you may find that even dork-walking is too strenuous for you. In this case, you'll want to look into the ultimate aging-person activity, a "sport" that requires so little physical activity that major tournaments are routinely won by coma victims. I refer, of course, to:

Golf

Nobody knows exactly how golf got started. Probably what happened was, thousands of years ago, a couple of primitive guys were standing around, holding some odd-shaped sticks, and they noticed a golf ball lying on the grass, and they said, "Hey! Let's see if we can hit this into a hole!" And then they said, "Nah, let's just tell long, boring anecdotes about it instead."

Which is basically the object, in golf. You put on the most unattractive pants that money can buy, pants so ugly that they have to be manufactured by blind people in dark rooms, and you get together in the clubhouse with other golfers and drone away for hours about how you "bogeyed" your three-iron on the par six, or your six-iron on the par three, or whatever. Also you watch endless televised professional golf tournaments with names like the Buick Merrill Lynch Manufacturers Hanover Frito-Lay Ti-D-Bol Preparation H Classic, which consist entirely of moderately overweight men holding clubs and frowning into the distance while, in the background, two announcers hold interminable whispered conversations like this:

FIRST ANNOUNCER: Bob, he's lying about eighteen yards from the green with a fourteen-mile-per-hour wind out of the northeast, a relative humidity of seventy-two percent, and a chance of afternoon or evening thundershowers. He might use a nine-iron here.

SECOND ANNOUNCER: Or possibly an eight, Bill. Or even—this makes me so excited that I almost want to speak in a normal tone of voice—a seven.

FIRST ANNOUNCER: Or he could just keep on frowning into space. Remember that one time we had a professional golfer frown for five solid hours, never once hitting a ball, us whispering the whole time in between Buick commercials, and it turned out he'd had some kind of seizure and died, standing up, gripping his sand wedge?

SECOND ANNOUNCER: In that situation, Bill, I'd have used a putter.

If you *really* get into golf, you can actually try to play it some time, although this is not a requirement. I did it once, with a friend of mine named Paul, who is an avid golfer in the sense that if he had to choose between playing golf and ensuring permanent world peace, he'd want to know how many holes.

So we got out on the golf course in one of those little electric carts that golfers ride around in to avoid the danger that they might actually have to contract some muscle tissue. Also, we had an enormous collection of random clubs and at least 3,000 balls, which turned out to be not nearly enough.

The way we played was, first Paul would hit his ball directly toward the hole. This is basic golfing strategy: You want to hit the ball the least possible number of times so you can get back to the clubhouse to tell boring anecdotes and drink. When it was my turn, we'd drive the cart to wherever my ball was, which sometimes meant taking the interstate highway. When we finally arrived at our destination, Paul would examine the situation and suggest a club.

"Try a five-iron here," he'd say, as if he honestly believed it would make a difference.

Then, with a straight face, he'd give me very specific directions as to where I should hit the ball. "You want to aim it about two and a half yards to the right of that fourth palm tree," he'd say, pointing at a palm tree that I could not hit with a Strategic Defense Initiative laser. I'd frown, pro-golfer-style, at this tree, then I'd haul off and take a violent swing at the ball, taking care to keep my head down, which is an important part of your golf stroke because it gives you a legal excuse if the ball winds up lodged in somebody's brain.

Sometimes, after my swing, the ball would still be there, surrounded by a miniature scene of devastation, similar to the view that airborne politicians have of federal disaster areas. Sometimes the ball would be gone, which was the signal to look up and see how hard Paul was trying not to laugh. Usually he was trying very hard, which meant the ball had gone about as far as you would hide an Easter egg from a small child with impaired vision. But sometimes the ball had completely disappeared, and we'd look for it, but we'd never see it again. I think it went into another dimension, a parallel universe where people are still talking about the strange day when these golf balls started materializing out of thin air, right in the middle of dinner parties, concerts, etc.

So anyway, by following this golfing procedure, Paul and I were able to complete nine entire holes in less time than it would have taken us to memorize *Moby Dick* in Korean. We agreed that nine holes was plenty for a person with my particular level of liabil-

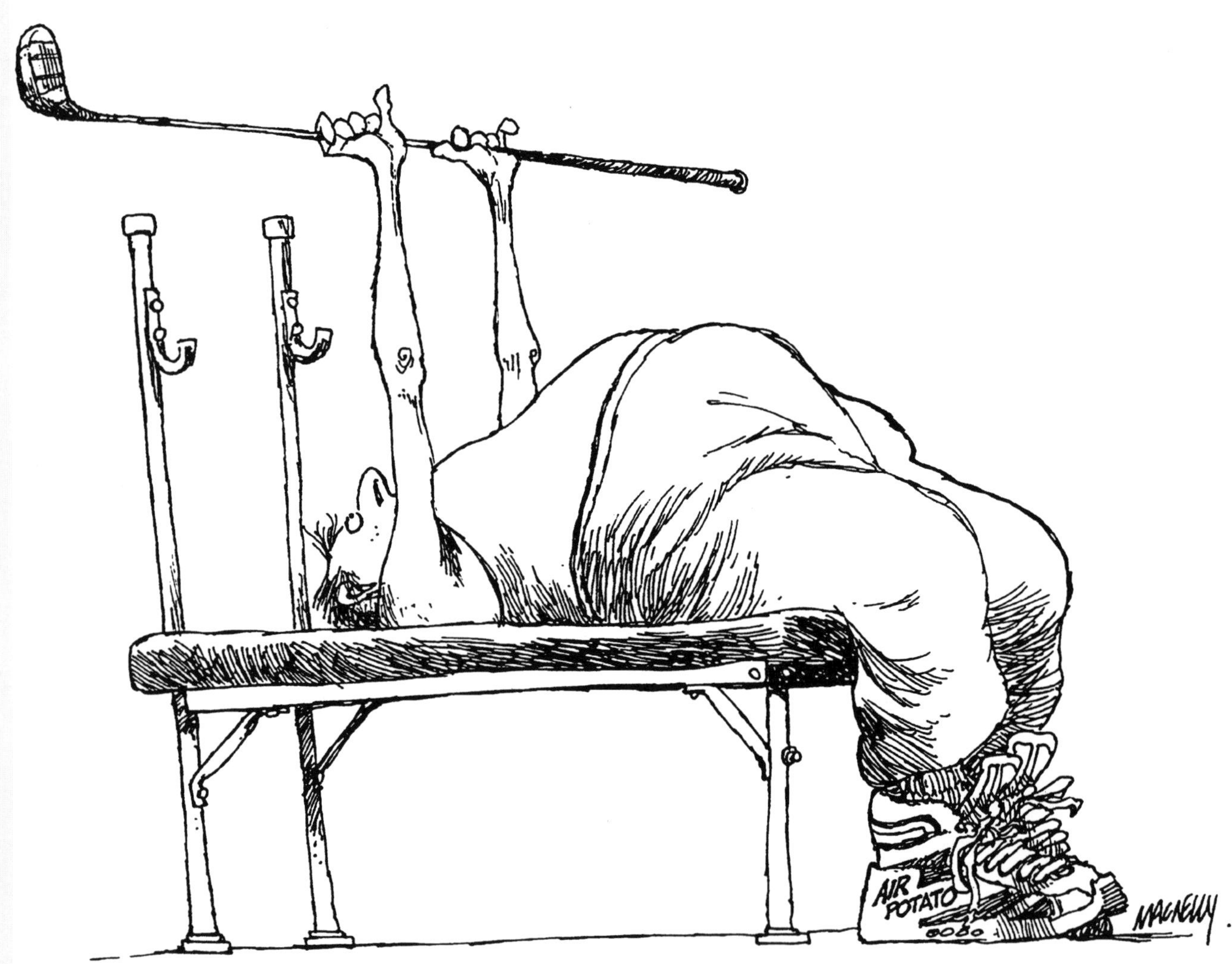
AIR POTATO
MACNELLY

ity insurance, so we headed back to the clubhouse for a beer, which, despite being a novice at golf, I was able to swallow with absolutely no trouble. The trick is to keep your head up.

Speaking of drinking beer, another sport that you'll want to get into as you get older is:

Fishing

Fishing is very similar to golf because in both sports you hold a long skinny thing in your hand while nothing happens for days at a time. The major advantage of fishing is that you are somewhat less likely to be killed by a golf ball; the disadvantage is that you have to become involved with bait, which consists of disgusting little creatures with a substance known to biologists as "bait glop" constantly oozing out of various orifices. The function of the bait is to be repulsive and thereby reduce the chances that a fish will bite it and wind up in your boat thrashing and gasping piteously and occasionally whispering, in a quiet but clear voice, "Please help me!" If you were to put a nice roast-beef sandwich on your hook, or an egg roll, you'd have fish coming from entirely different time zones to get caught. But not so with bait. "He's so dumb, he'd eat bait," is a common fish expression, which means that the only fish you're in any danger of catching are the total morons of the marine community, which is why, when you see them mounted on people's walls, they always have a vaguely vice-presidential expression. Not that I am naming names.

Skiing

If you're bored by slower activities such as fishing and golf, and you're looking for the kind of youth-recapturing, action-packed sport that offers you the opportunity to potentially knock down a tree with your face, you can't do better than skiing.

The key to a successful ski trip, of course, is planning, by which I mean *money*. For openers, you have to buy a special outfit that meets the strict requirements of the Ski Fashion Institute, namely:

1. It must cost as much as a medium wedding reception.
2. It must make you look like the Giant Radioactive Easter Bunny From Space.
3. It must be made of a mutant fiber with a name that sounds like the villain on a Saturday-morning cartoon show, such as "Gore-Tex," so as to provide the necessary resistance to moisture—which, trust me, will be gushing violently from all of your major armpits once you start lunging down the mountain.

You also have to buy ski goggles costing upwards of fifty dollars per eyeball that are specially designed not to not fog up under any circumstances except when you put them on, at which time they become approximately as transparent as the Los Angeles telephone directory, which is why veteran skiers recommend that you do not pull them down over your eyes until just before you make contact with the tree. And you'll need ski boots, which are made from melted bowling balls and which protect your feet by preventing your blood, which could contain dangerous germs, from traveling below your shins.

As for the actual skis, you should rent them, because of the feeling of confidence you get from reading the fine print on the lengthy legal document that the rental personnel make you sign, which is worded as follows: "The undersigned agrees that skiing is an INSANELY DANGEROUS ACTIVITY, and that the rental personnel were just sitting around minding their OWN BUSINESS when the undersigned, who agrees that he or she is a RAVING LOON, came BARGING IN UNINVITED, waving a LOADED REVOLVER and demanding that he or she be given some rental skis for the express purpose of suffering SERIOUS INJURY OR DEATH, leaving the rental personnel with NO CHOICE but to . . ." etc.

Okay! Now you're ready to "hit the slopes." Ski experts recommend that you start by taking a group lesson, because otherwise they would have to get real jobs. To start the lesson, your instructor, who is always a smiling 19-year-old named Chip, will take you to the top of the mountain and explain basic ski safety procedures until he feels that the cold has killed enough of your brain cells that you will cheerfully follow whatever lunatic command he gives you. Then he'll ski a short distance down the mountain, just to the point where it gets very steep, and swoosh to a graceful stop, making it look absurdly easy. It *is* absurdly easy for Chip, because underneath his outfit he's wearing an antigravity device. All the expert skiers wear them. You don't actually believe that "ski jumpers" can go off those ridiculously high ramps and just float to the ground unassisted without breaking into walnut-sized pieces, do you? Like Tinkerbell or something? Don't be a cretin.

After Chip stops, he turns to the group, his skis hovering as much as three inches above the snow, and orders the first student to copy what he did. This is the fun part. Woodland creatures often wake up from hibernation just to watch this part, because even they understand that the laws of physics, which are strictly enforced on ski slopes, do not permit a person to simply stop on the side of a snow-covered mountain if his feet are encased in bowling balls attached to what are essentially large pieces of Teflon. Nevertheless, the first student, obeying Chip's command, cautiously pushes himself forward, and then, making an unusual throat sound, passes Chip at Warp Speed and proceeds on into the woods, flailing his arms like a volunteer in a highly questionable nerve-gas experiment.

"That was good!" shouts Chip, grateful that he is wearing waterproof fibers inasmuch as he will be wetting his pants repeatedly during the course of the lesson. Then he turns to the rest of the group and says, "Next!"

The group's only rational response, of course, would be to lie down in the snow and demand a rescue helicopter. But these are not rational beings; these are ski students. And so, one by one, they, too, ski into the woods, then stagger out, sometimes with branches sticking out, antler-like, from their foreheads, and do it *again*. "Bend your knees this time!" Chip advises, knowing that this will actually make them go *faster*. He loves his work.

Eventually, of course, you get better at it. If you stick with your lessons, you'll become an "intermediate" skier, meaning you'll learn to fall *before* you reach the woods. That's where I am now, in stark contrast to my 9-year-old son, who has not yet studied gravity in school and therefore became an expert in a matter of hours. Watching him flash effortlessly down the slope, I experience, as a parent, feelings of both pride and hope: pride in his accomplishment, and hope that someday, somehow, he'll ski near enough to where I'm lying that I'll be able to trip him with my poles.

Important Final Word of Advice

Whatever sport you decide to become involved in, you should not plunge into it without first consulting with your physician. You can reach him on his cellular phone, in a dense group of trees, somewhere in the vicinity of the fourteenth hole.

CHAPTER TWELVE

Your Aging Parents: Getting Even With You for Teething

Back in the old days, most families were close-knit. Grown children and their parents continued to live together, under the same roof, sometimes in the same small, crowded room, year in and year out, until they died, frequently by strangulation.

No! Please excuse my cynical remark. Family life was wonderful back in those days, because there were no cars or televisions or microwave ovens or flush toilets or vaccines of any kind, plus there were wolves, so people really had to stick together. The family unit was organized according to what anthropologists call "The Beverly Hillbillies Principle," wherein the oldest member of the clan, played by Granny Clampett, had the most authority and received the most respect. In the evening the entire family would gather 'round and listen as this person handed down generations-old and oft-repeated stories of family history and lore:

GRANDMA: Tonight I think I'll hand down the oft-repeated story about how great-great-great-grandfather Lester bonked his head on the plow handle and then started dressing as a woman.

LITTLE BEATRICE: Oh shit, not again.

MAMA (whapping little Beatrice affectionately with the churn handle)**:** You hush up and listen, child, or someday you'll be unable to inflict this particular wad of lore on *your* grandchildren.

GRANDMA: Well, it seems that one day, great-great-great-grandfather Lester set out toward the avocado field, and he AWWWKKKK

LITTLE BEN: Look! Grandma's being dragged off by a wolf!

PAPA: Big one, too. That's at least as big as the one that got Grandpa.

MAMA: Well, Uncle Webster, I guess *you're* the eldest in the family now!

UNCLE WEBSTER: I guess so! So it seems that one day great-great-great-grandfather Lester set out toward the avocado field . . .

And so it went, from generation to generation. Things are very different now. Members of your modern nuclear family do not spend a quiet evening together unless they are trapped in an elevator. And your modern young people do not view their elders as sources of wisdom. Our generation certainly didn't. We got all our wisdom from songs written by currently deceased rock stars whose bloodstreams contained the annual narcotics outputs of entire Third World nations. We viewed our parents as bizarre alien life-forms whose sole biological function was to provide us with money so we could go off and live in the geographically opposite end of the country. We deeply resented any effort by our parents to meddle in our lives: we were furious when they urged us to become dentists or—God forbid—lawyers, instead of pursuing careers in fields that we considered to be truly fulfilling and meaningful, such as zither repair; we were outraged when they questioned our decisions to get married to people we had known for only a few days and had never seen in direct sunlight.

And of course we were *really* annoyed at our parents when, a few years later, we got divorced and enrolled in law school.

But eventually there came a reconciliation. As we grew older and more mature, as we started having children of our own, we began to see our parents in a new light, to realize that they were not, really, so different from us, and that only they could provide us with something very precious, something that had been missing from our lives: reliable babysitting.

So most of us are spending at least some time with our parents again. But this is not easy. For one thing, your parents naturally have trouble accepting the fact that you are a genuine grownup. You may view yourself as a mature, self-reliant person, but your mom views you as a person who once got lost in the department store and got so scared that you pooped your pants, which caused you to become so ashamed that you tried to hide in the Ladies' Lingerie Department, where the nice clerk was able to find you because she noticed the highly unromantic aroma emanating from somewhere inside a rack of negligees. Likewise your dad still has occasional back pain related to the time you fell asleep on the Jungle Cruise ride at Disneyland and he had to carry you for the rest of the day, covering an estimated 450 miles. It's because of many vivid memories like this that, on a fundamental level of your parents' psyche, you're always three years old. Everything that has happened to you since infancy—puberty, marriage, career, parenthood—is just a temporary phase you're going through. This is why, even though you're the president of a large corporation with a personal helicopter and authority over thousands of people and millions of dollars, your mom still, automatically, when you leave her house, zips your jacket all the way up to your chin.

But while your parents continue to view you as the child you were in 1952, you're starting to notice definite changes in them. Your mom, for example, seems to be much more into cleanliness. She's no longer accustomed to having small children around. It's been years since she has discovered a large, unexplained deposit of hardened Zoo-Roni on the sofa. She has nice, unspoiled furniture now, and it has stayed nice for a long time, and when you visit her, especially with your kids, she becomes edgy. She gets the vacuum cleaner out a lot, trying to look casual about it, but definitely not comfortable, trailing along after the kids with the motor running. She'll cook an elaborate meal, but she won't eat any of it. She'll claim she's not hungry, as she prowls around the dining room on Full Crumb Alert, attempting to conceal the Dust Buster under her apron. "Don't mind me, you just go ahead and eat," she'll say, sometimes from under the table. You wind up using as many as four plates per meal because your mom keeps snatching them up and washing them between bites.

Your dad seems different, too. You remember him as a competent, authoritative, worldly guy, usually very busy, and now he schedules his entire day around "Wheel of Fortune." He repeats things a lot and his shirts look way too big and he doesn't know who won the World Series and when you go somewhere together you try to make sure it's in your car because he drives way below the speed limit and hits the brakes hard for everything, including mailboxes. Also, he and your mom have both become abnormally attached to some kind of pet, a dog or a cat that they got after all the kids left home. They buy it sweaters and birthday presents and they have conversations with it that are often longer and more meaningful than the ones they have with you.

So, as much as you love your parents, your relationship with them tends to be uneasy. It can get a lot worse if your parents reach the point where they can no longer completely care for themselves, and the roles are reversed and the authority figure in the relationship suddenly becomes you. Little Poopy Pants. You become impatient with your parents, and you catch yourself talking to them exactly the way you talk to your children: a little too loud, a little too slow, a little too simple.

If you'll forgive me, I'm not going to make any jokes about this particular aspect of getting older. I'm going to depart from my smartass tone, just briefly, to make the one serious statement I plan to make in this whole book, which is this: No matter how out-of-it your parents may seem to you, they're still your parents. They're not your children. They're going through something you've never gone through, and although you can probably help them with it, you are damned sure not an expert on it. I learned this, very painfully, a few years ago. I'll end this chapter with something I wrote at the time, for whatever good it does. Then I promise to go back to being irresponsible and vicious.

Lost in America

My mother and I are driving through Hartford, Connecticut, on the way to a town called Essex. Neither of us has ever been to Essex, but we're both desperately hoping that my mother will want to live there.

She has been rootless for several months now, moving from son to son around the country, ever since she sold the house she had lived in for forty years, the house she raised us in, the house my father built. The house where he died, April 4, 1984. She would note the date each year on the calendar in the kitchen.

"Dave died, 1984," the note would say. "Come back, Dave."

The note for July 5, their anniversary, said: "Married Dave, 1942. Best thing that ever happened to me."

The house was too big for my mother to handle alone, and we all advised her to sell it. Finally she did, and she shipped all her furniture to Sunnyvale,

California, where my brother Phil lived. Her plan was to stay with him until she found a place of her own out there.

Only she hated Sunnyvale. At first this seemed almost funny, even to her. "All my worldly goods," she would say, marveling at it, "are in a warehouse in Sunnyvale, California, which I hate." She always had a wonderful sense of absurdity.

After a while it didn't seem so funny. My mother left Sunnyvale to live for a while with my brother Sam, in San Francisco, and then with me, in Florida; but she didn't want to stay with us. What she wanted was a home.

What she really wanted was her old house back.

With my father in it.

Of course, she knew she couldn't have that, but when she tried to think of what else she wanted, her mind would just lock up. She started to spend a lot of time watching soap operas. "You have to get on with your life," I would tell her, in this new, parental voice I was developing when I talked to her. Dutifully, she would turn off the TV and get out a map of the United States, which I bought her to help her think.

"Maybe Boulder would be nice," she would say, looking at Colorado. "I was born near Boulder."

"Mom," I would say in my new voice. "We've talked about Boulder fifty times, and you always end up saying you don't really want to live there."

Chastened, she would look back at her map, but I could tell she wasn't really seeing it.

"You have to be realistic," I would say. The voice of wisdom.

When she and I had driven each other just about crazy, she went back out to California, and repeated the process with both of my brothers. Then one night she called to ask, very apologetically, if I would go with her to look at Essex, Connecticut, which she had heard was nice. It was a bad time for me, but of course I said yes, because your mom is your mom. I met her in Hartford and rented a car.

I'm driving; my mother is looking out the window. "I came through Hartford last year with Frank and Mil, on the way to Maine," she says. Frank was my father's brother; he has just died. My mother loved to see him. He reminded her of my father.

"We were singing," my mother says. She starts to sing:

"I'm forever blowing bubbles
Pretty bubbles in the air."

I can tell she wants me to sing, too. I know the words; we sang this song when I was little.

"First they fly so high, nearly reach the sky
Then like my dreams, they fade and die."

But I don't sing. I am all business.

"I miss Frank," says my mother.

Essex turns out to be a beautiful little town, and we look at two nice, affordable apartments. But I can tell right away that my mother doesn't want to be there. She doesn't want to say so, after asking me to fly up from Miami, but we both know.

The next morning, in the motel coffee shop, we have a very tense breakfast.

"Look, Mom," I say, "you have to make some kind of decision." Sounding very reasonable.

She looks down at her map. She starts talking about Boulder again. This sets me off. I lecture her, tell her she's being childish. She's looking down at her map, gripping it. I drive her back to Hartford, neither of us saying much. I put her on a plane; she's going to Milwaukee, to visit my dad's sister, then back to my brother in Sunnyvale, California. Which she hates.

The truth is, I'm relieved that she's leaving.

"You can't help her," I tell myself, "until she decides what she wants." It is a sound position.

About a week later, my wife and I get a card from my mother.

"This is to say happy birthday this very special year," it says. "And to thank you for everything."

Our birthdays are weeks away.

About two days later, my brother Phil calls, crying, from a hospital. My mother has taken a massive overdose of Valium and alcohol. The doctors want permission to turn off the machines. They say there's no hope.

We talk about it, but there really isn't much to say. We give the permission.

It's the only logical choice.

The last thing I saw my mother do, just before she went down the tunnel to her plane, was turn and give me a big smile. It wasn't a smile of happiness; it was the same smile I give my son when he gets upset listening to the news, and I tell him don't worry, we're never going to have a nuclear war.

I can still see that smile anytime I want. Close my eyes, and there it is. A mom, trying to reassure her boy that everything's going to be okay.

CHAPTER THIRTEEN

How to Cope With . . . With . . . Wait, It's Right on the Tip of my Tongue . . .

As you get older, you've probably noticed that you tend to forget things. You'll be talking with somebody at a party, and you'll *know* that you know this person, but no matter how hard you try, you can't remember his or her name. This can be very embarrassing, especially if he or she turns out to be your spouse.

The first few times you commit this kind of *faux pas* (literally, "hors d'oeuvre"), you tend to gloss it over. But eventually you start to worry, to wonder if maybe you could be coming down with Whatshisname's Disease. Well, let me offer you these kind words of gentle reassurance: Don't be such a moron. The odds are that you're merely suffering from a very common middle-aged-person condition known technically to medical professionals as "having a brain cluttered up with useless crap left over from thirty years ago." For example, to this very day I can remember the words and tune to an incredibly irritating song sung long ago by Annette Funicello called "Pineapple Princess."

I hated this song when it came out. I still hate this song. I favor the death penalty for whoever wrote it. So naturally my brain has assigned it Priority One Status and placed it on a special E-Z Access Memory Circuit, which means that whenever I'm trying desperately to remember the name of the party hostess, or where I left my car keys, or how old I am, there's old Annette, yammering away in the forefront of my brain lobes.

And if I manage to mentally shove "Pineapple Princess" out of the way, my memory, always looking to help me out, alertly provides me with: a cigarette commercial jingle from 1959. Of *course!* The very thing I need! While I'm nearing panic at the shopping mall, racking my brain, trying to remember whether I had my son with me when I left home, it is very convenient that my brain is shrieking:

> *Every Parliament gives you . . .*
> *EXTRA MARGIN!*
> *The filter's recessed and made to stay*
> *A neat, clean quarter-inch away!*

Of course, your brain doesn't remember *everything* from your youth. Your brain shrewdly elects to remember only the truly *useless* things. This is why you can no longer do long division, but you remember the name of the kid who ate the worm in third grade (Charlie Ringwold). When I was in high school I read large wads of Shakespeare, but all I can quote is:

> *To be, or not to be, that is the question.*
> *Whether 'tis something, etc.*
> *And alas poor Yorick doesn't look so good either.*

Whereas I will go to my grave being able to recite flawlessly:

> *I'm a choice M&Ms peanut*
> *Fresh-roasted to a golden tan,*
> *Drenched in creamy milk chocolate,*
> *And covered with a thin candy shell.*

Is that pathetic, or what? And I'm not alone. If you surveyed a hundred typical middle-aged Americans, I bet you'd find that only two of them could tell you their blood types, but every last one would know the theme song from "The Beverly Hillbillies." Right? Even as you read these words, your brain, which cannot remember more than two words of your wedding vows, is cheerfully singing:

> *Come and listen to my story 'bout a man named Jed,*
> *A poor mountaineer barely kept his fam'ly fed . . .*

What can you do about this useless brain clutter? Unfortunately, the only known cure is a painful medical procedure wherein doctors drill a hole in your skull so the stored-up information can escape. If the patient is a middle-aged man, the doctors have to leap out of the way to avoid being hit by a high-pressure blast of numbers such as the batting averages for the entire Toronto Blue Jays lineup for 1979 and all the other vital pieces of information that guys tend to remember in lieu of trivia such as the full names of their children. The main drawback with this procedure is that if the doctors don't plug up your skull hole in time, you can lose your entire brain contents and wind up as a pathetic drooling cretin with no hope for meaningful employment outside of the state legislature.

So you're probably better off just learning how to cope with your memory problem. Sometimes you can cover it up by means of clever techniques such as the one suggested by famous etiquette expert Marjabelle Young Stewart in her book, *The New Etiquette*. She suggests that, in situations where people are having trouble remembering names, the ticket is for somebody to just step forward and introduce himself. As Marjabelle Young Stewart puts it:

> If you say "I'm Joshua Wright," the other person invariably responds with, "I'm Sally Jones," and the introductions are accomplished, at no loss of face to anyone.

There! It couldn't be simpler! Of course, some of you are saying, "But what if my name *isn't* Joshua Wright?" The answer is—and I'm sure I speak for Marjabelle Young Stewart as well as many other famous etiquette experts when I say this—tough shit. Because sometimes, for etiquette's sake, we have to tell "little white lies," such as when we tell a friend we're sorry that her cat died even though the truth is we would cheerfully have thrust the vicious little hairball into the trash compactor ourselves if we ever could have gotten our hands on it. It just so happens that, in social situations, it's easier for everybody involved if you agree to be "Joshua Wright" and the other person agrees to be "Sally Jones," unless of course the other person is the Pope, in which case you would refer to him as "Your Holiness Sally Jones."

Another memory aid that is recommended by leading memory experts is to use a "Mnemonic device." Let's say you want to remember that a certain business associate is named Ralph. Here's how a mnemonic device could help:

YOU: I don't know! I swear it!

LEADING MEMORY EXPERT: Perhaps if we increased the Mnemonic Device to *650 volts* . . .

YOU: RALPH!! HIS NAME IS RALPH!!!

So you see that there's no reason why you can't lead a normal and highly productive life despite the fact that your brain has turned into a festering dumpster of informational waste. In the next chapter we'll explore yet another exciting facet of the aging process, the name of which escapes me at the moment.

CHAPTER FOURTEEN

Aging Gracelessly: The Joys of Geezerhood

The central point of this final chapter is that—follow my logic carefully here—unless you die, you will continue to get older (It's insights like this that separate the professional book author from the person with a real job.)

Of course, we can't say exactly *how* old you're going to get without knowing certain scientific facts about you, such as your genetic makeup, your medical history, and your tendency to wager large sums of money with men named "Snake." But if you pick up any current actuarial table and look up the average life span for a person of your particular age, sex, and weight, you'll realize that, statistically, you have to squint like hell to read the numbers. This proves that you're *already* older than you think. And it's just going to get worse, because of a law of physics discovered by Albert Einstein, the brilliant physicist who not only invented the White Guy Afro haircut, but also discovered the Theory of Decade Relativity, which states: "Each decade goes exactly twice as fast as the decade before." This is why so much more seemed to happen in the sixties than in the seventies, and why your only truly enduring memory of the eighties, when all is said and done, will be Tammy Faye Bakker.

So now here we are in the nineties, which means that regardless of how many gallons of Oil of Olay you smear on yourself, you're going to start aging faster than a day-old bagel in a hot dumpster. You need to think about this. You need to decide how you're going to deal with the fact that you're becoming an Older Person.

One way is to deny it. This is the Peter Pan approach, and it has a powerful appeal. Remember when you were a kid, and you saw the legendary TV musical version of *Peter Pan,* and Peter was striding around the stage declaring, "I WON'T grow up!"? Remember what you thought, in your innocent, naïve, trusting childlike way? You thought: *"That's* not a little boy. That's obviously middle-aged actress Mary Martin making a fool out of herself."

So we see that although age-denial is appealing, it can generally make a person look ridiculous. Oh, some people try to get away with it, the best example being the Rolling Stones. As I write these words, the remaining non-deceased Stones, some of whom were born during the Hundred Years War, are still out there on tour, still rockin' and rollin' and putting on an electrifying act that reaches its exciting climax during "Satisfaction," when drummer Charlie Watts hurls his dentures into the crowd.

But is this really working, even for the Stones? To find out, I went to see them when they came to Miami. I'd seen them once before, when we were all a *lot* younger, back in the sixties. That was one of those classic sixties rock concerts, the kind where even the police dogs were stoned, and where the show would be scheduled to start at 9:00 P.M., but nothing would happen until maybe 11:30, when one of the promoters would get up on stage and announce that there would be a slight delay because the band was still at the airport in New Zealand.

The concert I saw in Miami was very different. For one thing, it started on time, probably because if it hadn't, one of the estimated 13,000 attorneys in the audience would have filed a lawsuit. Also it was a much older crowd, a lot of middle-aged soft-rockers like myself, stylishly decked out in our casual-wear beepers, taking bold swigs of Diet Pepsi. Sure, some of us were high, but it was not so much the high of ingesting hallucinogenic substances as the high of knowing that you had a babysitter on a weekday night.

But the most striking difference, for me, was in the Stones themselves. I had remembered them as awesome, larger-than-life, near-mystical figures, so I was filled with anticipation when, two decades later, I took my seat high in the upper deck of the Orange Bowl in Miami. My excitement mounted as the stadium darkened, and the giant speakers started playing dramatic buildup music, and clouds of smoke poured onto the stage. And then, when the crowd was about to explode with excitement, there was a blinding flash of light, and we heard the slashing, driving opening guitar riff of "Start Me Up," and suddenly, out of the darkness, came . . . these *little teeny* Rolling Stones. Maybe 14 inches tall. Talk about your comical letdowns. They looked like the Decadent Rock Band Action Figure Set from Toys "Я" Us.

I realize that this impression was partly due to the altitude of my seat, but it also had something to do with getting older. It's one thing when you're 19 and unemployed and mad at the world, and the Stones are these godlike outlaw rebels; but it's a whole different thing when you have a family and a mortgage and disability insurance, and the Stones have become essentially a corporation whose members are the same average age as the justices of the U.S. Supreme Court. I still enjoyed their music, but watching them strut around down there, smallish, aging men preening in their pants purchased at the Rock-'n'-Roll Superstar Extremely Tight Clothing Outlet, I couldn't help but think that they looked a little bit—this is difficult for me to write, about the Stones—silly.

Of course, I'd act silly too, if somebody was paying me millions of dollars. But nobody is, which is exactly my point. There's still a market demand for

Mick and the boys to act the way they acted twenty-five years ago. But there is zero demand for the rest of us to do this, and if we try, we look silly, and we don't get paid for it. So I'm recommending against trying to deny the aging process, unless you're a Certified Rolling Stone. If you're a Certified Public Accountant, you have to accept the fact that you're not going to suddenly transform yourself into the vibrant, youthful person you once were by getting a snake tattooed on your butt. You're going to transform yourself into a Certified Public Accountant with a snake on his butt, and you're going to feel stupid when you visit your proctologist.

So how *should* you cope with the fact that you're getting older? One approach, taken by millions of people, is to age gracefully, to enjoy the serenity that the golden years can bring, with their gifts of maturity and wisdom.

Or you can turn into a crusty old fart. This is definitely my plan. I figure that one of the major advantages of getting old is that you're allowed, even expected, to be eccentric and crotchety and just generally weird. Why not take advantage of this? Older people, if they play their cards right, can get away with almost anything.

The all-time example of this is, of course, Ronald Reagan. Here's a man who was twice elected to the most powerful position on Earth despite needing a TelePrompTer to correctly identify what year it was. But no matter how out-of-it he seemed to be, the people loved him. It was as if we were in an airplane, and the pilot got sick, so our kindly old Uncle Bob had to take the controls. We didn't *expect* as much from President Uncle Bob. We considered it a major triumph if he didn't crash.

Remember how he handled the Iran-contra Never-Ending Scandal from Hell? He went on national television, the President of the United States, and said it wasn't his fault, because *he was not aware, at the time, of what his foreign policy was.* In fact he had to appoint a Distinguished Commission to *find out* what his foreign policy was, and report back to him.

Now if he'd been a *young* President, some little Mister Competence right-on-top-of-everything jogging fact-spouting pissant whippersnapper like Jimmy Carter, his own *wife* would have called for his impeachment. But with Ronald Reagan, the voters, who also have never had the vaguest idea what our foreign policy was, were very forgiving. "Yeah," they said. "How's he supposed to remember *every darned time* he authorizes the sale of weapons to enemy nations? Why don't you medias leave him alone?!" And Ron went right on grinning and being popular and pretty much limiting his executive actions to signing stuff and having polyps removed until the end of his wildly successful term in office.

But an older person doesn't have to be the President to get away with things. I once knew a very sharp elderly lady who used to amuse herself, at parties, by trapping people's feet with her cane. She'd sidle up next to a victim, looking sweet and harmless and out-of-it, and she'd plant her cane tip right on the victim's shoe top and lean on it. The victim, not wishing to embarrass her, would say nothing while trying, subtly, to work his foot free, but as soon as he did, she'd shift over a little bit and harpoon him again. This would go on for fifteen minutes, the two of them moving around the room in a hilarious silent dance. It made for fine entertainment, and a younger person could never have pulled it off.

A certified geezer is also freer to express displeasure. Once I was walking in midtown Manhattan at rush hour, and I came to a massive traffic jam, horns honking everywhere, and right in the middle of a major intersection, the center of the whole mess, was a taxi driver honking at a very elderly man who was standing directly in front of the cab, blocking its path, and hitting it with his umbrella.

WHAP the umbrella would go, on the hood. Then, very slowly, the elderly man would raise it into the air, over his head, where it would waver for a second and then . . .

WHAP it would come down on the hood again. I stopped to watch, along with a large crowd of New Yorkers, who have an inbred genetic hatred of taxi drivers and who cheered louder with every WHAP. Nobody made any effort to move the elderly man out of the way. He was doing exactly what we'd all wanted to do a million times, but we couldn't because we'd get run over or arrested. I finally had to leave, but I like to think that the reason New York traffic is always so screwed up is that the elderly man is still in that intersection, whapping away.

So for my money, geezerhood is definitely the way to go. In fact, you might want to start practicing right now.

How to Geeze

Fashion Men should wear hats at all times, including in the bath. They should always have their top shirt button buttoned, but not necessarily all of the lower ones. For a casual summer look, men should wear a comfort-inducing, armpit-revealing sleeveless undershirt, Bermuda shorts, and—this is *very* important—black knee socks with wingtipped shoes. Women should wear a "house dress" large enough to cover an actual house. It should always be the same one, and it should be worn everywhere, including to the beach and funerals. Women should also give their hair a very natural and pleasing look by dying it exactly the same color as a radioactive carrot.

Dealing With Your Children and Grandchildren When they come to see you, spend the entire time complaining to them about how they never come to see you.

Driving The geezer car should be as large as possible. If a fighter jet can't land on it, you don't want to drive it. If necessary, you should get *two* cars and have them welded together. You should grip the wheel tightly enough so that you cannot be detached from it without a surgical procedure, and you should sit way down in the seat so that you're looking directly ahead at the speedometer. You should select a speed in advance—23 miles per hour is very popular—and drive this speed at all times, regardless of whether you're in your driveway or on the interstate. Always come to a full stop when you notice a Potentially Hazardous Road Condition such as an intersection or a store or a sidewalk or a tree. If you're planning to make a turn at any point during the trip, you should plan ahead by putting your blinker on as soon as you start the car. Never park the car without making a minimum of seventeen turns.

Announcing Your Intimate Medical Problems This is an excellent way to make new friends, especially in restaurants. "I can't eat that spicy food," you should announce to nobody in particular in a voice loud enough to direct military field operations. "I got this armpit cyst the size of a regulation softball, and that spicy food plays hell with it. One time I was eating chili and, bang, the damn thing *exploded,* and there was cyst contents flying *everywhere,* you had people diving under tables and . . . Hey! How come everybody's leaving? Can I have your egg roll?"

And so on. You get the idea. The main thing is, *don't be discreet.* We Boomers have never been a discreet generation, and I see no reason why we should fade quietly away just because we're getting old. Let's not go out with a whimper. Let's go out proudly whapping the umbrella of defiance on the taxicab hood of time. Let's remember the words of that rock song from the sixties, the anthem of our entire generation, the unforgettable song that spoke for all of us when it said . . . when it said . . . ummm . . .

Jeez, how the hell *did* that song go?

DAVE
BARRY'S
GREATEST
HITS

To
Beth & Gene

Contents

Why Humor is Funny

As a professional humorist, I often get letters from readers who are interested in the basic nature of humor. "What kind of a sick, perverted, disgusting person are you," these letters typically ask, "that you make jokes about setting fire to a goat?"

And that, of course, is the wonderful thing about humor. What may seem depressing or even tragic to one person may seem like an absolute scream to another person, especially if he has had between four and seven beers. But most people agree on what is funny, and most people like to be around a person with a great sense of humor, provided he also has reasonable hygiene habits. This is why people so often ask me: "Dave, I'd like to be popular, too. How can I get a sense of humor like yours, only with less of a dependence on jokes that are primarily excuses to use the word 'booger'?"

This is not an easy question. Ever since prehistoric times, wise men have tried to understand what exactly makes people laugh. That's why they were called wise men. All the other prehistoric people were out puncturing each other with spears, and the wise men were back in the cave saying: "How about: Here's my wife, please take her right now. No. How about: Would you like to take something? My wife is available. No. How about . . ."

Mankind didn't develop a logical system of humor until thousands of years later when Aristotle discovered, while shaving, the famous Humor Syllogism, which states, "If A is equal to B, and B is equal to C, then it would not be particularly amusing if the three of them went around poking each other in the eyes and going 'Nyuk nyuk nyuk.' At least *I* don't think it would be."

By the Elizabethan era, humor had become extremely popular. The works of Shakespeare, for example, are filled with scenes that English teachers always claim are real thigh-slappers, although when you actually decode them, it turns out they mostly depend on the use of the Elizabethan word for "booger." In America today, of course, our humor is much more sophisticated, ranging all the way from television shows featuring outtakes of situation comedies where the actors can't get the words right to television shows featuring outtakes of *commercials* where the actors can't get the words right. Also we have Woody Allen, whose humor has become so sophisticated that nobody gets it anymore except Mia Farrow. All those who think Mia Farrow should go back to making movies where the devil gets her pregnant and Woody Allen should go back to dressing up as a human sperm, please raise your hands. Thank you.

If you want to develop a sense of humor of your own, you need to learn some jokes. Notice I do not say "puns." Puns are little "plays on words" that a certain breed of person loves to spring on you and then look at you in a certain self-satisfied way to indicate that he thinks that *you* must think that he is by far the cleverest person on Earth now that Benjamin Franklin is dead, when in fact what you are thinking is that if this person ever ends up in a lifeboat, the other passengers will hurl him overboard by the end of the first day even if they have plenty of food and water.

So what you want is *real* jokes. The best source for these is the authoritative *Encyclopedia Britannica* article entitled "Humor and Wit," which is in volume 99 (Humidity—Ivory Coast). This is where Carson gets all his material. It's a regular treasure trove of fun. Here's a real corker from right at the beginning:

"A masochist is a person who likes a cold shower in the morning, so he takes a hot one."

Whoooeee! That is one authoritative joke! Tell that one at a dull party, and just watch as the other guests suddenly come to life and remember important dental appointments!

But it is not enough merely to know a lot of great jokes. You also have to be able to tell them properly. Here are some tips:

1. When you tell vicious racist jokes, you should first announce that you were a liberal back when it was legal to be one.

2. Men have a certain body part that women do not have, and men always think jokes about it are a stone riot, but if you tell such a joke to a woman, she will look at you as though you are a Baggie filled with mouse remains. I don't know why this is, but it never fails. So you want to avoid this particular type of joke in coeducational social settings such as Windsor Castle.

3. If, after you tell a joke, somebody attempts to tell you one back, you should keep assuring him that you haven't heard it, and then, when he gets to the punchline, no matter how funny it is, you should react as though he just told you the relative humidity and say: "Yeah, I heard that."

4. Never attend a large dinner party with my former mother-in-law, because she will shout across the table at you: "Tell the one about the man who's seeking the truth and he finally gets all the way to Tibet and the wise man tells him that a wet bird doesn't fly at night," and then she'll *insist* that you tell it, and then she'll tell you you told it wrong, and you might have to kill her with a fork.

Snews

Readers are sometimes critical of me because just about everything I write about is an irresponsible lie. But now I'm going to write a column in which everything is true. See how you like it.

Our first true item comes from a news release from the J I Case company. For the benefit of those of you who have real jobs and are not involved in the news business, I should first explain that a *news release* is an article that has been typed up by a public-relations professional hired by a client who wants to get certain information published, which is then mailed out to several thousand newspapers, almost all of which throw it away without reading it. If you ever commit a really horrible crime and you want to keep it out of the papers, you should have a public-relations professional issue a news release about it.

You ask: "Wouldn't it be more efficient if the public-relations professionals simply threw the releases away themselves?" Frankly, that is the kind of ignorant question that makes us journalists want to forget about trying to inform the public and instead just sit around awarding journalism prizes to each other. But I'll tell you the answer: Because this is America. Because two hundred years ago, a band of brave men got extremely cold at Valley Forge so that the press would have the freedom to throw away its own releases without prior censorship, that's why.

Anyway, this release from the J I Case company opens with this statement: "J I Case and Burlington, Iowa, the loader/backhoe capital of the world, today jointly celebrated the production of the 175,000th Case loader/backhoe." The release said they had a nice ceremony attended by the mayor of Burlington, a person named Wayne W. Hogberg, so I called him up to confirm the story. He works at the post office.

"Does Burlington really call itself the loader/backhoe capital of the world?" I asked. Newsmen are paid to ask the hard questions. "Oh yes," replied Mayor Hogberg. "We definitely lay claim to that. We use it whenever we have the opportunity. As a mayor I sort of rub it in with any other mayors I have occasion to meet." I bet that really steams the other mayors, don't you? I bet they are consumed with jealousy, when mayors get together.

Our second completely true news item was sent to me by Mr. H. Boyce Connell Jr. of Atlanta, Georgia, where he is involved in a law firm. One thing I like about the South is, folks there care about tradition. If somebody gets handed a name like "H. Boyce," he hangs on to it, puts it on his legal stationery, even passes it on to his son, rather than do what a lesser person would do, such as get it changed or kill himself.

What H. Boyce sent was a copy of a decision handed down by the Georgia Court of Appeals in the case of Apostol-Athanasiou vs. White. It seems the former had hired the latter to mow her lawn. What happened next, in the words of the court, is that "White allegedly slipped on some dog feces concealed in the tall grass, and his left foot was severely cut as it slid under the lawnmower." I am not going to tell you how this case came out, because you'll want to find out for yourself in the event that it is released as a major motion picture, but I will say, by way of a hint, that in the court's opinion "neither party had actual knowledge of the specific deposit of dog feces on which White apparently slipped."

Our next item comes from a release sent out by the Vodka Information Bureau, in New York City. The Vodka Information Bureau has learned that a whopping 42 percent of the women surveyed consider themselves "primary decision makers" in deciding what brand of vodka to buy. This raises in my mind, as I am sure it does in yours, a number of questions, primarily: What, exactly, do we mean by the verb "to whop"? So I looked it up in the *Oxford English Dictionary,* and there I found—remember, this is the column where we are not making things up—these helpful examples:

- "In less time than you can think whop comes a big black thing down, as big as the stone of a cheese-press."
- "Mother would whop me if I came home without the basket."

So I called my mother, who said, and I quote, "I always make the vodka-buying decision as follows: the largest bottle for the smallest amount of money." So I called the Vodka Information Bureau and told them what my mother said, and they said, sure, you can buy the cheapest vodka if you don't mind getting a lot of impurities, but if you want a nice clean vodka, you want a brand such as is manufactured by the company that sponsors the Vodka Information Bureau.

Finally, and sadly, we have received word of the death, at age 85, of Sir Seewoosagur Ramgoolam, who of course was governor general of the island nation of Mauritius from 1968 to 1982. Mauritius has an area of 720 square miles and was once the home of the dodo bird, which is now extinct. It is hard, at a time of such tragedy—I refer to the demise of Sir Seewoosagur Ramgoolam—to find words to express our feelings, but I think that I speak for all of us when I say that a cheese-press is "an apparatus for pressing the curds in cheese-making."

Public-Spirited Citizens Such as You

I love jokes. The worse the better. Among the happiest moments of my life were those at summer camp when I was 11, lying in my bunk at night just after the counselor, Mr. Newton, had gone off to play cards with the other counselors, which meant that Eugene was going to tell the joke whose punchline is: "Ding dong, dammit! Ding DONG!" Maybe you know this joke. It involves marital infidelity and a closet. By the second week of camp, Eugene had developed a half-hour version, and campers were creeping over from the other cabins to hear it.

So there we'd all be, listening in the dark with lunatic grins of anticipation on our faces, barely able to restrain ourselves, until finally Eugene would reach the punchline. "Ding dong, dammit," he'd say, and we'd start vibrating like tuning forks, and then Eugene would say "Ding DONG," and we'd dive down into the depths of our sleeping bags, out of control, howling and snorting, thinking nobody could hear us, although of course in the peaceful stillness of the forest night we must have sounded like water buffalo giving birth over a public-address system.

Mr. Newton would slam his cards down and come storming over, and he'd tell us that he was really sick of this, night after night, and if he heard one more sound out of us we'd have to clean the latrine the next day. This was a serious threat, because it was the kind of highly odorous summer-camp latrine where you wondered how it could possibly be so disgusting when nobody ever had the courage to use it. Evidently somewhere along the line it had reached Critical Latrine Mass and developed a life-style of its own.

After making this threat, Mr. Newton would stalk off back to his cards, and there would be silence for maybe a minute, and then there would be this tiny whisper from Eugene's direction, so faint that only a trained ear could discern it:

"Ding," said the whisper, "DONG."

And of course this resulted in a situation where, never mind having to clean the latrine, never mind that Mr. Newton was now standing in the middle of the cabin clutching a weighty flashlight and threatening to break everybody's heads, the only thing any of us could think about was whether we would ever be able to draw breath again.

And so we had a terrific summer, and all because of one idiot joke, which, although I would not tell it in public except under the influence of sodium pentothal, still does a better job of cheering me up than any major religion. I'd like to meet the person who made that joke up, but of course that's always one of the big mysteries about jokes: Nobody knows who makes them up. They're just *there,* floating around and lowering the productivity of offices and factories everywhere. And they've been there throughout human history. Archaeologists found this joke in an Egyptian tomb:

HE: Did you hear about the Sumerian?
SHE: No. What about the Sumerian?
HE: He was extremely stupid. Ha ha!
SHE: No, I had not heard about him.

This, of course, is a primitive version of the modern "ethnic joke," which still carries the same basic message, although it has become much more sophisticated over the years thanks to the introduction of such innovations as the light bulb. But who introduced them?

Other mysteries about jokes are: How come you can remember extremely complex jokes involving a minister, a priest, and a rabbi, but you can't remember your mother's birthday? How do jokes travel so fast, and so far? (The Apollo 7 astronauts found traces of a joke on the moon!) Also: Does Queen Elizabeth ever hear any jokes? Who tells them to her? What about the pope?

To answer these and other questions, I think we should set up a research project wherein we scientifically track the progress of a specified joke, similar to the way the flight patterns of birds are tracked by scientists called ornithologists, who attach metal wires and rubber bands to the birds' beaks and make them come back every week for appointments. No! Hold it! My mistake! I'm thinking of "orthodontists." What ornithologists do is attach bands of metal to a bird's leg, then toss it gently off the roof of a tall building and watch it splat into the pavement below at upwards of 100 miles an hour. People try to tell the ornithologists that the metal bands they're using are too heavy, but they just laugh. Recently they dropped a common wood warbler to which they had attached a 1983 Chevette.

But the theory is sound, and I was thinking maybe we could come up with some kind of similar system for tracking a joke. What I propose to do is inject a brand-new joke into the population at certain known places and times. This joke will have a distinguishing characteristic, so that as it spreads around the country, public-spirited citizens such as yourself can act as spotters. As soon as you hear this joke, I want you to report it via postal card to: The Joke Tracking Center, P.O. Box 011509, Miami, FL 33101.

Please include a summary of the joke, where and when you heard it, who told it to you, and any other helpful background information such as whether you were drinking liquor right out of the bottle at the time.

Obviously, I cannot reveal the joke here, but its distinguishing characteristic is that it answers the question: "Why is Walter Mondale nicknamed

'Fritz'?" Everybody got that? I have tested this joke on a carefully selected panel of lowlifes, all sworn to secrecy, and they assure me that it is in very poor taste and should spread like wildfire.

So let's all Simonize our watches and keep a sharp ear out for this joke. I'm very serious about this. Trained personnel are standing by now at the Joke Tracking Center. So report those sightings! Together, we have a chance here to obtain scientific findings of great significance, and possibly a large federal grant. Remember: This chain has never been broken.

The Snake

The way I picture it, adulthood is a big, sleek jungle snake, swimming just around the bend in the River of Life. It swallows you subtly, an inch at a time, so you barely notice the signs: You start reading the labels on things *before* you eat them, rather than to pass the time *while* you eat them; you find yourself listening to talk radio because the hit songs they play on the rock stations (can this really be *you,* thinking this?) all begin to *sound the same.* Before you know it, you have monogrammed towels in your bathroom, and all your furniture is nice. And suddenly you realize it's too late, that you'd rather sit around on your furniture and talk about the warning signs of colon cancer with other grown-ups than, for example, find out what happens when you set one of those plastic milk jugs on fire. And if your *kid* sets a milk jug on fire, you yell at him, "Somebody could get *hurt,*" and really mean it, from inside the snake.

I mention all this to explain how I came to buy, at age 38, an electric guitar. I had one once before, from 1965 through 1969 when I was in college. It was a Fender Jazzmaster, and I played lead guitar in a band called The Federal Duck, which is the kind of name that was popular in the sixties as a result of controlled substances being in widespread use. Back then, there were no restrictions, in terms of talent, on who could make an album, so we made one, and it sounds like a group of people who have been given powerful but unfamiliar instruments as a therapy for a degenerative nerve disease.

We mainly played songs like "Gloria," which was great for sixties bands, because it had only three chords; it had a solo that was so simple it could be learned in minutes, even by a nonmusical person or an advanced fish; and it had great lyrics.

My band career ended late in my senior year when John Cooper and I threw my amplifier out the dormitory window. We did not act in haste. First we checked to make sure the amplifier would fit through the frame, using the belt from my bathrobe to measure, then we picked up the amplifier and backed up to my bedroom door. Then we rushed forward shouting "The WHO! The WHO!" and we launched my amplifier perfectly, as though we had been doing it all our lives, clean through the window and down onto the sidewalk, where a small but appreciative crowd had gathered. I would like to be able to say that this was a symbolic act, an effort on my part to break cleanly away from one stage in my life and move on to another, but the truth is, Cooper and I really just wanted to find out what it would sound like. It sounded OK.

Unlike The Who, I couldn't afford a new amplifier, and playing an unamplified electric guitar is like strumming on a picnic table, so I sold my Jazzmaster and got a cheap acoustic guitar, which I diddled around on for 16 years. It was fine for "Kum By Yah," but ill-suited for "My Baby Does the Hanky Panky." So there's been this void in my life, which I've tried to fill by having a career, but I see now I was kidding myself.

So recently, *Ms* magazine sent me a check for $800 for an article I wrote about sex. This seemed like such a bizarre way to get hold of $800 that I figured I should do something special with it, so I thought about it, and what came to mind is—this is the scary part of the story, coming up now—*a new sofa.* Our primary living-room sofa looks like a buffalo that has been dead for some time, and I thought: "Maybe we should get a nicer sofa." Which is when I felt the snake of adulthood slithering around my leg.

So I said to my wife: "I am going to take this money and buy an electric guitar." And she said—I believe I married her in anticipation of this moment —"Fine."

I have never been so happy. My amplifier has a knob called overdrive, which, if you turn it all the way up to 10, makes it so that all you have to do is touch a string to make a noise that would destroy a greenhouse. My wife and son and dog spend more time back in the bedroom these days. Out in the living room, I put the Paul Butterfield Blues Band on the stereo, and when they do "Got My Mojo Workin'," I play the guitar solo at the same time Mike Bloomfield does. I am not as accurate as he is in terms of hitting the desired notes, but you can hear me better because I have "overdrive."

I bet I know what you're thinking: You're thinking my electric guitar is a Midlife Crisis Object that I bought in the Midlife Crisis Store filled with middle-aged guys who wear jogging shoes and claim they love Bruce Springsteen but really think he's merely adequate. And you may be right. I don't care if you are. To me, my guitar is a wonderful thing. It's a Gibson, with the classic old electric-guitar shape. It looks like a modernistic oar, which you could use, in a pinch, to row against the current in the River of Life, or at least stay even with it for a while.

Ye Olde Humor Columne

We need to do something about this national tendency to try to make new things look like they are old.

First off, we should enact an "e" tax. Government agents would roam the country looking for stores whose names contained any word that ended in an unnecessary "e," such as "shoppe" or "olde," and the owners of these stores would be taxed at a flat rate of $50,000 per year per "e." We should also consider an additional $50,000 "ye" tax, so that the owner of a store called "Ye Olde Shoppe" would have to fork over $150,000 a year. In extreme cases, such as "Ye Olde Barne Shoppe," the owner would simply be taken outside and shot.

We also need some kind of law about the number of inappropriate objects you can hang on walls in restaurants. I am especially concerned here about the restaurants that have sprung up in shopping complexes everywhere to provide young urban professionals with a place to go for margaritas and potato skins. You know the restaurants I mean: they always have names like Flanagan's, Hanrahan's, O'Toole's, or O'Reilley's, as if the owner were a genial red-faced Irish bartender, when in fact it is probably 14 absentee proctologists in need of tax shelter.

You have probably noticed that inevitably the walls in these places are covered with objects we do not ordinarily attach to walls, such as barber poles, traffic lights, washboards, street signs, and farm implements. This decor scheme is presumably intended to create an atmosphere of relaxed old-fashioned funkiness, but in fact it creates an atmosphere of great weirdness. It is as if a young urban professional with telekinetic powers, the kind Sissy Spacek exhibited in the movie *Carrie,* got really tanked up on margaritas one night and decided to embed an entire flea market in the wall.

I think it's too much. I think we need to pass a

law stating that the only objects that may be hung on restaurant walls are those that God intended to be hung on restaurant walls, such as pictures, mirrors, and the heads of deceased animals. Any restaurant caught violating this law would have to get rid of its phony Irish-bartender name and adopt a name that clearly reflected its actual ownership. ("Say, let's go get some potato skins at Fourteen Absentee Proctologists in Need of Tax Shelter.")

And I suppose it goes without saying that anybody caught manufacturing "collectible" plates, mugs, or figurines of any kind should be shipped directly to Devil's Island.

Now I know what you're thinking. You're thinking: "Dave, I hear what you're saying, but wouldn't laws such as these constitute unwarranted government interference in the private sector?"

The answer is: Yes, they would. But unwarranted government interference in the private sector is a small price to pay if it draws the government away from its efforts to revitalize decaying urban areas. The government inevitably tries to do this by installing 60 billion new red bricks and several dozen vaguely old-fashioned streetlights in an effort to create a look I would call "Sort of Colonial or Something."

The government did this to a town right near where I used to live, West Chester, Pennsylvania. This is a nice little old town, with a lot of nice little old houses, but about 10 years ago some of the downtown merchants started getting really upset because they were losing business to the "shopping malls," a phrase the merchants always say in the same tone of voice you might use to say "Nazi Germany." Now, as a consumer, I would argue that the reason most of us were going to the shopping malls was that the downtown stores tended to have window displays that had not been changed since the Truman administration, featuring crepe paper faded to the color of old oatmeal, accented by the occasional dead insect. And the actual merchandise in these stores was not the kind you would go out of your way to purchase or even accept as gifts. We are talking, for example, about clothing so dowdy that it could not be used even to clean up after a pet.

What I am saying is that the problem with the downtown West Chester stores, from this consumer's point of view, was that they didn't have much that anybody would want to buy. From the merchants' point of view, however, the problem was that the entire downtown needed to be Revitalized, and they nagged the local government for years until finally it applied for a federal grant of God knows how many million dollars, which was used to rip up the streets for several years, so as to discourage the few remaining West Chester shoppers. When they finally got it all together again, the new revitalized West Chester consisted of mostly the same old stores, only in front of them were (surprise!) red brick sidewalks garnished with vaguely old-fashioned streetlights. The whole effect was definitely Sort Of Colonial or Something, and some shoppers even stopped by to take a look at it on their way to the mall.

I gather this process has been repeated in a great many towns around the country, and it seems to me that it's a tremendous waste of federal time and effort that could otherwise be spent getting rid of the extra "e." I urge those of you who agree with me to write letters to your congresspersons, unless you use that stationery with the "old-fashioned" ragged edges, in which case I urge you to go to your local Flanagan's and impale yourself on one of the farm implements.

A Boy and His Hobby

Recently, I began to feel this void in my life, even after meals, and I said to myself: "Dave, all you do with your spare time is sit around and drink beer. You need a hobby." So I got a hobby. I make beer.

I never could get into the traditional hobbies, like religion or stamp collecting. I mean, the way you collect stamps is: Every week or so the Postal Service dreams up a new stamp to mark National Peat Bog Awareness Month, or whatever, and you rush down and clog the Post Office lines to buy a batch of these stamps, but instead of putting them to a useful purpose such as mailing toxic spiders to the Publisher's Clearing House, you take them home and just sort of *have* them. Am I right? Have I left any moments of drama out of this action sequence? And then the *biggest* thrill, as I understand it, the real *payoff,* comes when you get lucky and collect a stamp on which the Postal Service has made a *mistake,* such as instead of "Peat Bog" it prints "Beat Pog," which causes stamp collectors to just about wet their polyester pants, right?

So for many years I had no hobby. When I would fill out questionnaires and they would ask what my hobbies were, I would put "narcotics," which was of course a totally false humorous joke. And then one day my editor took me to a store where they sell beer-making equipment. Other writers, they have editors who inspire them to new heights of literary achievement, but the two major contributions my editor has made to my artistic development are (1) teaching me to juggle and (2) taking me to his beer-making store where a person named Craig gave me free samples until he could get hold of my Visa card.

But I'm glad I got into beer-making, because the beer sold here in the United States is sweet and watery and lacking in taste and overcarbonated and just generally the lamest, wimpiest beer in the entire known world. All the other nations are drinking Ray

Charles beer, and we are drinking Barry Manilow. This is why American TV beer commercials are so ludicrously masculine. It's a classic case of overcompensation. You may have seen, for example, the Budweiser or Miller commercial where some big hairy men are standing around on the side of a river when a barge breaks loose and starts drifting out of control. Now *real* men, men who drink *real* beer, would have enough confidence in their own masculinity to say: "Don't worry; it's probably insured."

But the men in the commercial feel this compulsion to go racing off on a tugboat and capture the barge with big hairy ropes, after which they make excited masculine hand gestures at each other to indicate they have done a task requiring absolute *gallons* of testosterone. Then they go to a bar where they drink Miller or Budweiser and continue to reassure themselves that they are truly a collection of major stud horses, which is why you don't see any women around. The women have grown weary of listening to the men say: "Hey! We sure rescued THAT barge, didn't we?!" And: "You think it's easy, to rescue a barge? Well, it's NOT!" and, much later at night: "Hey! Let's go let the barge loose again!" So the women have all gone off in search of men who make their own beer.

Some of you may be reluctant to make your own beer because you've heard stories to the effect that it's difficult to make, or it's illegal, or it makes you go blind. Let me assure you that these are falsehoods, especially the part about making you go bleof nisdc dsdf,sdfkQ$$%"%.

Ha ha! Just a little tasteless humor there, designed to elicit angry letters from liberals. The truth is, homemade beer is perfectly safe, unless the bottle explodes. We'll have more on that if space permits. Also it's completely legal to make beer at home. In fact, as I read the current federal tax laws—I use a strobe light—if you make your own beer, you can take a tax credit of up to $4,000, provided you claim you spent it on insulation!

And it's very easy to make your own beer: You just mix your ingredients and stride briskly away. (You may of course vary this recipe to suit your own personal taste.) Your two main ingredients are (1) a can of beer ingredients that you get from Craig or an equivalent person, and (2) yeast. Yeast is a wonderful little plant or animal that, despite the fact that it has only one cell, has figured out how to convert sugar to alcohol. This was a far greater accomplishment than anything we can attribute to giant complex multicelled organisms such as, for example, the Secretary of Transportation.

After the little yeasts are done converting your ingredients into beer, they die horrible deaths by the millions. You shouldn't feel bad about this. Bear in mind this is *yeast* we're talking about, and there's plenty more available, out on the enormous yeast ranches of the Southwest. For now, your job is to siphon your beer into bottles. This is the tricky part, because what can happen is the phone rings and you get involved in a lengthy conversation during which your son, who is 4½, gets hold of the hose and spews premature beer, called "wort," all over the kitchen and himself, and you become the target of an investigation by child welfare authorities because yours is the only child who comes to preschool smelling like a fraternity carpet.

But that's the only real drawback I have found, and the beer tastes delicious, except of course on those rare occasions when it explodes. Which leads us to another advantage: If you make your own beer, you no longer need to worry about running out if we have a nuclear war of sufficient severity to close the commercial breweries.

Daze of Wine and Roses

I have never gotten into wine. I'm a beer man. What I like about beer is you basically just drink it, then you order another one. You don't sniff at it, or hold it up to the light and slosh it around, and above all you don't drone on and on about it, the way people do with wine. Your beer drinker tends to be a straightforward, decent, friendly, down-to-earth person who enjoys talking about the importance of relief pitching, whereas your serious wine fancier tends to be an insufferable snot.

I realize I am generalizing here, but, as is often the case when I generalize, I don't care.

Nevertheless, I decided recently to try to learn more about the wine community. Specifically, I engaged the services of a rental tuxedo and attended the Grand Finale of the First Annual French Wine Sommelier Contest in America, which was held at the famous Waldorf-Astoria hotel in New York. For the benefit of those of you with plastic slipcovers, I should explain that a "sommelier" is a wine steward, the dignified person who comes up to you at expensive restaurants, hands you the wine list, and says "Excellent choice, sir," when you point to French writing that, translated, says "Sales Tax Included."

Several hundred wine-oriented people were on hand for the sommelier competition. First we mingled and drank champagne, then we sat down to eat dinner and watch the competition. I found it immensely entertaining, especially after the champagne, because for one thing many of the speakers were actual French persons who spoke with comical accents, which I suspect they practiced in their hotel rooms ("Zees epeetomizes zee hrole av zee sommelier sroo-out ees-tory . . . ," etc.) Also we in the audience got to drink just gallons of wine. At least I did. My policy with wine is very similar to my policy with beer, which is just pretty much drink it and look around for more. The people at my table, on the other hand, leaned more toward the slosh-and-sniff approach, where you don't so much *drink* the wine as you frown and then make a thoughtful remark about it such as you might make about a job applicant ("I find it ambitious, but somewhat strident." Or: "It's lucid, yes, but almost Episcopalian in its predictability.") As it happened, I was sitting next to a French person named Mary, and I asked her if people in France carry on this way about wine. "No," she said, "they just drink it. They're more used to it."

There were 12 sommeliers from around the country in the contest; they got there by winning regional competitions, and earlier in the day they had taken a written exam with questions like: "Which of the following appellations belong to the Savoie region? (a) Crepy; (b) Seyssel; (c) Arbois; (d) Etoile; (e) Ripple." (I'm just kidding about the Ripple, of course. The Savoie region would not use Ripple as an insecticide.)

The first event of the evening competition was a blind tasting, where the sommeliers had to identify a mystery wine. We in the audience got to try it, too. It was a wine that I would describe as yellow in color, and everybody at my table agreed it was awful. "Much too woody," said one person. "Heavily oxidized," said another. "Bat urine," I offered. The others felt this was a tad harsh. I was the only one who finished my glass.

Next we got a nonmystery wine, red in color, with a French name, and I thought it was swell, gulped it right down, but one of the wine writers at my table got upset because it was a 1979, and the program said we were supposed to get a 1978. If you can imagine. So we got some 1978, and it was swell, too. "They're both credible," said the wine writer, "but there's a great difference in character." I was the only one who laughed, although I think Mary sort of wanted to.

The highlight of the evening was the Harmony of Wine and Food event, where the sommelier contestants were given a menu where the actual nature of the food was disguised via French words ("Crochets sur le Pont en Voiture," etc.), and they had to select a wine for each of the five courses. This is where a sommelier has to be really good, because if he is going to talk an actual paying customer into spending as much money on wine for one meal as it would cost to purchase a half-dozen state legislators for a year, he has to say something more than, "A lotta people like this here chardonnay."

Well, these sommeliers were good. They were *into* the Harmony of Wine and Food, and they expressed firm views. They would say things like: "I felt the (name of French wine) would have the richness to deal with the foie gras," or "My feeling about Roquefort is that. . . ." I thought it was fabulous entertainment, and at least two people at my table asked how I came to be invited.

Anyway, as the Harmony event dragged on, a major issue developed concerning the salad. The salad was Lamb's-Lettuce with—you are going to be shocked when I tell you this—Walnut Vinaigrette. A lot of people in the audience felt that this was a major screw-up, or "gaffe," on the part of the contest organizers, because of course vinaigrette is just going to fight any wine you try to marry it with. "I strongly disagree with the salad dressing," is how one wine writer at my table put it, and I could tell she meant it.

So the contestants were all really battling the vinaigrette problem, and you could just feel a current of unrest in the room. Things finally came to a head, or "tete," when contestant Mark Hightower came right out and said that if the rules hadn't prevented him, he wouldn't have chosen any wine at all with the salad. "Ideally," he said, "I would have liked to have recommended an Evian mineral water." Well, the room just erupted in spontaneous applause, very similar to what you hear at Democratic Party dinners when somebody mentions the Poor.

Anyway, the winning sommelier, who gets a trip to Paris, was Joshua Wesson, who works at a restaurant named Huberts in New York. I knew he'd win, because he began his Harmony of Wine and Food presentation by saying: "Whenever I see oysters on a menu, I am reminded of a quote. . . ." Nobody's ever going to try buying a moderately priced wine from a man who is reminded of a quote by oysters.

It turns out however, that Wesson is actually an OK guy who just happens to have a God-given ability to lay it on with a trowel and get along with the French. I talked to him briefly afterwards, and he didn't seem to take himself too seriously at all. I realize many people think I make things up, so let me assure you ahead of time that this is the actual, complete transcript of the interview:

ME: So. What do you think?

WESSON: I feel good. My arm felt good, my curve ball was popping. I felt I could help the ball team.

ME: What about the vinaigrette?

WESSON: It was definitely the turning point. One can look at vinaigrette from many angles. It's like electricity.

I swear that's what he said, and furthermore at the time it made a lot of sense.

Randomly Amongst the Blobs

Without my eyeglasses, I have a great deal of trouble distinguishing between house fires and beer signs. I wear the kind of glasses that they never show in those eyeglasses advertisements where the lenses are obviously fake because they don't distort the attractive model's face at all. My lenses make the entire middle of my head appear smaller. When professional photographers take my picture, they always suggest that I take my glasses off, because otherwise the picture shows this head with the normal top and bottom, but in the middle there's this little perfect miniature human head, maybe the size of an orange, staring out from behind my glasses.

People like photographers and dentists and barbers are always asking me to take my glasses off, and I hate it because it makes me stupid and paranoid. I worry that the dentist and his aides are creeping up on me with acetylene torches, or have sneaked out of the room and left me chatting away at the dental spittoon. So I use a sonar technique originally developed by bats, wherein I fire off a constant stream of idiot conversational remarks designed to draw replies so I can keep track of which blobs in the room represent people. This makes it very hard to work on my teeth.

Swimming at the beach is the worst. If I go into the ocean with my glasses off, which is the traditional way to go into the ocean, I cannot frolic in the surf like a normal person because (a) I usually can't see the waves until they knock me over and drag me along the bottom and fill my mouth with sand, and (b) the current always carries me down the beach, away from my wife and towel and glasses. When I emerge from the water, all I can see is this enormous white blur (the beach?) covered with darkish blobs (people?), and I run the risk of plopping down next to a blob that I think is my wife and throwing my arm over it in an affectionate manner, only to discover that it is actually horseshoe crabs mating, or a girlfriend of an enormous violent jealous weightlifter, or, God help me, the violent weightlifter himself.

So what I do in these circumstances is wander randomly amongst the blobs, making quiet semidesperate noises designed not to bother any civilians, yet to draw the attention of whatever blob might be my wife. "Well, here I am!" I say, trying to appear as casual as possible. "Yes, here I am! Dave Barry! Ha ha! Help!" And so forth. I'm not sure I'm all that unobtrusive on account of my mouth is full of sand.

Mostly these days when I go to the beach I just stay out of the water altogether. I sit on the shore and play cretin, sand-digging games with my three-year-old son, and I watch the lifeguards, who sit way up on the beach with their 20-20 vision and blow their whistles at swimmers I couldn't see even with the aid of a radio telescope, off the coast of France somewhere.

At least I no longer have to worry about necking on dates, the way I did in high school. That was awful. See, you have to take your glasses off when you neck, lest you cause facial injury to the other necker. So I'd be sitting on the sofa with a girl, watching a late movie on television, and I'd figure the time was right, and I'd very casually remove my glasses, rendering myself batlike, and lean toward the blob representing the girl and plant a sensuous kiss on the side of her head owing to the fact that she was still watching the movie. Now what? Do I try again, on the theory that she has been aroused by being kissed on the side of the head? Or is she angry? Is she still watching television? Is she still on the sofa? There was no way to tell. The world was a blur. So I'd have to very casually grope around for my glasses and put them back on for a little reconnaissance, but by the time I found them likely as not the potential co-necker had fallen asleep.

I suppose I could wear contact lenses, but people who wear contact lenses are always weeping and blinking, and their eyes turn red, as though their mothers had just died. You want to go up to them on the street and say "There, there," and maybe give them money. Also, you never hear of anybody who wears them successfully for more than maybe three weeks. People are always saying, "I really liked them, but my hair started to fall out," or, "I had this girlfriend, Denise, and one of her contacts slid up under her eyelid and went into her bloodstream and got stuck in her brain and now she never finishes her sentences."

I guess I should be grateful that I can see at all, and I am. I just felt like wallowing in self-pity for a while, is all. I promise I won't do it again. Those of you with worse afflictions than mine, such as migraine headaches or pregnancy, are welcome to write me long, descriptive letters. I promise to look them over, although not necessarily with my glasses on.

Valuable Presidential Freebies!

My wife recently got two offers in the mail, one from Ed McMahon and one from President Reagan. Ed's offer is that if my wife will stick some little stickers on a card and send it back, he'll give her $2 million. I figure there has to be a catch. Maybe there's some kind of espionage chemical on the back of the sticker so that when you lick it your nasal passages swell up and explode and you can't collect your two million. Because otherwise it just seems too easy, you know?

President Reagan's offer looks better. He's offering my wife the opportunity to be on a special Presidential Task Force. Apparently this is a limited offer being made only to a select group consisting of all current and former Republicans, living or dead, in the world. My wife used to be a Republican before she quit voting altogether, except for when there are judicial candidates with humorous names.

According to the colorful brochure my wife got, her primary task as a member of the Presidential Task Force is to send in $120. President Reagan is going to use this money to prevent the government from falling into the hands of the Democrats, who, according to the brochure, are all disease-ridden vermin. As tokens of the president's gratitude, my wife will receive a number of Valuable Gifts, including (I swear I am not making this up):

- A "Medal of Merit" in a "handsome case," in recognition for highly meritorious service to the nation in the form of coming up with the 120 beans.
- A lapel pin, which the brochure says will "signify your special relationship with President Reagan."
- An embossed Presidential Task Force Membership Card, which "reveals your toll-free, members-only, Washington hotline number; your

direct line to important developments in the United States Senate; your superfast way to contact President Reagan and every Republican in the United States Senate."

Except for the time that our dog was throwing up what appeared to be squirrel parts in the living room, I can't honestly think of any occasion in recent years when we needed to get hold of President Reagan and every Republican in the senate on short notice. Nevertheless, I think the embossed Task Force card hotline number could come in mighty handy.

Let's say my wife and I are at the department store and we're trying to get waited on by a small clot of sales personnel who are clearly annoyed that some idiot has gone and left the doors open again, thus permitting members of the public to get into the store and actually try to purchase things, if you can imagine, right in the middle of a very important sales personnel discussion about hair design.

Ordinarily what my wife and I do in these situations is stand around in an obvious manner for several minutes, after which we ask politely several times to be waited on, after which we escalate to rude remarks, after which we discharge small arms in the direction of the ceiling, after which we give up and go home. But if my wife were a Task Force member, the sales personnel would notice her lapel pin and say to each other in hushed tones: "That pin signifies that she has a special relationship with President Reagan! We had best make an exception in her case, and permit her to make a purchase!" For they would know that if they didn't, my wife would be on the horn pronto, contacting President Reagan and all the senate Republicans, and heaven only knows what kind of strong corrective action they would take, except that it would probably involve the shipment of missiles to camel-oriented nations.

So all in all I think the president has made my wife a fine offer. Not only does she get the valuable Free Gifts, but she gets to keep the government in Republican hands and thus save the Republic and ensure a brighter future for the entire Free World for generations to come. Of course we must weigh this against the fact that $120 will buy you enough beer to last nearly two weeks in mild weather.

Valuable Scam Offer

So I got this letter, which said I had been selected by a "merchandise distribution organization" to receive some merchandise. The way the letter sounded, these people just woke up one day and said, "Hey! We have some merchandise! Let's form an organization and *distribute* it!" The letter said I could receive as much as $1,000 in cash, but I was not so naive as to think I would get that. I figure I'd have a better shot at the Disney World vacation, or the 24-karat gold bracelet with the rubies and diamonds, or maybe even—you never can tell—the *five function LCD watch.*

So I made an appointment to go get the merchandise, and they told me that, while I was there, they would tell me about a new Leisure Concept, and I had to bring my spouse. This is a normal legal precaution they take to avoid a situation where you sign a contract, and when you get home your spouse finds out and stabs you to death with a potato peeler, which could void the contract.

So we went to the appointed place and sat for a while in a room filled with other couples, and every now and then a person would come in, call out a name, and lead a couple off, and the rest of us would wonder what was going to happen to them. I thought maybe it would be like a fraternity initiation, in which they'd shove us into a darkened room where sales representatives would taunt us and poke us with sharp sticks, then give us our merchandise. But it turns out they don't let you off that easy.

Finally, our name was called by a person named Joe. Joe is the kind of person who cannot begin a sentence without saying, "Let me be honest with you," and cannot end one without grasping your forearm to let you know he is your best personal friend in the world. When Joe was born, the obstetrician examined him briefly and told the nurse: "Do not sign *anything* this baby gives you."

Joe told us his organization didn't invite just any old set of spouses out there to offer this new Leisure Concept to. He said they had already spent somewhere between $400 and $700 on us—not that we should feel obligated or anything!—to check us out thoroughly to make sure we were not convicted felons, because he knew that nice people like us certainly didn't want to be part of any Leisure Concept that allowed convicted felons to join, right? (Grasp.) So my wife asked exactly how they could check on something like that, which made Joe very nervous. I think it suddenly occurred to him that we might actually *be* convicted felons, because he launched into a murky speech about "extenuating circumstances," the gist of which seemed to be that when he said they didn't allow convicted felons, he didn't mean *us*.

Next we found out how you can get AIDS from hotel bedsheets. The way this came up is, Joe asked us where we liked to stay during vacations, and we said, hotels. So Joe went over the pluses and minuses of hotels for us, and the only plus he could think of was that hotels have maid service, but even then, being honest, he had to admit that you never know who has been sleeping on those sheets, and you have to worry when you read all these newspaper stories about AIDS. You know? (Grasp.) This was when we realized that, whatever Joe's Leisure Concept was, it didn't have maid service.

So finally Joe let it slip out that his Leisure Concept was "resorts." As he explained it, basically, we were supposed to give them $11,000 plus annual dues, and then we could spend our Leisure Time at these resorts, which Joe's company had already built some of and plans to build lots more of. To help illustrate their resort in Virginia, for example, they had a nice picture of the dome of the U.S. Capitol, although when we asked Joe about it, he admitted that the Capitol was not, to be honest, technically on the resort property per se.

My wife, a picky shopper, said that yes, these were certainly very attractive photographs but generally before she spends $11,000 on resorts she likes to see at least one in person. So Joe told us they had one right outside, which he showed us. What it was, to be honest with you, was a campground. It was one of those modern ones with swimming pools and miniature golf and video games, the kind that's popular with people whose idea of getting close to nature is turning the air conditioning in their recreational vechicles down to medium. My reaction was that I would spend my Leisure Time there only if this were one of the demands made by people who had kidnapped my son.

So we went back inside, and Joe lunged at us with a Special Offer, good only that day: For only $8,000, we could join his resorts! Plus annual dues! Plus we could stay at affiliated resorts! For a small fee! There are thousands of them! They litter the nation! Plus we could get discounts at condominiums! Waikiki Beach! Air fares! A castle in Germany! Rental cars! *Several* castles in Germany! Snorkeling! Roy Orbison's Greatest Hits! But we had to act today! Right now! For various reasons! Did we have any questions?!!

My major question was, essentially, did they think we had the same Scholastic Aptitude Test scores as mayonnaise. My wife's questions were: What are you talking about? What resorts? What condominiums? How much of a discount? Joe didn't know. He was more of a specialist in bedsheet hygiene. So he called the Sales Manager, who hauled over a batch of travel brochures, which he kept on his side of the table while he flipped through them at great speed, pausing occasionally to read parts of headlines to us as if they contained actual information.

The whole ordeal took over three hours, and it was not easy, but we got our merchandise: a calculator of the kind that you have eight or twelve dead ones at the bottom of your sock drawer at any given time because it's easier and cheaper to buy a new one than to try to put in new batteries, and an LCD watch that really does have five functions, if you count telling time as two functions (telling hours, and telling minutes).

I would say, even though the watch stopped working the next day, that it was a fun family outing, and I recommend that you try it, assuming you are fortunate enough to get through the strict screening procedure and receive an invitation. Those of you who are convicted felons might want to use your illegal handguns to bypass the Leisure Concept altogether and ask for the $1,000 cash up front.

&*@##%$(!?,.<
>+*&'%$!!@@#$$%%^$

I got to thinking about dirty words this morning when I woke up and looked at the clock, realized I had once again overslept, and said a popular dirty word that begins with "S," which will hereinafter be referred to as "the S-word."

I say the S-word every morning when I look at the clock, because I'm always angry at the clock for continuing to run after I've turned off the alarm and gone back to sleep. What we need in this country, instead of Daylight Savings Time, which nobody really understands anyway, is a new concept called Weekday Morning Time, whereby at 7 A.M. every weekday we go into a space-launch-style "hold" for two or three hours, during which it just remains 7 A.M. This way we could all wake up via a civilized gradual process of stretching and belching and scratching, and it would still be only 7 A.M. when we were ready to actually emerge from bed.

But so far we are stuck with this system under which the clock keeps right on moving, which is what prompts me each morning to say the S-word. The reason I raise this subject is that this particular morning I inadvertently said it directly into the ear of my son, who is almost four and who sometimes creeps into our bedroom during the night because of nightmares, probably caused by the fact that he sleeps on *Return of the Jedi* sheets with illustrations of space creatures such as Jabba the Hut, who looks like a 6,000-pound intestinal parasite.

I felt pretty bad, saying the S-word right into my son's ear, but he was cool. "Daddy, you shouldn't say the S-word," he said. Only he didn't say "the S-word," you understand; he actually said the S-word. But he said it in a very mature way, indicating that he got no thrill from it, and that he was merely trying to correct my behavior.

I don't know where kids pick these things up.

Here's what strikes me as ironic: When I said

the S-word this morning, I was in no way thinking of or trying to describe the substance that the S-word literally represents. No, I was merely trying to describe a feeling of great anguish and frustration, but I'd have felt like a fool, looking at the alarm clock and saying: "I feel great anguish and frustration this morning." So in the interest of saving time, I said the S-word instead, and I got a condescending lecture from a person who consistently puts his underpants on backwards.

The other irony is that for thousands of years, great writers such as William Shakespeare have used so-called dirty words to form literature. In *Romeo and Juliet,* for example, the following words appear in Act II, Scene VI, Row A, Seats 4 and 5:

> "O Romeo, Romeo;
> "Where the F-word art thou, Romeo?"

Today, of course, it is considered very poor taste to use the F-word except in major motion pictures. When we do use it, we are almost always expressing hostility toward somebody who has taken our parking space. This is also ironic, when you consider what act the F-word technically describes, and I imagine you psychiatrists out there could drone on for hours about the close relationship between sex and hostility, but frankly I think you psychiatrists are up to your necks in S-word.

What I think is that the F-word is basically just a convenient nasty-sounding word that we tend to use when we would really like to come up with a terrifically witty insult, the kind Winston Churchill always came up with when enormous women asked him stupid questions at parties. But most of us don't think of good insults until weeks later, in the shower, so in the heat of the moment many of us tend to go with the old reliable F-word.

I disapprove of the F-word, not because it's dirty, but because we use it as a substitute for thoughtful insults, and it frequently leads to violence. What we ought to do, when we anger each other, say, in traffic, is exchange phone numbers, so that later on, when we've had time to think of witty and learned insults or look them up in the library, we could call each other up:

YOU: Hello? Bob?

BOB: Yes?

YOU: This is Ed. Remember? The person whose parking space you took last Thursday? Outside of Sears?

BOB: Oh, yes! Sure! How are you, Ed?

YOU: Fine, thanks. Listen, Bob, the reason I'm calling is: "Madam, you may be drunk, but I am ugly, and . . ." No, wait. I mean: "You may be ugly, but I am Winston Churchill, and . . ." No, wait. (Sound of reference book thudding onto the floor.) S-word. Excuse me. Look, Bob, I'm going to have to get back to you.

BOB: Fine.

This would be much more educational than the F-word approach, plus it would eliminate a lot of unnecessary stabbings. On the other hand, to get back to my original point, we really ought to repeal any laws we have on the books against the S-word, which should henceforth be considered a perfectly acceptable and efficient way of expressing one's feelings toward alarm clocks and cars that break down in neighborhoods where a toxic-waste dump could be classified as urban renewal.

Molecular Homicide

We have the flu. I don't know if this particular strain has an official name, but if it does, it must be something like Martian Death Flu. You may have had it yourself. The main symptom is that you wish you had another setting on your electric blanket, up past "HIGH," that said: "ELECTROCUTION."

Another symptom is that you cease brushing your teeth because (a) your teeth hurt and (b) you lack the strength. Midway through the brushing process, you'd have to lie down in front of the sink to rest for a couple of hours, and rivulets of toothpaste foam would dribble sideways out of your mouth, eventually hardening into crusty little toothpaste stalagmites that would bond your head permanently to the bathroom floor, which is where the police would find you.

You know the kind of flu I'm talking about.

I spend a lot of time lying very still and thinking flu-related thoughts. One insight I have had is that all this time scientists have been telling us the truth: Air really *is* made up of tiny objects called "molecules." I know this because I can feel them banging against my body. There are billions and billions and billions of them, but if I concentrate, I can detect each one individually, striking my body, especially my eyeballs, at speeds upwards of a hundred thousand miles per hour. If I try to escape by pulling the blanket over my face, they attack my hair, which has become almost as sensitive as my teeth.

There has been a mound of blankets on my wife's side of the bed for several days now, absolutely motionless except that it makes occasional efforts to spit into a tissue. I think it might be my wife, but the only way to tell for sure would be to prod it, which I wouldn't do even if I had the strength, because if it turned out that it was my wife, and she were alive, and I prodded her, it would kill her.

Me, I am leading a more active life-style. Three or four times a day, I attempt to crawl to the bathroom. Unfortunately this is a distance of nearly 15 feet, with a great many air molecules en route, so at about the halfway point I usually decide to stop and get myself into the fetal position and hope for nuclear war. Instead, I get Earnest. Earnest is our dog. She senses instantly that something is wrong, and guided by that timeless and unerring nurturing instinct that all female dogs have, she tries to lick my ears off.

For my son, Robert, this is proving to be the high point of his entire life to date. He has had his pajamas on for two, maybe three days now. He has a sense of joyful independence a five-year-old child gets when he suddenly realizes that he could be operating an acetylene torch in the coat closet and neither parent would have the strength to object. He has been foraging for his own food, which means his diet consists entirely of "food" substances that are advertised only on Saturday morning cartoon shows; substances that are the color of jukebox lights and that, for legal reasons, have their names spelled wrong, as in New Creemy Chock-'n'-Cheez Lumps o' Froot ("part of this complete breakfast").

Crawling around, my face inches from the carpet, I sometimes encounter traces of colorful wrappers that Robert has torn from these substances and dropped on the floor, where Earnest, always on patrol, has found them and chewed them into spit-covered wads. I am reassured by this. It means they are both eating.

The Martian Death Flu has not been an entirely bad thing. Since I cannot work, or move, or think, I have been able to spend more Quality Time with Robert, to come up with creative learning activities that we can enjoy and share together. Today, for example, I taught him, as my father had taught me, how to make an embarrassing noise with your hands. Then we shot rubber bands at the contestants on "Divorce Court." Then, just in case some parts of our brains were still alive, we watched professional bowling. Here's what televised professional bowling sounds like when you have the flu:

PLAY-BY-PLAY MAN: He left the 10-pin, Bob.

COLOR COMMENTATOR: Yes, Bill. He failed to knock it down.

PLAY-BY-PLAY MAN: It's still standing up.

COLOR COMMENTATOR: Yes. Now he must try to knock it down.

PLAY-BY-PLAY MAN: You mean the 10-pin, Bob?

The day just flew by. Soon it was 3:30 P.M., time to crawl back through the air molecules to the bedroom, check on my wife or whoever that is, and turn in for the night.

Earnest was waiting about halfway down the hall.

"Look at this," the police will say when they find me. "His ears are missing."

Way to Go, Roscoe!

Well, it looks like we've finally gotten some tax reform. We've been trying to get tax reform for over 200 years, dating back to 17-something, when a small, brave band of patriots dressed up as Indians and threw tea into the Boston Harbor. Surprisingly, this failed to produce tax reform. So the brave patriots tried various other approaches, such as dressing up as tea and throwing Indians into the harbor, or dressing up as a harbor and throwing tea into Indians, but nothing worked.

And so, today, the tax system is a mess. To cite some of the more glaring problems:

- The big corporations pay nothing.
- The rich pay nothing.
- The poor pay nothing.
- I pay nothing.
- Nobody pays anything except you and a couple of people where you work.
- The commissioner of the Internal Revenue Service is named "Roscoe."

This unfair system has increasingly resulted in calls for reform. I personally called for reform nearly two years ago, when I proposed a simple and fair three-pronged tax system called the You Pay Only $8.95 Tax Plan, which worked as follows:

PRONG ONE: You would pay $8.95 in taxes.

PRONG TWO: Cheating would be permitted.

PRONG THREE: Anybody who parked his or her car diagonally across two parking spaces would be shot without trial. (This prong is not directly related to tax reform, but everybody I discussed it with feels it should be included anyway.)

The other major plan was proposed by President Reagan, who made tax reform the cornerstone of his second term, similar to the way he made tax reduction the cornerstone of his first term. Remember that? It was back when everybody was talking about "supply-side economics," which is the mysterious curve that became famous when an economist named Arthur Laffer drew it at a party, on a napkin belonging to U.S. Congressman Jack Kemp. I'm not making this up.

What the Laffer curve allegedly showed, when you held it in a certain light, was that if the government reduced everybody's taxes, it would make *more money,* and the federal budget deficit would go away. I admit that, looking back on it, this theory seems even stupider than throwing beverages into Boston Harbor, but, at the time, it had a very strong appeal. Congressman Kemp started showing his napkin around Washington and soon many people were excited about supply-side economics. It was similar to those stories you sometimes see in the newspaper about how some Third World village gets all riled up when a peasant woman discovers a yam shaped exactly like the Virgin Mary. President Reagan made tax reduction his first-term cornerstone, and Congress enacted it, and everybody waited for the budget deficit to go down, and it wasn't until recently that economists realized Kemp had been holding his napkin sideways.

So that was tax reduction. Now we're on tax *reform,* which as I said earlier is the president's second-term cornerstone. For a while, however, it appeared to be in big trouble in Congress, because of the PACs. PACs are lobbying organizations with names like the American Nasal Inhaler Industry Committee for Better Government, which make large contributions to your elected representatives so they can afford to make TV campaign commercials where they stand around in shirt sleeves pretending that they actually care about ordinary bozo citizens such as you.

The PACs did not care for the president's plan. They were very concerned that the term "tax reform" might be interpreted to mean "reforming the tax system in some way," which of course would destroy the economy as we now know it. So they had all these amendments introduced, and, before long, the president's tax-reform plan had been modified so much that its only actual legal effect, had it been enacted, would have been to declare July as Chalk Appreciation Month. And so it looked as though the president might have to come up with a new cornerstone for his second term, something like: "Ronald Reagan: He never bombed Canada." Or: "Ronald Reagan: Most of his polyps were benign."

And then a wonderful thing happened. The Senate Finance Committee, a group of men who are not famous for standing up to the special interests, a group of men who have little slots in their front doors for the convenience of those PACs wishing to make large contributions at night, suddenly got their courage up. They took a hard look at themselves, and they said: "Wait a minute. What are we? Are we a bunch of prostitutes, taking large sums of money from the PACs and giving them what they want? No! Let's take large sums of their money and *not* give them what they want!" It was a courageous step, a step that took the senators beyond prostitution, into the realm of fraud. All the editorial writers of course hailed it as a Positive Step. And that is how we came to have tax reform.

How will tax reform affect you? It will change your life dramatically. Let's say you're a typical family of four with both parents working and occasional car problems. Under the new system, each year you'll get a bunch of unintelligible forms from the government, and you'll put off doing anything about them until mid-April, and you'll be confused by the directions, and you'll miss a lot of deductions, and you'll worry about being audited. Other than that things will remain pretty much the same. Roscoe will still be in charge.

Tax Attacks

NOTE: *This is my annual column on how to fill out our income-tax return. As you read it, please bear in mind that I am not a trained accountant. I am the Chief Justice of the United States Supreme Court. Nevertheless, if you have any questions whatsoever about the legality of a particular tax maneuver, you should call the special Toll-Free IRS Taxpayer Assistance Hotline Telephone Number in your area and listen to the busy signal until you feel you have a better understanding of the situation.*

There are a number (23,968,847) of significant differences between this year's tax form and last year's, but let's first look at the two things that have *not* changed:

1. The commissioner of Internal Revenue is *still* named "Roscoe," and

2. Roscoe is evidently still doing situps under parked cars, because he once again devotes the largest paragraph on page one to telling us taxpayers how we can send in "voluntary contributions to reduce the federal debt." As I interpret this statement, Roscoe, by using the word "voluntary," is saying that even though your government finds itself in serious financial trouble owing to the fact that every time an Acting Assistant Deputy Undersecretary of Something changes offices, he spends more on new drapes than your whole house is worth, the IRS does not *require* you to send in extra money, beyond what you actually owe. No sir. You also are allowed to send in jewelry, stocks, canned goods, or clothing in good condition. Roscoe is a 42 regular.

Everything else about the tax form is different this year, but it shouldn't be too much trouble as long as you avoid Common Taxpayer Errors. "For example," reminds IRS Helpful Hint Division Chief Rexford Pooch, Jr., "taxpayers who make everything up should use numbers that sound sort of accurate, such as $3,847.62, rather than obvious fictions like

$4,000. Also, we generally give much closer scrutiny to a return where the taxpayer gives a name such as Nick 'The Weasel' Testosterone."

With those tips in mind, let's look at some typical tax cases, and see how they would be handled under the new tax code.

TAX CASE ONE: Mrs. Jones, a 71-year-old widow living on social security with no other income, is sound asleep one night when she has an incredibly vivid dream in which her son dies in an automobile crash in California. Suddenly, she is awakened by the telephone; it is a member of the California Highway Patrol, calling to remind her that she does not have a son. Stunned, she suffers a fatal heart attack.

QUESTION: Does Mrs. Jones still have to file a tax return?

ANSWER: Yes. Don't be an idiot. She should use Form DPFS-65, "Dead Person Filing Singly," which she can obtain at any of the two nationwide IRS Taxpayer Assistance Centers during their normal working hour.

TAX CASE TWO: Mr. and Mrs. Smith, both 32, are a working couple with two dependent children and a combined gross net abstracted income of $27,000. During the first fiscal segment of the 1984 calendar year, they received IRS Form YAFN-12, notifying them that according to the federal computer, they owe $179 billion in taxes. They have a good laugh over this and show the notice to their friends, thinking that it is such an obvious mistake that the IRS will correct it right away and they might even get their names in the newspaper as the victims of a typical humorous government bonehead computer bungle.

QUESTION: Can the Smiths deduct the cost of the snake-related injuries they suffered when they were fleeing the federal dogs through the wilderness?

ANSWER: They may deduct 61 percent of the base presumptive adjusted mean allocated cost that is greater than, but not exceeding, $1,575, provided they kept accurate records showing they made a reasonable effort to save little Tina's ear. Except in states whose names consist of two words.

TAX CASE THREE: Mr. A. Pemberton Trammel Snipe-Treadwater IV has established a trust fund for his six children under which each of them, upon reaching the age of 21, will receive a subcontinent. One afternoon while preparing to lash a servant, Mr. Snipe-Treadwater has a vague recollection that in 1980—or perhaps it was in 1978, he is not sure—he might have paid some taxes.

QUESTION: What should Mr. Snipe-Treadwater do?

ANSWER: He should immediately summon his various senators and congressmen to soothe his brow with damp compresses until he can be named ambassador to France.

Yup the Establishment

Obviously, we—and when I say "we," I mean people who no longer laugh at the concept of hemorrhoids—need to come up with some kind of plan for dealing with the yuppies. In a moment I'll explain my personal proposal, which is that we draft them, but first let me give you some background.

If you've been reading the trend sections of your weekly newsmagazines, you know that "yuppies" are a new breed of serious, clean-cut, ambitious, career-oriented young person that probably resulted from all that atomic testing. They wear dark, natural-fiber, businesslike clothing even when nobody they know has died. In college, they major in Business Administration. If, to meet certain academic requirements, they have to take a liberal-arts course, they take Business Poetry.

In short, yuppies are running around behaving as if they were real grown-ups, and they are doing it at an age when persons of my generation were still playing Beatles records backwards and actively experimenting to determine what happens when you drink a whole bottle of cough syrup.

NOTE TO IMPRESSIONABLE YOUNG READERS: *Don't bother. All that happens is you feel like you could never, ever cough again, even if professional torturers armed with X-acto knives ordered you to, then you develop this intense, 10-to-12-hour interest in individual carpet fibers. So it's not worth it, plus I understand the manufacturers have done something wimpy to the formulas.*

What bothers me about the yuppies is, they're destroying the normal social order, which is that people are supposed to start out as wild-eyed radicals, and then gradually, over time, develop gum disease and become conservatives.

This has always been the system. A good example is Franklin Roosevelt, who when he was alive was considered extremely liberal, but now is constantly being quoted by Ronald Reagan. Or take the Russian leaders. When they were young, they'd pull any kind of crazy stunt, kill the czar, anything, but now they mostly just lie around in state.

So I say the yuppies represent a threat to society as we know it, and I say we need to do something about them. One possibility would be to simply wait until they reproduce, on the theory that they'll give their children the finest clothing and toys and designer educations, and their children will of course grow up to absolutely loathe everything their parents stand for and thus become defiant, ill-dressed, unwashed, unkempt, violently antiestablishment drug addicts, and society will return to normal. The problem here is that yuppies have a very low birth rate, because apparently they have to go to Aspen to mate.

So we'll have to draft them. Not into the Armed Forces, of course; they'd all make colonel in about a week, plus they'd be useless in an actual war, whapping at the enemy with briefcases. Likewise we cannot put them in the Peace Corps, as they would cause no end of ill will abroad, crouching among the residents of some poverty-racked village in, say, Somalia, and attempting to demonstrate the water-powered Cuisinart.

No, what we need for the yuppies is a national Lighten Up Corps. First they'd go through basic training, where a harsh drill sergeant would force them to engage in pointless nonproductive activities, such as eating moon pies and watching "Days of Our Lives." Then they'd each have to serve two years in a job that offered no opportunity whatsoever for career advancement, such as:

- bumper-car repairman;
- gum-wad remover;
- random street lunatic;
- bus-station urinal maintenance person;
- lieutenant governor;
- owner of a roadside attraction such as "World's Largest All-Snake Orchestra."

During their time of service in the Lighten Up Corps, the yuppies would of course be required to wear neon-yellow polyester jumpsuits with the name "Earl" embroidered over the breast pocket.

Pain & Suffering

As an American, you are very fortunate to live in a country (America) where you have many legal rights. Bales of rights. And new ones are being discovered all the time, such as the right to make a right turn on a red light.

This doesn't mean you can do just *anything*. For example, you can't shout "FIRE!" in a crowded theater. Even if there *is* a fire, you can't shout it. A union worker has to shout it. But you can—I know this, because you always sit right behind me—clear your throat every 15 seconds all the way through an entire movie, and finally, at the exact moment of greatest on-screen drama, hawk up a gob the size of a golf ball. Nobody can stop you. It's your *right*.

The way you got all these rights is the Founding Fathers fought and died for them, then wrote them down on the Constitution, a very old piece of paper that looks like sick puppies have lived on it, which is stored in Washington, D.C., where you have the right to view it during normal viewing hours. The most important part of the Constitution, rightswise, appears in Article IX, Section II, Row 27, which states:

If any citizen of the United States shall ever at any time for any reason have any kind of bad thing happen to him or her, then this is probably the result of Negligence on the part of a large corporation with a lot of insurance. If you get our drift.

What the Constitution is trying to get across to you here is that the way you protect your rights, in America, is by suing the tar out of everybody. This is an especially good time to sue, because today's juries hand out giant cash awards as if they were complimentary breath mints.

So you definitely want to get in on this. Let's say your wedding ring falls into your toaster, and when you stick your hand in to retrieve it, you suffer Pain and Suffering as well as Mental Anguish. You would sue:

- The toaster manufacturer, for failure to include, in the instructions section that says you should never never never never *ever* stick your hand in the toaster, the statement: "Not even if your wedding ring falls in there."
- The store where you bought the toaster, for selling it to an obvious cretin like yourself.
- The Union Carbide Corporation, which is not directly responsible in this case, but which is feeling so guilty that it would probably send you a large cash settlement anyway.

Of course you need the help of a professional lawyer. Experts agree the best way to select a lawyer is to watch VHF television, where more and more of your top legal talents are advertising:

"Hi. I'm Preston A. Mantis, president of Consumers Retail Law Outlet. As you can see by my suit and the fact that I have all these books of equal height on the shelves behind me, I am a trained legal attorney. Do you have a car or a job? Do you ever walk around? If so, you probably have the makings of an excellent legal case. Although of course every case is different, I would definitely say that, based on my experience and training, there's no reason why you shouldn't come out of this thing with at least a cabin cruiser. Remember, at the Preston A. Mantis Consumers Retail Law Outlet, our motto is: "It is very difficult to disprove certain kinds of pain."

Another right you have, as an American, is the right to Speedy Justice. For an example of how Speedy Justice works, we turn now to an anecdote told to me by a friend who once worked as a clerk for a judge in a medium-sized city. My friend swears this is true. It happened to an elderly recent immigrant who was hauled before the judge one day. The thing to bear in mind is, this man was *not actually guilty of anything.* He had simply gotten lost and confused, and he spoke very little English, and he was wandering around, so the police had picked him up just so he'd have a warm place to sleep while they straightened everything out.

Unfortunately, this judge, who got his job less on the basis of being knowledgeable in matters of law than on the basis of attending the most picnics, somehow got the *wrong folder* in front of him, the folder of a person who had done something semiserious, so he gave the accused man a stern speech, then sentenced him to *six months in jail.* When this was explained to the man, he burst into tears. He was thinking, no doubt, that if he had only known they had such severe penalties for being elderly and lost in America, he would never have immigrated here in the first place.

Finally, about an hour later, the police figured out what happened, and after they stopped rolling around the floor and wetting their pants, they told the judge, and he sent them to fetch the prisoner back from jail. By now, of course, the prisoner had no *idea* what they're going to do to him. Shoot him, maybe. He was terrified. So put yourself in the judge's position. Here you have a *completely innocent* man in front of you, whom you have scared half to death and had carted off to jail because *you* made a stupid mistake. What is the only conceivable thing you can do? Apologize, right?

This just shows you have no legal training. What this judge did was give a speech. "*America,*" it began. Just the one word, very dramatically spoken. My friend, who saw all this happen, still cannot recount this speech without falling most of the way out of his chair. The gist of it was that this is a Great Country, and since this was a First Offense, he, the judge, had had a Change of Heart, and had decided to give the accused a Second Chance.

Well. Once they explained *this* to the prisoner, that he was not going to jail after all, that he was to be shown all this *mercy*, he burst into tears again, and rushed up and *tried to kiss the judge's hand.* Who could blame him? This was probably the greatest thing that had ever happened to him. What a *great* country! What *speedy* justice! I bet he still tells his grandchildren about it. I bet they tell him he should have sued.

The Deadly Wind

What prospective buyers said, when they looked at our house, was: "Huh! This is . . . *interesting.*" They *always* said this. They never said: "What a nice house!" Or: "We'll take this house! Here's a suitcase filled with money!!" No, they said our house is *interesting.* What they meant was: "Who installed this paneling? Vandals?"

Sometimes, to cheer us up, they also said: "Well it certainly has a lot of possibilities!" Meaning: "These people have lived here for 10 years and *they never put up any curtains.*"

We were trying to sell our house. We had elected to move voluntarily to Miami. We wanted our child to benefit from the experience of growing up in a community that is constantly being enriched by a diverse and ever-changing infusion of tropical diseases. Also they have roaches down there you could play polo with.

The first thing we did, when we decided to move, was we rented a dumpster and threw away the majority of our furniture. You think I am kidding, but this is only because you never saw our furniture. It was much too pathetic to give to The Poor. The Poor would have taken one look at it and returned, laughing, to their street grates.

What we did give to The Poor was all my college textbooks, which I had gone through, in college, using a yellow felt marker to highlight the good parts. You college graduates out there know what I'm talking about. You go back, years later, when college is just a vague semicomical memory, and read something you chose to highlight, and it's always a statement like: "Structuralized functionalism represents both a continuance of, and a departure from, functionalistic structuralism." And you realize that at one time you actually had *large sectors* of your brain devoted to this type of knowledge. Lord only knows what The Poor will use it for. Fuel, probably.

One book we did keep is called *Survive the Deadly Wind.* I don't know where we got it, but it's about hurricanes, and so we thought it might contain useful information about life in Miami. "Any large pieces of aluminum left in a yard are a definite hazard," it states. "Each piece has a potential for decapitation. Hurled on the tide of a 150-mile-an-hour wind, it can slice its way to, and through, bone." Ha ha! Our New Home!

After we threw away our furniture, we hired two men, both named Jonathan, to come over and fix our house up so prospective buyers wouldn't get to laughing so hard they'd fall down the basement stairs and file costly lawsuits. The two Jonathans were extremely competent, the kind of men who own winches and freely use words like "joist" and can build houses starting out with only raw trees. The first thing they did was rip out all the Homeowner Projects I had committed against our house back when I thought I had manual dexterity. They were trying to make the house look as nice as it did before I started improving it. This cost thousands of dollars.

I think there should be a federal law requiring people who publish do-it-yourself books to include a warning, similar to what the Surgeon General has on cigarette packs, right on the cover of the book, stating:

WARNING: ANY MONEY YOU SAVE BY DOING HOMEOWNER PROJECTS YOURSELF WILL BE OFFSET BY THE COST OF HIRING COMPETENT PROFESSIONALS TO COME AND REMOVE THEM SO YOU CAN SELL YOUR HOUSE, NOT TO MENTION THE EMOTIONAL TRAUMA ASSOCIATED WITH LISTENING TO THESE PROFESSIONALS, AS THEY RIP OUT LARGE CHUNKS OF A PROJECT, LAUGH, AND YELL REMARKS SUCH AS: "HEY! GET A LOAD OF THIS."

After the Jonathans took out all my projects, the house mostly consisted of holes, which they filled up with spackle. When prospective buyers asked: "What kind of construction is this house?" I answered: "Spackle."

The only real bright spot in the move was when I got even with the television set in our bedroom, which had been broken for years. My wife and I have had the same argument about it maybe 200 times, wherein I say we should throw it away, and she says we should get it repaired. My wife grew up in a very sheltered rural Ohio community and she still believes you can get things repaired.

Over the years, this television had come to believe that as long as my wife was around, it was safe, and it had grown very smug, which is why I wish you could have seen the look on its face when, with my wife weakened by the flu, I took it out and propped it up at the end of the dumpster, execution-style, and, as a small neighborhood crowd gathered, one of the Jonathans hurled a long, spear-like piece of Homeowner Project from 20 feet away right directly through the screen, into the very heart of its picture tube. It made a sound that I am sure our other appliances will not soon forget.

But the rest were mostly low points. I looked forward to the day when somebody bought our house, perhaps to use as a tourist attraction (SPACKLE KINGDOM, 5 MI.), and we could pack our remaining household possessions—a piano and 48,000 "He-Man" action figures—into cardboard boxes and move to Miami to begin our new life, soaking up the sun and watching the palm trees sway in the tropical breeze. At least until the aluminum sliced through them.

The House of the Seven Figures

Before my wife, Beth, left on the jet airplane to buy us a new house, we sat down and figured out what our Price Range was. We used the standard formula where you take your income and divide it by three, which gives you the amount you would spend annually on housing if you bought a house that is much cheaper than the one you will actually end up buying.

With that figure in mind, Beth took off for our new home-to-be, South Florida, and my son and I, who had never been in charge of each other for this long before, embarked on the following rigorous nutritional program:

BREAKFAST: Frozen waffles heated up.

LUNCH: Hot dogs heated up.

DINNER: Choice of hot dogs or frozen waffles heated up.

Also in the refrigerator were many health-fanatic foods such as presliced carrot sticks placed there by Beth in hopes that we would eat something that did not have a label stating that it met the minimum federal standard for human armpit hair, but we rejected these because of the lengthy preparation time.

Some of you may be wondering why, considering that this is the most important financial transaction of our lives, I didn't go with Beth to buy the house. The answer is that I am a very dangerous person to have on your side in a sales situation. I develop great anxiety in the presence of salespeople, and the only way I can think of to make it go away is to buy whatever they're selling. This is not a major problem with, for example, pants, but it leads to trouble with cars and houses.

Here is how I bought our last car. I didn't dare go directly to the car dealership, so, for several consecutive days—this is the truth—I would park at a nearby Dairy Queen, buy a chocolate cone, then amble over to the car lot, disguised as a person just ambling around with a chocolate cone, and I would try to quickly read the sticker on the side of the car where they explain that the only part of the car included in the Base Sticker Price is the actual sticker itself, and you have to pay extra if you want, for example, transparent windows. After a few minutes, a salesman would spot me and come striding out, smiling like an entire Rotary Club, and I would adopt the expression of a person who had just remembered an important appointment and amble off at speeds approaching 40 miles per hour. What I'm saying is, I shopped for this car the way a squirrel hunts for acorns in a dog-infested neighborhood.

When I finally went in to buy the car, I was desperate to get it over with as quickly as possible. Here is how I negotiated:

SALESPERSON: (showing me a sheet of paper with figures on it): OK, Dave. Here's a ludicrously inflated opening price that only a person with Rice-A-Roni for brains would settle for.

ME: You got a deal.

I am worse with houses. The last time we were trying to buy a house, I made Beth crazy because I was willing to make a formal offer on whatever structure we were standing in at the time:

ME: This is perfect! Isn't this perfect?!

BETH: This is the real-estate office.

ME: Well, how much are they asking?

So this is why Beth went to Miami without me. Moments after she arrived, she ascertained that there were no houses there in our Price Range. Our Price Range turned out to be what the average homeowner down there spends on roach control. (And we are not talking about *killing* the roaches. We are talking about sedating them enough so they let you into your house.)

Fortunately, Beth found out about a new financial concept they have in home-buying that is tailor-made for people like us, called Going Outside Your Price Range. This is where she started looking, and before long she had stumbled onto an even *newer* financial concept called Going Way Outside Your Price Range. This is where she eventually found a house, and I am very much looking forward to seeing it someday, assuming we get a mortgage.

They have developed a new wrinkle in mortgages since the last time we got one, back in the seventies. The way it worked then was, you borrowed money from the bank, and every month you paid back some money, and at the end of the year the bank sent you a computerized statement proving you still owed them all the money you borrowed in the first place. Well, they're still using that basic system, but now they also have this wrinkle called "points," which is a large quantity of money you give to the bank, right up front, for no apparent reason. It's as though the *bank* is the one trying to buy the house. You ask real-estate people to explain it, and they just say: "Oh yes, the points! Be sure to bring an enormous sum of money to the settlement for those!" And of course we will. We consumers will do almost anything to get our mortgages. Banks know this, so they keep inventing new charges to see how far they can go:

MORTGAGE OFFICER: OK, at your settlement you have to pay $400 for the preparation of the Certificate of Indemption.

CONSUMER: Yes, of course.
MORTGAGE OFFICER: And $430 for pastries.

But it will all be worth it, to get to our house. It sounds, from Beth's description, as though it has everything that I look for in a house: (1) a basketball hoop and (2) a fiberglass backboard. I understand it also has rooms.

Can New York Save Itself?

At the Miami Herald we ordinarily don't provide extensive coverage of New York City unless a major news development occurs up there, such as Sean Penn coming out of a restaurant. But lately we have become very concerned about the "Big Apple," because of a story about Miami that ran a few weeks ago in the Sunday magazine of the *New York Times.* Maybe you remember this story: The cover featured an upbeat photograph of suspected Miami drug dealers being handcuffed face-down in the barren dirt next to a garbage-strewn sidewalk outside a squalid shack that probably contains roaches the size of Volvo sedans. The headline asked:

CAN MIAMI SAVE ITSELF?

For those readers too stupid to figure out the answer, there also was this helpful hint:

A City Beset by Drugs and Violence

The overall impression created by the cover was: *Sure Miami can save itself! And some day trained sheep will pilot the Concorde!*

The story itself was more balanced, discussing the pluses as well as the minuses of life in South Florida, as follows:

- *Minuses:* The area is rampant with violent crime and poverty and political extremism and drugs and corruption and ethnic hatred.
- *Pluses:* Voodoo is legal.

I myself thought it was pretty fair. Our local civic leaders reacted to it with their usual level of cool maturity, similar to the way Moe reacts when he is poked in the eyeballs by Larry and Curly. Our leaders held emergency breakfasts and issued official statements pointing out that much of the information in the *New York Times* story was Ancient History dating all the way back to the early 1980s, and that we haven't had a riot for what, *months* now, and that the whole drugs-and-violence thing is overrated. Meanwhile, at newsstands all over South Florida, crowds of people were snapping up all available copies of the *New York Times,* frequently at gunpoint.

All of which got us, at the *Miami Herald,* to thinking. "Gosh," we thought. "Here the world-famous *New York Times,* with so many other things to worry about, has gone to all this trouble to try to find out whether Miami can save itself. Wouldn't they be thrilled if we did the same thing for them?" And so it was that we decided to send a crack investigative team consisting of me and Chuck, who is a trained photographer, up there for a couple of days to see what the situation was. We took along comfortable walking shoes and plenty of major credit cards, in case it turned out that we needed to rent a helicopter, which it turned out we did. Here is our report:

DAY ONE: We're riding in a cab from La Guardia Airport to our Manhattan hotel, and I want to interview the driver, because this is how we professional journalists take the Pulse of a City, only I can't, because he doesn't speak English. He is not allowed to, under the rules, which are posted right on the seat:

NEW YORK TAXI RULES

1. DRIVER SPEAKS NO ENGLISH.
2. DRIVER JUST GOT HERE TWO DAYS AGO FROM SOMEPLACE LIKE SENEGAL.
3. DRIVER HATES YOU.

Which is just as well, because if he talked to me, he might lose his concentration, which would be very bad because the taxi has some kind of problem with the steering, probably dead pedestrians lodged in the mechanism, the result being that there is a delay of 8 to 10 seconds between the time the driver turns the wheel and the time the taxi actually changes direction, a handicap that the driver is compensating for by going 175 miles per hour, at which velocity we are able to remain airborne almost to the far rim of some of the smaller potholes. These are of course maintained by the crack New York Department of Potholes (currently on strike), whose commissioner was recently indicted on corruption charges by the Federal Grand Jury to Indict Every Commissioner in New York. This will take some time, because New York has more commissioners than Des Moines, Iowa, has residents, including the Commissioner for Making Sure the Sidewalks Are Always Blocked by Steaming Fetid Mounds of Garbage the Size of Appalachian Foothills, and, of course, the Commissioner for Bicycle Messengers Bearing Down on You at Warp Speed with Mohawk Haircuts and Pupils Smaller Than Purely Theoretical Particles.

After several exhilarating minutes, we arrive in downtown Manhattan, where the driver slows to 125 miles so he can take better aim at wheelchair occupants. This gives us our first brief glimpse of the city we have come to investigate. It looks to us, whizzing past, as though it is beset by serious problems. We are reminded of the findings of the 40-member Mayor's Special Commission on the Future of the City of New York, which this past June, after nearly two years of intensive study of the economic, political, and social problems confronting the city, issued a 2,300-page report, which reached the disturbing conclusion that New York is "a nice place to visit" but the commission "wouldn't want to live there."

Of course they probably stayed at a nicer hotel than where we're staying. We're staying at a "medium-priced" hotel, meaning that the rooms are more than spacious enough for a family of four to stand up in if they are slightly built and hold their arms over their heads, yet the rate is just $135 per night, plus of course your state tax, your city tax, your occupancy tax, your head tax, your body tax, your soap tax, your ice bucket tax, your in-room dirty movies tax, and your piece of paper that says your toilet is sanitized for your protection tax, which bring the rate to $367.90 per night, or a flat $4,000 if you use the telephone. A bellperson carries my luggage—one small gym-style bag containing, primarily, a set of clean underwear—and I tip him $2, which he takes as if I am handing him a jar of warm sputum.

But never mind. We are not here to please the bellperson. We are here to see if New York can save itself. And so Chuck and I set off into the streets of Manhattan, where we immediately detect signs of a healthy economy in the form of people squatting on the sidewalk selling realistic jewelry. This is good, because a number of other businesses, such as Mobil Corp., have recently decided to pull their headquarters out of New York, much to the annoyance of Edward Koch, the feisty, cocky, outspoken, abrasive mayor who really gets on some people's nerves, yet at the same time strikes other people as a jerk. "Why would *anybody* want to move to some dirt-bag place like the Midwest?" Mayor Koch is always asking reporters. "What are they gonna do at *night?* Huh? *Milk the cows?* Are they gonna wear bib overalls and sit around *canning their preserves?* Huh? Are they gonna . . . Hey! Come back here!"

But why *are* the corporations leaving? To answer this question, a polling firm recently took a scientific telephone survey of the heads of New York's 200 largest corporations, and found that none of them were expected to arrive at work for at least two more hours because of massive transit delays caused by a wildcat strike of the 1,200-member Wildcat Strikers Guild. So you can see the corporations' point: It *is* an inconvenience, being located in a city where taxes are ludicrously high, where you pay twice your annual income to rent an apartment that could easily be carried on a commercial airline flight, where you spend two-thirds of your work day trying to get to and from work, but as Mayor Koch philosophically points out, "Are they gonna *slop the hogs?* Are they gonna. . . ."

Despite the corporate exodus, the New York economy continues to be robust, with the major industry being people from New Jersey paying $45 each to see *A Chorus Line*. Employment remains high, with most of the new jobs opening up in the fast-growing fields of:

- Person asking everybody for "spare" change.
- Person shrieking at taxis.
- Person holding animated sidewalk conversation with beings from another dimension.
- Person handing out little slips of paper entitling the bearer to one free drink at sophisticated nightclubs with names like The Bazoom Room.

As Chuck and I walk along 42nd Street, we see a person wearing an enormous frankfurter costume, handing out coupons good for discounts at Nathan's Famous hot dog stands. His name is Victor Leise, age 19, of Queens, and he has held the position of giant frankfurter for four months. He says he didn't have any connections or anything; he just put in an application and, boom, the job was his. Sheer luck. He says it's OK work, although people call him "Frank" and sometimes sneak up and whack him on the back. Also there is not a lot of room for advancement. They have no hamburger costume.

"Can New York save itself?" I ask him.

"If there are more cops on the street, there could be a possibility," he says, through his breathing hole.

Right down the street is the world-famous Times Square. Although this area is best known as the site where many thousands of people gather each New Year's Eve for a joyous and festive night of public urination, it also serves as an important cultural center where patrons may view films such as *Sex Aliens, Wet Adulteress,* and, of course, *Sperm Busters* in comfortable refrigerated theaters where everybody sits about 15 feet apart. This is also an excellent place to shop for your leisure product needs, including The Bionic Woman ("An amazingly lifelike companion") and a vast selection of latex objects, some the size of military pontoons. The local residents are very friendly, often coming right up and offering to engage in acts of leisure with you. Reluctantly, however, Chuck and I decided to tear ourselves away, for we have much more to see, plus we do not wish to spend the rest of our lives soaking in vats of penicillin.

As we leave the area, I stop briefly inside an Off-Track Betting parlor on Seventh Avenue to see if I can obtain the Pulse of the City by eavesdropping on native New Yorkers in casual conversation. Off-Track Betting parlors are the kinds of places where you never see signs that say, "Thank You for Not Smoking." The best you could hope for is, "Thank You for Not Spitting Pieces of Your Cigar on My Neck." By listening carefully and remaining unobtrusive, I am able to overhear the following conversation:

FIRST OFF-TRACK BETTOR: I like this *(very bad word)* horse here.

SECOND OFF-TRACK BETTOR: That *(extremely bad word)* couldn't *(bad word)* out his own *(comical new bad word).*

FIRST OFF-TRACK BETTOR: *(bad word).*

Listening to these two men share their innermost feelings, I sense concern, yes, but also an undercurrent of hope, hope for a Brighter Tomorrow, if only the people of this great city can learn to work together, to look upon each other with respect and even, yes, love. Or at least stop shoving one another in front of moving subway trains. This happens a fair amount in New York, so Chuck and I are extremely alert as we descend into the complex of subway tunnels under Times Square, climate-controlled year-round at a comfortable 172 degrees Fahrenheit.

Although it was constructed in 1536, the New York subway system boasts an annual maintenance budget of nearly $8, currently stolen, and it does a remarkable job of getting New Yorkers from point A to an indeterminate location somewhere in the tunnel leading to point B. It's also very easy for the "out-of-towner" to use, thanks to the logical, easy-to-understand system of naming trains after famous letters and numbers. For directions, all you have to do is peer up through the steaming gloom at the informative signs, which look like this:

A 5 N 7 8 C 6 AA MID-DOWNTOWN 7 3/8
EXPRESS LOCAL ONLY LL 67♦
DDD 4♠ 1K☆AAAA 9 ONLY
EXCEPT CERTAIN DAYS BB ®®3
MIDWAY THROUGH TOWN 1 7 D
WALK REAL FAST AAAAAAAAA 56
LOCALIZED EXPRESS-6
"YY" ♣ 1,539
AAAAAAAAAAAAAAAAAA

If for some reason you are unsure where to go, all you have to do is stand there looking lost, and within seconds a helpful New Yorker will approach to see if you have any "spare" change.

Within less than an hour, Chuck and I easily located what could well be the correct platform, where we pass the time by perspiring freely until the train storms in, colorfully decorated, as is the tradition in New York, with the spray-painted initials of all the people it has run over. All aboard!

Here is the correct procedure for getting on a New York subway train at rush hour:

1. As the train stops, you must join the other people on the platform in pushing forward and forming the densest possible knot in front of each door. You want your knot to be so dense that, if the train were filled with water instead of people, not a single drop would escape.

2. The instant the doors open, you want to push forward as hard as possible, in an effort to get onto the train *without letting anybody get off.* This is *very important.* If anybody does get off, it is legal to tackle him and drag him back on. I once watched three German tourists—this is a true anecdote—attempt to get off the northbound No. 5 Lexington Avenue IRT train at Grand Central Station during rush hour. "Getting off please!" they said, politely, from somewhere inside a car containing approximately the population of Brazil, as if they expected people to actually *let them through.* Instead of course, the incoming passengers propelled the Germans, like gnats in a hurricane, *away* from the door, deeper and deeper into the crowd, which quickly compressed them into dense little wads of Teutonic tissue. I never did see where they actually got off. Probably they stumbled to daylight somewhere in the South Bronx, where they were sold for parts.

Actually, there is reason to believe the subways are safer now. After years of being fearful and intimidated, many New Yorkers cheered in 1985 when Bernhard Goetz, in a highly controversial incident that touched off an emotion-charged nationwide debate, shot and killed the New York subway commissioner. This resulted in extensive legal proceedings, culminating recently when, after a dramatic and highly publicized trial, a jury voted not only to acquit Goetz, but also to dig up the commissioner and shoot him again.

Chuck and I emerge from the subway in Lower Manhattan. This area has been hard hit by the massive wave of immigration that has threatened to rend the very fabric of society, as the city struggles desperately to cope with the social upheaval caused by the huge and unprecedented influx of a group that has, for better or for worse, permanently altered the nature of New York: young urban professionals. They began arriving by the thousands in the 1970s, packed two and sometimes three per BMW sedan, severely straining the city's already-overcrowded gourmet-ice cream facilities. Soon they were taking over entire neighborhoods, where longtime residents watched in despair as useful businesses such as bars were replaced by precious little restaurants with names like The Whittling Fig.

And still the urban professionals continue to come, drawn by a dream, a dream that is best expressed by the words of the song "New York, New York," which goes:

Dum dum da de dum
Dum dum da de dum
Dum dum da de dum
Dum dum da de dum dum.

It is a powerfully seductive message, especially if you hear it at a wedding reception held in a Scranton, Pennsylvania, Moose Lodge facility and you have been drinking. And so you come to the Big

Apple, and you take a peon-level position in some huge impersonal corporation, an incredibly awful, hateful job, and you spend $1,250 a month to rent an apartment so tiny that you have to shower in the kitchen, and the only furniture you have room for—not that you can afford furniture anyway—is your collection of back issues of *Metropolitan Home* magazine, but you stick it out, because this is the Big Leagues *(If I can make it there, I'll make it anywhere),* and you know that if you show them what you can do, if you really *go for it,* then, by gosh, one day you're gonna wake up, in The City That Never Sleeps, to find that the corporation has moved its headquarters to Plano, Texas.

Now Chuck and I are in Chinatown. We pass an outdoor market where there is an attractive display consisting of a tub containing I would estimate 275,000 dead baby eels. One of the great things about New York is that, if you ever need dead baby eels, you can get them. Also there is opera here. But tonight I think I'll just try to get some sleep.

At 3:14 A.M. I am awakened by a loud crashing sound, caused by workers from the city's crack Department of Making Loud Crashing Sounds during the Night, who are just outside my window, breaking in a new taxicab by dropping it repeatedly from a 75-foot crane. Lying in bed listening to them, I can hardly wait for . . .

DAY TWO: Chuck and I decide that since we pretty much covered the economic, social, political, historical and cultural aspects of New York on Day One, we'll devote Day Two to sightseeing. We decide to start with the best-known sight of all, the one that, more than any other, exemplifies what the Big Apple is all about: the Islip Garbage Barge. This is a barge of world-renowned garbage that originated on Long Island, a place where many New Yorkers go to sleep on those occasions when the Long Island Railroad is operating.

The Islip Garbage Barge is very famous. Nobody really remembers *why* it's famous; it just *is,* like Dick Cavett. It has traveled to South America. It has been on many television shows, including—I am not making this up—"Donahue." When we were in New York, the barge—I am still not making this up—was on trial. It has since been convicted and sentenced to be burned. But I am not worried. It will get out on appeal. It is the Claus von Bülow of garbage barges.

Chuck and I find out from the Director of Public Affairs at the New York Department of Sanitation, who is named Vito, that the barge is anchored off the coast of Brooklyn, so we grab a cab, which is driven by a man who of course speaks very little English and, as far as we can tell, has never heard of Brooklyn. By means of hand signals we direct him to a place near where the barge is anchored. It is some kind of garbage-collection point.

There are mounds of garbage everywhere, and if you really concentrate, you can actually see them giving off smell rays, such as you see in comic strips. Clearly no taxi has ever been here before, and none will ever come again, so we ask the driver to wait. "YOU WAIT HERE," I say, speaking in capital letters so he will understand me. He looks at me suspiciously. "WE JUST WANT TO SEE A GARBAGE BARGE," I explain.

We can see the barge way out on the water, but Chuck decides that, to get a good picture of it, we need a boat. A sanitation engineer tells us we might be able to rent one in a place called Sheepshead Bay, so we direct the driver there ("WE NEED TO RENT A BOAT"), but when we get there we realize it's too far away, so we naturally decide to rent a helicopter, which we find out is available only in New Jersey.

("NOW WE NEED TO GO TO NEW JERSEY. TO RENT A HELICOPTER.") Thus we end up at the airport in Linden, New Jersey, where we leave the taxi driver with enough fare money to retire for life, if he ever finds his way home.

Chuck puts the helicopter on his American Express card. Our pilot, Norman Knodt, assures me that nothing bad has ever happened to him in a helicopter excepting getting it shot up nine times, but that was in Vietnam, and he foresees no problems with the garbage-barge mission. Soon we are over the harbor, circling the barge, which turns out to be, like so many celebrities when you see them up close, not as tall as you expected. As I gaze down at it, with the soaring spires of downtown Manhattan in the background gleaming in the brilliant sky, a thought crosses my mind: I had better write at *least* 10 inches about this, to justify our expense reports.

Later that day, I stop outside Grand Central Station, where a woman is sitting in a chair on the sidewalk next to a sign that says:

TAROT CARDS
PALM READINGS

I ask her how much it costs for a Tarot card reading, and she says $10, which I give her. She has me select nine cards, which she arranges in a circle. "Now ask me a question," she says.

"Can New York save itself?" I ask.

She looks at me.

"That's your question?" she asks.

"Yes," I say.

"OK," she says. She looks at the cards. "Yes, New York can save itself for the future."

She looks at me. I don't say anything. She looks back at the cards.

"New York is the Big Apple," she announces. "It is big and exciting, with very many things to see and do."

After the reading I stop at a newsstand and pick up a copy of *Manhattan Living* magazine, featuring a guide to condominiums. I note that there are a number of one-bedrooms priced as low as $250,000.

Manhattan Living also has articles. "It is only recently," one begins, "that the word 'fashionable' has been used in conjunction with the bathroom."

DAY THREE: Just to be on the safe side, Chuck and I decide to devote Day Three to getting back to the airport. Because of a slip-up at the Department of Taxi Licensing, our driver speaks a fair amount of English. And it's a darned good thing he does, because he is kind enough to share his philosophy of life with us, in between shouting helpful instructions to other drivers. It is a philosophy of optimism and hope, not just for himself, but also for New York City, and for the world:

"The thing is, you got to look on the lighter side, because HEY WHAT THE HELL IS HE DOING! WHAT THE HELL ARE YOU DOING YOU *(very bad word)!* Because for me, the thing is, respect. If a person shows me respect, then HAH! YOU WANT TO SQUEEZE IN FRONT NOW?? YOU S.O.B.!! I SQUEEZE YOU LIKE A LEMON!! So I am happy here, but you Americans, you know, you are very, you know WHERE IS HE GOING?? You have to look behind the scenery. This damn CIA, something sticky is going on WHERE THE HELL IS THIS STUPID S.O.B. THINK HE IS GOING??? behind the scenery there, you don't think this guy what his name, Casey, you don't LOOK AT THIS S.O.B. you don't wonder why he *really* die? You got to look behind the scenery. I don't trust *nobody.* I don't trust my own *self.* WILL YOU LOOK AT . . .

By the time we reach La Guardia, Chuck and I

have a much deeper understanding of life in general, and it is with a sense of real gratitude that we leap out of the cab and cling to the pavement. Soon we are winging our way southward, watching the Manhattan skyline disappear, reflecting upon our many experiences and pondering the question that brought us here:

Can New York save itself? Can this ultrametropolis—crude yet sophisticated, overburdened yet wealthy, loud yet obnoxious—can this city face up to the multitude of problems besetting it and, drawing upon its vast reserves of spunk and spirit, as it has done so many times before, emerge triumphant?

And, who cares?

A Boy and His Diplodocus

We have been deeply into dinosaurs for some time now. We have a great many plastic dinosaurs around the house. Sometimes I think we have more plastic dinosaurs than plastic robots, if you can imagine.

This is my son's doing, of course. Robert got into dinosaurs when he was about three, as many children do. It's a power thing: Children like the idea of creatures that were much, much bigger and stronger than mommies and daddies are. If a little boy is doing something bad, such as deliberately pouring his apple juice onto the television remote-control device, a mommy or daddy can simply snatch the little boy up and carry him, helpless, to his room. But they would not dare try this with Tyrannosaurus Rex. No sir. Tyrannosaurus Rex would glance down at Mommy or Daddy from a height of 40 feet and casually flick his tail sideways, and Mommy or Daddy would sail directly through the wall, leaving comical cartoon-style Mommy-or-Daddy–shaped holes and Tyrannosaurus Rex would calmly go back to pouring his apple juice onto the remote-control device.

So Robert spends a lot of time being a dinosaur. I recall the time we were at the beach and he was being a Gorgosaurus, which, like Tyrannosaurus Rex, is a major dinosaur, a big meat-eater (Robert is almost always carnivorous). He was stomping around in the sand and along came an elderly tourist couple, talking in German. They sat down near us. Robert watched them.

"Tell them I'm a Gorgosaurus," he said.

"*You* tell them," I said.

"Gorgosauruses can't talk," Robert pointed out, rolling his eyes. Sometimes he can't believe what an idiot his father is.

Anybody who has ever had a small child knows what happened next. What happened was Robert, using the powerful whining ability that Mother Nature gives to young children to compensate for the fact that they have no other useful skills, got me to go over to this elderly foreign couple I had never seen before, point to my son, who was looking as awesome and terrifying as a three-year-old can look lumbering around in a bathing suit with a little red anchor sewn on the crotch, and say: "He's a Gorgosaurus."

The Germans looked at me the way you would look at a person you saw walking through a shopping mall with a vacant stare and a chain saw. They said nothing.

"Ha ha!" I added, so they would see I was in fact very normal.

They continued to say nothing. You could tell this had never happened to them over in Germany. You could just tell that in Germany, they have a strict policy whereby people who claim their sons are dinosaurs on public beaches are quickly sedated by the authorities. You could also tell that this couple agreed with that policy.

"Tell them I'm a meat-eater," the Gorgosaurus whispered.

"He's a meat-eater," I told the couple. God only knows why.

They got up and started to fold their towels.

"Tell them I can eat more in ONE BITE than a mommy and a daddy and a little boy could eat in TWO WHOLE MONTHS," urged the Gorgosaurus, this being one of the many dinosaur facts he got from the books we read to him at bedtime. But by then the Germans were already striding off, glancing back at me and talking quietly to each other about which way they would run if I came after them.

"Ha ha!" I called after them, reassuringly.

Gorgosaurus continued to stomp around, knocking over whole cities. I had a hell of a time getting him to take a nap that day.

Sometimes when he's tired and wants to be cuddled, Robert is a gentle plant-eating dinosaur. I'll come into the living room, and there will be this lump on my wife's lap, whimpering, with Robert's blanket over it.

"What's that?" I ask my wife.

"A baby Diplodocus," she answers. (Diplodocus looked sort of like Brontosaurus, only sleeker and cuter.) "It lost its mommy and daddy."

"No!" I say.

"So it's going to live with us forever and ever," she says.

"Great!" I say.

The blanket wriggles with joy.

Lately, at our house we have become interested in what finally happened to the dinosaurs. According to our bedtime books, all the dinosaurs died quite suddenly about 60 million years ago, and nobody knows why. Some scientists—this is the truth, it was in *Time* magazine—think the cause was a Death Comet that visits the earth from time to time. Robert thinks this is great. A Death Comet! That is *serious* power. A Death Comet would *never* have to brush its teeth. A Death Comet could have pizza *whenever it wanted.*

Me, I get uneasy, reading about the Death Comet. I don't like to think about the dinosaurs disappearing. Yet another reminder that nothing lasts forever. Even a baby Diplodocus has to grow up sometime.

Young Frankincense

My most vivid childhood memory of Christmas that does not involve opening presents, putting batteries in presents, playing with presents, and destroying presents before sundown, is the annual Nativity Pageant at St. Stephen's Episcopal Church in Armonk, New York. This was a major tradition at St. Stephen's, which had quite a few of them. For example, at Easter, we had the Hoisting of the Potted Hyacinths. Each person in the congregation was issued a potted hyacinth, and we'd sing a song that had a lot of "alleluias" in it, and every time we'd get to one, we'd all hoist our pots over our heads. This is the truth. Remember it next time somebody tells you Episcopalians never really get loose.

But the big event was the Nativity Pageant, which almost all the Sunday School kids were drafted to perform in. Mrs. Elson, who had experience in the Legitimate Theater, was the director, and she would tell you what role you would play, based on your artistic abilities. Like, if your artistic abilities were that you were short, you would get a role as an angel, which involved being part of the Heavenly Host and gazing with adoration upon the Christ Child and trying not to scratch yourself. The Christ Child was played by one of those dolls that close their eyes when you lay them down because they have weights in their heads. I know this because Neil Thompson and I once conducted a research experiment wherein we scientifically opened a doll's head up with a hammer. (This was not the doll that played the Christ Child, of course. We used a doll that belonged to Neil's sister, Penny, who once tied her dog to the bumper of my mother's car roughly five minutes before my mother drove the car to White Plains. But that is another story.)

Above your angels, you had your three shepherds. Shepherd was my favorite role, because you got to carry a stick, plus you spent most of the pageant waiting back in the closet with a rope that led up to the church bell and about 750,000 bats. Many were the happy rehearsal hours we shepherds spent back there, in the dark, whacking each other with sticks and climbing up the ladder so as to cause bat emission products to rain down upon us. ("And lo, when the shepherds did looketh towards the heavens, they did see, raining down upon them, a multitude of guano. . . .")

When it was our turn to go out and perform, we shepherds would emerge from the closet, walk up the aisle, and hold a conference to determine whether or not we should go to Bethlehem. One year when I was a shepherd, the role of First Shepherd was played by Mike Craig, who always, at every rehearsal, would whisper: "Let's ditch this joint." Of course this does not strike *you* as particularly funny, but believe me, if you were a 10-year-old who had spent the past hour in a bat-infested closet, it would strike you as amusing in the extreme, and it got funnier every time, so that when Mike said it on Christmas Eve *during the actual pageant,* it was an awesome thing, the hydrogen bomb of jokes, causing the shepherds to almost pee their garments as they staggered off, snorting, toward Bethlehem.

After a couple of years as shepherd, you usually did a stint as a Three King. This was not nearly as good a role, because (a) you didn't get to wait in the closet, and (b) you had to lug around the gold, the frankincense, and of course the myrrh, which God forbid you should drop because they were played by valuable antique containers belonging to Mrs. Elson. Nevertheless, being a Three King was better than being Joseph, because Joseph had to hang around with Mary, who was played by (YECCCCCHHHHHHH) a girl. You had to wait backstage with this girl, and walk in with this girl, and needless to say you felt like a total wonk, which was not helped by the fact that the shepherds and the Three Kings were constantly suggesting that you *liked* this girl. So during the pageant Joseph tended to maintain the maximum allowable distance from Mary, as though she were carrying some kind of fatal bacteria.

On Christmas Eve we were all pretty nervous, but thanks to all the rehearsals, the pageant generally went off with only 60 or 70 hitches. Like, for example, one year Ernie Dobbs, a Three King, dropped the frankincense only moments before showtime, and he had to go on carrying, as I recall, a Rolodex. Also there was the famous incident where the shepherds could not get out of the bat closet for the longest while, and thus lost their opportunity for that moment of dramatic tension where they confer and the audience is on the edge of its pews, wondering what they'll decide. When they finally emerged, all they had time to do was lunge directly for Bethlehem.

But we always got through the pageant, somehow, and Mrs. Elson always told us what a great job we had done, except for the year Ernie broke the frankincense. Afterwards, whoever had played Joseph would try to capture and destroy the rest of the male cast. Then we would go home to bed, with visions of Mattel-brand toys requiring six "D" cell batteries (not included) dancing in our heads. Call me sentimental, but I miss those days.

Peace on Earth, But No Parking

Once again we find ourselves enmeshed in the Holiday Season, that very special time of year when we join with our loved ones in sharing centuries-old traditions such as trying to find a parking space at the mall. We traditionally do this in my family by driving around the parking lot until we see a shopper emerge from the mall, then we follow her, in very much the same spirit as the Three Wise Men, who 2,000 years ago followed a star, week after week, until it led them to a parking space.

We try to keep our bumper about four inches from the shopper's calves, to let the other circling cars know that she belongs to us. Sometimes two cars will get into a fight over whom the shopper belongs to, similar to the way great white sharks will fight over who gets to eat a snorkeler. So we follow our shoppers closely, hunched over the steering wheel, whistling "It's Beginning to Look a Lot Like Christmas" through our teeth, until we arrive at her car, which is usually parked several time zones away from the mall. Sometimes our shopper tries to indicate that she was merely planning to drop off some packages and go back to shopping, but when she hears our engine rev in a festive fashion and sees the holiday gleam in our eyes, she realizes she would never make it.

And so we park and clamber joyously out of our car through the windows, which is necessary because the crack Mall Parking Space Size Reduction Team has been at work again. They get out there almost every night and redo the entire parking lot, each time making the spaces smaller, until finally, they are using, say, a Jell-O box to mark the width between lines. "Let's see them fit in there," they say, laughing, because they know we will try. They know that if necessary, we will pull into the parking space balanced on two left-side wheels, like professional stunt drivers, because we are holiday shoppers.

I do not mean to suggest that the true meaning of the holiday season is finding a parking space. No, the true meaning of the holiday season is finding a sales clerk. The way to do this is, look around the store for one of those unmarked doors, then burst through it without warning. There you will find dozens of clerks sitting on the floor, rocking back and forth and whimpering from weeks of exposure to the holiday environment. Of course as soon as they see you, a shopper, they will bolt for the window. This is why you must carry a tape recorder.

"Hold it!" you shout, freezing them in their tracks. "I have a tape recorder here, and unless somebody lets me make my holiday purchases, I'm going to play 'Frosty the Snowman.' "

Cruel? Inhuman? Perhaps. But you have no choice. Because this is the holiday season, and you have to buy thoughtful gifts for all of your Loved Ones, or they will hate you. Here are some helpful suggestions:

GIFTS FOR CHILDREN: To find out what children want this year, I naturally called up the headquarters of the Toys Backward 'R' Us Corporation, which as you parents know is now larger than the Soviet Union. I talked with a spokesperson who told me that last year the corporation's net sales were $2.4 billion (I assume she meant in my immediate neighborhood).

The spokesperson told me that one of the hot toys for boys this year, once again, is the G.I. Joe action figure and "accessories," which is the toy-industry code word for "guns," as in: "Don't nobody move! I got an accessory!" The little boy on your list can have hours of carefree childhood fun with this G.I. Joe set, engaging in realistic armed-forces adventures such as having G.I. Joe explain to little balding congressional committee figures how come he had to use his optional Action Shredder accessory.

Another hot item is Captain Power and the Soldiers of the Future, a toy system that—here is a coincidence for you—is featured on a Saturday-morning TV show. The heart of this system is an electronic accessory that the child shoots at the TV screen to actually kill members of the Bio Dread Empire. The spokesperson did not say whether it also would work on Geraldo Rivera.

For little girls, the toy industry is once again going way out on a limb and offering a vast simpering array of dolls. The big news this year, however, is that many of these dolls have computer chips inside them, so they can do the same things that a real baby would do if it had a computer chip inside it. Some dolls even respond according to the time of day. In the morning, they say: "I'm hungry!" In the evening, they say: "I'm sleepy!" And late at night, when the house is dark and quiet, they whisper into the child's ear: "I think I hear Mr. Eyeball Plucker in the closet again!"

GIFTS FOR GROWN-UPS: I don't want to get too corny here, but I think the nicest gift you can give a grown-up, especially one you really care about, is not something you buy in a store. In fact, it costs nothing, yet it is a very precious gift, and one that only you can give. I'm talking about your parking space.

Hey Babe Hum Babe Hum Babe Hey . . .

The crack of the bat . . . the roar of the crowd . . . the sight of slug-shaped, saliva-drenched gobs of tobacco seeping into the turf and causing mutations among soil-based life forms. . . .

Baseball. For me, it's as much a part of summer as sitting bolt upright in bed at 3:30 A.M. and trying to remember if I filed for an extension on my tax return. And the memories baseball season brings back! Ebbetts Field, for example. That's all I remember: Ebbetts Field. What the hell does it mean? Is it anything important? Maybe one of you readers can help.

Why does baseball hold such great appeal for Americans? A big factor, of course, is that the Russians can't play it. Try as they might, they can't seem to master infield chatter, which is what the members of the infield constantly yell at the pitcher. A typical segment of infield chatter would be:

Hey babe hum babe hum babe hey no batter hey fire that ball hum that pellet whip that hose baby sling that sphere c'mon heave that horsehide right in there c'mon dammit we're bored we're really bored bored bored bored out here hunched over in these cretin pants c'mon let's fling that orb let's unload that globe you sum-bitch let's THROW that ball please for God's sake let's . . .

The infield's purpose in chattering at the pitcher like this is to get him so irritated that he deliberately throws the ball at the batter's face, which minimizes the danger that the batter will swing and thus put the infield in the position of having to stand in the path of a potentially lethal batted ball. American boys learn infield chatter as very young children, but the Russians have tremendous trouble with it. The best they've been able to do so far is "Holy mackerel, you are putting forth some likely shots now, ho ho!" which is pretty good for only five years' effort, but hardly the level of chatter they'll need in international competition.

Another reason why Americans are Number One in baseball is the phrases yelled by fans to encourage the players. American fans generally use the three basic phrases:

- Boo.
- You stink.
- You really stink, you stupid jerk.

These phrases of encouragement have dominated baseball since the 1920s, when the great George Herman Ruth made baseball history at Yankee Stadium by pointing his bat at the stands and correctly identifying them in only four attempts. But in recent years, a large cold-air mass of change has begun to form in the North, where fans of the Montreal Expos, who all know how to speak French because there's nothing else to do in Canada after 4 P.M., have developed some new and very competitive phrases, such as:

- Vous bumme, il y a un poisson dans votre bibliotheque. (You bum, there is a fish in your library.)
- Boux. (Boo.)

Thus encouraged, the Expos have become a baseball powerhouse. They probably would have won the World Series by now except that the players refuse to return from spring training until Labor Day.

So the United States is still the best, and you can bet the mortgage that the World Series, which is open to any city in the world that has a major-league franchise, will this year be won once again by a team consisting of U.S. citizens plus maybe two dozen guys named Julio from friendly spider-infested nations to the south. In fact, the only real problem facing major-league baseball at the moment is that everybody associated with it in any way is a drug addict. This is beginning to affect the quality of the game:

ANNOUNCER: For those viewers who are just joining us, the game has been delayed slightly because the umpires really wanted some nachos, and also the Yankees keep turning into giant birds. I can't remember seeing that happen before in a regular season game, can you, Bob?

COLOR COMMENTATOR *(shrieking)*: THESE aren't my crayons!

So baseball has problems. So who doesn't? It's still a very national pastime, and I for one always feel a stirring of tremendous excitement as we approach the All-Star Game. I'm assuming here that we haven't already passed the All-Star Game.

What I like about the All-Star Game is that the teams aren't picked by a bunch of experts who use computers and care only about cold statistics—what a player's batting average is, how well he throws, whether he's still alive, etc. No, the All-Star teams are chosen by the fans, the everyday folks who sit out in the hot sun hour after hour, cursing and swilling beer that tastes like it has been used to launder jockstraps. The fans don't care about statistics: They vote from the heart, which is why last year's starting American League lineup included Lou Gehrig, O.J. Simpson, and Phil Donahue.

And what lies ahead, after the All-Star break? I look for several very tight pennant races, with many games ending in scores of 4–2, 5–1, and in certain instances 2–0. In the National League, I think we'll see a sharp late-season increase in the number of commercials wherein players employ inappropriate baseball imagery, such as, "Hit a home run against nasal discharge." And in the American League, I look for Dave Winfield to be attacked by seagulls. As always, pitching will be the key.

Red, White, and Beer

Lately I've been feeling very patriotic, especially during commercials. Like, when I see those strongly pro-American Chrysler commercials, the ones where the winner of the Bruce Springsteen Sound-Alike Contest sings about how The Pride Is Back, the ones where Lee Iacocca himself comes striding out and practically challenges the president of Toyota to a knife fight, I get this warm, proud feeling inside, the same kind of feeling I get whenever we hold routine naval maneuvers off the coast of Libya.

But if you want to talk about *real* patriotism, of course, you have to talk about beer commercials. I would have to say that Miller is the most patriotic brand of beer. I grant you it tastes like rat saliva, but we are not talking about taste here. What we are talking about, according to the commercials, is that Miller is by God an *American* beer, "born and brewed in the U.S.A.," and the men who drink it are American men, the kind of men who aren't afraid to perspire freely and shake a man's hand. That's mainly what happens in Miller commercials: Burly American men go around, drenched in perspiration, shaking each other's hands in a violent and patriotic fashion.

You never find out exactly why these men spend so much time shaking hands. Maybe shaking hands is just their simple straightforward burly masculine American patriotic way of saying to each other: "Floyd, I am truly sorry I drank all that Miller beer last night and went to the bathroom in your glove compartment." Another possible explanation is that, since there are never any women in the part of America where beer commercials are made, the burly men have become lonesome and desperate for any form of physical contact. I have noticed that sometimes, in addition to shaking hands, they hug each other. Maybe very late at night, after the David Letterman show, there are Miller commercials in which the burly men engage in slow dancing. I don't know.

I do know that in one beer commercial, I think this is for Miller—although it could be for Budweiser, which is also a very patriotic beer—the burly men build a house. You see them all getting together and pushing up a brand-new wall. Me, I worry some about a house built by men drinking beer. In my experience, you run into trouble when you ask a group of beer-drinking men to perform any task more complex than remembering not to light the filter ends of cigarettes.

For example, in my younger days, whenever anybody in my circle of friends wanted to move, he'd get the rest of us to help, and, as an inducement, he'd buy a couple of cases of beer. This almost always produced unfortunate results, such as the time we were trying to move Dick "The Wretch" Curry from a horrible fourth-floor walk-up apartment in Manhattan's Lower East Side to another horrible fourth-floor walk-up apartment in Manhattan's Lower East Side, and we hit upon the labor-saving concept of, instead of carrying The Wretch's possessions manually down the stairs, simply dropping them out the window, down onto the street, where The Wretch was racing around, gathering up the broken pieces of his life and shrieking at us to stop helping him move, his emotions reaching a fever pitch when his bed, which had been swinging wildly from a rope, entered the apartment two floors below his through what had until seconds earlier been a window.

This is the kind of thinking you get, with beer. So I figure what happens, in the beer commercial where the burly men are building the house, is they push the wall up so it's vertical, and then, after the camera stops filming them, they just keep pushing, and the wall crashes down on the other side, possibly onto somebody's pickup truck. And then they all shake hands.

But other than that, I'm in favor of the upsurge in retail patriotism, which is lucky for me because the airwaves are saturated with pro-American commercials. Especially popular are commercials in which the newly restored Statue of Liberty—and by the way, I say Lee Iacocca should get some kind of medal for that, or at least be elected president—appears to be endorsing various products, as if she were Mary Lou Retton or somebody. I saw one commercial strongly suggesting that the Statue of Liberty uses Sure brand underarm deodorant.

I have yet to see a patriotic laxative commercial, but I imagine it's only a matter of time. They'll show some actors dressed up as hardworking country folk, maybe at a church picnic, smiling at each other and eating pieces of pie. At least one of them will be a black person. The Statue of Liberty will appear in the background. Then you'll hear a country-style singer singing:

"Folks 'round here they love this land;
They stand by their beliefs;
An' when they git themselves stopped up;
They want some quick relief."

Well, what do you think? Pretty good commercial concept, huh?

Nah, you're right. They'd never try to pull something like that. They'd put the statue in the *foreground.*

Why Not the Best?

Excellence is *the* trend of the eighties. Walk into any shopping-mall bookstore, go to the rack where they keep the bestsellers such as *Garfield Gets Spayed,* and you'll see a half-dozen books telling you how to be excellent: *In Search of Excellence, Finding Excellence, Grasping Hold of Excellence, Where to Hide Your Excellence at Night So the Cleaning Personnel Don't Steal It,* etc.

The message of these books is that, here in the eighties, "good" is no longer good enough. In today's business environment, "good" is a word we use to describe an employee whom we are about to transfer to a urinal-storage facility in the Aleutian Islands. What we want, in our eighties business executive, is somebody who demands the best in *everything;* someone who is *never satisfied;* somebody who, if he had been in charge of decorating the Sistine Chapel, would have said: "That is a good fresco, Michelangelo, but I want a *better* fresco, and I want it by tomorrow morning."

This is the kind of thinking that now propels your top corporations. Take the folks at Coca-Cola. For many years, they were content to sit back and make the same old carbonated beverage. It was a *good* beverage, no question about it; generations of people had grown up drinking it and doing the experiment in sixth grade where you put a nail into a glass of Coke and after a couple of days the nail dissolves and the teacher says: "Imagine what it does to your *teeth!*" So Coca-Cola was solidly entrenched in the market, and the management saw no need to improve.

But then along came Pepsi, with the bold new marketing concept of saying that its carbonated beverage was *better,* a claim that Pepsi backed up by paying $19 trillion to Michael Jackson, the most excellent musical genius of all time according to the cover story in *Newsweek* magazine. And so the folks at Coca-Cola suddenly woke up and realized that, hey, these are the *eighties,* and they got off their butts and *improved* Coke by letting it sit out in vats in the hot sun and adding six or eight thousand tons of sugar, the exact amount being a trade secret.

Unfortunately, the general public, having failed to read the market surveys proving that the new Coke was better, refused to drink it, but that is not the point. The point is, the Coke executives decided to *strive for excellence,* and the result is that the American consumer is now benefiting from the most vicious carbonated-beverage marketing war in history. It wouldn't surprise me if, very soon, one side or the other offered to pay $29 trillion to Bruce Springsteen, who according to a *Newsweek* magazine cover story is currently the most excellent musical genius of all time, preceded briefly by Prince.

This striving for excellence extends into people's personal lives as well. When eighties people buy something, they buy the best one, as determined by (1) price and (2) lack of availability. Eighties people buy imported dental floss. They buy gourmet baking soda. If an eighties couple goes to a restaurant where they have made a reservation three weeks in advance, and they are informed that their table is available, they stalk out immediately, because they know it is not an excellent restaurant. If it were, it would have an enormous crowd of excellence-oriented people like themselves, waiting, their beepers going off like crickets in the night. An excellent restaurant wouldn't have a table ready immediately for anybody below the rank of Liza Minnelli.

An excellence-oriented eighties male does not wear a regular watch. He wears a Rolex, because it weighs nearly six pounds and is advertised only in excellence-oriented publications such as *Fortune* and *Rich Protestant Golfer Magazine.* The advertisements are written in incomplete sentences, which is how advertising copywriters denote excellence:

"The Rolex Hyperion. An elegant new standard in quality excellence and discriminating handcraftsmanship. For the individual who is truly able to discriminate with regard to excellent quality standards of crafting things by hand. Fabricated of 100 percent 24-karat gold. No watch parts or anything. Just a great big chunk of gold on your wrist. Truly a timeless statement. For the individual who is very secure. Who doesn't need to be reminded all the time that he is very successful. Much more successful than the people who laughed at him in high school. Because of his acne. People who are probably nowhere near as successful as he is now. Maybe he'll go to his twentieth reunion, and they'll see his Rolex Hyperion. Hahahahyahahahahaha."

Nobody is excused from the excellence trend. *Babies* are not excused. Starting right after they get out of the womb, modern babies are exposed to instructional flashcards designed to make them the best babies they can possibly be, so they can get into today's competitive preschools. Your eighties baby sees so many flashcards that he never gets an unobstructed view of his parents' faces. As an adult, he'll carry around a little wallet card that says "$7 \times 9 = 63$," because it will remind him of mother.

I recently saw a videotape of people who were teaching their babies while they (the babies) were *still in the womb.* I swear I am not making this up. A group of pregnant couples sat in a circle, and, under the direction of an Expert in These Matters, they crooned instructional songs in the direction of the women's stomachs. Mark my words: We will reach the point, in our lifetimes, where babies emerge from their mothers fully prepared to assume entry-level management positions. I'm sure I'm not the only person who has noticed, just wandering around the shopping mall, that more and more babies, the really brand-new modern ones, tend to resemble Lee Iacocca.

Making the World Safe for Salad

I've been thinking about technology of late, because, as you are no doubt aware (like fudge, you are), we recently celebrated the 25th anniversary of the Etch-a-Sketch. I think we can all agree that, except for long-lasting nasal spray, this is the greatest technological achievement of all time. Think, for a moment, of the countless happy childhood hours you spent with this amazing device: Drawing perfect horizontals; drawing perfect verticals; drawing really spastic diagonals; trying to scrape away the silver powder from the window so you could look inside and try to figure out how it works (Mystery Rays from space, is what scientists now believe); and just generally enjoying the sheer childhood pleasure of snatching it away from your sister and shaking it upside down after she had spent 40 minutes making an elaborate picture of a bird.

Think how much better off the world would be if everybody—young and old, black and white, American and Russian, *Time* and *Newsweek*—spent part of each day playing with an Etch-a-Sketch. Think how great it would be if they had public Etch-a-Sketches for you to use while you were waiting in line at the Department of Motor Vehicles. And imagine what would happen if, instead of guns, our young soldiers carried Etch-a-Sketches into battle! They would be cut down like field mice under a rotary mower! So we can't carry this idea too far.

So anyway, as I said, this got me to thinking about technology in general. Too often—three or four times a week, according to some figures—we take technology for granted. When we drop our money into a vending machine at our place of employment and press the button for a tasty snack selection of crackers smeared with "cheez," a nondairy petroleum subproduct approved for use on humans, we are blithely confident that the machine will automatically, much of the time, hurl our desired selection down into the pickup bin, using a computerized electronic snack-ejection device that gives our snack a bin impact velocity of nearly 70 miles an hour, which is what is required to reduce our crackers to a fine, dayglow-orange grit. We rarely stop to consider that without this device, the only way the vending-machine manufacturers would be able to achieve this kind of impact velocity would be to use gravity, which means the machines would have to be 40 feet tall!

Of course, not all technology is good. Some is exactly the opposite (bad). The two obvious examples of this are the hydrogen bomb and those plastic "sneeze shields" they put over restaurant salad bars for your alleged hygiene protection. I have said this before, but it needs to be said again: *Sneeze shields actually spread disease,* because they make it hard for a squat or short-armed person to reach back to the chick peas and simulated bacon, and some of these people inevitably are going to become frustrated and spit in the House Dressing (a creamy Italian).

But this does not mean we should be against technology in general. Specifically, we should not be so hostile toward telephone-answering machines. I say this because I own one, and I am absolutely sick unto death of hearing people say—they *all* say this; it must be Item One on the curriculum in Trend College—"I just *hate* to talk to a *machine!*" They say this as though it is a major philosophical position, as opposed to a description of a minor neurosis. My feeling is, if you have a problem like this, you shouldn't go around *trumpeting* it; you should stay home and practice talking to a machine you can feel comfortable with, such as your Water Pik, until you are ready to assume your place in modern society, OK?

Meanwhile, technology marches on, thanks to new inventions conceived of by brilliant innovative creative geniuses such as a friend of mine named Clint Collins. Although he is really a writer, Clint has developed an amazingly simple yet effective labor-saving device for people who own wall-to-wall carpeting but don't want to vacuum it. Clint's concept is, you cut a piece of two-by-four so it's as long as your vacuum cleaner is wide, and just before company comes, you drag it across your carpet, so it leaves parallel marks similar to the ones caused by a vacuum. Isn't that great? The only improvement I can think of would be if they wove those lines into the carpet right at the factory, so you wouldn't even need a two-by-four.

Another recent advantage in technology comes from Joseph DiGiacinto, my lawyer, who has developed a way to fasten chopsticks together with a rubber band and a little wadded-up piece of paper in such a way that you can actually pick up food with them one-handed. You don't have to ask your waiter for a fork, which makes you look like you just tromped in from Des Moines and never even heard of sweet and sour pork. If you'd like to get in on this high-tech culinary advance, send an envelope with your address and a stamp on it to: Chopstick Concept, c/o Joseph DiGiacinto, Legal Attorney at Law, 235 Main Street, White Plains, NY 10601, and he'll send you, free, a Chopstick Conversion Kit—including a diagram, a rubber band, and instructions that can be wadded up for use as your paper wad—just as soon as I let him know that he has made this generous offer. He also does wills.

And what other advances does the future hold, technologywise? Even as you read these words, white-coated laboratory geeks are working on a revolutionary new camera that not only will focus automatically, set the exposure automatically, flash automatically, and advance the film automatically, but will also automatically refuse to take stupid pictures, such as of the wing out the airplane window.

Trouble on the Line

I want them to stop explaining my long-distance options to me. I don't want to *know* my long-distance options. The more I know about my long-distance options, the more I feel like a fool.

They did this to us once before, with our financial options. This was back in the seventies. Remember? Up until then, if you had any excess money, you put it in a passbook savings account paying 5¼ percent interest, and your only financial options were, did you want the toaster or the electric blanket. For a really slick high-finance maneuver, you could join the Christmas Club, where you gave the bank some money each week, and, at the end of the year, the bank gave you your money *back*. These were simple, peaceful times, except for the occasional Asian land war.

And then, without warning, they made it legal for consumers to engage in complex monetary acts, many of them involving "liquidity." Today, there are a whole range of programs in which all that happens is people call up to ask what they should do with their money:

"Hi, Steve? My wife and I listen to you all the time, and we just love your show. Now here is the problem: We're 27 years old, no kids, and we have a combined income of $93,000, and $675,000 in denatured optional treasury instruments of accrual, which will become extremely mature next week."

Now to me, those people do not have a problem. To me, what these people need in the way of financial advice is: "Lighten up! Buy yourself a big boat and have parties where people put on funny hats and push the piano into the harbor!" But Mr. Consumer Radio Money Advisor, he tells them complex ways to get even *more* money and orders them to tune in next week. These shows make me feel tremendously guilty, as a consumer, because I still keep my money in accounts that actually get smaller, and sometimes disappear, like weekend guests in an old murder mystery, because the bank is always taking out a "service charge," as if the tellers have to take my money for walks or something.

So I feel like a real consumer fool about my money, and now I have to feel like a fool about my phone, too. I liked it better back when we all had to belong to the same Telephone Company, and phones were *phones*—black, heavy objects that were routinely used in the movies, as murder weapons (try *that* with today's phones!). Also, they were permanently attached to your house, and only highly trained Telephone Company personnel could "install" them. This involved attaching four wires, but the Telephone Company always made it sound like brain surgery. It was part of the mystique. When you called for your installation appointment, the Telephone Company would say: "We will have an installer in your area between the hours of 9 A.M. October 3 and the following spring. Will someone be at home?" And you would say yes, if you wanted a phone. You would stay at home, the anxious hours ticking by, and you would wait for your Phone Man. It was as close as most people came to experiencing what heroin addicts go through, the difference being that heroin addicts have the option of going to another supplier. Phone customers didn't. They feared the power of the Telephone Company.

I remember when I was in college, and my roommate Rob somehow obtained a phone. It was a Hot Phone. Rob hooked it up to our legal, wall-mounted phone with a long wire, which gave us the capability of calling the pizza-delivery man without getting up off the floor. This capability was essential, many nights. But we lived in fear. Because we knew we were breaking the rule—not a local, state, or federal rule, but a *Telephone Company* rule—and that any moment, agents of the Telephone Company, accompanied by heavy black dogs, might burst through the door and seize the Hot Phone and write our names down and *we would never be allowed to have phone service again*. And the dogs would seize our pizza.

So the old Telephone Company could be tough, but at least you knew where you stood. You never had to think about your consumer long-distance options. Whereas today you cannot turn on the television without seeing Cliff Robertson, standing in some pathetic rural community with a name like Eye Socket, Montana, telling you that if you don't go with his phone company, you won't be able to call people in rural areas like this, in case you ever had a reason to, such as you suddenly needed information about heifers. Which sounds reasonable, but then Burt Lancaster tells you what a jerk you are if you go with Cliff because it costs more. But that's exactly what Joan Rivers says about Burt! And what about Liz? Surely Liz has a phone company!

So it is very confusing, and yet you are expected to somehow make the right consumer choice. They want you to fill out a *ballot*. And if you don't fill it out, they're going to *assign you a random telephone company*. God knows what you could wind up with. You could wind up with the Soviet Union Telephone Company. You could wind up with one of those phone companies where you have to crank the phone, like on "Lassie," and the operator is always listening in, including when you call the doctor regarding intimate hemorrhoidal matters.

So you better fill out your ballot. I recommend that you go with Jim & Ed's Telephone Company &

Radiator Repair. I say this because Jim and Ed feature a service contract whereby you pay a flat $15 a month, and if you have a problem, Jim or Ed will come out to your house (Jim is preferable, because after 10 A.M. Ed likes to drink Night Train wine and shoot at religious lawn statuary) and have some coffee with you and tell you that he's darned if *he* can locate the problem, but if he had to take a stab, he'd guess it was probably somewhere in the wires.

Read This First

Congratulations! You have purchased an extremely fine device that would give you thousands of years of trouble-free service, except that you undoubtedly will destroy it via some typical bonehead consumer maneuver. Which is why we ask you to PLEASE FOR GOD'S SAKE READ THIS OWNER'S MANUAL CAREFULLY BEFORE YOU UNPACK THE DEVICE. YOU ALREADY UNPACKED IT, DIDN'T YOU? YOU UNPACKED IT AND PLUGGED IT IN AND TURNED IT ON AND FIDDLED WITH THE KNOBS, AND NOW YOUR CHILD, THE SAME CHILD WHO ONCE SHOVED A POLISH SAUSAGE INTO YOUR VIDEOCASSETTE RECORDER AND SET IT ON "FAST FORWARD," THIS CHILD ALSO IS FIDDLING WITH THE KNOBS, RIGHT? AND YOU'RE JUST STARTING TO READ THE INSTRUCTIONS, RIGHT??? WE MIGHT AS WELL JUST BREAK ALL THESE DEVICES RIGHT AT THE FACTORY BEFORE WE SHIP THEM OUT, YOU KNOW THAT?

We're sorry. We just get a little crazy sometimes, because we're always getting back "defective" merchandise where it turns out that the consumer inadvertently bathed the device in acid for six days. So, in writing these instructions, we naturally tend to assume that your skull is filled with dead insects, but we mean nothing by it. OK? Now let's talk about:

1. UNPACKING THE DEVICE: The device is encased in foam to protect it from the Shipping People, who like nothing more than to jab spears into the outgoing boxes. PLEASE INSPECT THE CONTENTS CAREFULLY FOR GASHES OR IDA MAE BARKER'S ENGAGEMENT RING WHICH SHE LOST LAST WEEK, AND SHE THINKS MAYBE IT WAS WHILE SHE WAS PACKING DEVICES. Ida Mae really wants that ring back, because it is her only proof of engagement, and her fiancé, Stuart, is now seriously considering backing out on the whole thing inasmuch as he had consumed most of a bottle of Jim Beam in Quality Control when he decided to pop the

question. It is not without irony that Ida Mae's last name is "Barker," if you get our drift.

WARNING: DO NOT EVER AS LONG AS YOU LIVE THROW AWAY THE BOX OR ANY OF THE PIECES OF STYROFOAM, EVEN THE LITTLE ONES SHAPED LIKE PEANUTS.

If you attempt to return the device to the store, and you are missing one single peanut, the store personnel will laugh in the chilling manner exhibited by Joseph Stalin just after he enslaved Eastern Europe.

Besides the device, the box should contain:

- Eight little rectangular snippets of paper that say: "WARNING"
- A plastic packet containing four $5/17''$ pilfer grommets and two chub-ended $6/93''$ boxcar prawns.

YOU WILL NEED TO SUPPLY: a matrix wrench and 60,000 feet of tram cable.

IF ANYTHING IS DAMAGED OR MISSING: You *immediately* should turn to your spouse and say: "Margaret, you know why this country can't make a car that can get all the way through the drive-thru at Burger King without a major transmission overhaul? Because nobody cares, that's why." (Warning: This Is Assuming Your Spouse's Name Is Margaret.)

2. PLUGGING IN THE DEVICE: The plug on this device represents the latest thinking of the electrical industry's Plug Mutation Group, which, in the continuing effort to prevent consumers from causing hazardous electrical current to flow through their appliances, developed the Three-Pronged Plug, then the Plug Where One Prong Is Bigger Than the Other. Your device is equipped with the revolutionary new Plug Whose Prongs Consist of Six Small Religious Figurines Made of Chocolate. DO NOT TRY TO PLUG IT IN! Lay it gently on the floor near an outlet, but out of direct sunlight, and clean it weekly with a damp handkerchief.

WARNING: WHEN YOU ARE LAYING THE PLUG ON THE FLOOR, DO NOT HOLD A SHARP OBJECT IN YOUR OTHER HAND AND TRIP OVER THE CORD AND POKE YOUR EYE OUT, AS THIS COULD VOID YOUR WARRANTY.

3. OPERATION OF THE DEVICE:

WARNING: WE MANUFACTURE ONLY THE ATTRACTIVE DESIGNER CASE. THE ACTUAL WORKING CENTRAL PARTS OF THE DEVICE ARE MANUFACTURED IN JAPAN. THE INSTRUCTIONS WERE TRANSLATED BY MRS. SHIRLEY PELTWATER OF ACCOUNTS RECEIVABLE, WHO HAS NEVER ACTUALLY BEEN TO JAPAN BUT DOES HAVE MOST OF *SHOGUN* ON TAPE.

INSTRUCTIONS: For results that can be the finest, it is our advising that: Never to hold these buttons two times!! Except the battery. Next, taking the (something) earth section may cause a large occurrence! However. If this is not a trouble, such rotation is a very maintenance action, as a kindly (something) viewpoint from Drawing B.

4. WARRANTY: Be it hereby known that this device, together with but not excluding all those certain parts thereunto, shall be warrantied against all defects, failures, and malfunctions as shall occur between now and Thursday afternoon at shortly before 2, during which time the Manufacturer will, at no charge to the Owner, send the device to our Service People, who will emerge from their caves and engage in rituals designed to cleanse it of evil spirits. This warranty does not cover the attractive designer case.

WARNING: IT MAY BE A VIOLATION OF SOME LAW THAT MRS. SHIRLEY PELTWATER HAS *SHOGUN* ON TAPE.

The Urban Professionals

I'm going to start a rock 'n' roll band. Not a *good* band, where you have to be in tune and wear makeup. This will be a band consisting of people who are Approaching Middle Age, by which I mean they know the words to "Wooly Bully." This will be the kind of band whose members often miss practice for periodontal reasons and are always yelling at their kids for leaving Popsicles on the amplifiers. We will be called the "Urban Professionals." I will be lead guitar.

I miss being in a band. The last band I was in, the "Phlegmtones," dissolved a couple of years ago, and even that was not truly a formal band in the sense of having instruments or playing them or anything. What it was, basically, was my friend Randall and myself drinking beer and trying to remember the words to "Runaround Sue," by Dion and the Belmonts.

Before that, the last major band I was in was in college, in the sixties. It was called the "Federal Duck," which we thought was an extremely hip name. We were definitely 10 pounds of hipness in a 5-pound bag. We had the first strobe light of any band in our market area. We were also into The Blues, which was a very hip thing to be into, back in the sixties. We were always singing songs about how our woman she done lef' us and we was gon' jump into de ribba an' drown. This was pretty funny, because we were extremely white suburban-style college students whose only actual insight into the blues came from experiences such as getting a C in Poli Sci.

In terms of musical competence, if I had to pick one word to describe us, that word would be "loud." We played with the subtlety of aboveground nuclear testing. But we made up for this by being cheap. We were so cheap that organizations were always hiring us sight unseen, which resulted a number of times in our being hired by actual grown-ups whose idea of a good party band was elderly men in stained tuxedos playing songs from *My Fair Lady* on accordions at about the volume of a drinking fountain.

When we would come in and set up, with our mandatory long hair and our strobe light and our 60,000 pounds of amplifiers, these people would watch us in wary silence. But once we started to play, once the sound of our pulsating beat filled the air, something almost magical would happen: They would move farther away. They'd form hostile little clots against the far wall. Every now and then they'd send over an emissary, who would risk lifelong hearing damage to cross the dance floor and ask us if we knew any nice old traditional slow-dance fox-trot-type songs such as "Smoke Gets In Your Eyes," which of course we didn't, because it has more than four chords. So we'd say: "No, we don't know that one, but we do know another one you might like." Then we'd play "Land of 1,000 Dances," a very big hit by Cannibal and the Headhunters on Rampart Records. This is a song with only one chord (E). Almost all of the lyrics consist of the statement, *I said a na,* as follows:

I said a na
Na na na na
Na na na na, na na na, na na na;
Na na na na.

Our best jobs were at fraternity parties. The only real problem we'd run into there was that every now and then they'd set fire to our equipment. Other than that, fraternity brothers made for a very easygoing audience. Whatever song they requested, we'd play "Land of 1,000 Dances," and they'd be happy. They were too busy throwing up on their dates to notice. They are running the nation today.

Me, I am leading a quiet life. Too quiet. This is why I'm going to form the Urban Professionals. Right now I am actively recruiting members. So far I've recruited one, an editor named Tom whose musical qualifications are that he is 32 years old. He's going to play some instrument of the type you got handed in rhythm band in elementary school, such as the tambourine. Just judging from my circle of friends, I think The Urban Professionals are going to have a large tambourine section.

Once we start to catch on, we'll make a record. It will be called: "A Moderate Amount of Soul." After it comes out, we'll go on a concert tour. We'll stay in Holiday Inns, and sometimes we'll "trash" our rooms by refusing to fill out the Guest Questionnaire. Because that's the kind of rebels the Urban Professionals will be. But our fans will still love us. When we finish our act, they'll be overcome by emotion. They'll all rise spontaneously to their feet, and they'll try, as a gesture of appreciation, to hold lighted matches over their heads. Then they'll all realize they quit smoking, so they'll spontaneously sit back down.

The Plastic, Fantastic Cover

I have just about given up on the Tupperware people. I've been trying to get them interested in a song I wrote, called "The Tupperware Song," which I am sure would be a large hit. I called them about it two or three times a week for several weeks.

"You wrote a song?" they would say.

"Yes," I would say.

"About Tupperware?" they would say.

"Yes," I would say. "It's kind of a blues song."

"We'll have somebody get back to you," they would say.

For quite a while there I thought I was getting the run-around, until finally a nice Tupperware executive named Dick called me up. He was very honest with me. "There's a fairly limited market for songs about Tupperware," he said.

"Dick," I said. "This is a killer song." Which was true. It gets a very positive reaction whenever I perform it. Of course, I perform it only in those social settings where people have loosened up to the point where they would react positively if you set their clothing on fire, but I still think this song would have widespread appeal.

I wrote it a while back, when friends of mine named Art and Dave had a big Tupperware party in their apartment. It was the social event of the month. Something like 50 people showed up. When the Tupperware Lady walked in, you could tell right away from her facial expression that this was not the kind of Tupperware crowd she was used to. She was used to a subdued all-female crowd, whereas this was a large coeducational crowd with some crowd members already dancing on the refrigerator. The

Tupperware Lady kept saying things like: "Are you sure this is supposed to be a Tupperware party?" And: "This doesn't look like a Tupperware party." She wanted to go home.

But we talked her into staying, although she never really accepted the fact that Art and Dave were her Tupperware hostesses. She wanted to deal with a woman. All of her communications with Art and Dave had to go through a woman interpreter:

TUPPERWARE LADY *(speaking to a woman)***:** Where do you want me to set up?

WOMAN *(speaking to Art, who is standing right there)***:** Art, where do you want her to set up?

ART: How about right over here on the coffee table?

WOMAN *(to the Tupperware Lady)***:** Art says how about right over here on the coffee table.

TUPPERWARE LADY: Fine.

Once we got everybody settled down, sort of, the Tupperware Lady wanted us to engage in various fun Tupperware party activities such as "brain teasers" wherein if we could name all the bodily parts that had three letters, we would win a free grapefruit holder or something. We did this for a while, but it was slowing things down, so we told the Tupperware Lady we had this song we wanted to perform.

The band consisted of me and four other highly trained journalists. You know what "The Tupperware Song" sounds like if you ever heard the song "I'm a Man" by Muddy Waters, where he sings about the general theme that he is a man, and in between each line the band goes Da-DA-da-da-DUM, so you get an effect like this:

MUDDY WATERS: *I'm a man.*
BAND: Da-DA-da-da-DUM
MUDDY WATERS: *A natural man.*
BAND: Da-DA-da-da-DUM
MUDDY WATERS: *A full-grown man.*

And so on. This is the general approach taken in "The Tupperware Song," except it is about Tupperware. It starts out this way:

Some folks use waxed paper
Some folks use the Reynolds Wrap
Some folks use the Plastic Baggie
To try to cover up the gap
You can use most anything
To keep your goodies from the air
But nothing works as well
As that good old Tupperware

(CHORUS)

'Cause it's here
Whooaaa
Take a look at what we got
If you don't try some and buy some
Don't blame me when your turnips rot.

It has two more verses covering other important Tupperware themes. Verse Two stresses the importance of "burping" the air out of your container to make sure your lid seals securely, and Verse Three points out that you can make money by holding a Tupperware party in your home.

As you might imagine, the crowd was completely blown away by this song. The Tupperware Lady herself was near tears. But the important thing was, people bought a *lot* of Tupperware that night. People bought Tupperware they would never in a million years need. Single men who lived in apartments and never cooked anything, ever, that could not be heated in a toaster, were ordering Tupperware cake transporters. It was obvious to me right then and there that "The Tupperware Song" was a powerful marketing tool.

I explained all this to Dick, of the Tupperware company, and he said I could send him a cassette tape of the song. Which I did, but I haven't heard a thing. Not that I'm worried. I'm sure there are plenty of other large wealthy corporations out there that would be interested in a blues song about Tupperware. In fact, I'm getting offers in the mail almost every day. Most of them are for supplementary hospitalization insurance, but that's obviously just a negotiating ploy.

Bang the Tupperware Slowly

When I die, I want my obituary to read as follows:

"Dave Barry is dead. Mr. Barry and his band, the Urban Professionals, once performed 'The Tupperware Song' before 1,000 Tupperware distributors."

This is the truth. We really did perform before 1,000 Tupperware distributors, and they gave us a standing ovation, although in the interest of accuracy, I should tell you that just before we performed, they also gave a standing ovation to a set of ovenware. But I don't care. This was without question the highlight of my entire life.

The way it came about was, the Tupperware people finally saw the musical light and decided to invite me to perform my original composition, "The Tupperware Song," before a large sales conference at Tupperware headquarters, located in Orlando, Florida, right next to Gatorland, an attraction where (this is true) alligators jump into the air and eat dead chickens hung from wires. Naturally I accepted the invitation. A break like this comes along once in your career.

I formed a new band, the Urban Professionals, especially for this performance. I chose the members very carefully, based on their ability to correctly answer the following question: "Do you want to go to Orlando at your own expense and perform before Tupperware distributors?" (The correct answer was: "Yes.") Using this strict screening procedure, I obtained three band members, all trained members of the *Miami Herald* staff. I'm the lead guitar player and singer and also (I'm not bragging here; these are simply facts) the only person in the band who knows when the song has started or ended. The other members of the band just sort of stand around looking nervous until I've been going for a while, and then, after it penetrates their primitive musical consciousnesses that the song has begun, they become startled and lurch into action. Likewise it takes them up to 30 seconds to come to a complete stop after the song is technically over.

The only other normal instrument in the band is a harmonica, played by Gene. Gene has been attempting to play the harmonica for a number of years, and has developed a repertoire of several songs, all of which sound exactly like "Oh, Susannah!" "Here's another one!" he'll say, and then he plays "Oh, Susannah!" He plays it very rapidly, totally without pauses, as if he's anxious to get back to journalism, so if you tried to sing along, you'd have to go: "Icomefromalabamawithmybanjoonmyknee," etc., and pretty soon you'd run out of oxygen and keel over onto your face, which Gene wouldn't notice because he'd be too busy trying to finish the song on schedule.

The other two instruments in the band are actually Tupperware products, played rhythmically by Tom and Lou, who also dance. How good are they? Let me put it this way: If you can watch them perform and not wet your pants then you are legally blind. For one thing, they are both afflicted with severe rhythm impairment, the worst cases I have ever seen, worse even than Republican convention delegates. You ask Lou and Tom to clap along to a song and not only will they never once hit the beat, but they will also never, no matter how eternally long the song goes on, both clap at the same time. On top of which you have the fact that they do not have your classic dancer's build, especially Lou, who is, and I say this with all due respect, the same overall shape as a Krispy Kreme jelly doughnut.

When we got to the Tupperware convention center we became a tad nervous, because (a) it turns out that Tupperware is a large business venture that many people take very seriously and (b) we had never even practiced as a total band. The bulk of our musical preparation to that point had consisted of deciding that our band outfits should include sunglasses.

Fortunately, the Tupperware distributors turned out to be extremely peppy people, prone to applauding wildly at the slightest provocation. They especially loved Lou and Tom lunging around waving their Tupperware products in what they presumably thought was unison, looking like the Temptations might look if they were suddenly struck onstage with severe disorders of the central nervous system.

After we got off the stage, Lou announced that it was the most exciting thing he had ever done. Gene kept saying: "A professional musician. I'm a *professional musician.*" A Tupperware person came up and asked if we'd be willing to perform again, and of course we said yes, although I am becoming concerned. Tom has announced, several times, that he thinks next time the dancers should get a singing part. I can see already that unless we hold our egos in check, keeping this thing in perspective, we could start having the kind of internal conflicts that broke up the Beatles, another very good band.

Bite the Wax Tadpole!

Now we're going to look at some important new developments in the U.S. advertising industry, which continues to be a hotbed of innovation as well as a source of pride to all Americans regardless of intelligence. This country may no longer be capable of manufacturing anything more technologically sophisticated than breakfast cereal, but by God when it comes to advertising, we are still—and I mean this sincerely—Number One.

Our first bit of advertising news will come as a happy surprise to those of you who lie awake nights asking yourselves: "Whatever happened to Mikey, the lovable chubby-cheeked child who hated everything until he tasted Life brand breakfast cereal in the heartwarming television commercial that we all saw 63,000 times back in the seventies?"

The good news is: Mikey is coming back, as part of a major advertising campaign! The Quaker Oats Co. sent me *two* large press kits on this, both quoting a Quaker Oats executive as saying: "We've received thousands of letters over the years asking what's become of him. . . . We thought it would be fun to satisfy America's curiosity by conducting a nationwide search to reveal his present-day identity."

Ha ha! Fun is hardly the word! I don't know about you, but I'm going to be waiting on tenterhooks until the big moment comes when the Quaker Oats Co., in a national press conference, finally reveals what "tenterhooks" are. No, seriously, they're going to reveal who Mikey is, so that the thousands of people who wrote to them about this important matter can go back to learning how to eat with real utensils.

Speaking of adorable and talented young actors whose moving commercial performances have tugged at the heartstrings of our minds, I wonder whatever happened to that little boy who used to do the Oscar Mayer commercials. Remember? The one who claimed his baloney had a first name, and it was O-S-C-A-R? I wonder if that child didn't run into problems later in life. ("OK, pal. You and Oscar there are under arrest.").

Another commercial personality I was wondering about is the man who used to promote Ti-D-bol brand automatic commode freshener by rowing his boat around inside the tank of a giant toilet. I mean, it must have been difficult for him, going back to normal life after having reached a show business pinnacle like that. So I called the Knomark company, which makes Ti-D-bol, and I found out an amazing fact: The role of the original Ti-D-bol man was played by none other than "Miami Vice" 's Don Johnson! Isn't that an incredible celebrity gossip tidbit? I hope to see it reprinted in leading supermarket tabloids everywhere, although in the interest of fairness and objectivity I should point out that I just now made it up.

The actual truth, according to Bill Salmon, Knomark's marketing director, is that there were a number of Ti-D-bol men. "The Ti-D-bol man," he said, "was anybody who put on the blazer and the white hat and got in the boat." The current Ti-D-bol man, he said, is a cartoon character who remains on dry land. "Right now he is not in a toilet tank in a rowboat, but that does not mean we would not use the Ti-D-bol man in the tank again at a future time," Salmon stressed.

By the way, I was disappointed to learn from Salmon that the rowboat commercials were done with trick photography, meaning there never was a 50-foot-high toilet. I think they should build one, as a promotional concept. Wouldn't that be great? They could split the cost with the Jolly Green Giant. I bet he sure could use it. I bet he's making a mess out of his valley. Ho ho ho!

I found our next news item in the *Weekly World News,* a leading supermarket tabloid, and it is just so wonderful that I will reprint it verbatim:

"The Coca-Cola Company has changed the name of its soft drink in China after discovering the words mean 'bite the wax tadpole' in Chinese."

I called Coca-Cola, and a woman named Darlene confirmed this item. She also said the company decided to go with a different name over in China, which I think is crazy. "Bite the Wax Tadpole" is the best name I ever heard for a soft drink. Think of the commercials:

(The scene opens up with a boy in a Little League uniform, looking very sad. His father walks up.)

FATHER: What's the matter, Son?

SON *(bursting into tears)***:** Oh Dad, I struck out and lost the big game. *(Sobs.)*

FATHER *(putting his arm around the boy's shoulders)***:** Hey! Forget it! Let's have a nice cold can of Bite the Wax Tadpole!

SON: And then I murdered a policeman.

The Rules

Recently I read this news item stating that the U.S. Senate Finance Committee had printed up 4,500 copies of a 452-page document with every single word crossed out. The Senate Finance Committee did this on purpose. It wasn't the kind of situation where they got the document back from the printer and said: "Hey! Every single word in this document is crossed out! We're going to fire the zitbrain responsible for this!" No. A 452-page document with all the words crossed out was exactly what the Senate Finance Committee wanted.

This news item intrigued me. I said to myself: There has to be a logical explanation for this. So I called Washington, D.C., and over the course of an afternoon I spoke to, I don't know, maybe 15 or 20 people, and sure enough it turned out there was an extremely logical explanation: The Senate Finance Committee was following the Rules. As well it should. You have to have rules. This is true in government just as much as in sports. Think what professional baseball would be like if the pitcher could just throw the ball right at the batter whenever he felt like it, or the batter could turn around after a called third strike and try to whomp a major cavity in the umpire's skull. It would be great. I'd buy season tickets. But you can't have that kind of behavior in your government.

This is why, back when we bombed Libya, the Reagan administration made such a large point of the fact that we were *not* trying to kill Moammar Khadafy. I think most of us average citizens had assumed, since the administration had been going around announcing that it had absolute proof that Khadafy was an international baby-murdering scumball, that the whole *point* of the raid was to kill him, and although we didn't want to see innocent persons hurt, we certainly wouldn't have minded if say a half dozen fatal bombs had detonated inside Moammar's personal tent.

So I, for one, was quite surprised when right after the raid, President Reagan himself said, and this is a direct quote: "We weren't out to kill anybody." My immediate reaction, when I read this statement, was to assume that this was another of those unfortunate instances where the president's advisers, caught up in the excitement of planning a major military operation, had forgotten to advise the president about it. But then other top administration officials started saying the same thing, that we weren't trying to kill anybody, and specifically we *weren't trying to kill Khadafy*. You following this? We announced we have proof the guy is a murderer; we announce that we are by God going to Do Something about It; we have large military airplanes fly over there and drop bombs all over his immediate vicinity; but *we weren't trying to kill him*. You want to know why? I'll tell you why: The Rules.

That's right. It turns out that we have this law, signed in 1976 by Gerald Ford, who coincidentally also pardoned Richard M. Nixon, under which it is illegal for our government to assassinate foreign leaders. So we can't just hire a couple of experienced persons named Vito for 100 grand to sneak over there one night in dark clothing and fill up Moammar's various breathing apertures with plumber's putty. No, that would be breaking a Rule. So what we do is spend several hundred million dollars to crank up the entire Sixth Fleet and have planes fly over from as far away as England, not to mention that we lose a couple of airmen, to achieve the purpose of *not* killing Moammar Khadafy. We did kill various other random Libyans, but that is OK, under the Rules. Gerald Ford signed nothing to protect them.

OK? Everybody understand the point here? The point is: You have to follow the Rules. Without Rules, you would have *anarchy*.

And that is exactly why the Senate Finance Committee had to print up 4,500 copies of a 452-page document with every single word crossed out. What this document was, originally, was the tax-reform bill passed by the House of Representatives. It seemed the Senate Finance Committee didn't like it, so they wrote a whole new bill, with all different words. Their new bill is 1,489 pages long. Also they wrote another 1,124 pages to explain how it works. (Sounds like our new reformed tax system is going to be mighty simple, all right! I can't wait!)

OK. So the Finance Committee had 2,613 pages worth of tax reform to print up, but that was not all. They also printed the entire House bill, the one they rejected, with all the words crossed out to show where they disagreed with it. According to the 15 or 20 people I talked to on the phone, the committee had to do this. I asked them if maybe it wouldn't have been more economical, and just as informative, if the Finance Committee had stuck a note on the front of their bill saying something like: "We thought the whole House Bill was pig doots and we chucked it," but the 15 or 20 people assured me that, no, this was not possible, under the Rules. I was skeptical at first, but I heard this same explanation over and over, all afternoon, from people who all sounded like very bright college graduates, so that by the end of the day I was beginning to think that, yes, of course, it made perfect sense to print 4,500 copies of a document with every word crossed out. I felt like a fool for even bothering to think about it.

By the way: This document is for sale. This is the truth. You can actually buy a document that your government has used your tax money to print up with all the words crossed out. It's called HR 3838

As Reported in the Senate, Part I. The Government Printing Office is selling it for—I swear—$17. So far they have sold *1,800 copies.* And I *don't even want to know* who is buying them. I am sure that whoever they are, they're going to claim *every single cent they spent on these documents as a tax deduction.* But I don't *care.* I'm *through* asking questions.

I also don't want to know how much we spend each year for the upkeep on Richard M. Nixon.

The $8.95 Tax Plan

I'd like to take just a moment here to discuss my tax plan, which I call the You Pay Only $8.95 Tax Plan, because the way this particular plan works, you would pay only $8.95 in taxes. There would be no deductions, but you would still be permitted to cheat.

I imagine many of you have questions about the details of this plan, so I'll try to answer them here in the informative question-and-answer format:

Q. How much money will your tax plan raise?

A. To answer your question, I punched some figures into my personal home computer, using the following "Basic" computer language program:

ME: HOW MUCH WOULD WE RAISE IF EVERYBODY PAID $8.95 IN TAXES? ROUGHLY.

COMPUTER: SYNTAX ERROR.

ME: NO, A SYNTAX ERROR WOULD BE "ME HIT COMPUTER IN SCREEN WITH BIG ROCK."

COMPUTER: ROUGHLY $2 BILLION.

ME: THANK YOU.

Q. But the federal government wishes to spend $830 billion this year. Where will the other $828 billion come from?

A. It would come from people who elect to purchase the new American Express Platinum Card, which costs $250, making it even more prestigious than the Gold Card, which is of course much more prestigious than the Green Card, which is advertised to lowlife scum like yourself on television. According to the American Express brochure, the new Platinum Card is "beyond the aspirations and reach of all but a few of our Cardmembers," and "sets its possessor on a new plateau of recognition." Under my plan, people who buy the Platinum Card would be taxed $500 million each, and if they complained the slightest little bit they would be thrown into federal prisons so lonely that inmates pay spiders for sex.

Q. What about nuns?

A. Nuns would be taxed at a reduced rate of $5.95, because they do so little damage to our nation's crumbling infrastructure. For example, you have probably noticed that they drive really slow. This makes quite a difference, as the following statistical analysis shows:

ME: WHAT PERCENTAGE OF THE DAMAGE TO THE INTERSTATE HIGHWAY SYSTEM IS CAUSED BY NUNS?

COMPUTER: WHAT?

ME: PERHAPS THIS HOT SOLDERING IRON WILL REFRESH YOUR MEMORY.

COMPUTER: A VERY SMALL PERCENTAGE.

Q. What about Mark Goodson and Bill Todman?

A. Who?

Q. The highly successful game-show producers. How would they be affected by your new tax plan?

A. They would have their bowels ripped out by wolves.

Q. Good. In the cartoon series "Tom and Jerry," which one is Tom?

A. Well, I say it's the cat. My four-year-old son says it's the mouse, but he also says dinosaurs could talk.

COMPUTER: IT'S DEFINITELY THE CAT, AS IN "TOM CAT."

A. Yes, that's what I say, but my son claims he knows of mice named Tom.

COMPUTER: HA HA! WHAT A CRETIN.

Q. What are the steps involved in getting this tax plan passed by Congress?

A. Well, first it has to be formally introduced as a bill on "Meet the Press"; then various congressional committees and subcommittees have to go to Aruba with their spouses for several weeks to see if there are any similar tax plans operating in the Caribbean; then interested groups such as the American Eggplant Council have to modify it so that members of the eggplant industry are exempt from paying any taxes ever and get flown free wherever they want on Air Force jets; then Senator Jesse Helms has to attach an amendment making it legal, during the months of May and June, to shoot homosexuals for sport, except of course for homosexual tobacco farmers; then the bill has to be signed by President Reagan; then the Supreme Court has to check it to make sure he didn't forget and sign "Best Wishes, Ron" again.

Q. Dave, the You Pay Only $8.95 Tax Plan makes a lot of sense to me. How can I let my Congressperson know how I feel on this issue?

A. The easiest way is to simply steal into his bedroom in the dead of night and stand over his sleeping form until he senses your presence and wakes up, then express your views clearly.

Q. Fine.

A. Be sure to use sweeping arm gestures.

Mutant Fleas Terrorize Midwest

I was going to write about how the president's revolutionary new tax plan will affect you, but it occurred to me that I really don't care how the president's revolutionary new tax plan will affect you. So instead I'm going to write about the giant vampire fleas that are on this pet-killing rampage in the Midwest.

You probably read about these fleas recently in the *Sun*, a weekly supermarket newspaper with a circulation of 18 trillion. According to the *Sun* article, what happened was that the American farmer, all the while we were feeling sorry for him, was deluging the soil with herbicides, despite the known scientific fact that chemicals cause insects to mutate and become enormous, as has been documented in countless Japanese movies. So the result is that the Midwest is now infested with giant mutant fleas that, according to the *Sun*, "are themselves as large as the small dogs they kill, draining them dry of life fluids in as little as two minutes." The *Sun* even printed an actual artist's depiction of a dog being attacked by a flea the size of Sylvester Stallone.

Of course you don't believe a word of it. You think publications like the *Sun* make everything up. I used to think that, too, before I checked into a story the *Sun* published a few months ago headlined "GIANT FLYING CAT TERRIFIES STATES." Remember? The article that featured the actual artist's depiction of an enormous cat? Flying? With wings? Well, I did some checking, and you will be interested to learn that every single word in the headline is true except for "GIANT," "FLYING," "TERRIFIES," AND "STATES." It turns out that some people in Harrington, Delaware, have indeed seen a largish cat. The local editor says he thinks it's an escaped exotic pet, because it has a collar and has been declawed. He said it does not have any actual wings per se, but it jumps pretty well, especially considering that, to judge from its tracks, it has only three legs. They think it eats birds.

But the point is that the central thrust of the *Sun* headline ("CAT") was right on target, which gives us every reason to accept the giant-mutant-flea article at face value. Nevertheless, I thought I should check it out, so I called the Midwest, which is in Iowa, and talked with Donald Lewis, extension entomologist for Iowa State University. He said: "I haven't heard anything even remotely similar to that. We do have periodic flea outbreaks, but each flea is still small." Naturally, this made me suspicious, so I called Lysle Waters of the University of Iowa, who said: "I haven't heard anything about that. And I definitely would have heard about giant fleas."

And that was all the proof I needed. Because when two men from separate universities that are miles apart and have completely different nicknames ("Cyclones" vs. "Hawkeyes") used *almost exactly the same words*—"I haven't heard anything"—to deny having heard anything, then you don't have to be a seasoned journalist such as myself to know they are covering up a giant mutant flea rampage. My guess is they don't want to scare off the seven or eight tourists who flock to the Midwest each summer looking for directions.

How serious is this problem? To help answer that question, the *Sun* has published a direct quotation from a "Cornbelt sheriff" who, as you can well imagine, asked not to be identified. He states that these giant fleas "are almost impossible to catch" because "they can jump 50 times their own height without warning."

The Cornbelt sheriff does not specify *why* he would wish to catch the giant mutant flea or what kind of warning he feels the flea should give. ("Stand back! I am about to jump 50 times my own height!") But he does point out that once the fleas have eaten all the smaller animals in the Midwest, they "will have to go somewhere else to eat the larger livestock, chicken ranches, city streets, and homes."

"Little children will be completely at their mercy," he notes.

I have mixed feelings about all this. On the one hand, I have never liked small dogs. There are these two in particular that live near me, both about the size of the wads of cotton they put in aspirin bottles to keep you from getting at the aspirin. They're always yapping at me when I go by, and quite frankly the only thing I would enjoy more than watching them have all their life fluids sucked out by a giant mutant flea would be watching this happen in slow motion. But I draw the line at larger livestock, chicken ranches, and most little children.

Step One, of course, is to send Vice President Bush out there to the Midwest to frown at the affected area from a federal helicopter. Step Two is to develop a plan. I think we should try an approach that has been used on other insect pests in the past, namely: You get a hold of a whole bunch of the males, sterilize them, and drop them from airplanes onto the affected area, where they mate with the females, who don't get pregnant, and there you are.

Of course, we have to solve some technical problems first. We need to figure out a way to sterilize giant mutant fleas. My guess is this job will call for highly paid personnel with soothing voices and tremendous manual dexterity. Also, we will need some kind of special parachute system, because otherwise we're going to have giant, federally neutered fleas crashing through the roofs of cornbelt dwellings, thus further depressing the American farmer. Of course, all of this will cost money, which fortunately is the very thing the government will continue to relieve you of in large amounts under the president's revolutionary new tax plan.

Booked to Death

I'm on a book tour. I'm going on radio and TV shows, being a Guest, selling a book. I've been on this tour two, maybe three weeks now. Maybe 10 weeks. Hard to tell. Been in a lot of time zones. Been on a lot of planes. Had a lot of complimentary honey-roasted peanuts whapped onto my tray table by hostile flight attendants. "Would you care for some peanuts, sir?" WHAP. Like that. The flight attendants hate us passengers, because we're surly to them because our flight is delayed. Our flight is always delayed. The Russians will never be able to get their missiles through the dense protective layer of delayed flights circling over the United States in complex, puke-inducing holding patterns.

Our flight is also always very crowded. This is because air fares are now assigned by a machine called the Random Air Fare Generator, which is programmed to ensure that on any given flight (1) no two people will pay the same fare, and (2) everybody else will pay less than you. People are flying across the country for less than you paid for your six-week-old corn muffin at the airport snack bar. Anybody can afford to fly these days. You see Frequent Flyers with bare feet and live carry-on chickens.

And so the planes are crowded and noisy and late, and everybody hates everybody. If armed terrorists had tried to hijack any of the flights I've been on lately, we passengers would have swiftly beaten them to death with those hard rolls you get with your in-flight meal. Funny, isn't it? The airlines go to all that trouble to keep you from taking a gun on board, then they just hand you a dinner roll you could kill a musk ox with.

Me, I eat the roll. Got to eat. Got to keep my strength up, on the book tour, so I can be perky when I get interviewed by the cheerful talk-show host. You want to sound as perky and enthusiastic as possible, on a book tour, so your listening audience won't suspect that you really, deep down inside, don't want to talk about your book ever ever ever again. You have come to hate your book. Back at the beginning, you kind of liked it, but now you think of it as a large repulsive insect that cheerful hosts keep hauling out and sticking in your face and asking you to pet.

But you do it, because the alternative is gainful employment. You put on your perky face, and you chat with the host about why you wrote the book. Why you wrote it, of course, is money. I'm very up front about this. "Buy my book," I always advise the listening audience. "Or just send me some money in a box."

I've had some fun times, on my various book tours. The most fun was when I was promoting a book about do-it-yourself home repair. This book was, of course, totally worthless, not a single fact in it, but I ended up on a whole bunch of radio shows where the hosts, who had not had time to look at the book personally, thought I had written a *real* book about home repair. So the interviews went like this:

HOST: Dave, what's the best place to add insulation?

ME: Bob, I recommend the driveway.

HOST: Ha ha! Seriously, Dave.

ME: I am serious, Bob.

HOST: My guest has been Dave Barry.

I have also been on some very interesting TV shows. I was on a show in Cleveland where the other guests were a sex therapist and a Swedish gynecologist, who were supposed to have a sensitive discussion about the Male Perspective on sexuality with an all-male audience that had been bused in especially for the show. It turned out, however, that there was also beer on the bus, so the Male Perspective on sexuality consisted almost entirely of hooting and snickering. Somebody would ask the sex-therapist where the "G-spot" was, and she'd start to answer, and somebody in the back would yell: "It's in Germany!" Then there would be a violent eruption of hoots and snickers and we'd break for a commercial.

Recently, in Boston, I was on a show where the other two guests were—this is true—a police officer who explained how to avoid getting your purse snatched, and a woman named "Chesty Morgan" who once served in the Israeli army and currently dances topless and has the largest natural bosom in the world. She said she wears a size double-P bra. She has it made specially in Waco, Texas. She has a very interesting and tragic life story, and I wouldn't be surprised if, in the near future, she comes out with a book.

Hot Books and Hot Coals

Time now for the annual literary survey and firewalking report:

First, I am pleased to report that millions of units of new literature will soon be arriving at bookstores near you. I know this because I recently went to San Francisco to attend the American Booksellers Association's annual convention, at which all the big publishing companies reveal their fall literary lines. And on hand were a number of top authors such as Mister T, who was there to stress to the young people of America that they should read a lot of books or he will break all the bones in their faces; and Mary Lou Retton, who discussed a new book she has written about (get ready!) physical fitness. This is certainly a topic we need a *lot* more books on, because at present we have only enough fitness books to cover the Midwest to a depth of 60,000 feet.

Some other exciting book concepts you can look forward to seeing this fall include:

- A great many books telling you how to become so extremely successful in business, so totally *excellent,* that one day, during a budget meeting, you just *vanish* in a blinding flash of total managerial perfection, and the next thing you know you are on a distant misty mountain top wearing a white robe and talking about motivation with Lee Iacocca;
- Biographies of two of the three Stooges;
- A book called *How to Find a Husband in 30 Days* (Get Ready . . . Get Set . . . Get Married!), which is a terrific literary concept, the only problem being that it is written by the same person who wrote the best-selling *Thin Thighs in 30 Days,* which also seemed like a terrific con-

cept except that it did not work, in the sense that if you glance around with your eyes angled slightly downward you will note that the general population continues to have thighs the size of research submarines.

And here is a major piece of literary excitement for you; Parker Brothers has unveiled a new group of cute licensed characters for children. This is the one thing we need even *more* than we need another fitness book. These licensed characters are called "The Hugga Bunch," and I am pleased to report that they are just about the most lovable little wads of cuteness to mince down the pike since Rainbow Brite. You parents of preschool children are definitely going to hear a *lot* of high-pitched whining about these exciting characters.

Which brings us to the firewalking portion of our report. One of the authors at the convention was a person named Tolly Burkan, who is one of the top, if not *the* top firewalker in the United States. For the benefit of those of you who do not watch "Donahue," I should explain that firewalking is a very important new emerging growth trend where people walk on hot coals in bare feet. You will never in a million jillion years guess what state this concept has gained great popularity in: California(!). Out in California, you can pay people money, and they let you walk on their hot coals.

Besides doing firewalking seminars, Tolly Burkan has produced various cassette tapes and books, including his hardcover book *Dying to Live,* in which he explains how he used to be really messed up and try to kill himself all the time, but now he is all straightened out and goes around encouraging people to walk barefoot on hot coals. Also he supervises fasting. According to a brochure I got at his firewalking demonstration, you pay him $35 a day, in return for which you get not to eat under his personal supervision. Also for $500 he will whack you in both kneecaps with a ballpeen hammer.

Ha ha! Just kidding! I think!

The firewalking demonstration took place at a parking lot near the convention hall, and there were maybe a hundred of us on hand to watch. Tolly, who had a wireless microphone and who has that extremely mellow California-spiritual-leader style of speech similar to what you would get if you gave Mister Rogers a horse tranquilizer, explained the basic theory of firewalking, which as I understand it is that if you really believe you can do something, then by golly you can just *do* it, even if it seems impossible. I happen to agree with this theory. I think it explains, for example, how large heavy commercial airplanes get off the ground despite the fact that they are clearly too heavy to fly, especially when their beverage carts are fully loaded.

So anyway, at the firewalking demonstration, Tolly raked out a six-foot-long bed of very hot coals from a bed of cedar and oak logs (he has also walked on mesquite) and taught the onlookers a little chant they were supposed to chant when the walkers walked across the coals. This being San Francisco, they chanted it. In New York, they would have stolen his wireless microphone. Then Tolly brought on some of his veteran walkers, who each took a couple of quick steps across the coals the way you would step if you were walking on some very hot coals. Then Tolly walked on the coals a couple of times for a newspaper photographer, including once when he pretended that while he was walking he was reading his book, which by the way is for sale.

These people actually do walk across hot coals. It is quite impressive. To find something comparable in my experience I have to go back to when I was eight years old, and Charles Ringwald ate a worm, only he did it without any assistance in the form of chanting. So if you're looking for a way to find total happiness in your life, I urge you to walk on hot coals as soon as possible, provided of course that you have taken a seminar run by a responsible professional.

Also, Charles Ringwald, if you're out there, please get in touch with me as soon as possible, because I have a terrific idea for a book.

The Hair Apparent

I have a letter here from Mrs. Belle Ehrlich, of San Jose, California, who feels I should get a new hairdo. To quote her directly: "I enjoy reading most of your columns . . . but your hairdo in your photo sure looks DATED and NOT at all flattering or becoming, to say the least. If you are still sporting that awful hairdo, I suggest you go to a good hair stylist to give you a new and better hairdo. I hope you don't mind my criticism, it's nothing personal—just a suggestion."

Mind? Ha ha! MIND? Of course not, Mrs. Belle Ehrlich of San Jose! As a journalist who seeks to inform his readers about topics of vital concern to the nation and the world, I *welcome* insulting remarks about my hair!

OK, perhaps I am a bit sensitive about my hair. I have been sensitive about my hair since second grade, when the Kissing Girls first swung into action. You probably had Kissing Girls at your elementary school too: they roamed the playground, chasing after selected boys and trying to kiss them. We boys carried on as though we would have preferred to undergo the Red-Ants-Eat-Your-Eyelids-Off Torture than get kissed, but of course we wanted desperately to be selected. And I almost never was. The boys who were selected had wavy hair. Wavy hair was big back then, and I did not have it. I had straight hair, and it did not help that my father cut it.

You should know that my father was a fine, decent, and sensitive man, but unfortunately he had no more fashion awareness than a baked potato. His idea of really el snazzo dressing was to wear a suit jacket and suit pants that both originated as part of the same suit. He would have worn the same tie to work for 42 consecutive years if my mother had let him. So, the way he would cut my hair is, he'd put me on a stool, and he'd start cutting hair off one side of my head with the electric clippers, then he'd walk around me and attempt, relying on memory, to make the other side of my head look similar. Which, of course, he could never quite do, so he would head back around to take a stab at Side One again, and he'd keep this up for some time, and all I can say is, thank heavens they had a little plastic guard on the electric clippers so that you couldn't make the hair any shorter than a quarter-inch, because otherwise my father, with the best of intentions, trying to even me up, would have started shaving off slices of actual tissue until eventually I would have been able to turn my head sideways and stick it through a mail slot. As it was, in photographs taken back then, I look like an extremely young Marine, or some kind of radiation victim.

It also did not help that in third grade I became the first kid in the class to get glasses, and we are talking serious 1950s horn rims of the style that when you put them on a third-grade child, especially one with a comical haircut, you get a Mister Peepers effect such that everybody assumes the child must be a Goody-Two-Shoes Teacher's Pet science-oriented little dweeb. And it also did not help that I was a late developer, pubertywise. I was *ready* for puberty. All of us boys were. We wanted to catch up to the girls, who about two years earlier had very suddenly, in fact I think it was all on the same day, shown up at school a foot taller than us and with bosoms and God knows what else. So I was definitely looking forward to puberty as the Dawn of a New Era in the looks department, and you can just imagine how *betrayed* I felt when it started happening to the other boys, even boys whom I had considered my friends, well before it happened to me. They got ahead of me then, and sometimes I think I never really caught up. I am 38 years old now, and I have yet to develop hair on my arms. Isn't that supposed to happen, in puberty? I see men much younger than myself, with hairy arms, and I think: Does this mean I'm not done with puberty *yet?*

I realize I sound insecure here, but if you really wanted to see insecure, you should have seen me in eighth grade. I was a mess. That was why I developed a sense of humor. I needed something to do at parties. The other boys, the boys who had wavy hair and reasonable hormone-activity levels, would be necking with girls, and I would be over by the record player, a short radiation victim in horn-rimmed spectacles, playing 45s and making jokes to entertain the 10-year-old brother of whoever was holding the party. Now that I'm grown up, I keep reading magazine articles about these surveys where they ask you women what you really want most in a man, and you always say: A Sense of Humor. And I think to myself: Right. Sure. Great. *Now* you want a sense of humor. But back in the eighth grade, back when it really mattered, what you wanted was puberty.

And I am not even going to mention here that for several years my hands were covered with warts.

So anyway, Mrs. Belle Ehrlich of San Jose, what I'm trying to say here is: Thanks, thanks a million for taking the time to drop me a note informing me that my hair looks awful. Because now I'm grown up (except in terms of arm hair) and have contact lenses, and I have finally come to think of myself as very nearly average in appearance, I can handle this kind of helpful criticism, and I will definitely see if I can't find a good hair stylist. This is assuming that I ever leave my bedroom again.

TV or Not TV

The turning point, in terms of my giving in to the concept of being a Television Personality, was when I let them put the styling mousse on my hair. Hair has always been my dividing line between television personalities and us newspaper guys. We newspaper guys generally have hair that looks like we trim it by burning the ends with Bic lighters. We like to stand around and snicker at the TV guys, whose hair all goes in the same direction and looks as though it's full-bodied and soft, but which in fact has been permeated with hardened petrochemical substances to the point where it could deflect small-caliber bullets. We newspaper guys think these substances have actually penetrated the skulls and attacked the brain cells of the TV guys, which we believe explains why their concept of a really major journalistic achievement is to interview Mr. T.

So I need to explain how I became a Television Personality. A while back, a public-television station asked me to be the host of a new TV series they want to start for parents of young children, and I said, sure, what the heck. I remember saying, "Sounds like fun." And thus I became a talent. That's what TV people call you if you go in front of the camera: a "talent." They call you that right to your face. Only after a while you realize they don't mean that you have any actual *talent*. In fact, it's sort of an insult. In the TV business, "talent" means "not the camera, lighting, or sound people, all of whom will do exactly what they're supposed to do every single time, but the bonehead with the pancake makeup who will make us all stay in the studio for two extra hours because he cannot remember that he is supposed to say 'See you next *time*' instead of 'See you next *week*.'" It reminds me of the way people in the computer industry use the word "user," which to them means "idiot."

When you are a TV talent, you are meat. People are always straightening your collar, smearing things on your face, and talking about you in the third person, saying things like: "What if we had him sitting down?" and "Can we make his face look less round?" and "Can we do anything about his nose?" This is how my hair came to contain several vats of styling mousse, which is this gunk that looks like shaving cream and which you can just tell was invented by a French hair professional whom, if you met him, you would want to punch directly in the mouth. The TV people felt it made me look older. I felt it made me look like a water bed salesman, but hey, I'm just a talent.

Still, I thought I'd be all right, once we got into the studio. What I pictured was, I would saunter in front of the camera, and say something like, "Hi! Welcome to our show! Here's an expert psychological authority to tell you what it means when your child puts the cat in the Cuisinart! And sets it on 'mince'!" Then I would just sit back and listen to the expert, nodding my head and frowning with concern from time to time. And every now and then I might say something spontaneous and riotously funny.

As it turns out, *nothing* happens spontaneously in a television studio. Before anything can happen, they have to spend several hours shining extremely bright lights on it from different angles, then they have to stand around frowning at it, then they have to smear it and dust it with various substances to get it to stop the glare from those bright lights that they are shining on it, and then they have to decide that it has to be moved to a completely different place so they can start all over.

Once they get all set up, once they're satisfied that the lights are as bright and as hot as they can possibly get them, it's time for the talent to come in and make a fool out of itself. On a typical day, I would have to do something like walk up to a table, lean on it casually, say some witty remarks to one camera, turn to the right and say some more witty remarks to another camera, and walk off. This sounds very easy, right? Well, here's what would happen. I would do my little performance, and there would be a lengthy pause while the director and the producer and the executive producer and all the assistant producers back in the control room discussed, out of my hearing, what I had done wrong.

Now I can take criticism. I'm a writer and my editor is always very direct with me. "Dave, this column bites the big one," is the kind of thing he'll say by way of criticism. And I can handle it. But in the TV world, they never talk to you like that. They talk to you as though you're a small child, and they're not sure whether you're just emotionally unbalanced or actually retarded. They take tremendous pains not to hurt your feelings. First of all, they *always* tell you it was great.

"That was great, Dave. We're going to try it again, with just a little more energy, OK? Also, when you walk in, try not to shuffle your feet, OK? Also, When you turn right, dip your eyes a bit, then come up to the next camera, because otherwise it looks odd, OK? Also, don't bob your head so much, OK? And try not to smack your lips, OK? Also, remember you're supposed to say next *time,* not next *week,* OK? So just try to be natural, and have some fun with it, OK? I think we're almost there."

So I had to do everything a great many times, and of course all my jokes, which I thought were absolute killers when I wrote them in the privacy of my home, soon seemed, in this studio where I was telling them over and over to camera persons who hadn't even laughed the first time, remarkably stupid, or even the opposite of jokes, antihumor, somber remarks that you might make to somebody who had just lost his whole family in a boat explosion. But I kept at it, and finally after God knows how many attempts, would come the voice from the control room: "That was perfect, Dave. Let's try it again with a little more energy. Also you forgot to say your name."

The Embarrassing Truth

Have you ever really embarrassed yourself? Don't answer that, stupid. It's a rhetorical question. Of course you've embarrassed yourself. Everybody has. I bet the pope has. If you were to say to the pope: "Your Holy Worshipfulness, I bet you've pulled some blockheaded boners in your day, huh?" he'd smile that warm, knowing, fatherly smile he has, and then he'd wave. He can't hear a word you're saying, up on that balcony.

But my point is that if you've ever done anything humiliating, you've probably noticed that *your brain never lets you forget it.* This is the same brain that never remembers things you *should* remember. If you were bleeding to death and the emergency-room doctor asked you what blood type you were, you'd say: "I think it's B. Or maybe C. I'm pretty sure it's a letter." But if your doctor asked you to describe the skirt you were wearing when you were doing the Mashed Potatoes in the ninth-grade dance competition in front of 350 people, and your underwear, which had holes in it, fell to your ankles, you'd say, without hesitating for a millisecond, "It was gray felt with a pink flocked poodle."

Your brain cherishes embarrassing memories. It likes to take them out and fondle them. This probably explains a lot of unexplained suicides. A successful man with a nice family and a good career will be out on his patio, cooking hamburgers, seemingly without a care in the world, when his brain, rummaging through its humiliating-incident collection, selects an old favorite, which it replays for a zillionth time, and the man is suddenly so overcome by feelings of shame that he stabs himself in the skull with his barbecue fork. At the funeral, people say how shocking it was, a seemingly happy and well-adjusted person choosing to end it all. They assume he must have had a terrible dark secret involving drugs or organized crime or dressing members of the conch family in flimsy undergarments. Little do they know he was thinking about the time in Social Studies class in 1963 when he discovered a hard-to-reach pimple roughly halfway down his back, and he got to working on it, subtly at first, but with gradually increasing intensity, eventually losing track of where he was, until suddenly he realized the room had become silent, and he looked up, with his arm stuck halfway down the back of his shirt, and he saw that *everybody in the class, including the teacher, was watching what he was doing,* and he knew they'd give him a cruel nickname that would stick like epoxy cement for the rest of his life, such as when he went to his 45th reunion, even if he had been appointed Chief Justice of the U.S. Supreme Court, the instant his classmates saw him, they'd shriek: "Hey look! It's ZIT!"

Everybody has incidents like this. My mother is always reliving the time she lost her car in a shopping-center parking lot, and she was wandering around with several large shopping bags and two small children, looking helpless, and after a while other shoppers took pity on her and offered to help. "It's a black Chevrolet," she told them, over and over. And they searched and searched and searched for it. They were extremely nice. They all agreed that it can be darned easy to lose your car in these big parking lots. They had been there for an hour, some of them, searching for this black Chevrolet, and it was getting dark, when my mother remembered that several days earlier we had bought a new car. "I'm sorry!" she told the people, smiling brightly so they would see what a humorous situation this was. "It's *not* a black Chevrolet! It's a yellow Ford!" She kept on smiling as they edged away, keeping their eyes on her.

My own personal brain is forever dredging up the time in 11th grade when I took a girl, a very attractive girl on whom I had a life-threatening crush, to a dance. I was standing in the gym next to her, holding her hand, thinking what a sharp couple we made—Steve Suave and His Gorgeous Date—when one of my friends sidled up to me and observed that, over on the other side, my date was using her spare hand to hold hands with another guy. This was of course a much better-looking guy. This was Paul Newman, only taller.

Several of my friends gathered to watch. I thought: What am I supposed to do here? Hit the guy? That would have been asking for a lifetime of dental problems. He was a varsity football player; I was on the Dance Committee. I also had to rule out hitting my date. The ideal move would have been to spontaneously burst into flames and die. I have read that this sometimes happens to people. But you never get a break like that when you need it.

Finally I turned to my date, dropped her hand, looked her square in the eye, and said: "Um." Just like that: "Um." My brain absolutely loves to remember this. "Way to go, Dave!" it shrieks to me, when I'm stopped at red lights, 23½ years later. Talk about eloquent! My brain can't get over what a jerk I was. It's always coming up with much better ideas for things I could have said. I should start writing them down, in case we ever develop time travel. I'd go back to the gym with a whole Rolodex file filled with remarks, and I'd read them to my date over the course of a couple of hours. Wouldn't *she* feel awful! Ha ha!

It just occurred to me that she may be out there right now, in our reading audience, in which case I wish to state for the record that I am leading an absolutely wonderful life, and I have been on the Johnny Carson show, and I hope things are equally fine with you.

Twice. I was on Carson twice.

A Million Words

It was time to go have my last words with my father. He was dying, in the bedroom he built. He built our whole house, even dug the foundation himself, with a diaper tied around his head to keep the sweat out of his eyes. He was always working on the house, more than 35 years, and he never did finish it. He was first to admit that he really didn't know how to build a house.

When I went in to see him, he was lying in the bedroom, listening to the "People's Court." I remember when he always would be on those Sunday-morning television talk shows, back in the fifties and sixties. Dr. Barry, they called him. He was a Presbyterian minister, and he worked in inner-city New York. They were always asking him to be on those shows to talk about Harlem and the South Bronx, because back then he was the only white man they could find who seemed to know anything about it. I remember when he was the Quotation of the Day in the *New York Times.* The Rev. Dr. David W. Barry.

His friends called him Dave. "Is Dave there?" they'd ask, when they called to talk about their husbands or wives or sons or daughters who were acting crazy or drinking too much or running away. Or had died. "Dave," they'd ask, "what can I do?" They never thought to call anybody but him. He'd sit there and listen, for hours, sometimes. He was always smoking.

The doctor told us he was dying, but we knew anyway. Almost all he said anymore was thank you, when somebody brought him shaved ice, which was mainly what he wanted, at the end. He had stopped putting his dentures in. He had stopped wearing his glasses. I remember when he yanked his glasses off and jumped in the Heyman's pool to save me.

So I go in for my last words, because I have to go back home, and my mother and I agree I probably won't see him again. I sit next to him on the bed, hoping he can't see that I'm crying. "I love you, Dad," I say. He says: "I love you, too. I'd like some oatmeal."

So I go back out to the living room, where my mother and my wife and my son are sitting on the sofa, in a line, waiting for the outcome and I say, "He wants some oatmeal." I am laughing and crying about this. My mother thinks maybe I should go back in and try to have a more meaningful last talk, but I don't.

Driving home, I'm glad I didn't. I think: He and I have been talking ever since I learned how. A million words. All of them final, now. I don't need to make him give me any more, like souvenirs. I think: Let me not define his death on my terms. Let him have his oatmeal. I can hardly see the road.

Subhumanize Your Living Room

Today we're going to talk about redecorating your home. My guess is you're unhappy with your current decor, especially if you have small children around, the result being that all of your furniture and carpeting, no matter what the original color scheme, is now the color of mixed-fruit juice.

Fortunately for you, home decor is an area I happen to know a great deal about, as I have done my own decorating, without professional assistance, ever since my college days, when I shared a dormitory suite with several other design-conscious young men. Our watchword, decorwise, was "functionality." For the floor covering in our bedrooms, we chose the comfortable, carefree casualness of unlaundered jockey shorts. By the end of a semester, there would be six, maybe seven hundred pairs of shorts per bedroom, forming a pulsating, bed-high mound.

For our living-room-wall treatment we opted for a very basic, very practical, and very functional decorating concept called "old college dormitory paint, the color of the substance you might expect to see oozing from an improperly treated wound." We highlighted this with an interesting textural effect that you can obtain by having a Halloween party and throwing wads of orange and black crepe paper soaked in beer up against the wall and then leaving it there for a couple of months to harden and trying to scrape it off with the edge of an economics textbook.

But our *pièce de résistance* (French, meaning "piece of resistance") was our living-room furniture, which was a two-piece grouping consisting of:

- An orange emergency light that flashed when you plugged it in.
- A "Two-Man Submarine," which we purchased for only $9.95 via an advertisement in a Spider-

Man comic book. It was made of sturdy cardboard and measured five feet long when fully assembled. It was not only very attractive but also quite functional inasmuch as you could sit inside it and pretend you were actually deep beneath the ocean surface, driving a real submarine made of sturdy cardboard.

As you might imagine, the overall effect created by these design elements was quite impressive, especially when we had dates and we really spruced up the place. We'd stack the deceased pizza boxes in the corner, and we'd create a romantic atmosphere by spraying a couple of cans of Right-Guard brand deodorant on the jockey-short mounds, and believe me it was a real treat to see the look on the face of a date as she entered our suite for the first time and, seeing the striking visual effect created by the orange emergency light flashing on the "Two-Man Submarine," she realized what a suave kind of college man she was having a date with.

But enough about my qualifications. Let's talk about your own home. Clearly you need new furniture. To select exactly what you want, you need to have some Creative Decorating Ideas, which you get by purchasing about $65 worth of glossy magazines with names like *Unaffordable Home Design.* Inside these magazines will be exquisite color photographs of the most wondrously perfect, profoundly clean rooms anybody has ever seen, rooms where even the air molecules are arranged in attractive patterns. How, you ask yourself, can rooms look like this? Where are the hand smudges? Where is the dark spot on the carpet where the dog threw up the unidentified reptile? And how come there are *never any people* in these photographs?

The answer is: *These rooms are only four inches high.* The magazines have them built by skilled craftsmen solely for the purpose of making your home look, by comparison, like a Roach Motel. In fact, occasionally a magazine will slip up, and you'll see through the window of what is allegedly a rich person's living room, what appears to be a 675-pound thumb.

OK! Now that you have your Creative Decorating Ideas, you get a sheet of graph paper, and you make an elaborate scale drawing of your existing floor plan, showing exactly to the inch where you would put all your nice new furniture, if you were a major cocaine dealer and could afford nice new furniture. Unfortunately the furniture you can afford comes from places with names like Big Stu's World of Taste and is made of compressed bran flakes. So, frankly, if I were you, I'd spread my glossy interior-design magazines around so they covered as much of my current decor as possible.

The Lure of the Wild

The first time I taught my son, Robert, how to fish was when he was two. I did it the old-fashioned way: I took him to the K-Mart with Uncle Joe, our old friend and lawyer, to pick out a Complete Fishing Outfit for $12.97. Then we went to a pond, where Robert sat in the weeds and put pond muck in his hair while Uncle Joe and I tried to bait the hook with a living breathing thinking feeling caring earthworm. This is a very difficult thing emotionally, and not just for the earthworm. It would be different if worms gave you some reason to feel hostile toward them, such as they had little faces that looked like Geraldo Rivera. That would be no problem. "Let's go bait some worms purely for amusement," you would frequently hear me call out.

But the way worms are now, they make it very hard, writhing around and conveying, by means of body language and worm guts squirting out, the concept of "Please please oh PLEASE Mr. Human Being don't stick this hook into me." For my money, worms are far better at this kind of nonverbal communication than those people called "mimes," who paint their faces all white and repeatedly attempt to entertain you at street festivals, although to be absolutely certain, we would have to run an experiment wherein we baited a hook with a live mime. (All those in favor of doing this, raise your hands. I thought so!)

I think it would be more humane if we just forgot about bait altogether and shot the fish directly with guns, the way we do with rabbits and deer. I saw Roy Scheider take this approach to angling in the movie *Jaws I,* and he got himself a real prize trophy shark using a rifle for a weapon and Richard Dreyfuss for bait. Unfortunately, this turned out to be a violation of our outmoded game laws, so Roy had to *throw the shark back,* which turned out to be highly fatal to several dozen teen-agers and a helicopter in *Jaws II.* This is a totally unnecessary outrage, if you ask me, especially when you consider that it is *not* illegal to catch deer with rod and reel in most states. *(Editor's Note: He's raving. Pay no attention.)*

Nevertheless, Robert and Uncle Joe and I did manage to land a fish, the kind veteran anglers call a "bluegill." It was three to four ounces of well-contained fury, and it fought like a frozen bagel. Many times at airport newsstands I have examined sportsperson-oriented magazines with names like *Tackle 'n' Bait,* and I have noted that the covers often feature pictures of bold sportspersons struggling to land extremely muscular, violent-looking fish the size of guest bathrooms, whose expressions say: "Yes, you had better kill me, Mr. Sportsperson, because otherwise I will evolve legs and lungs and talons and fangs and come to your suburban home and wreck your riding mower and *have my way with your women hahahahahaha.*"

But the fish we caught was a cute fish, a fish that would star in a Walt Disney animated cartoon feature called *Billy Bluegill Learns the True Meaning of Christmas.* Robert looked at it, then he looked at Uncle Joe and me with a look of great upsettedness in his two-year-old eyes and we realized, being responsible grown-ups, that it was time to lie.

"The fish doesn't feel it!" we announced brightly, almost in unison. "You see this sharp barbed metal hook going right through his lip?! It doesn't hurt a bit! Ha ha!!" Meanwhile Billy the Bluegill was of course edging out the worm for the Academy Award for Best Performance by a Cold-Blooded Animal Gasping and Writhing Around to Indicate Extreme Pain. And so Uncle Joe, being an attorney, got Billy off the hook (get it?) and we put him (Billy) back into the pond.

After that Robert and I didn't go fishing for several years, until last Christmas, when we went up to New York and Uncle Phil—who is not our attorney but Robert affectionately calls him "uncle" anyway because he is my brother—bought Robert *another fishing rod,* meaning I had to teach him *again.* Fortunately, there were no worms available, as they had all formed up into characteristic V-shaped patterns and attempted to migrate South, getting as far as the toll booths on the New Jersey Turnpike.

So Robert and I used "lures," which are these comical devices that veteran anglers instinctively buy from catalogs. You would think that, to be effective, lures would have to look like creatures that a fish might actually eat, but, in fact, they look like what you would expect to see crawling around on the Planet Zork during periods of intense radioactivity. For example, many lures have propellers, which you rarely see in the Animal Kingdom. In my opinion, the way lures actually work is that the fish see one go by, and they get to laughing so hard and thrashing around that occasionally one of them snags itself on the hook. Back in the Prepuberty Era I used to spend hundreds of hours lure-fishing with my friend Tom Parker and his faithful dog Rip, and the only distinct memory I have of us catching anything besides giant submerged logs was the time Tom was using a lure called a Lazy Ike and it was attacked with stunning ferocity by his faithful dog Rip, resulting in a very depressing situation, veterinarianwise.

So, fortunately Robert and I didn't catch anything the second time I taught him to fish, and I think he's now old enough to remember it clearly and thus never ask me to teach him again. That's the good news. The bad news is, I am sure that one of these days he's going to want to have a "catch."

Earning a Collie Degree

We have a new dog, which means we're going through this phase where we spend a lot of time crouching and stroking and going "Yessss! That's a GOOD girl!" and otherwise practically awarding a Nobel Prize to her for achievements such as not pooping on the rug.

Her name is Earnest, which I realize is not a traditional girl's name, but it describes her very well. Most dogs are earnest, which is why most people like them. You can say any fool thing to a dog, and the dog will give you this look that says, "My God, you're RIGHT! I NEVER would have thought of that!" So we come to think of dogs as being understanding and loving and compassionate, and after a while we hardly even notice that they spend the bulk of their free time circling around with other dogs to see which one can sniff the other the most times in the crotch.

We are not sure yet whether Earnest has a working brain. You can't tell, early on, with dogs. When we got our previous dog, Shawna, we thought she was smart as a whip, because she was a purebred German shepherd who had this extremely *alert* look. At first we took this to mean that she was absorbing every tiny detail of her environment with her keen senses and analyzing it with computerlike speed, but it turned out to be her way of expressing the concept: "What?"

Shawna would be sitting in our yard, looking very sharp, and a squirrel would scurry *right* past her, a squirrel whose presence was instantly detected by normal, neighborhood dogs hundreds of yards away, causing them to bark rigorously, and also by us humans, causing us to yell helpfully: "Look! Shawna! A *squirrel!!*" And after a few seconds of delay, during which her nervous system would send the message via parcel post from her ears to her brain that something was going on, Shawna would turn in the exact opposite direction from whichever way the squirrel was, adopt a pose of great canine readiness, and go: "What?"

The only dog I ever met that was dumber than Shawna belongs to my editor. This dog, a collie named Augie, also *looks* smart, if you grew up watching "Lassie." Lassie looked brilliant, in part because the farm family she lived with was made up of idiots. Remember? One of them was always getting pinned under the tractor, and Lassie was always rushing back to the farmhouse to alert the other ones. She'd whimper and tug at their sleeves, and they'd always waste precious minutes saying things: "Do you think something's *wrong?* Do you think she wants us to *follow* her? What *is* it girl?" as if this had never happened before, instead of every week. What with all the time these people spent pinned under the tractor, I don't see how they managed to grow any crops whatsoever. They probably got by on federal crop supports, which Lassie filed the applications for.

So anyway I thought Augie, being a collie, would have at least some intelligence, despite the fact that when my editor and I would walk into his house, Augie would not notice us, sometimes for upwards of a half hour. When she finally did notice us, talking and drinking beer, she would bark as though the Manson gang had just burst in, so my editor would have to go over and sort of say, "Look! It's me! The person you have lived with for 10 years!" This would cause Augie's lone functioning brain cell to gradually quiet down and go back to sleep.

But I still thought she was roughly on par with Shawna, IQ-wise, until the night—you may remember the night; it was the longest one we ever had—that I slept on my editor's couch in his living room, which is also where Augie sleeps. Only she doesn't sleep. What she does is, first, she lies down. Then she scratches herself. Then she engages in loud personal hygiene. Then she thinks, "Maybe I can go out!" and she walks across the floor, which is made of a special kind of very hard wood so that when a dog walks on it, it goes TICK TICK TICK TICK at exactly the volume you would use to get maximum benefit from the Chinese Ticking Torture. When Augie gets to the front door, which is of course closed—it is always closed at night; even the domestic insects have learned this by now—she bumps into it with her head. Then she backs up and bumps into it with her head a couple more times, in case there has been some mistake. Then she senses, somehow, that there is a person sleeping on the couch, and she has the most innovative idea she has ever thought of, which is: "Maybe *he* will let me out!" So she walks over to me and noses me in the face, using the same nose she uses for hygiene, and I say, "Dammit, Augie! Go to sleep!" So she lies down for *one minute,* which is how long it takes for her brain cell to forget everything that has ever happened to her since she was born. And then she starts again: SCRATCH SCRATCH SCRATCH SLURP SLURP SLURP (think) TICK TICK TICK TICK BUMP (think) BUMP (think) BUMP (think) TICK TICK TICK NOSE "DAMMIT, AUGIE! GO TO SLEEP!" TICK TICK TICK TICK (pause) SCRATCH . . .

I don't know yet about Earnest. One day soon I will give her the dog intelligence test, where you show her the ball, then you put the ball under a blanket, and then you see if she can find the ball. Shawna never could find the ball. I doubt Augie could find the blanket. I'm hoping Earnest does better, but I'm not counting my chickens. I am also not looking forward to receiving a lot of violent letters from you dog lovers out there, the ones with the "I (heart) my (breed of dog)" bumper stickers, asking how dare I say dogs are stupid when your dog can add, subtract, land the space shuttle, etc. So please note, dog lovers: I never said *your* dog is stupid. I said *my* dog might be stupid. I know for a fact that she can't be *too* intelligent, because here I've written a fairly insulting column about her species, and despite the fact that she's lying right at my feet, it hasn't occurred to her to pull the plug on my word proces

Some Thoughts on the Toilet

Both of our household toilets broke recently, on the same day. They work together, toilets. You know those strange sounds your plumbing makes at night? The ones that worry you much more than, for example, the threat of nuclear war? Those are your toilets, talking to each other. They communicate via plumbing sounds, similar to whales. "It's New Year's Eve," they'll say. "We break tonight."

I happen to know a great deal about toilets, although that was not the original plan. The original plan was for me to become profoundly wealthy by investing in real estate. I had read a book about it, which made the whole process sound as easy as getting insurance offers from Ed McMahon by mail. The trick, according to this book, was that when you purchase your real estate, you *never used your own money*. You used *other people's* money. The way the book described it, you strode into the bank, and you said: "Hi! I'd like to become filthy rich via real estate, but I don't wish to use my own money!" And the bank would say: "Well then! Here! Take some of ours!!"

So I got some partners who also had a sincere interest in becoming rich, and we hatched a plan wherein we would, using other people's money, buy a couple of small apartment buildings, after which we would sit around drinking gin and tonic and amassing great wealth due to Depreciation and Leverage, two characters who appeared often in the real-estate book, performing amazing financial feats. They reminded me of Batman and Robin.

So my partners and I went around presenting our proposal to various bankers, and they thought it was the greatest thing they had every heard. They would set up extra chairs and invite all their banker friends over, and they'd make us go through our proposal again and again, and when we'd get to the part about not using any of our own money, they'd fall over backwards and hurl their loan application forms into the air and laugh until there was spittle all over their vests. They had evidently not read the book.

So eventually we worked out a compromise arrangement whereby my partners and I would each provide our life's savings, and the bank would provide a Closing Ceremony, which is when you go into a little room with unfamiliar lawyers and you sign every piece of paper they have managed to acquire in their lives, including book reports. This is how we came to acquire, as an investment, eight toilets. The Head Toilet, of course, immediately fired off an urgent message to the others. "We have been purchased," the message said, "by people who have read *a real estate investment book.*" As you can imagine, the sound of hysterical gurgling went on well into the night.

I became intimately familiar with every single one of these investment toilets. See, my partners all had useful skills, such as carpentry, whereas my only area of proven competence was listening to the radio, so we agreed that I would learn how to be the plumber. Gradually, I learned that there are two major toilet facts:

TOILET FACT NUMBER ONE: The only way to prevent a toilet part from leaking is to tighten it until it breaks.

TOILET FACT NUMBER TWO: Circling the Earth, at this very moment, is an alien spacecraft that is sending down powerful radio beams that affect the brains of tenants in such a way that they *must put inappropriate objects in the toilet.* They cannot help themselves. "Find an inappropriate object!" the beam commands them. "Put it in the toilet RIGHT NOW!" You landlords out there, you know I'm telling the truth, right? And the tenants, they don't even remember what they have done. "How in the world did THAT get in there?" they say, when you show them, for example, a harmonica. "Ha ha!" they add. "Ha ha," you agree, all the while calculating the various angles and forces involved in killing them with your wrench.

Because of these two facts, I soon got to know all eight toilets personally, as individuals. I would call them by name. "So, Bob," I would say. "Leaking again, eh? How would you like to be *replaced,* Bob? How would you like to be taken outside and have your smooth white porcelain body *smashed repeatedly with a hammer?* Because there are plenty more toilets, down at the Home Center, who would *love* to have your job." But Bob would just chuckle, knowing that even if I could somehow manage to install an entire new toilet, it would quickly become part of the cadre.

This went on for several years, during which I amassed the world's largest privately held collection of broken toilet parts, but not, surprisingly enough, great wealth, so finally I ceased playing an active role in the investment property. But I have used the knowledge I acquired, in my home. When our toilets break, I call the plumber, and I am able to describe the problem in technical plumbing terms. "It's our toilets," I say. "They are broken." And he comes out and fixes them, and I don't care how much he charges. "That will be $68,000," he could tell me, and I would come up with it, somehow, because anything is better than having to deal with the toilets directly. Particularly the one in the hall bathroom. Norman.

The Elements of Elegance

Today we're going to talk about how you can hold an elegant dinner party in your home. Well, not really *your* home, of course. You'll need a much more elegant home, one where there is fine nonvelveteen art on the walls and a harp in the corner of the living room and some effort has been made over the years to clean behind the toilets.

You'll also need elegant guests, by which I mean not your friends. You want to invite socially prominent people, which means people who do not object to being called Thad and Bootsie right to their faces and who are directly affected by oil-company mergers. The best way to lure such people to your dinner party is to tell them it has something to do with disease. Socially prominent people are very fond of disease, because it gives them a chance to have these really elaborate charity functions, and the newspaper headlines say "EVENING IN PARIS BALL RAISES MONEY TO FIGHT GOUT" instead of "RICH PEOPLE AMUSE THEMSELVES."

Now let's plan your menu. The most elegant and sophisticated dishes are those that involve greasy little unsanitary birds with no meat and about 60 billion bones, such as grouse. If your local supermarket doesn't carry grouse, your best bet is to go into the woods and tramp around the underbrush until you hear something rustling, then cut loose with 30-second bursts from an automatic weapon until all rustling ceases. Then you merely squat down and scoop up anything that looks like a grouse or some other protein-based life form. It would also be a good idea to take along a pig, which will automatically without any prior training root around for truffles, a kind of delicacy that is very popular among pigs and French people. When you see the pig chewing something, fire a few warning shots over its head and collect whatever it spits out in a Mason jar.

To prepare your grouse, remove the feathers or fur, open up the bodies, remove the organs and parasites and mulch them in the blender until they turn to pâté. Now place the grouse corpses on a stout pan and insert them into a heated oven, dousing them from time to time with A-1 sauce.

When your guests arrive, your first responsibility is to make them feel at ease. I strongly suggest you get a copy of the *Complete Book of Games and Stunts* published in MCLVI by Bonanza Books and authored by Darwin A. Hindman, Ph.D., professor of physical education at the University of Missouri, available at garage sales everywhere. I especially recommend the "Funnel Trick" described in Chapter Four ("Snares"), wherein you tell the victim that the object is to place a penny on his forehead and tilt his head forward so the penny drops into a funnel stuck into his pants. However—get this—while he's got his head tilted back, you pour a pitcher of water into the funnel and get his pants soaking wet! Be sure to follow this with a lighthearted remark ("You look like a cretin, Thad!") and offer everybody a swig from the liqueur bottle.

Once your guests are loosened up, have them sit around the dinner table, and start by serving them each a small wad of truffles with a side wad of pâté. Then bring on the grouse, after whanging each corpse briskly against the kitchen table so as to knock off the char. As your guests enjoy their meal, show great facial interest in whatever conversational topics they choose ("Grouse don't have any teeth, do they?" "These aren't truffles! These are cigarette filters drenched in pig saliva!") Dessert should be something that has been set on fire.

After dinner, the men will gather around the radial-arm saw for cigars and brandy while the women head for the bathroom en masse to make pasta or whatever it is they do in there. Then you should herd everybody back into the living room for a cultural activity, such as humming and paging through one of those enormous $26.95 coffee-table books with names like *The Tractors of Spain* that people give you for Christmas when they get desperate.

Your guests will signal when they're ready to leave by darting out of the room the instant you turn your back; be sure to intercept them at the door to say goodbye and obtain written statements to the effect that they had a wonderful time and will invite you over on a specific date. You really shouldn't have to do this, but unfortunately many people today have forgotten even the basics of etiquette.

Restrooms and Other Resorts

What we had in mind was a fun and spontaneous getaway weekend in Key West with our son, Robert, our friends Gene and Arlene, and their two children, Molly and Danny. So we tossed several thousand child-related objects into our two cars and off we went in a little spontaneous convoy, and, after a couple of hours, we stopped at a nice restaurant for lunch, Except, of course, the children didn't want to eat lunch. Children never want to eat in restaurants. What they want to do is to play under the table until the entrées arrive, then go to the bathroom.

And so we grown-ups sat there, trying to be relaxed, while our table, possessed from below by unseen forces, shrieked and vibrated like the furniture in the little girl's bedroom in *The Exorcist.* In accordance with federal restaurant regulations, the people seated around us had no children of any kind whatsoever, probably never had, probably were there to discuss important corporate mergers, and so occasionally we'd dart our heads under the table and hiss "STOP THAT!" like some deranged type of duck. We kept this up until the entrées arrived, and it was time to accompany the children to the restroom.

The men's room was very small and had not been cleaned since the Westward Expansion. Robert, seeing this, immediately announced that he had to do Number Two, and of course he insisted that I stand right outside the stall. I hate this situation, because when strangers come in to pee, there I am, apparently just hanging around for fun in this tiny repulsive bathroom. So to indicate that I'm actually there on official business, guarding a stall, I feel obligated to keep a conversation going with Robert, but the only topic I can ever think of to talk about, under the circumstance, is how the old Number Two is coming along. You'd feel like a fool in that situation, talking about, say, Iran. So I say: "How're you doing in there, Robert?" in a ludicrously interested voice. And Robert says: "You just ASKED me that!" which is true. And I say "Ha ha!" to reassure the peeing stranger that I am merely engaging in parenthood and there is no cause for alarm.

And so, finally, we all got out of the restrooms, and we parents grabbed quick violent bites from our nice cold entrées in between checking young Danny's head for signs of breakage after he walked into adjacent tables. Eventually, the waitress took the children's plates, untouched, back to the kitchen to be frozen and reused hundreds of times as entrees for other children. Many modern efficient restaurants are now making their children's entrées entirely out of plastic.

Eventually, we got ourselves back on the road, which was the signal for the children to announce that they were hungry, and, of course, they ate potato chips all the rest of the way to Key West. Once at the hotel we were totally unpacked in a matter of hours, and we decided to go to a restaurant, thus proving that long car trips do indeed damage your brain. We found a charming Italian place with fairly clean restrooms and a lovely illuminated fountain with a dangerous electrical cord to attract the children, especially young Danny, who is only two, but has already figured out hundreds of ways to kill himself.

At the sight of the entrées arriving, the children of course fled like startled deer, so we had one of those restaurant meals where you are constantly whirling your head around as you eat, trying to locate the children, with the ever-present danger that you'll get your timing off and stab yourself in the side of the head with your fork. And then it was time to go back to the hotel for an intimate evening of sitting on the floor drinking beer and watching the older children bounce on the bed and eat potato chips while young Danny located bureaus to bang his head into.

For breakfast we found a charming buffet-style restaurant with medium restrooms and a cigarette machine that three small children, if they worked together, could pull over onto their heads.

After breakfast, we went back to our hotel so the children could get something to eat, and then we decided that the women would go shopping and the men, being Caring and Sharing eighties-style males, would take the children. Gene and I thought it would be fun to go to the beach, so off we went, unfortunately forgetting to take any of the items usually associated with the beach, such as toys, suntan lotion, rafts, or bathing suits. We did, however, remember to bring the children. Call it instinct.

Of course, as soon as we got to the beach, little Molly announced that she had to go to the bathroom, and so I watched Danny and Robert fill their shorts with beach muck while Gene and Molly hiked off in search of a restroom, which they eventually found a half-mile away. It took them a long time to get back, because Molly refused to go into the men's room and Gene can't go into the women's room, so he had to hang around right outside like a sex offender while Molly went in alone, only she came back five minutes later and reported that she couldn't find the toilets. You wonder how we got this far as a species.

Finally, they got back, and we decided we'd better head back to the hotel, because one of the many things we had forgotten was young Danny's diaper bag, and he was wearing his Big Boy underpants, making him, in Gene's words, a "time bomb."

That night, spontaneously, we hired a babysitter.

Revenge of the Pork Person

Ok, ladies, I want you all to line up according to height and prepare to receive your fashion orders for the fall season. You ladies want to be up-to-date, right? You don't want to show up at work dressed in some dowdy old thing from last year, looking like Beaver Cleaver's mother, do you? Of course not! You want to look the very best you possibly can, given your various physical deformities.

Ha ha! I'm just teasing you ladies, because I know how sensitive you tend to be about the way you look. I have never met a woman, no matter how attractive, who wasn't convinced, deep down inside, that she was a real woofer. Men tend to be just the opposite. A man can have a belly you could house commercial aircraft in and a grand total of eight greasy strands of hair, which he grows real long and combs across the top of his head so that he looks, when viewed from above, like an egg in the grasp of a giant spider, plus this man can have B.O. to the point where he interferes with radio transmissions, and he will still be convinced that, in terms of attractiveness, he is borderline Don Johnson.

But not women. Women who look perfectly fine to other people are always seeing horrific physical flaws in themselves. I have this friend, Janice, who looks very nice and is a highly competent professional with a good job and a fine family, yet every now and then she will get very depressed, and do you want to know why? Because she thinks she has *puffy ankles.* This worries her much more than, for example, the arms race. Her image of herself is that when she walks down the street, people whisper: "There she goes! The woman with the *puffy ankles!*"

Likewise my wife, who it goes without saying has a great figure and excellent legs, is convinced, and nothing will change her mind, that she has inadequate calves. This has resulted in a situation where

—I can produce documentation to prove this—the number of lifetime fitness-club memberships she has purchased *actually exceeds the total number of her legs.*

What women think they should look like, of course, is the models in fashion advertisements. This is pretty comical, because when we talk about fashion models, we are talking about mutated women, the results of cruel genetic experiments performed by fashion designers so lacking in any sense of human decency that they think nothing of putting their initials on your eyeglass lenses. These experiments have resulted in a breed of fashion models who are 8 and sometimes 10 feet tall, yet who weigh no more than an abridged dictionary due to the fact that they have virtually none of the bodily features we normally associate with females such as hips and (let's come right out and say it) bosoms. The leading cause of death among fashion models is falling through street grates. If a normal human woman puts on clothing designed for these unfortunate people, she is quite naturally going to look like Revenge of the Pork Person.

This was particularly true last year, when the Fashion Concept that we here in the fashion industry decided to thrust upon you ladies was the Big Shoulder Look. Remember that? What fun! I cannot tell you how many hours of enjoyment we got from watching you trying to have serious business careers while looking like Green Bay Packers in drag. At one point, we considered having you wear actual helmets, but we couldn't figure out how to fit all our initials on them.

But that was last year. This year we, of course, have an entirely new concept. We have been working on it for just months and months now, and we are extremely proud of it, because it is so highly innovative. Are you ready? Here it is:

Gray.

Everybody got that? Better write it down! If we find any ladies out on the street without their gray on, we are going to be *very upset.* Also we are asking you to purchase certain mandatory accessories in the form of several thousand dollars worth of handbags, shoes, belts, and watch straps made from dead crocodiles. NO, YOU MAY *NOT* ASK WHY! JUST *DO* IT!

Sorry for that emotional outburst, ladies. It's just that we work so hard to come up with these concepts, and it really frosts our shorts when we find ourselves being questioned by some bimbo *consumer,* pardon our French.

Looking ahead to the future, we see some very exciting developments looming on the fashion horizon for you ladies. Here, for example, is a real quotation from a recent issue of *Vogue* magazine, which uses capital letters for important fashion bulletins:

"THE LOOK OF THE MODERN WOMAN? IN MODERNIST ANDRÉE PUTMAN'S EYES, SHE'S STRONG-SHOULDERED, HIGH-BREASTED, ALMOST AMAZONIAN AND COMES WITH BUILT-IN HIGH HEELS. AT LEAST, THAT'S THE LOOK OF THE NEW PUTMAN-DESIGNED MANNEQUINS MAKING THEIR FIRST PUBLIC APPEARANCE NOW AT BARNEY'S NEW YORK. COME FALL, THE CREATURES WILL PROLIFERATE TO OTHER STORES, OTHER CITIES."

Isn't this *exciting,* ladies? There could come a time, perhaps in your very lifetimes, when we are no longer designing clothes even for mutated fashion models, but for mannequins based on *entirely new concepts of what the female body really should look like,* from deep thinkers such as Andrée Putman. You could see the day when you can't even buy shoes without getting large heel implants! Let's all toss our hats into the air with joy! Our hats, by the way, should be gray porkpies.

Slope Flake

As those of you who own digital watches are already aware, the winter months are approaching, which means now is the time to start planning that ski vacation.

I understand that some of you may be reluctant to plan ski vacations because you've seen the snippet of film at the beginning of "Wide World of Sports" wherein the Agony of Defeat is depicted by an unfortunate person who loses control of himself going off the end of a ski-jump launcher and various organs come flying out of his body. If you're concerned that something like this could happen to you, here's a statistic from the National Ski Resort Association that should be very reassuring: the so-called castorbean tick, which sucks blood from sheep, will respond to a temperature change of as little as 0.5 degrees centigrade! Wait a minute, there seems to be a mistake here: that reassuring statistic actually comes from the *Encyclopedia Britannica.* Perhaps someone in our reading audience can come up with something more closely related to skiing safety.

Meanwhile, the rest of you should decide what kind of skiing you want to engage in. One option is cross-country skiing, which has become very popular in recent years because it is highly "aerobic," a term health experts use to describe how dull an activity is. What you do is find a patch of country and slog across on skis for no apparent reason in a manner very much reminiscent of a herd of cattle, except of course that cattle have the excuse that if they stop, armed men will ride up and kick them with pointed boots. A more fun option is downhill skiing, which is when a machine takes you up a hill and you have to get down.

Whatever kind of skiing you decide to do, your next important task—in fact, your most important task—is to make sure you have proper ski equipment. When your great grandfather was a boy, of course, he'd simply take two barrel staves and tie them to his feet. This could well be an indication that there is some kind of congenital mental illness in your family, and I urge you to look into it immediately.

Next you'll want to select a ski resort. The important thing here is to decide whether or not you are rich. If you are, you'll want to ski at an exclusive resort, the kind your congressperson goes to, where you have to examine your pillow before you go to bed at night lest you wind up with a complimentary miniature Swiss chocolate lodged in your ear. But even if you belong to the middle or lower class, there are plenty of newer resorts with names like "Large Rugged Wolf Mountain Ski Resort and Driving Range" that entrepreneurs have constructed in places such as South Carolina by piling industrial sludge on top of discarded appliances.

Just before you leave home, you should call the resort and ask for a frank and honest appraisal of the slope conditions, because it would make little sense to go and spend money if the resort operator did not frankly and honestly feel it would be worth your while. Most resorts use the Standardized Ski Resort Four-Stage Slope Condition Description System:

"REALLY INCREDIBLY SUPERB": This means the entire slope is encased in a frozen substance of some kind.

"REALLY SUPERB": This means there are large patches of bare industrial sludge, but persons with good motor skills can still slide all the way to the bottom.

"SUPERB:" This means persons wishing to get to the bottom will have to remove their skis at several points and clamber over rusted dishwashers with sharp exposed edges.

"EXCELLENT": This means it is July.

OK! You've reached the resort, and now it's finally time to "hit the slopes." Not so fast! First attach skis of approximately equal length to each of your feet, discarding any leftovers, and check the bindings to make sure they release automatically just before your ankles break. Now grasp your poles and try to stand up. We'll wait right here.

(Three-hour pause.)

Ha ha! It's not as easy as it looks, is it? I mean, here are all these people around you, and *they* can do it, and their *kids* can do it, really *little* kids, *babies* practically, skiing past you without a care in the world, and there you are, thrashing around on your back in the snow right smack in front of the ski lodge, making an even bigger fool of yourself than Richard Nixon did the time he resigned and made that speech about his mother! Ha ha! Years from now you'll look back on this and laugh, but for now you can lash out with your poles and try to inflict puncture wounds on the other skiers' legs.

Now that you're comfortable with the equipment, summon several burly ski patrol persons and have them carry you over to the chairlift. While you're riding up to the summit, you'll have an opportunity to admire the spectacular sweeping panoramic view of the little tiny wire that you and the chairs and the other skiers are all hanging from. It looks far too frail to hold all that weight, doesn't it? But you can rest assured that it was designed and built on the basis of countless careful measurements and calculations done by scientists and engineers who are not currently up there hanging from the wire with you.

Shark Treatment

I have come up with a sure-fire concept for a hit television show, which would be called "A Live Celebrity Gets Eaten by a Shark." To help you understand why I think this show would be a success, let me give you a little background.

The human race has been fascinated by sharks for as long as I can remember. Just like the bluebird feeding its young, or the spider struggling to weave its perfect web, or the buttercup blooming in spring, the shark reveals to us yet another of the infinite and wonderful facets of nature, namely the facet that can bite your head off. This causes us humans to feel a certain degree of awe.

I know what I'm talking about here, because I once had—this is the truth—an encounter with a shark. It was in 1973, in the Bahamas, where I was sailing with a group of friends. One day, we were anchored near a little island that had a vast shallow sandy-bottomed lagoon next to it, maybe a foot deep, and a friend of mine named Richard and I were wading around in there, and lo and behold we saw this shark. It was a small shark, less than two feet long. The only conceivable way it could have been a threat to a human being would be if it somehow got hold of, and learned to use, a gun.

So Richard and I decided to try to catch it. With a great deal of strategy and effort and shouting, we managed to maneuver the shark, over the course of about a half-hour, to a sort of corner of the lagoon, so that it had no way to escape other than to flop up onto the land and evolve. Richard and I were inching toward it, sort of crouched over, when all of a sudden it turned around and—I can still remember the sensation I felt at that moment, primarily in the armpit area—*headed right straight toward us.*

Many people would have panicked at this point. But Richard and I were not "many people."

We were experienced waders, and we kept our heads. We did exactly what the textbook says you should do when you're unarmed and a shark that is nearly two feet long turns on you in water up to your lower calves: We sprinted I would say 600 yards in the opposite direction, using a sprinting style such that the bottoms of our feet never once went below the surface of the water. We ran all the way to the far shore, and if we had been in a Warner Brothers cartoon you would have seen these two mounds of sand racing across the island until they bonked into trees and coconuts fell onto their heads.

So I know the fascination of the shark, and thus I have been particularly interested in all these shark documentaries on television. You've probably noticed them. Any given night, you tune into a channel at random and odds are you'll see divers hurling themselves into shark-infested waters. The narrator always claims this is for Scientific Research, which is blatant horse waste. I mean, if that were true, you'd figure that after two or three thousand documentaries, they'd know all they needed to know about sharks, and they'd move on to another variety of sea life. But they don't, because they know darned good and well that the viewers aren't going to remain glued to their seats to watch divers paddling around in waters infested by, for example, clams.

So the documentary-makers stick with sharks. Generally, their procedure is to scatter bleeding fish pieces around their boat, so as to infest the waters. I would estimate that the primary food source of sharks today is bleeding fish pieces scattered by people making documentaries. Once the sharks arrive, they are generally fairly listless. The general shark attitude seems to be: "Oh, God, another documentary." So the divers have to somehow goad them into attacking, under the guise of Scientific Research. "We know very little about the effect of electricity on sharks," the narrator will say, in a deeply scientific voice. "That is why Todd is going to jab this Great White in the testicles with a cattle prod." The divers keep this kind of thing up until the shark finally gets irritated and snaps at them, and then they act as though this was a totally unexpected and very dangerous development, although clearly it is what they wanted all along.

Shark documentaries took an important stride forward recently with a series called "Ocean Quest," in which, instead of using trained divers, the documentary maker rented a former beauty queen, Shawn Weatherly, and spent a year dropping her into various shark-infested waters. The idea was that she, being a regular person just like me and you except she has a great body, would be able to convey to us viewers the various human emotions she was feeling. This was pretty funny, inasmuch as Shawn's acting ability is such that she could not convey the concept of falling if you pushed her off a cliff. But the point is, here was a shark documentary that barely even pretended to be scientific, and instead focused on the excitement involved in watching somebody act as bait.

So I say it's time to take this one step farther. I say the public is ready to drop the Scientific Research aspect altogether, and to get past all the usual shark-documentary foreplay. I don't think it would be a problem, getting the celebrities. You look for somebody whose career really needs a boost—a Telly Savalas, for example, or a Zsa Zsa Gabor—and you point out what exposure like this could do for a person. I don't think you could keep Zsa Zsa *out* of the water. Ed McMahon could be the host. Your only real problem would be getting a shark. Most of your top sharks probably have commitments to do documentaries.

Electro-Maggots

Today's science question comes from eight-year-old Bobby Johnson, an imaginary child who lives in Maryland. Bobby asks: "What good are insects, anyway? You know?"

ANSWER: It's a shame, Bobby, but for far too many people, the usual reaction upon encountering an insect is to want to smash it with a rock. That's certainly *my* immediate reaction, although there are certain insects I would prefer to use a flame-thrower on, such as those large tropical-style spiders that appear to be wearing the pelts of small mammals.

Oh, I can hear you junior-high-school science teachers out there now, spitting out your cafeteria entrée ("Tuna Warmed Up") and shouting: "Wait a minute! Spiders aren't insects! Spiders are *arachnids!*" That's exactly what's wrong with our junior high schools today: all those snotty science teachers going around telling our young people that spiders are not insects, when they (the science teachers) could be leading voluntary organized prayers. Of *course* spiders are insects. The very word "insect" is a combination of two ancient Greek words: "in," meaning "a," and "sect," meaning "repulsive little creature." Thus not only are spiders insects but so are crabs, jellyfish, the late Truman Capote, bats, clams, olives and those unfortunate little dogs, "pugs," I believe they are called, that appear to have been struck repeatedly in the face with a heavy, flat object such as the *Oxford English Dictionary*.

So, Bobby, we can see that . . . Bobby? Bobby! Take that finger out of your nose and pay attention when I answer your Science Question! Whose finger *is* that, anyway?! Put it back where you found it this instant!!

All right. So, Bobby, we can see that the insect family is very large and varied indeed. Just sitting here thinking about it, I would estimate that there are over 600 billion species of insect in my basement alone, which is a real puzzle because we pay $16 a month to have a man come and spray an allegedly lethal chemical all over the place. What I think has happened is that the insects got to this man somehow. Maybe a group of wasps met him at the end of our driveway one afternoon and made it clear to him by gesturing with their feelers that they wouldn't want to see him or his wife or God forbid his small children get stung in the eyeballs, and so what he has actually been spraying around our basement all this time is Liquid Insect Treat.

This is probably good. We cannot simply destroy insects in a cavalier manner, because, as many noted ecology nuts have reminded us time and time again, they (the insects) are an essential link in the Great Food Chain, wherein all life forms are dependent on each other via complex and subtle interrelationships, as follows: Man gets his food by eating cows, which in turn eat corn, which in turn comes from Iowa, which in turn was part of the Louisiana Purchase, which in turn was obtained from France, which in turn eats garlic, which in turn repels vampires, which in turn suck the blood out of Man. So we can see that without insects there would be no . . . Hey, wait a minute! I just noticed that there are *no insects* in the Great Food Chain. Ha ha! Won't *that* be a kick in the pants for many noted ecology nuts! I bet they all race right out and buy 4,000-volt patio insect-electrocution devices!

Nevertheless, we do need insects for they perform many useful functions. Without insects, for example, we would have no reliable way to spread certain diseases. Also, in some part of Africa that I saw in a documentary film once, they have this very, very large insect, called the Goliath beetle, which grows to almost a foot in length, and the children actually use these beetles to pull their little toy carts. Wouldn't that be fun, Bobby, to have a foot-long beetle of your own, pulling a cart around and clambering into bed with you? Perhaps I'll get you one!

Of course most of us find it difficult to talk about insects without bringing up the subject of sex. According to scientists who study insects (known as "entomologists," or "Al"), the male insect initiates reproduction by rubbing his legs together to produce a distinctive sound, which attracts a bird, which eats the male, then throws up. The female insect then lays 1.5 billion eggs, eating them as she goes along so she will have the strength she will need to suckle them when they hatch. The young insects, called "maggots," enjoy a carefree childhood, writhing playfully under their mother's 76,806,059 watchful eyes and engaging in maggot games that teach them skills they will need to survive as adults, such as scurrying under the refrigerator when the kitchen light comes on. Eventually, they reach a point where their mother can teach them no more, so they eat her, and the males start rubbing their legs together. This life cycle takes about 18 minutes, slightly less in my basement.

So there you have it, Bobby, a fascinating look at the jillions of tiny life forms that inhabit Spaceship Earth with us, and that will still be around long after we're all dead from nuclear war! Of course the insects know this, too, and they do everything they can to promote international tension. They send their top-rated chiggers to all the nuclear-arms-reduction talks, so after a few minutes the negotiators for both sides are so welt-covered and irritated that they lunge across the table and try to punch each other in the mouth. It's just one more way these amazing little creatures adapt to the world around them. So the next time you're about to stomp on an insect, Bobby, remember this: A sudden, jerky motion can lead to serious muscle strain!

Well, kids, that's it for this month's science question. Tune in next month, when a child from Ohio named "Suzy," or perhaps "Mark," will write in to ask about the Six Basic Rules of cattle-prod safety.

The Lesson of History

The difficult thing about studying history is that, except for Harold Stassen, everybody who knows anything about it firsthand is dead. This means that our only source of historical information is historians, who are useless because they keep changing everything around.

For example, I distinctly remember learning in fifth grade that the Civil War was caused by slavery. So did you, I bet. As far as I was concerned, this was an excellent explanation for the Civil War, the kind you could remember and pass along as an important historical lesson to your grandchildren. ("Gather 'round boys and girls, while Grandpa tells you what caused the Civil War. Slavery. Now go fetch Grandpa some more bourbon.")

Then one day in high school, out of the blue, a history teacher named Anthony Sabella told me that the Civil War was caused by economic factors. I still think this was a lie, and not just because Anthony Sabella once picked me up by my neck. I mean, today we have more economic factors than ever before, such as the Dow Jones Industrial Average, but you don't see the North and the South fighting each other, do you? Which is good, because the South has 96 percent of the nation's armed pickup trucks, whereas the North mainly has Fitness Centers, so it would be over in minutes.

DISCUSSION QUESTION: What kind of a name is "Dow" Jones? *Explain.*

Nevertheless, I had to pretend I thought the Civil War was caused by economic factors, or I never would have escaped from Mr. Sabella's class and got into college, where the history professors sneered openly at the primitive high-school-teacher notion that the Civil War had been caused by anything so obvious as economic factors. No, they said, the Civil War was caused by acculturalized regionalism. Or maybe it was romantic transcendentalism, or behavioristic naturalism, or structuralized functionalism. I learned hundreds of terms like these in college, and I no longer even vaguely remember what they mean. As far as I know, any one of them could have caused the Civil War. Maybe we should lock them all in a small room and deny them food and water until one of them confesses.

DISCUSSION QUESTION: Was the author "just kidding" when he made that last "off-the-wall" suggestion? Cite specific examples.

What is the cause of all this disagreement among the experts over basic historical issues? Economic factors. If you're a historian and you want to write a best-selling book, you have to come up with a new wrinkle. If you go to a publisher and say you want to write that Harry Truman was a blunt-spoken Missourian who made some unpopular decisions but was vindicated by history, the publisher will pick you up by your neck and toss you into the street, because there are already bales of such books on the market. But if you claim to have uncovered evidence that Harry Truman was a Soviet ballerina, before long you'll be on national morning television, answering earnest questions from David Hartman in a simulated living room.

DISCUSSION QUESTION: Don't you think David Hartman is just a little *too* avuncular? Why?

So I propose that we laypersons forget about historians and agree among ourselves to believe in a permanent set of historical facts once and for all. Specifically, I propose we use the facts contained in a book I found in my basement recently, called *Civilization Past and Present,* which was apparently one of my wife's high-school textbooks.

DISCUSSION QUESTION: Did she steal it? Or what?

Civilization Past and Present combines the advantage of having a snappy title with the advantage of ending in 1962, just before history starts to get really depressing. It's easy to understand, because my wife has underlined all the important words and phrases (*Germany,* for example). And it doesn't beat around the bush. For example, on page 599 it makes the following statement in plain black and white: "The causes of the American Civil War are complex."

Since some of you laypersons out there may not have *Civilization Past and Present* in your basements, here's a brief summary to tide you over until you can get your own copies:

HISTORY
5,000,000,000 B.C.—1962

After the Earth cooled, it formed an extremely fertile crescent containing primitive people such as the Hittites who believed in just the stupidest things you ever heard of. Then came Greece and Rome, followed by Asia. All of this came to a halt during the Middle Ages, which were caused by the Jutes and featured the following terms underlined by my wife: *the steward, the bailiff, and the reeve.* Next the Turks got way the hell over into France, after which there were towns. And the Magna Carta. Then France and England fought many wars that involved dates such as 1739 and were settled by the Treaty of Utrecht, which also was used to harness water power. By then the seeds had been sown for several World Wars and the Louisiana Purchase, but fortunately we now have a fairly peaceful atom. Now go fetch Grandpa some more bourbon.

DEFINE THE FOLLOWING: "Avuncular."

Sock it to Me

I woke up this morning experiencing several important concerns, which I would like to share with you here in the hope that they will add up to a large enough total word count so that I can go back to bed.

CONCERN NUMBER ONE: Mr. Lyndon H. LaRouche, Jr.

As you probably know, Mr. LaRouche is this person who has started his own political party and wishes to take over the country, which troubles many people because his views are somewhat unorthodox. (What I mean of course, is that he is as crazy as a bedbug. Where you have a brain, Lyndon H. LaRouche, Jr., has a Whack-a-Mole game. But I am not about to state this in print, as I do not wish to have his ardent followers place poison snakes in my sock drawer.)

Those of you who are frequent airline travelers are no doubt already familiar with Mr. LaRouche's views, because they are displayed on posters attached to card tables at most major airports. Somehow, a year or so ago, the LaRouche people managed to get the lucrative Airport Lunatic concession away from the Moonies. What I suspect happened is that one day, on a prearranged signal, the LaRouche people sneaked up behind the Moonies and strangled them with their own little book bags, probably in full view of thousands of air travelers, who of course would not have objected. Many of them probably helped out by whapping the Moonies with their carry-on luggage. I know I would have.

But then, two of Mr. LaRouche's ardent followers won the Illinois Democratic primary nominations for secretary of state and lieutenant governor. This caused massive nationwide anxiety because of the unorthodoxy of their views, which, as far as we have been able to tell, involve shooting Jane Fonda with a laser beam from space. Not that I personally see anything wrong with these views! No sir! I don't even *have* a sock drawer!

But we do have to ask ourselves if we truly can afford, as a nation, to elect crazy people to a vital state office like lieutenant governor, which involves weighty responsibilities such as wearing a suit and phoning the governor every day to see if he's dead. Because mark my words, if these people win in Illinois, they'll go after higher and higher offices, until someday—I do not wish to alarm you, but we must be aware of the danger—we could have a situation where our top national leaders are going around babbling about laser beams from space. So I have called on you Illinois voters to come to your senses before the general election and take responsible citizen action in the form of moving to a more intelligent state. This is the perfect time to do so, thanks to declining oil prices.

CONCERN NUMBER TWO: Declining oil prices

Like many of you, I did not realize at first that the decline in oil prices was something to be concerned about. In fact, I viewed it as the first really positive development in this nation since Jimmy Carter was attacked by the giant swimming rabbit. But then I started reading articles by leading nervous economists stating that the oil-price decline is a very bad thing, because it is causing severe hardships for the following groups:

1. The OPEC nations.
2. The U.S. oil industry.
3. The big banks.
4. Texans in general.

When I read this, naturally my reaction as a concerned American, was hahahahahahahahaha.

No, seriously, we need to be worried about declining oil prices, and I am going to explain why. The international economy is based on the U.S. dollar, which is trusted and respected throughout the world because it is the only major currency that does not look like it was designed by preschool children. The value of the dollar, in turn, depends on the investment savvy of big U.S. banks, which lend their dollars to the oil-rich Third World, which loses them gambling on rooster fights.

This system worked well until the late 1970s, when the price of oil started to fall. This was caused by a decline in demand, which was caused by the fact that people couldn't get their cars repaired, which was caused by the fact that the oil companies had bought all the independent garages and turned them into "self-service" stations selling a mutant assortment of retail goods and staffed by surly teenagers, so that God forbid you should have actual *car* trouble at one of these service stations because they would tow you away for blocking the access of customers wishing to purchase nasal spray and Slim Jims.

So now the banks are stuck with a lot of oil, which they are trying to get rid of by converting it into VISA cards, which they offer to my wife. She gets six or seven VISA offers from desperate banks per business day. She got one recently from—I am not making this up—a bank in *South Dakota.* I didn't even know they *had* banks in South Dakota, did you? What would people keep in them? Pelts?

Well I don't know about you, but I am uncomfortable with the idea of having a world economy dependent upon the VISA needs of my wife. She is only one person. That is the law. So I think we need to revamp the whole world economic structure, and the obvious first step is to require banks to repair cars. The supermarkets, which already cash checks, could take over the remaining functions currently performed by banks, such as lending money to the Third World and being closed. You would get your food at service stations, which would be required to get some new sandwiches. You would continue to buy gas at "convenience" stores. Illinois would be sold to wealthy Japanese investors. All these regulations would be enforced by laser beams from space.

The D-Word

There's this sensitive issue that we in the news media are very reluctant to bring up.

No. It isn't condoms. We are totally comfortable, these days, doing lengthy stories about condoms: ("PASTELS OUT, EARTH TONES IN, FOR FALL CONDOM"). You will soon see condom commercials on television. Fortunately we can assume, based on television's track record with this kind of thing, that these commercials will be tasteful and informative:

FIRST MAN: What's the matter, Ted?

SECOND MAN: I think I have a horrible sexually transmitted disease!

FIRST MAN: Here. Try some of my condoms.

SECOND MAN: Thanks.

(The Next Day:)

FIRST MAN: Feeling better, Ted?

SECOND MAN: You bet! Thanks to condoms! And I got that big promotion!

No, the issue we are reluctant to talk about is even more sensitive (ha ha!) than condoms. The issue—and I will try to be tasteful here—is that sometimes it seems like maybe the president of the United States is kind of d**b. If you get what I mean. What I mean is, I am not totally confident that the president would get what I mean, unless several aides explained it to him. And even then, he might forget.

This is unsettling, although I don't know why it should be. For the past 25 years, the presidency had been a remarkable parade of hanky-panky, comical incompetence, and outright weirdness, and the country has done OK. In fact, once you got into the spirit of it, it was kind of fun. I don't know about you, but I *loved* it when Jimmy Carter reported that he'd been attacked by a giant swimming rabbit. I *loved* it when Richard Nixon made speeches wherein he looked as though a large and disorganized committee of alien beings had taken over his body and were just learning how to operate it: ("OK. Let's try to wave. Who's operating the arms?" "Me!" "No, me!" "NO . . . ," etc.).

So I don't mind the president being *bizarre,* but that's not the same as accepting that he might be kind of d**b. Yet it's getting harder and harder to think of any other explanation, not with this Iran-Contra scandal. I realize you out there in Readerland are sick to death of this scandal, but it's still causing multiple orgasms here in the news media, because of all these shocking revelations, the most amazing one being that the president apparently viewed foreign policy as a sort of family station wagon, which he, in the role of Ozzie Nelson, would cheerfully lend to his teen-age son, Ricky, played by Oliver North.

RICKY: Hey Dad, can I take the foreign policy down to the Malt Shoppe and deal with Iranians?

OZZIE: The Iranians?

RICKY: Don't worry, Dad. They're moderates.

OZZIE: Well in that case, OK. Just don't trade arms for hostages!

The president, apparently, was so totally unaware of where his foreign policy was that he had to appoint a distinguished commission to help him locate it, and when the commissioners called him in to testify, he told them, essentially, that *he couldn't remember what it looked like.* Now, if Richard Nixon had claimed something like that you would at least have had the comfort of knowing he was lying. You could trust Nixon that way. But with this president, you have this nagging feeling that he's telling the *truth.*

This bothers us media people, which is why we have developed this euphemistic way of describing the president's behavior, namely, we say he has a "hands-off management style." As in: "How many people with a hands-off management style does it take to change a light bulb?"

Of course the president's aides, in an effort to show that he is a Take-Charge Guy, have arranged to have him star in a number of Photo Opportunities: The President Shakes Hands with People Wearing Suits; the President Sits Down with People Wearing Suits; the President, Wearing a Suit, Signs His Own Name; etc. I think this is good, as far as it goes. My concern is that it should not go any further. My concern is that we could have a sudden eruption of "hands-on" management, for example in the nuclear-arms talks, and we'll end up with Soviet Troops in Des Moines.

Catching Hell

Call me a regular American guy if you want, but baseball season is kind of special to me. For one thing, it means ice hockey season will be over in just a few short months. But it also brings back a lot of memories, because I, like so many other regular American guys, was once a Little Leaguer. I was on a team called the "Indians," although I was puny of chest, so if you saw me in my uniform you'd have thought my team was called the "NDIAN," because the end letters got wrinkled up in my armpits. I had a "Herb Score" model glove, named for a player who went on to get hit in the eye by a baseball.

I remember particularly this one game: I was in deep right field, of course, and there were two out in the bottom of the last inning with the tying run on base, and Gerry Sinnott, who had a much larger chest, who already had to *shave,* was at bat. As I stood there waiting for the pitch, I dreamed a dream that millions of other kids had dreamed: that someday I would grow up, and *I wouldn't have to be in Little League anymore.* In the interim, my feelings could best be summarized by the statement: "Oh please please PLEASE God don't let Gerry Sinnott hit the ball to me."

And so of course God, who as you know has a terrific sense of humor, had Gerry Sinnott hit the ball to me. Here is what happened in the next few seconds: Outside of my body, hundreds of spectators, *thousands* of spectators, arrived at the ball field at that very instant via chartered buses from distant cities to see if I would catch the ball. Inside my body, my brain cells hastily met and came up with a Plan of Action, which they announced to the rest of the body parts. "Listen up, everybody!" they shouted. "We're going to MISS THE BALL! Let's get cracking!!"

Instantly my entire body sprang into action, like

a complex, sophisticated machine being operated by earthworms. The command flashed down from Motor Control to my legs: "GET READY TO RUN!" And soon the excited reply flashed back: "WHICH LEG FIRST?!" Before Motor Control could issue a ruling, an urgent message came in from Vision Central, reporting that the ball *had already gone by,* in fact was now a good 30 to 40 yards behind my body, rolling into the infield of the adjacent game. Motor Control, reacting quickly to this surprising new input, handled the pressure coolly and decisively, snapping out the command: "OK! We're going to FALL DOWN!!" And my body lunged violently sideways, in the direction opposite the side where the ball had passed a full two seconds earlier, flopping onto the ground like some pathetic spawning salmon whose central nervous system had been destroyed by toxic waste, as Gerry Sinnott cruised toward home.

Those boyhood memories! I have them often, although I can control them pretty well with medication.

Actually, when I got older I continued to play organized baseball in the form of "league softball," a game in which after work you put on a comical outfit and go to a public park to argue with strangers. For the first several years the team I was on had a nice, relaxed attitude, by which I mean we were fairly lenient if a player made a mental error. For example, if the ball was hit to the shortstop, and he threw it to first base, but the first baseman wasn't there because he was rooting through the ice cooler looking for a non-"light" beer, we'd say to the person who brought the beer: "Hey! NEVER make the mental error of bringing 'light' beer to a softball game! It can cost a fielder valuable seconds!" But we wouldn't *fine* him or anything.

In later years, however, we got more and more young guys on the team who really wanted to *win;* guys who wore cleats and batting gloves and held *practices* where they were always shrieking about the importance of "hitting" somebody called the "cutoff man"; guys who hated to let women play, apparently for fear that one of them might, during a crucial late-inning rally, go into labor; guys who (this was the last straw) drank *Gatorade* during the game. I had to quit.

But I'm getting back into it. I have a son of my own now, and, being an American guy, I've been teaching him the basics of the game. One recent bright sunny day I took him out in the yard with a Whiffle ball, and I gave him a few pointers. "Robert," I said, "did you know that if we use a magnifying glass to focus sunlight on the Whiffle ball, we can actually cause it to melt?" So we did this, and soon we had advanced to complex experiments involving candy wrappers, Popsicle sticks, and those little stinging ants. Although I drew the line at toads. You have to teach sportsmanship, too.

Mrs. Beasley Froze for Our Sins

One of the issues that we professional newspaper columnists are required by union regulations to voice grave concern about is the federal budget deficit, which we refer to as the "mounting" deficit, because every extra word helps when you have to produce a certain number of gravely concerned newsprint inches. The point we try to get across in these columns is: "You readers may be out driving fast boats and having your fun, but we columnists are sitting in front of our word processors, worried half to death about the nation's financial future." Then we move on to South Africa.

So anyway, I have decided to fret briefly about the deficit, which according to recent reports continues to mount. A while back I proposed a very workable solution to the whole deficit problem, namely that the government should raise money by selling national assets we don't really need: metric road signs, all the presidential libraries, the Snail Darter, the House of Representatives, North Dakota, etc. Unfortunately, the only concrete result of this proposal was that I got an angry letter from everybody in North Dakota, for a total of six letters, arguing that if we're going to sell anything, we should sell New York City.

This probably wouldn't work. There would be major cultural adjustment problems. Suppose, for example, that we sold New York to Switzerland. Now Switzerland is a very tidy, conservative nation, and the first thing it would do is pass a lot of laws designed to make New York more orderly, such as no public muttering, no lunging into the subway car as though it were the last helicopter out of Saigon, no driving taxis over handicapped pedestrians while they are in the crosswalk, no sharing loud confidences regarding intestinal matters to strangers attempting to eat breakfast. These laws would be very difficult for New Yorkers to adjust to. Switzerland would have to send in soldiers to enforce them, and this would inevitably lead to tragic headlines in the *New York Times:*

ENTIRE SWISS ARMY
FOUND STABBED TO DEATH
WITH OWN LITTLE
FOLDING KNIVES

Pedestrians Step Right over
Rotting Corpses

So I'm afraid that, appealing as the idea may be, we can't reduce the deficit by selling New York.

What the government desperately needs is an innovative new concept for getting money from people, and we can all be grateful that such a concept appears to be oozing over the fiscal horizon at this very moment: a national lottery game. A number of congresspersons have already proposed that we start one. It would be similar to the lotteries currently operating in the really advanced states. Here's how they work:

1. First you pass strict laws that say it is totally illegal for private citizens to operate lotteries, because they encourage the poor and the stupid to gamble away their money against ludicrously bad odds. If you find private citizens operating such lotteries, you call them "numbers racketeers" and you throw them in prison.
2. Next you set up an official state lottery with even more ludicrous odds. You give it a perky name like the "Extremely Lucky Digits Game," and you run cheerful upbeat ads right on television strongly suggesting that the poor and the stupid could make no wiser investment than to spend their insulin money on lottery tickets. A nice touch is to say you're using the lottery proceeds to fund a popular program that the state would have to pay for anyway, such as senior citizens or baby deer. In Pennsylvania, for example, they drag an actual senior citizen in front of the camera to perform the ritual televised Daily Number drawing. The senior citizen usually looks kind of frightened, like a hostage being displayed by the Red Brigades. The clear implication is that if the viewers don't purchase Daily Number tickets, Pennsylvania will have to throw old Mrs. Beasley out into the snow headfirst.

   The news media help out by regularly running heart-warming front-page stories about how a man who was broke and starving won $800 million in his state lottery and suddenly could afford nice teeth and many new friends.

So anyway, the plan now is to run something like this on a nationwide scale, which I think would be great, especially if it keeps the federal government from doing something really desperate to raise money, such as selling drugs or making snuff movies. The only potential problem with a national lottery, as some states have pointed out, is that it might siphon off a lot of poor and stupid from the state lotteries. But if this happens, we could have a bailout system, where the federal government would step in and purchase so many million dollars worth of lottery tickets from the troubled state. I mean, hey, why do we have governments in the first place, if not to help each other out?

The Columnist's Caper

I figured out why I'm not getting seriously rich. I write newspaper columns. Nobody ever makes newspaper columns into Major Motion Pictures starring Tom Cruise. The best you can hope for, with a newspaper column, is that people will like it enough to attach it to their refrigerators with magnets shaped like fruit.

So I have written a suspense novel. It has everything. Sex. Violence. Sex. Death. Russians. Dead Russians. Here's what the newspaper critics are saying:

"A very short novel."—the *Waco, Texas, Chronic Vegetable*

"This is it? This is the entire novel?—the *Arkansas Dependent-Statesperson*

"Not enough sex."—the *Evening Gonad*

No doubt you motion-picture producers out there would like to see the novel these critics are raving about, so you can send me lucrative film offers. Here it is:

CHAPTER ONE

Carter Crater strode into the Oval Office. He looked like Tom Cruise, or, if he is available, Al Pacino.

Behind the desk sat the president of the United States. To his left, in the corner, stood the secretary of state. Crater sensed that something was wrong.

"Unless we act quickly," the president said, "within the next few hours the world will be blown to pieces the size of Smith Brothers cough lozenges."

Crater frowned. "We had better act quickly," he said.

The president looked thoughtful. "That just might work," he said. "Use whatever means you consider necessary, including frequent casual sex."

CHAPTER TWO

In the Kremlin, General Rasputin Smirnov frowned at Colonel Joyce Brothers Karamazov Popov.

"It is absolutely essential that the Americans do not suspect anything," Smirnov said.

"Yes," agreed Popov.

Smirnov frowned.

"Shouldn't we be speaking Russian?" he asked.

Popov looked thoughtful.

"We should at least have accents," he said.

CHAPTER THREE

Suddenly, it struck Crater: The Oval Office doesn't *have* corners.

CHAPTER FOUR

Some 2,347 miles away in East Berlin, a man and a woman walked briskly eastward on Volkswagenkindergarten-pumpernikelstrasse. Talking intently, they did not notice the sleek black Mercedes sedan, its windows tinted almost black, as it turned off Hamburgerfrankfurterwienerschnitzelstrasse and came toward them from behind, picking up speed until, traveling at 130 kilometers per microgram, it roared into a parked garbage truck.

"Too much window tint," the woman said.

CHAPTER FIVE

Some 452.5 miles away, Crater had sex.

CHAPTER SIX

"Ach," said General Smirnov. "Zees American agent, ve must keel heem."

"Dat's de troof," agreed Popov. "Les'n we do, he gon' mess up de plan to blow up de worl'."

CHAPTER SEVEN

Crater handed the microfilm to crack intelligence expert Lieutenant Ensign Sergeant Commander Monica Melon.

She studied it carefully for about 15 minutes. Finally she spoke.

"There's something written on here," she said, frowning, "but it's really teensy."

CHAPTER EIGHT

Smirnov frowned at Popov.

"Blimey," he said.

CHAPTER NINE

In the darkened room, Crater could see the shadowy figure who threatened to destroy the world, who had led Crater on this desperate chase across nine continents, a race filled with terror and death and women whose thighs could have been the basis for a major world religion, and all leading to this moment, Crater and the shadowy figure, alone in the gloom. Slowly, almost reluctantly, Crater reached for the light switch. He flicked it on. The shadowy figure turned, slowly, slowly. At last, Crater could see the figure's face.

It was a big surprise.

CHAPTER TEN

"Good job of saving the entire world, Crater," the president said. "But I have one question: How did you know Miss Prendergast never heard the cathedral bell?"

"Easy, sir," answered Crater. "You see, Lord Copperbottom is *left-handed,* so the gardener couldn't possibly have taken the key from the night stand."

"I never thought of that," said the president. He frowned at the names coming up out of the floor and drifting toward the ceiling so the audience would know who had played what parts.

"Hey," the president said. "These names are *backwards.*"

A Rash Proposal

Lately I have been thinking a lot about the defense of Western Europe. It keeps my mind off this rash in my right armpit. When I think about it, I reach the point where all I want to do is quit my job and move to an isolated cave so I can devote full time to scratching myself. Eventually it reached the point where I threw caution to the winds and went to an actual skin doctor. I was hoping he'd give me one of those hand-held garden implements with the three sharp prongs I forget what you call them, and say: "Dave, I want you to rake this implement across your rash every 10 seconds or as needed." But no, he gave me some wimpy little white pills and came up with a bizarre treatment program under which—this is the truth—I was supposed to *try to grow a new rash.* Really. He thinks my rash is caused by a rash-causing chemical that large corporations put in deodorants, apparently out of sheer hatred for the consumer, and to test this theory he wants me to rub some of this very same chemical onto my arm and see if I develop a new rash. I'm not going to do it, of course, because (a) I don't even want the rash I brought him in the first place, let alone a new one, and (b) if he thinks I'm stupid enough to deliberately rub rash-causing chemicals on myself, his next move will be to ask me to rub them on my family and friends.

Sometimes you have to wonder what's happening to the medical profession. A recent edition of the *Weekly World News,* which I feel is probably the best newspaper your money can buy in a supermarket, carried a story headlined "HUMAN HEAD TRANSPLANT." The story concerns an operation performed by doctors in Communist China who got hold of this unfortunate man with a large brain tumor, and they treated him by amputating his head and replacing it with one they got from a person who had lost his body in a factory accident and consequently died. I would very much like to know how the doctors explained this operation to the patient ("The only possible side effect we can foresee, Loo Ping, will be some neck stiffness, plus the fact that you will have the head of a dead factory worker.")

Of course you have an entirely different set of problems to confront when you talk about defending Western Europe. The main one is that it is filled with Western Europeans, who are not in the least bit interested in defending themselves. They have discovered, over the past thousand years or so, that every time they get military, they wind up having a lengthy and extremely complicated war in which the various countries have tremendous trouble remembering whose side they're on:

BRITISH SOLDIER: Taste my sword, French person!

FRENCH SOLDIER: No! Wait! We are allies! This is World War I!

BRITISH SOLDIER: I'm terribly sorry! I thought it was the Hundred Years War! Does this mean I can kill Italians?

FRENCH SOLDIER *(consulting manual)***:** No, I'm afraid not. Not until World War II.

So eventually the Western Europeans stopped forming armies altogether and decided to become third-rate powers, which means we have to defend them from the Russians. We're available to defend foreign continents because we have no urgent need to defend our own. I mean, the Mexicans certainly aren't going to attack us, seeing as how most of them already work here. I suppose the Canadians could attack us, but the entire population of Canada is maybe the size of the audience on "Donahue," only quieter, so even if they did attack, nobody would know, especially if it was during rush hour.

So we're over there defending Western Europe, which is very, very expensive. For one thing, we have to get up an army, which means we have to pay for all those commercials wherein we suggest to young people that the whole point of the army is to teach them valuable electronics skills, with no mention whatsoever of getting shot at or getting cretin haircuts and being ordered to do pushups by a person who has never read anything longer than a Dr Pepper bottle. For another thing, to defend Western Europe we have to let the Pentagon buy all these tanks and guns and things, and the Pentagon is unable to buy any object that costs less than a condominium in Vail. If the Pentagon needs, say, fruit, it will argue that it must have fruit that can withstand the rigors of combat conditions, and it will wind up purchasing the FX-700 Seedless Tactical Field Grape, which will cost $160,000 per bunch, and which will have an 83 percent failure rate.

So I have come up with this plan for defending Western Europe much more economically, which is to pull our armed forces out of there altogether. They could come home and fix our videocassette recorders. In their place we would send over all our state highway departments and tell them we want them to repair the roads between Western Europe and Russia. Think about it: First they'd have their Cone Placement Division strew millions of traffic cones randomly all over the roads, then they'd have their Sign Erection Department put up signs explaining that all the lanes would be really messed up for the next 17 years to Help Serve You Better, then the Traffic Direction Division would get all kinds of low-life derelicts out there waving flags and directing motorists right into oncoming trucks, and within a few months it would be absolutely impossible for any vehicle, including Communist tanks, to get from Russia to Western Europe.

So that's my plan. What do you think? I think those wimpy little pills are starting to kick in.

He Knows Not What He Writes

The problem with writing about religion is that you run the risk of offending sincerely religious people, and then they come after you with machetes. So I am going to be very sensitive, here, which is not easy, because the thing about religion is that everybody else's always appears stupid.

For example, if you read about some religious sect in India that believes God wants people to drink their own urine, you don't say to yourself, "Isn't that amazing, the diversity of belief systems Man has developed in his neverending quest to understand and cope with the intricate moral dilemmas posed by a complex and uncertain world?" No, what you say to yourself is, "These people have the brains of trout."

Meanwhile, over in India, the sect members are getting a major chuckle over the fact that some American basketball players cross themselves before they take foul shots. "As if God cares about foul shots," the sect members howl, tears streaming down their faces. "Say, is this my urine or yours?"

That's the basic problem, of course: figuring out what God wants us to do. I will admit right up front here that I don't have the vaguest idea. All my religious training was in Sunday school maybe 25 years ago, and the main thing I remember was that God was always smiting the Pharisees. At least I think it was the Pharisees. It seemed that hardly a day went by when thay didn't get the tar smitten out of them, which is probably why you see so few of them around anymore.

My wife, who has bales of religious training, tells me that this was the Old Testament God, who was very strict, whereas the New Testament God is a genuinely mellow deity, the kind of deity who would never smite anybody or order you to smear goat's blood on your first-born son, which is the kind of thing the Old Testament God was always doing.

NOTE: The preceding paragraph is in no way intended to suggest that there is anything wrong with smearing goat's blood on your first-born son. As far as I'm concerned, this is an excellent ritual, and I would do it myself if not for the fact that my son might tell the school authorities. Please put away your machetes. Thank you.

It used to be much worse. Back in ancient Greece and Rome they had gods all over the place, and it was no fun at all being a mortal, as you know if you ever read any myths:

"One day two young lovers, Vector and Prolix, were walking in a garden. This angered Bruno, the god of gardens, so he turned Vector into a toad. Saddened, Prolix picked up her lover and squeezed him to her bosom, which caused him to secrete a toad secretion upon her garment. This angered Vito, the god of fabric, who turned Prolix into an exceedingly unattractive insect. Saddened, Vector hopped to his lover, which angered Denise, who was the goddess of municipal water supply and just happened to be in the neighborhood, so she hit them both with a rock."

And so on. So things are better now. Today most of us believe in just the one God, and He never turns people into toads or anything, unless you count Spiro Agnew. All He wants us to do is what He wants us to do, which is clearly revealed in the Bible.

(Sound of the machetes being unsheathed.)

And the Talmud and the Koran and the Book of Mormon and the works of L. Ron Hubbard. These holy writings tell us what God wants us to do, often in the form of revealing anecdotes:

"And Bezel saideth unto Sham: 'Sham,' he saideth, 'Thou shalt goest unto the town of Begorrah, and there shalt thou fetcheth unto thine bosom 35 talents and also shalt thou fetcheth a like number of cubits, provideth that they are nice and fresh.' "

The problem is that many of us don't have the vaguest idea what these anecdotes reveal. This is why we have broadcast preachers, who can take a religious anecdote and explain it over the course of a half-hour in such a manner that if you listened all the way through you would have no questions at all:

BROADCAST PREACHER: And so we can see that it was BEZEL who told SHAM to go to Begorrah. It was not SHAM who told BEZEL: It was BEZEL who told SHAM. Now people ask me, they say, "Brother Ray Bob Tom, what do you mean, it was Bezel who told Sham?" And I say, "What I mean is that when we're talking about who told who to go to Begorrah, we must understand that it was BEZEL who told . . ."

And so on. It can take upwards of a week to get through an entire sentence, which is why you often have to send in a Love Offering to get cassettes so you'll remember what it is that God wants you to do. This sometimes seems too complicated, so a lot of people have switched over to the more relaxed style of the Merv Griffin–type of broadcast preachers, who have bands and potted plants and sofas and everything. ("Our next guest is not only one of the top Christians in the business, but also a close personal friend of mine.")

So we have a number of ways of finding out what God wants us to do, and each of us must decide what the answer is in this wonderful country where we are free to believe as we choose, and where there are strict laws against assaulting people just because we don't like something they wrote.

Man Bites Dog

Today we begin a popular feature wherein we will address the major ethical questions of the day, starting with: Is it OK to eat your dog?

ANSWER: No. Not here in America. Oh, sure, most of us have heard the story about an American who *cooked* her dog in a microwave oven, but this was not for the purpose of eating it. What happened (according to the story) was this American had one of those little rodent-size dogs whose main purpose in the Great Chain of Life is to pee on people's ankles, and it got wet in the rain, so the American quite naturally did what any normal person would do if he or she had one lone kernel of candy corn for a brain, namely stick the dog in the microwave oven to dry out, but apparently the oven was on the wrong setting (it should have been set on "Dog"), so the dog ended up getting dried out to the point of Well Done. The story always stops right there, so we don't know what happened next. We don't know whether the spouse came home from a hard day at the office and went, "Mmmmmmm! Something smells dee-ee*licious!* I'll just look inside the microwave here and *GAAAACCCCKKKK!!!!*"

Of course, this needless tragedy could easily have been prevented via legislation requiring that microwave ovens carry a stern federal message such as

WARNING: THE SURGEON GENERAL HAS DETERMINED THAT YOU SHOULD NOT PUT A DOG IN THIS OVEN AND TURN IT ON.

On the other hand, this could be one of those stories that everybody tells even though it's not true, like the one about the teen-aged couple who is parking on a lonely country road and hears on the radio that a homicidal maniac who has a hook instead of a right hand has escaped from the mental institution, so the boy real quick starts the engine and drives right over Reggie Jackson, who was walking his Doberman because it was choking on an alligator from the New York City sewer system. This probably never happened. But it is a fact that my editor, Gene Weingarten, once ate a dog. This was at the 1964 World's Fair in Flushing, New York (which incidentally is how alligators got into the sewers), and Gene was at the pavilion of some Third World nation and he ordered a dish with an unusual name, and when he asked the waiter (who spoke little English) what it was, the waiter, in Gene's words, "made it clear by gestures and going 'woof woof,' that it was a dog." Gene said it wasn't bad. *Not that this is any excuse.* I want to stress that I personally have never eaten a dog, and I want to remind those of you who have already stopped reading this column to write violent letters to the editor that it was Gene Weingarten, c/o *Tropic* magazine, *Miami Herald,* Miami FL 33101, who ate the dog.

But it is an interesting ethical question, why we get so upset about this. I mean, most of us don't think twice about eating *cows,* which are genetically almost exactly the same as dogs in the sense of having four legs and being pretty stupid. Yet if somebody tried to dry a *cow* out in a microwave oven, we'd all laugh like the dickens and it would get on "Celebrity Bleeps and Boners." So this is a real puzzle, all right, which is why I am very grateful to Diane Eicher, an alert reader who sent me an article from *Nutrition Health Review* headlined: "Usefulness Keeps Pets Out of Oven." I am not making this article up. It concerns Marvin Harris, a University of Florida anthropologist who, according to the article, "studies and tries to make sense of human culture." (Ha ha!)

Harris is quoted in the article as saying that the reason we didn't eat dogs, cats, and horses is—get ready—"These animals are just too darned useful for us to eat."

Now I don't wish to be critical here, but a statement like that makes you wonder if Professor Harris has not accidentally been studying the culture on the planet Zoog, because the last word I would use to describe household pets here on Earth is "useful." I have owned a number of household pets, mostly dogs, and the only useful thing I can recall any of them ever doing was the time Germaine tried to bite the Amway representative. Other than that it has been basically a long series of indelible rug stains. And I defy anybody to point to a single instance of, for example, a tropical fish doing anything useful, as in

ALERT FISH
RESCUES WOMAN
FROM TRASH COMPACTOR

Yet we don't eat the tropical fish, do we? No! Not unless we have a very good reason, such as we have been sitting in our doctors' waiting room for the better part of the day without food or water. Then we might snack on a couple of guppies, but that is as far as it would go.

And I don't even want to *talk* about cats.

Nevertheless Professor Harris feels pets have many useful functions:

"Modern day household pets can't match the entertainment value of lions attacking elephants or people in the Roman circus," he said, "but cats chasing imaginary mice, or dogs retrieving bouncing balls are at least as amusing as the late night movie."

I think we can all agree that pets are not as entertaining as watching lions attack humans, but I have to wonder how many of you couples out there in our listening audience have ever said to each other: "The heck with *Casablanca*, let's watch Beaner retrieve a bouncing ball." So we indeed have a very complex ethical issue here, but unfortunately we no longer really care.

"Adventure Dog"

I have this idea for a new television series. It would be a realistic action show, patterned after the true-life experiences of my dog, Earnest. The name of the show would be "Adventure Dog."

The theme song would go:

Adventure dog,
Adventure dooooooggg
Kinda big, kinda strong
Stupid as a log.

Each episode would be about an exciting true adventure that happened to Earnest. For example, here's the script for an episode entitled: "Adventure Dog Wakes Up and Goes Outside":

It is 6:17 A.M. Adventure Dog is sleeping in the hall. Suddenly she hears a sound. Her head snaps up. Somebody is up! Time to swing into action! Adventure Dog races down the hall and, skidding on all four paws, turns into the bathroom, where, to her total shock, she finds: The Master! Whom she has not seen since LAST NIGHT! YAYYYYYY!!

ADVENTURE DOG: Bark!

MASTER: DOWN, dammit!

Now Adventure Dog bounds to the front door, in case the Master is going to take her outside. It is a slim chance. He has only taken her outside for the past 2,637 consecutive mornings. But just in case, Adventure Dog is ready.

ADVENTURE DOG: Bark!

Can it be? Yes! This is unbelievable! The Master is coming to the door! Looks like Adventure Dog is going outside! YAAAYYY!

MASTER: DOWN, dammit!

Now the Master has opened the door approximately one inch. Adventure Dog realizes that, at this rate, it may take the Master a full three-tenths of a second to open the door all the way. This is bad. He needs help. Adventure Dog alertly puts her nose in the crack and applies 600,000 pounds of force to the door.

MASTER: HEY!

DOOR: WHAM!

And now Adventure Dog is through the door, looking left, looking right, her finely honed senses absorbing every detail of the environment, every nuance and subtlety, looking for . . . Holy Smoke! There it is! The YARD! Right in the exact same place it was yesterday! This is turning out to be an UNBELIEVABLE adventure!

ADVENTURE DOG: Bark!

Adventure Dog is vaguely troubled. Some primitive version of a thought is rattling around inside her tiny cranium, like a BB in a tuna fish can. For she senses that there is some reason why the Master has let her outside. There is something he wants Adventure Dog to do. But what on Earth could it be? Before Adventure Dog can think of an answer, she detects . . . is this possible? Yes! It's a SMELL! Yikes! Full Red Alert!

ADVENTURE DOG: Sniff sniff sniff.

MASTER: Come *on*, Earnest.

ADVENTURE DOG: Sniff sniff sniff sniff sniff sniff sniff sniff.

No question about it. The evidence is clear. This is a smell, all right. And what's more, it's the smell of—this is so incredible—DOG WEEWEE! Right here in the yard!

MASTER: EARNEST!

ADVENTURE DOG: Sniff sniff sniff sniff sniff.

Adventure Dog is getting the germ of an idea. At first it seems farfetched, but the more she thinks about it, the more she thinks, hey, why not! The idea is—get ready—Adventure Dog is going to MAKE WEEWEE! Right now! Outside! It's crazy, but it just might work!

MASTER: Good GIRL.

What was that? It was a sound! Definitely. A sound coming from over there. Yes! No question about it. This is unbelievable! It's the MASTER out here in the yard! YAAAYY!

MASTER: DOWN, dammit!

THEME SONG SINGER: Adventure Dog, Adventure Dooooooggg . . .

ADVENTURE DOG: BARK!

MASTER: DOWN!

Bear in mind that this is only one episode. There are many other possibilities: "Adventure Dog Gets Fed," "Adventure Dog Goes for a Ride in the Car and Sees Another Dog and Barks Real Loud for the Next 116 Miles," etc. It would be the kind of family-oriented show your kids could watch, because there would be extremely little sex, thanks to an earlier episode, "Adventure Dog Has an Operation."

Slow Down and Die

I think it's getting worse. I'm talking about this habit people have of driving on interstate highways in the left, or "passing" lane, despite the fact that they aren't passing anybody. You used to see this mainly in a few abnormal areas, particularly Miami, where it is customary for everyone to drive according to the laws of his or her own country of origin. But now you see it everywhere: drivers who are not passing, who have clearly never passed anybody in their entire lives, squatting in the left lane, little globules of fat clogging up the transportation arteries of our very nation. For some reason, a high percentage of them wear hats.

What I do, when I come up behind these people, is the same thing you do, namely pass them on the right and glare at them. Unfortunately, this tactic doesn't appear to be working. So I'm proposing that we go to the next logical step: nuclear weapons. Specifically I'm thinking of atomic land torpedoes, which would be mounted on the front bumpers of cars operated by drivers who have demonstrated that they have the maturity and judgment necessary to handle tactical nuclear weapons in a traffic environment. I would be one of these drivers.

Here's how I would handle a standard left-lane blockage problem: I would get behind the problem driver and flash my lights. If that failed, I'd honk my horn until the driver looked in his rear-view mirror and saw me making helpful, suggestive hand motions indicating that he is in the passing lane, and if he wants to drive at 55, he should do it in a more appropriate place, such as the waiting room of a dental office. If *that* failed, I'd sound the warning siren, which would go, and I quote, *"WHOOP WHOOP WHOOP WHOOP."* Only if *all* these measures failed would I proceed to the final step, total vaporization of the car (unless of course there was a BABY ON BOARD!).

Too violent, you say? Shut up or I'll break your legs. No, wait, forgive me. I'm a little tense, is all, from driving behind these people. But something has to be done, and I figure if word got around among members of the left-lane slow-driver community, wherever they get together—hat stores would be my guess—that they had a choice of either moving to the right or turning into clouds of charged particles, many would choose the former.

It is not entirely their fault. Part of the problem is all those signs on the interstates that say SPEED LIMIT 55. I am no psychologist, but I believe those signs may create the impression among poorly informed drivers that the speed limit is 55. Which of course it is not. We Americans *pretend* 55 is the speed limit, similar to the way we're always pretending we want people to have a nice day, but it clearly isn't the real speed limit, since nobody, including the police, actually drives that slowly, except people wearing hats in the left lane.

So the question is, how fast are you *really* allowed to drive? And the answer is: Nobody will tell you. I'm serious. The United States is the only major industrialized democracy where the speed limit is a secret. I called up a guy I know who happens to be a high-ranking police officer, and I asked him to tell me the real speed limit, and he did, but only after—this is the absolute truth—he made me promise I wouldn't reveal his name, or his state, or above all *the speed limit itself.* Do you believe that? Here in the United States of America, home of the recently refurbished Statue of Liberty, we have an officer of the law who is afraid he could *lose his job for revealing the speed limit.*

When things get this bizarre, we must be dealing with federal policy. Specifically we are dealing with the U.S. Transportation Secretary, who is in charge of enforcing our National Pretend Speed Limit. The Transportation Secretary has learned—you talk about digging out the hard facts!—that motorists in a number of states are driving faster than 55 miles per hour, and she threatened to cut off these states' federal highway funds. So, to keep the Transportation Secretary happy, the police have to pretend they're enforcing the 55 limit, when in fact they think it's stupid and won't give you a ticket unless you exceed the *real* speed limit, which varies from state to state, and even from day to day, and which the police don't dare talk about in public for fear of further upsetting the Transportation Secretary.

I told my friend, the high-ranking police officer, that this system creates a lot of anxiety in us civilian motorists, never knowing how fast we're allowed to go, and he said the police like it, because they can make the speed limit whatever the hell they want it to be, depending on how they feel. "It used to be," he said, "that the only fun you had in police work was police brutality. Now the real fun is to keep screwing with people's heads about what the speed limit is."

Ha ha! He was just kidding, I am sure. Nevertheless, I think we need a better system, and fortunately I have thought one up. Here it is: The state should say the hell with the federal highway funds. They could make a lot more money if they set up little roadside stands where you could stop your car and pay $5, and a state employee would whisper the speed limit for that day in your ear. What do you think? I think it makes more sense than the system we have now. Of course, the Transportation Secretary wouldn't like it, but I don't see why we should care, seeing as how the Transportation Secretary probably gets chauffeured around in an official federal limousine that is, of course, totally immune from traffic laws. Although I imagine it would be vulnerable to atomic land torpedoes.

Sacking the Season

It's football season again, and I know I speak for everybody in North America when I make the following statement: rah. Because, to me, football is more than just a game. It is a potential opportunity to see a live person lying on the ground with a bone sticking out of his leg, while the fans, to show their appreciation, perform "the wave."

And football breeds character. They are constantly scrubbing the locker rooms because of all the character that breeds in there. This results in men the caliber of famed Notre Dame player George Gipp, played by Ronald Reagan, who, in a famous anecdote, looked up from his deathbed and told Pat O'Brien, played by Knute Rockne, that if things ever really got bad for the Fighting Irish, he (O'Brien) should tell "the boys" to win one for the Gipper. Which O'Brien did, and the boys said: "What for? He's dead." Ha ha! This is just one reason I am so excited about the upcoming season.

Before I unveil my Pigskin Preview, however, I must say a few serious words here about a problem that, regrettably, has reached epidemic proportions in the world of sports fans. I'm talking about male cheerleaders. I don't know where you grew up, but where I grew up, there were certain things a guy absolutely did not do, and cheerleading is about six of them. A guy who led cheers where I grew up would have been driven around for a few hours inside somebody's engine compartment. Most likely Steve Stormack's.

So you may call me insecure if you wish, but I am deeply troubled when I see young men on TV bouncing up and down on their tiptoes and clapping like sea lions, and the fact that they get to hug the female cheerleaders and sometimes pick them up by their personal regions is not, in my view, an adequate excuse. I am calling on you sports fans to write letters to U.S. Attorney General Edwin Meese urging him to appoint a federal commission to issue a concerned and bulky report about this issue, so that we sports writers can put it behind us once and for all and get back to writing stories about what should be the topic of interest on the sports pages: drugs.

Drug testing is very big in football. This is because football players are Role Models for young people. All you young people out there want to grow up and have enormous necks and get knee operations as often as haircuts. That's why the people in charge of football don't want you to associate their sport in any way with drugs. They want you to associate it with alcohol. During televised games, you'll see announcements wherein famous athletes urge you not to take drugs alternating with announcements wherein famous exathletes urge you to drink beer. Good luck, young people!

Now let's take a look at what kind of action we can expect to see this season on the actual "gridiron" per se. As in previous years, football will be divided into two major sectors, "college" and "professional," the difference being that professional players receive money, whereas college players also receive complimentary automobiles, although many teams will be hard-hit by strict new academic regulations requiring that a player cannot compete unless he can read most of the numbers on his gearshift knob. Nevertheless, I look for an action-packed college season in which major teams featuring linemen named Dwight who have the size and vocabulary skills of cement trucks trash a series of amateur schools by scores ranging as high as 175-0, which will earn them the right to play in such New Year's Day classics as the Rose Bowl, the Orange Bowl, and the Liquid You Drain Out of a Can of Artichoke Hearts Bowl, although unfortunately not against each other.

In professional football, I look for a very exciting and competitive season until about a third of the way through the first game, when Injuries will become a Factor. These injuries will of course all be caused by artificial turf, which is easily the most dangerous substance in the universe. If we really wanted to protect Europe, we would simply cover the border regions with artificial turf, and the Russians would all be writhing on the ground clutching their knees within seconds after they invaded. And then the Europeans could perform "the wave."

Here are some other predictions: I look for the TV networks to provide helpful expert analysis by explayers who utilize technological wizardry such as the "electronic chalkboard" to make simple running plays seem like brain surgery. I look for 19,000 third-down situations, all of them Crucial. In any group of five players, I look for four of them to be Probably the Most Underrated in the League. I look for Second Effort, Good Hang Time, and a Quick Release. I look for yet another Classic Super Bowl Matchup like the one we had last year between two teams whose names escape me at the moment.

I look for a video rental store that's open all weekend.

Why Sports Is a Drag

Mankind's yearning to engage in sports is older than recorded history, dating back to the time, millions of years ago, when the first primitive man picked up a crude club and a round rock, tossed the rock into the air, and whomped the club into the sloping forehead of the first primitive umpire. What inner force drove this first athlete? Your guess is as good as mine. Better, probably, because you haven't had four beers. All I know is, whatever the reason, Mankind is still nuts about sports. As Howard Cosell, who may not be the most likable person in the world but is certainly one of the most obnoxious, put it: "In terms of Mankind and sports, blah blah blah blah the 1954 Brooklyn Dodgers."

Notice that Howard and I both use the term "Mankind." Womankind really isn't into sports in the same way. I realize things have changed since my high-school days, when sports were considered unfeminine and your average girls' gym class consisted of six girls in those gym outfits colored Digestive Enzyme Green running around waving field-hockey sticks and squealing, and 127 girls on the sidelines in civilian clothing, claiming it was That Time of the Month. I realize that today you have a number of top female athletes such as Martina Navratilova who can run like deer and bench-press Chevrolet pickup trucks. But to be brutally frank, women as a group have a long way to go before they reach the level of intensity and dedication to sports that enables men to be such incredible jerks about it.

If you don't believe me, go to your local racquetball club and observe the difference between the way men and women play. Where I play, the women tend to gather on the court in groups of random sizes —sometimes three, sometimes five, as if it were a Jane Fonda workout—and the way they play is, one of them will hit the ball at the wall and the rest of them will admire the shot and compliment her quite sincerely, and then they all sort of relax, as if they're thinking, well, thank goodness *that's* over with, and they always seem very surprised when the ball comes *back*. If one of them has the presence of mind to take another swing, and if she actually hits the ball, everybody is *very* complimentary. If she misses it, the others all tell her what a *good* try she made, really, then they all laugh and act very relieved because they know they have some time to talk before the ball comes bouncing off that darned *wall* again.

Meanwhile, over in the next court, you will have two males wearing various knee braces and wrist bands and special leatheroid racquetball gloves, hurling themselves into the walls like musk oxen on Dexedrine, and after every single point one or both of them will yell "S______!" in the self-reproving tone of voice you might use if you had just accidentally shot your grandmother. American men tend to take their sports seriously, much more seriously than they take family matters or Asia.

This is why it's usually a mistake for men and women to play on teams together. I sometimes play in a coed slow-pitch softball league, where the rules say you have to have two women on the field. The teams always have one of the women play catcher, because in slow-pitch softball the batters hit just about every pitch, so it wouldn't really hurt you much if you had a deceased person at catcher. Our team usually puts the other woman at second base, where the maximum possible number of males can get there on short notice to help out in case of emergency. As far as I can tell, our second basewoman is a pretty good baseball player, better than I am anyway, but there's no way to know for sure because if the ball gets anywhere near her, a male comes barging over from, say, right field, to deal with it. She's been on the team for three seasons now, but the males still don't trust her. They know that if she had to choose between catching a fly ball and saving an infant's life, deep in her soul, she would probably elect to save the infant's life, without even considering whether there were men on base.

This difference in attitude between men and women carries over to the area of talking about sports, especially sporting events that took place long ago. Take the 1960 World Series. If we were to look at it objectively, we would have to agree that the outcome of the 1960 World Series no longer matters. You could make a fairly strong case that it didn't really matter in 1960. Women know this, which is why you almost never hear them mention the 1960 World Series, whereas you take virtually any male over age 35 and even if he can't remember which of his children has diabetes, he can remember exactly how Pirates shortstop Bill Mazeroski hit the ninth-inning home run that beat the Yankees, and he will take every available opportunity to discuss it at length with other males.

See that? Out there in Readerland, you females just read right through that last sentence, nodding in agreement, but you males leaped from your chairs and shouted: "Mazeroski wasn't a SHORTSTOP! Mazeroski played SECOND BASE!" Every male in America has millions of perfectly good brain cells devoted to information like this. We can't help it. We have no perspective. I have a friend named Buzz, a successful businessman and the most rational person you ever want to meet, and the high point of his entire life is the time he got Stan Albeck, the coach of the New Jersey Nets, to look directly at him during a professional basketball game and make a very personal remark rhyming with "duck shoe." I should explain that Buzz and I have season tickets to the Philadelphia 76ers, so naturally we hate the Nets a great deal. It was a great honor when Albeck singled

Buzz out of the crowd for recognition. The rest of us males congratulated Buzz as if he'd won the Nobel Prize for Physics.

It's silly, really, this male lack of perspective, and it can lead to unnecessary tragedy, such as soccer-riot deaths and the University of Texas. What is even more tragic is that women are losing perspective, too. Even as you read these words, women are writing vicious letters to the editor, expressing great fury at me for suggesting they don't take their racquetball seriously. Soon they will be droning on about the importance of relief pitching.

Batting Clean-Up and Striking Out

The primary difference between men and women is that women can see extremely small quantities of dirt. Not when they're babies, of course. Babies of both sexes have a very low awareness of dirt, other than to think it tastes better than food.

But somewhere during the growth process, a hormonal secretion takes place in women that enables them to see dirt that men cannot see, dirt at the level of *molecules,* whereas men don't generally notice it until it forms clumps large enough to support agriculture. This can lead to tragedy, as it did in the ill-fated ancient city of Pompeii, where the residents all got killed when the local volcano erupted and covered them with a layer of ash 20 feet deep. Modern people often ask, "How come, when the ashes started falling, the Pompeii people didn't just *leave?*" The answer is that in Pompeii, it was the custom for the men to do the housework. They never even *noticed* the ash until it had for the most part covered the children. "Hey!" the men said (in Latin). "It's mighty quiet around here!" This is one major historical reason why, to this very day, men tend to do extremely little in the way of useful housework.

What often happens in my specific family unit is that my wife will say to me: "Could you clean Robert's bathroom? It's filthy." So I'll gather up the Standard Male Cleaning Implements, namely a spray bottle of Windex and a wad of paper towels, and I'll go into Robert's bathroom, and it *always looks perfectly fine.* I mean, when I hear the word "filthy" used to describe a bathroom, I think about this bar where I used to hang out called Joe's Sportsman's Lounge, where the men's room had bacteria you could enter in a rodeo.

Nevertheless, because I am a sensitive and caring kind of guy, I "clean" the bathroom, spraying Windex all over everything including the 600 action figures each sold separately that God forbid Robert should ever take a bath without, and then I wipe it back off with the paper towels, and I go back to whatever activity I had been engaged in, such as doing an important project on the Etch-a-Sketch, and a little while later my wife will say: "I hate to rush you, but could you do Robert's bathroom? It's really *filthy.*" She is in there looking at the very walls I *just Windexed,* and she is seeing *dirt! Everywhere!* And if I tell her I already *cleaned* the bathroom, she gives me this look that she has perfected, the same look she used on me the time I selected Robert's outfit for school and part of it turned out to be pajamas.

The opposite side of the dirt coin, of course, is sports. This is an area where men tend to feel very sensitive and women tend to be extremely callous. I have written about this before and I always get irate letters from women who say they are the heavyweight racquetball champion of some place like Iowa and are sensitive to sports to the point where they could crush my skull like a ripe grape, but I feel these women are the exception.

A more representative woman is my friend Maddy, who once invited some people, including my wife and me, over to her house for an evening of stimulating conversation and jovial companionship, which sounds fine except that this particular evening occurred *during a World Series game.* If you can imagine such a social gaffe.

We sat around the living room and Maddy tried to stimulate a conversation, but we males could not focus our attention on the various suggested topics because we could actually *feel* the World Series television and radio broadcast rays zinging through the air, penetrating right into our bodies, causing our dental fillings to vibrate, and all the while the women were behaving *as though nothing were wrong.* It was exactly like that story by Edgar Allan Poe where the murderer can hear the victim's heart beating louder and louder even though he (the murder victim) is dead, until finally he (the murderer) can't stand it anymore, and he just *has* to watch the World Series on television. That was how we felt.

Maddy's husband made the first move, coming up with an absolutely brilliant means of escape: *He used their baby.* He picked up Justine, their seven-months-old daughter, who was fussing a little, and announced: "What this child needs is to have her bottle and watch the World Series." And just like that he was off to the family room, moving very quickly for a big man holding a baby. A second male escaped by pretending to clear the dessert plates. Soon all four of us were in there, watching the Annual Fall Classic, while the women prattled away about human relationships or something. It turned out to be an extremely pivotal game.

Snots at Sea

Like most Americans, I was thrilled to death last February when our wealthy yachting snots won the coveted America's Cup back from Australia's wealthy yachting snots.

It was not an easy victory. Our boys spent years experimenting with different designs for their boat before they came up with the innovative idea of having a submerged nuclear submarine tow it. "That was the real breakthrough," explained Captain Dennis Conner. "We could hit nearly 50 miles per hour without even putting up our sails. Plus we had torpedoes." It was American ingenuity at its best, and I think that, as a nation, we should be inspired to take up sailing as a popular mania, similar to the way, in previous years, we have taken up Bruce Springsteen and being Republican.

I have done some sailing myself, and let me tell you: There's nothing quite like getting out on the open sea, where you can forget about the hassles and worries of life on land, and concentrate on the hassles and worries of life on the sea, such as death by squid. My son, Robert, has this book entitled *Giants of Land, Sea, and Air, Past and Present,* which I like to read to him at bedtime to insure that he won't fall asleep until just after dawn. Here's what this book says regarding squid: "The giant squid may reach a length of 55 feet, including its 35-foot tentacles."

My point is that while you should of course enjoy your sailing experience, you should take the routine marine precaution of being constantly aware that a creature the size of Yonkers, New York, could be oozing and sliming along just beneath the surface, watching you with humongous eyes. Another one of Robert's books, *The Big Book of Animal Records,* states that the eye of a giant squid can get to be—this is an Amazing True Nature Fact, coming up here—16 inches across. Think about that. Think about the size of the whole *eyeball.* Think of the pranks you could play if you got hold of an eyeball like that.

DELIVERY ROOM DOCTOR: Well, Mr. and Mrs. Foonster, here's your newborn child!
NEW PARENTS: AIIIIEEEEEEEEEEEEEEEE.

But this is not the time for lighthearted humor. This is a time to learn Safe Boating Practices, so that your sailing experience will not be ruined in the event of a squid attack. Here is the procedure recommended by boating safety experts:

1. Do not panic. Remember that the squid does not necessarily want to eat you. Oh, sure, it wants to eat *somebody,* but this does not have to be *you.*
2. Shout: "Here! Eat Ralph!"

Boating safety experts recommend that you always keep a supply of unpopular guests on hand to push overboard as emergency marine sacrifices. They do not, however, have to be named Ralph. You can just *claim* they are named Ralph, because you are dealing with a squid.

OK, that takes care of boating safety. Now let's talk about the kind of boat you should select. There are many different kinds, the main ones being yachts, swoops, tankers, frigates, drawls, skeeters, fuggits, kvetches, and pantaloons. These are all basically the same. The only important factor to bear in mind, when selecting a boat, is that it should be "seaworthy," meaning that if for some reason you accidentally drive it into another boat, or a reef, or a Howard Johnson's Motor Lodge, *you will not be held financially responsible.* This means the type of boat you want is what veteran mariners refer to as a "stolen" boat, or, if this is not practical, a "rented" boat.

I rented a boat once, in the Virgin Islands. My wife and I did this with another couple, and we agreed that I should be the captain, because I had the most sailing experience, in the form of sitting on various people's sailboats drinking beer and remarking upon the weather. Fortunately the boat we rented had a motor in it. You will definitely want this feature on your sailboat too, because if you put up the sails, the boat tips way over, and you could spill your beer. This was a constant problem for Magellan. I put the motor on whenever we wanted to actually get somewhere, or if we came within two miles of something we might run into, such as another boat or a Virgin Island. On those rare occasions when I did attempt to sail, I was hampered by the fact that the only nautical commands my crew understood were:

1. "Pull on that thing."
2. "No, the OTHER thing."
3. "No, the thing over THERE, dammit."
4. "Never mind."

Our navigational policy was always to steer the boat in the direction of restaurants and hotels that had real bathrooms. Our boat allegedly had a bathroom (or as we say aboard ship, a "bathroom"), but it was about the size of those styrofoam containers you get Egg McMuffins in, and it was mostly filled with the marine toilet, a complex and punitive device that at any moment you expected to see a tentacle come snaking out of. Which is why the No. 1 rule of the sea is: If you absolutely have to use the marine toilet, you want to send Ralph in there first.

Sic, Sic, Sic

I would have to say that the greatest single achievement of the American medical establishment is nasal spray. Oh, I realize it can be overdone. A friend of mine named Tatnall claims he knew a woman who was so addicted to nasal spray that she carried some down the aisle on her wedding day. Her hand would go darting under her veil, and a snort would resound through the church. Tatnall swears this is true. So I fully agree that nasal-spray abuse is a serious problem and we certainly need some kind of enormous federal program to combat it.

But aside from that, I feel that nasal spray is a wondrous medical achievement, because it is supposed to relieve nasal congestion, and by gadfrey, it relieves nasal congestion. What I'm saying is that it actually works, which is something you can say about very few other aspects of the medical establishment.

This is especially true when it comes to figuring out what is wrong with sick people. My experience has been that doctors will give you a clear-cut, understandable diagnosis only if you wander in with, say, an ice pick protruding from your skull. And even then, you have to pretend that you don't know what's wrong. If you say, "I have an ice pick in my skull," the doctor will become irritated, because he spent all those years in medical school and he's damned if he's going to accept opinions from an untrained layperson such as yourself. "It conceivably could be an ice pick," he'll say, in a tone of voice that suggests he's talking to a very stupid sheep, "but just in case I'm going to arrange for a test in which we remove a little snippet of your liver every week for eight weeks." So your best bet is to keep your mouth shut and let the doctor diagnose the ice pick, which he will call by its Latin name.

If you have a subtler problem, however, you

may never find out what's wrong. For example, a few months back, one side of my tongue swelled up. I tried everything—aspirin, beer, nasal spray—but my tongue was still swollen. So I went to a doctor. His receptionist began my treatment by having me sit in the waiting room where I read a therapeutic article in a 1981 issue of *National Geographic.* That took me maybe an hour, during which I learned a great deal about this ancient tribe of people who managed to build a gigantic and photogenic temple in a jungle several thousand years ago despite the fact that they were extremely primitive at the time.

Step Two in the therapy was when a nurse put me in a little examination room with a paper-covered table, which evidently was emitting some kind of invisible healing rays because they had me sit there alone with it for 43 minutes by my watch. It wasn't as boring as it sounds because there was a scale in there, so I could weigh myself for amusement.

To culminate the treatment, the actual doctor took a few moments out from his busy schedule of renewing his subscription to *National Geographic* and renting additional space for people to wait in and came right into the room with me and actually looked at my tongue. He was in the room with me for 2 minutes and 30 seconds by my watch, at the end of which he told me that my problem was two Latin words, which I later figured out meant swollen tongue. He said I should come back in a week. I considered suggesting that, seeing how I had already been there for almost two hours, maybe I should just spend the week in the examination room, but I was afraid this would anger him and he would send me to the hospital for tests. I didn't want to go to the hospital, because at the hospital as soon as they find out what your Blue Cross number is they pounce on you with needles the size of turkey basters. Those are the two most popular doctor options: to tell you to come back in a week, or to send you to the hospital for tests. Another option would be to say, "it sure beats the heck out of me why your tongue is swollen," but that could be a violation of the Hippocratic Oath.

What I finally did was talk to a woman I know who used to be a nurse but had to quit because she kept wanting to punch doctors in the mouth, and she suggested that I gargle with salt water. I did, and the swelling went right away. Although of course this could also have been because of the paper-covered table.

I really envy my dog. When she gets sick or broken, we take her to the veterinarian, and he fixes her right up. No Latin words, no big deal. It's a very satisfying experience, except of course for my dog, who routinely tries to launch herself out of the examining room through closed windows. I find myself thinking: why can't I get medical care like this? How much more complicated can people be than dogs? I'm kind of hoping my dog's tongue will swell up, because I'm dying to see how the veterinarian treats her. If he has her gargle with salt water, I'm going to start taking my problems to him.

The Light Side of Smoking

As you are aware, each year the U.S. Surgeon General emerges from relative obscurity into the limelight of public attention and if he sees his shadow, we have six more weeks of winter. No, all kidding aside, what he does is issue his annual report, where he tells you that smoking is bad for you. In fact, for a while, previous surgeons general got so lazy that they were turning in the same report, over and over, until finally one year Richard Nixon got ketchup stains on it.

Anyway, the result of all this reporting is that the general public at large has gotten very strict about smoking. Hardly a day goes by when you don't read a newspaper story like this:

"SAN FRANCISCO—The city commissioners here yesterday approved a tough new antismoking ordinance under which if you see a person light a cigarette in a public place, you can spit in this person's face."

I agree with this new strictness. And I'm not one of those holier-than-thou types who go around condemning smoking, drinking and senseless murder without ever having even tried them. I used to smoke cigarettes, plenty of them, sometimes two and three at a time when I had Creative Block and was hoping to accidentally set my office on fire so I could write a column about it.

And then one morning, four years ago, something happened that I will never forget. I woke up, and I looked at myself in the mirror, because I happened to wake up in the bathroom, and I said to myself: "Dave, you have a wonderful wife, you have a newborn son, you have a good job, you have friends who care about you, you have a lawnmower that starts on the second or third pull—you have everything a man could possibly want, and a whole lifetime ahead of you to enjoy it in. Why not smoke a cigarette right now?" And so I did. I didn't quit until two years later, at Hannah Gardner's annual extravaganza eggnog party, when I was overcome by a giant weepy guilt attack while under the influence of Hannah's annual eggnog, the recipe for which we should all hope to God never falls into the hands of the Russians.

Not that it was easy to quit. Not at all. A few months back, I read a newspaper article that said the government, after much research, had decided that nicotine is an addictive drug, even worse than heroin, and I just had to laugh the bitter kind of laugh that Clark Gable laughs in *Gone With the Wind* when he realizes that the South has been reduced to a lump of carbon. I mean, surely the government has better things to spend its money on. Surely the government could have used these research funds to buy a military toilet seat, and just asked us former smokers about nicotine vs. heroin addiction. We could have simply pointed out that, when a commercial airliner takes off, the *instant* the wheels leave the ground, the pilot, who you would think would be busy steering or something, tells the smokers that they may light up. He does not tell the heroin addicts that they may stick their needles into themselves, does he? No, he doesn't, because heroin addicts have enough self-control to survive a couple of heroin-free hours. But the pilot knows that if he doesn't let the cigarette smokers get some nicotine into themselves *immediately,* they will sneak off to smoke in the bathroom, possibly setting it on fire, or, if already occupied by other smokers, they will try to get out on the wing.

So we are talking about a powerful addiction here, and I frankly feel the government's efforts to combat it are pathetic. The big tactic so far has been warnings on cigarette packages. The government seems to feel that smokers—these are people who, if they run out of cigarettes late at night in a hotel and have no change for the machine, will smoke used cigarettes from the sand-filled ashtrays next to the elevators, cigarettes whose previous owners could easily have diseases such as we associate with public toilet seats—the government believes that these same smokers will *read* their cigarette packages, as if they needed *instructions* on how to operate a cigarette, and then they'll remark, with great surprise: "Look here! It says that cigarette smoking is *Hazardous to Your Health!!* How very *fortunate* that I read this package and obtained this consumer information! I shall throw these away right now!"

No, we need something stronger than warnings. We need cigarette loads. For those of you who were never obnoxious 12-year-old boys, I should explain that a "load" is an old reliable practical joke device, a small, chemically treated sliver of wood that you secretly insert into a cigarette, and when the cigarette burns down far enough, the load explodes, and everybody laughs like a fiend except, of course, the smoker, who is busy wondering if his or her heart is going to start beating again. I think Congress ought to require the cigarette manufacturers to put loads in, say, one out of every 250 cigarettes. This would be a real deterrent to smokers thinking about lighting up, especially after intimate moments:

MAN: Was it good for you? *(inhales)*

WOMAN: It was wonderful. *(inhales)* Was it good for you?

MAN: Yes. *(inhales)* I have an idea: Why don't we BLAM!!

What do you think? I think it would be very effective, and if it doesn't work, we could have the Air Force spray something toxic on North and South Carolina.

Ear Wax in the Fog

When you talk about the postderegulation airline industry, the three issues that inevitably arise are smoking, fog, and earwax. We'll take them individually.

Follow me closely here. You know those little earphones they give you on airplanes so you can listen to old Bill Cosby routines? OK, let's assume that 20 million people have flown on earphone flights in the past 15 years. Let's further assume that each person leaves one-sixteenth of an ounce of earwax on these phones (this is an average, of course; Nancy Reagan leaves much less). This means that in the last 15 years alone, the airlines have collected nearly 600 tons. Do you have any idea how large a blob that makes? Neither do I, so I called the folks at the Miami Public Library, who did a little research and informed me that it was the most disgusting question they had ever been asked.

My question is this: Why do the airlines—why does *any* nonmilitary organization—need a blob of earwax that large? My personal theory is that they're going to drop it on the radar apparatus at O'Hare Airport in Chicago, just so they can see the looks on the faces of passengers all over America when the ticket-counter agents say: "I'm afraid your flight has been canceled due to earwax on the radar at O'Hare." Any problem at O'Hare, even a minor plumbing malfunction, inevitably paralyzes air travel all over the free world. Nobody really knows why this is, but if you ask the ticket agent, he'll come up with something just to drive you away: "Your flight is supposed to use the plane from flight 407, which is due in from Houston, only it couldn't take off because the crew was supposed to arrive on flight 395 from O'Hare, but that plane never got to O'Hare because the captain, the handsome, brooding Mark Crandall, had seen Nikki and Paul leave the party together arm in arm and in a rage of jealousy, had decided to seduce Paul's former lover Brenda, unaware that she had just found out about Steven's fatal liver disease. So we're looking at a delay of at least two hours."

But the airlines won't use the earwax just yet. No, that's their trump card, and they won't play it until more people wise up about the fog. I figured it out several years ago. See, I live in an area that is never blanketed by fog. People often remark on this at parties. "Say what you will," they remark, "but this area is never blanketed by fog, ha ha!" Except when I am trying to get back home from a distant airport, at which time it is always pea soup. "I'm afraid our destination is completely fogged in, Mr. Barry," the ticket agent says, in the tone of voice you use when somebody else's destination is fogged in and you're going home in a half-hour to have a drink and watch Johnny Carson.

Here's how they do it: They have an agent permanently assigned to lurk in the bushes outside my home, and when he sees me walk out the door carrying a suitcase, he gets on the walkie-talkie. "Looks like he's going to try to make a round trip via airplane again!" he whispers. This alerts his superiors back at airline headquarters that they should stop drilling holes into the heads of small furry woolen creatures and arrange to have a dense fog blanket transferred down from Canada via weather satellite.

Ask yourself this question: If Charles Lindbergh, flying with no instruments other than a bologna sandwich, managed to cross the Atlantic and land safely on a runway completely covered with French people, why are today's airplanes, which are equipped with radar and computers and individualized liquor bottles, unable to cope with fog? Are they concerned about passenger safety? Then why not let the passengers decide? Why not get on the public-address system and say: "Attention passengers. Your destination is very foggy. We think you'll make it, but there's always a chance you'll crash on a remote mountaintop and be eaten by wolves. Your other option is to stay here in the airport for God knows how long, sitting in these plastic seats and eating $3.50 cheese sandwiches manufactured during the Truman administration. What do you say?" The gate agents would have to leap up on the counter to avoid being trampled by the hordes barging onto the plane.

Which leads us to the question of whether smoking should be allowed on airplanes. The Founding Fathers, who had bales of foresight, specified in the U.S. Constitution that people could smoke on airplanes, but they had to sit near the toilets. Now, however, there's a move afoot to ban smoking altogether on flights that last less than two hours. The cigarette industry is against this ban, their argument being that there is no Hard Evidence that cigarettes are anything short of wonderful, according to the highly skilled research scientists that the cigarette industry keeps in small darkened cages somewhere. Another strong antiban argument was raised by Congressman Charlie Rose of North Carolina, who warned the Civil Aeronautics Board recently that people would sneak into the washrooms to smoke and might start fires. "There's a significant problem if they were to go into washrooms for a smoke and forget where the used paper towels are stored," observed Congressman Rose, who evidently feels that many smokers have extremely small brains.

But I think he has a point. I think that if the CAB decides to ban smoking, it should require the airlines to install smoke detectors in the washrooms, so that if a person sets one off, it will activate an unusually powerful toilet mechanism that will flush the smoker right out of the plane. Of course, if I know the airlines, they'll rig it so he lands on the radar apparatus at O'Hare.

1987: Look Back in Horror

January

2—In College Bowl action, the University of Miami loses the national championship to Penn State when Vinny Testaverde, after selecting the "History" category, identifies World War II as "a kind of fish."

3—Oral Roberts tells his followers that unless they send him $4.5 million by the end of the month, God will turn him into a hypocritical money-grubbing slime bag.

5—In response to growing pressure from the United States, the government of Colombia vows to track down its major drug dealers and, if necessary, remove them from the Cabinet.

8—The Federal Aviation Administration announces that, in response to a routine questionnaire, 63 percent of the nation's air traffic controllers stated that their primary career goal was "to defeat the forces of the Planet Wambeeno."

10—In the ongoing war against the federal deficit, the Reagan administration submits the first-ever $1 trillion budget.

14—In New York City, officials of the Justice Department's Organized Crime Task Force announce that Anthony "Grain Embargo" DiPonderoso and Jimmy "Those Little Pins They Put in New Shirts" Zooroni have agreed to enter the Federal Nickname Exchange Program.

16—In his first press conference since 1952, President Reagan, asked by reporters to comment on persistent allegations that he is "out of touch," responds: "Thanks, but I just had breakfast."

18—The People's Republic of China announces that "Deng Xiaoping" means "Big Stud Artichoke."

21—The Audi Corporation is forced to recall 250,000 cars after repeated incidents wherein parked Audis, apparently acting on their own, used their mobile phones to purchase stocks on margin.

26—President Reagan tells Iran-contra scandal investigators that he "might have" approved the sale of arms to Iran.

28—In the Middle East, Syria has its name legally changed to "Jordan." A welcome calm settles over Beirut as the six remaining civilians are taken hostage.

30—In Washington, the Internal Revenue Service unveils the new, improved W-4 form, which is such a big hit that the experts who thought it up are immediately put to work on developing a policy for the Persian Gulf.

February

1—A new policy requiring random drug testing of all airline pilots runs into a snag when nearly half of the Delta pilots are unable to hit the specimen bottle.

2—Miami City Commissioner Rosario Kennedy, responding to a *Herald* report that taxpayers spent $111,549 to decorate her office says—we are not making this quotation up—"there's not one item that really stands out. It's not the Taj Mahal." Donations of clothing and canned goods pour in from concerned taxpayers.

3—In the ongoing war against the federal budget deficit, Congress gives itself a pay raise.

4—The United States yacht *Stars and Stripes* recaptures the coveted America's Cup when the Australian entry, *Kookaburra,* is sunk by a Chinese-made "Silkworm" missile. The U.S. Sixth Fleet steams toward the troubled region with orders "to form humongous targets." Liberace goes to the Big Candelabra in the Sky.

6—In a White House ceremony marking his 76th birthday, President Reagan attempts to blow out the hot line.

7—Famed *Washington Post* reporter Bob Woodward reveals that, in a secret hospital interview, dying entertainer Liberace revealed that Woodward's upcoming book, *Veil,* would be "a real page-turner."

8—True item: Senator Lloyd Bentsen, chairman of the Senate Finance Committee, sends out a letter telling lobbyists that for $10,000 each, they can attend monthly breakfasts with him.

9—Representative Arnold LaTreece announces that for $15,000 each, lobbyists can kiss him on the lips.

10—George Bush announces that he is available for $12.50.

11—President Reagan tells Iran-contra scandal investigators that he did not approve of the arms sale to Iran.

15—George Bush reduces his price to $3.99, including the souvenir beverage mug.

17—In Colombia, police arrest Carlos Lehder for jaywalking and discover, during a routine search, that his pockets contain 1,265,000 pounds of cocaine. Lehder claims to have "no idea" how it got there.

19—Mario Cuomo announces that he doesn't want to be president and immediately becomes the Democratic front-runner.

22—George Bush announces that *he* doesn't want to be president, either.

22—Andy Warhol goes to the Big Soup Can in the Sky.

23—Panic grips the nation as a terrorist group seizes 150,000 new, improved W-4 forms and threatens to send them to randomly selected Americans through the mail.

23—Famed *Washington Post* reporter Bob Woodward reveals that, in a secret hospital interview, dying artist Andy Warhol revealed that Woodward's forthcoming book, *Veil,* would be "available in bookstores everywhere."

24—President Reagan announces that he cannot remember whether he approved the sale of arms to Iran. In a quotation that we are not making up, the president tells White House reporters: "Everybody that can remember what they were doing on August 8, 1985, raise your hand."

25—White House reporters examine their diaries and discover, to their shock, that on August 8, 1985, they approved the sale of arms to Iran. They are immediately arrested.

March

2—The Miami Grand Prix is won by Mrs. Rose Gridhorn, 83, of Hackensack, New Jersey, driving a 1976 Chrysler New Yorker with the left blinker on.

3—Comedian Danny Kaye dies moments after granting an interview to Bob Woodward.

7—In the widening scandal on Wall Street; the heads of three major investment firms rob a liquor store.

9—In Tallahassee, state legislators agree on a plan to tax professionals who perform services. A few hours later, they decide it also should apply to lawyers.

11—Florida Governor "Bob" Martinez, who ran for office on a platform of *opposing* taxes, announces that he will *support* the new tax on services, until it is passed, then he will call for a referendum so voters can vote *against* the tax, although he will campaign *for* the tax, but then he will change his mind and announce that he is calling a special session of the Legislature to *repeal* the tax. Everybody naturally assumes that the governor is joking.

13—Noncandidate Mario Cuomo, carrying out his normal duties as governor of New York state, meets with the heads of state of England, France, Norway, Sweden, and Germany.

15—A barge loaded with garbage sets out into the Atlantic under the command of explorer/author Thor Heyerdahl, who is seeking to prove his theory that South America could have been discovered by ancient mariners sailing from Islip, Long Island, in crude garbage barges.

18—The Southern Methodist University football team is suspended from intercollegiate athletics when National Collegiate Athletic Association investigators, after taking urine samples, determine that the school's leading rusher, majoring in communications, is a horse.

21—The IRS releases an even newer, simpler W-4 form in response to complaints from a number of taxpayers, all of whom will be audited for the rest of their lives.

23—The Southern Methodist University horse is drafted by the Kansas City Chiefs.

24—A place called Chad defeats Libya in some kind of war. This really happened.

27—In what is hailed as a major arms race breakthrough, United States and Soviet arms negotiators in Geneva agree to wear matching outfits.

30—In an illegal industrial waste dump somewhere in Louisiana, lightning strikes two adjacent putrid pools of festering corrosive toxic slime, setting off a bizarre chain of chemical reactions that cause the pools first to bubble, then slowly, horrifyingly, to solidify and pulsate upward, gradually forming themselves into shapes that, in the ghastly light of the flickering electrical storm, appear almost human.

"Hi!" they shriek cheerfully into the swampland emptiness. "We're Jim and Tammy Faye!"

April

1—Speaking in unison, an estimated three dozen congressmen, all of them age 43, all of them blond, and all of them named Dick, announce that they are seeking the Democratic presidential nomination.

3—In the Persian Gulf, Iranians attack the Islip garbage barge, but are driven off by courageous flies.

6—Noncandidate Mario Cuomo, in the pursuit of his normal gubernatorial duties, reaches a tentative pact with Soviet arms negotiators.

12—At an art auction, Vincent Van Gogh's *Sunflowers* fetches the highest price ever paid for a painting, $39.8 million, paid by grateful Miami taxpayers wishing to hang it in the office of City Commissioner Rosario Kennedy.

13—True Anecdote: In National League baseball action, the Atlanta Braves' Dion James hits a ball that would have been caught easily, except that in midair it strikes and kills a dove.

14—In Colorado, Gary Hart declares his candidacy for the presidential nomination, making the announcement while standing in front of a dramatic backdrop of soaring mountains, towering pine trees and four *Miami Herald* reporters disguised as rhododendrons.

15—The lifeless body of Atlanta Braves player Dion James is found under an enormous mound of dove droppings.

16—President and Mrs. Reagan release their tax returns.

19—The IRS sends back the Reagans' tax returns, gently pointing out that you're supposed to fill them out.

22—Crack U.S. counterintelligence agents in Moscow begin to suspect that the new U.S. Embassy in Moscow, constructed by Soviet labor, might be bugged, when one of them sneezes in the ambassador's office and six chairs say, "Gesundheit."

23—The National Basketball Association grants Miami a franchise. The new team will be named The Enormous Bloodsucking Insects.

26—Jack Kemp announces that he is running for president, pledging that, if elected, he will deepen his voice.

30—Following a lengthy and dramatic trial, a confused New Jersey jury awards custody of a 3-year-old boy to a 6-week-old girl.

May

2—Late at night on a Washington street, four *Miami Herald* reporters on routine patrol notice that Gary Hart appears to be spending the weekend with an attractive woman who is not his wife. The reporters confront Hart, who explains that there is no woman, and he hardly knows her, and she is actually his uncle, and the voters don't care about candidates' private lives anyway. Satisfied, the reporters decide to write a story about Hart's monetary policy.

3—Like a raging unquenchable forest fire, the Gary Hart story sweeps across the nation, as voters are consumed by a burning need to know more about the candidate's monetary views.

4—The Hart story becomes so hot that issue-oriented Phil Donahue devotes a show to it, preempting the sex-change lesbian surrogate-mother nude-dancer ex-priests.

5—The presidential campaign of Gary Hart experiences another "close call" when a *Miami Herald* reporter receives a tip that Hart spent a night in Bimini aboard a boat named *Monkey Business* with an attractive woman who is not his wife. Fortunately, Hart is able to explain that he has never been on a boat and there is no such place as "Bimini" and the person who went there with the woman was actually a being from the Planet Buppo who is able to take the form of leading presidential candidates. Satisfied, the reporter writes a lengthy analysis of Hart's views on the NATO alliance.

6—An angry Gary Hart is forced to withdraw from the race after word leaks out that the *Washington Post* has obtained documented evidence that he once proposed tying the prime rate to the Index of Leading Economic Indicators.

7—Citing alleged "bisexual activity," officials of the Assemblies of God Church vote to have Jim Bakker defrocked. Then they hastily vote to have him frocked again.

16—Rita Hayworth dies moments after confiding to Bob Woodward that his forthcoming book, *Veil,* would be out "just in time for Christmas gift giving."

29—Nineteen-year-old Mathias Rust, a German, flying a single-engine Cessna airplane, manages to cross 400 miles of Soviet airspace to reach Red Square in Moscow, where he narrowly avoids colliding with a Delta Air Lines flight en route from Pittsburgh to Cleveland.

30—Caspar Weinberger orders 5,000 single-engine Cessna airplanes.

June

1—The public responds with massive displays of sympathy to reports that a number of totally unsuspecting Dade County politicians were cruelly tricked into believing that a private duplex where a man allegedly sold stolen suits was in fact a major department store. "It was a mistake that anyone could have made," said a police spokesman, "provided that he had the IQ of Cheez Whiz."

2—True Item: In the ongoing Iran-contra hearings the committee learns that a country named Brunei contributed $10 million to help the contras, except Fawn Hall or somebody typed a wrong number, so the money ended up in the Swiss bank account of a total stranger. This helps explain why, despite all the elaborate assistance efforts with secret codes and passwords and everything, the only actual aid ever received by the contras was a six-month trial subscription to *Guns and Ammo.*

5—Another True Item: In Venice for the European Economic Summit, President Reagan, unaware that his words are being broadcast over an open microphone, tells a joke wherein God gradually reduces a gondolier's intelligence until the gondolier switches from singing *"O Sole Mio"* to *"When Irish Eyes are Smiling."*

7—Brunei receives 314,334 urgent personal mail solicitations from TV evangelists

8—In the most dramatic Iran-contra testimony to date, Fawn Hall, played by Farrah Fawcett, testifies that, as Justice Department investigators closed in, she and Oliver North stayed late in their White House basement office and "colorized" a number of classic black-and-white films.

13—After a highly controversial trial in New York, "subway vigilante" Bernhard Goetz is acquitted in connection with a subway shooting incident wherein he claims he was attacked by a gang of prominent Wall Street investors.

18—A survey of Florida residents reveals that their No. 1 concern about the state is that "not enough people are walking around with guns." Alarmed, the state Legislature passes a law under which all citizens who are not actually on Death Row will be *required* to carry revolvers.

22—Fred Astaire dies in the arms of Bob Woodward.

24—In a ground-breaking experiment, medical researchers reduce a gondolier's intelligence to the bare minimum required to sustain life, and the gondolier says: "Everybody that can remember what they were doing on August 8, 1985, raise your hand."

29—In Wimbledon action, John McEnroe kills a line judge and is given a stern warning.

July

1—In a contest sponsored by a pesticides company, a Broward County insect is declared the largest cockroach in the country, narrowly edging out Phyllis Schlafly.

4—The Hormel Company marks the 50th anniversary of Spam in festivities featuring a full-size, fully functioning suspension bridge constructed entirely out of the popular luncheon substance.

7—The central figure in the Iran-contra hearings, Lieutenant Colonel Oliver North, becomes an instant national folk hero when, with his eyes glistening and his voice cracking with emotion, he courageously admits, before a worldwide television audience, that he is very patriotic.

9—Oral Roberts reveals that he can raise the dead. He is rushed to the White House.

11—The Iran-contra hearings reach their dramatic peak when Lieutenant Colonel North, his eyes glistening and his voice cracking with emotion, makes a sweeping patriotic hand gesture and knocks over his bottle of Revlon Eye Glistener.

15—The giant Citicorp bank announces that it has agreed to forgive Mexico's $56.3 billion debt in exchange for 357.9 gazillion chickens.

18—In Hollywood, plans are formulated for a major motion picture based on the Oliver North story, starring Sylvester Stallone as North, Fawn Hall as herself and Helen Keller as the president.

21—The discovery of "superconductors"—materials that offer no resistance to electricity even at relatively high temperatures—creates a worldwide stir of excitement among the kind of dweebs who always had their Science Fair projects done early.

24—In the ongoing Iran-contra hearings, the committee hears two days of dramatic testimony from Mario Cuomo, who explains that he has decided to stay out of the presidential race so he can fulfill his obligations as governor of New York.

27—Officials at the National Zoo in Washington are saddened by the death of the tiny infant cub of rare giant pandas Ling-Ling and Hsing-Hsing, who are described as "distraught" by their close friend, Bob Woodward. Edwin Meese is linked to the Lincoln assassination.

30—In Moscow, the Embassy spy scandal deepens when it is learned that for the past six years, the "wife" of the U.S. ambassador has in fact been four male KGB agents wearing what State Department officials describe as "a very clever disguise."

August

2—South Florida's dreams of a first-class sports facility come true at last with the opening of Joe Robbie Stadium, featuring comfortable seating, excellent visibility, plenty of bathrooms, and nearly five parking spaces.

3—Political activist Donna Rice, in her continuing effort to avoid publicity, sells her story to ABC television.

6—As "Ollie-mania" continues to sweep the country, one of the most popular video-arcade games in the country is a new one called—this is true—"Contra." The way it works is, there are two soldiers on the screen, and when you put in a quarter, it never gets to them.

10—The U.S. space probe Meanderer II, after a journey of six years and many millions of miles, passes within 400 miles of the surface of Neptune, sending back dramatic color photographs of a Delta Air Lines jet.

16—On the 10th anniversary of Elvis Presley's death, tens of thousands of fans gather in Memphis to hear Bob Woodward discuss his final moments with the bulging superstar. At the same time, thousands of other people gifted with "New Age" consciousness celebrate the Harmonic Convergence by picking at their straitjacket straps with their teeth.

20—In Miami, alert Metrorail police arrest a woman for permitting her child to eat a Vienna sausage. Bystanders applaud this courageous law-enforcement action by firing their revolvers into the air.

22—Rumors circulate that Gary Hart will re-enter the presidential race. Johnny Carson places his writers on Full Red Alert.

25—In what is hailed as a landmark ruling, the Supreme Court decides, by a 7 to 2 vote, that you cannot count three oranges as one item in the express checkout lane "unless they are all in the same package."

27—Georgia Senator Sam Nunn announces that he doesn't want to be president. Cuomo challenges him to a debate.

28—In the Persian Gulf, tensions mount as a U.S. gunboat engages in a scuffle with actor Sean Penn.

September

1—The FAA, responding to consumer complaints, issues tough new rules under which airlines are required to notify passengers "within a reasonable period of time" if their plane has crashed.

2—In Washington, reporters notice that at some point—possibly during a speech by Senator Inouye, when everybody was asleep—the ongoing Iran-contra hearings turned into the ongoing confirmation hearings for Supreme Court nominee Robert Bork.

7—As the arrival of Pope John Paul II approaches, the South Florida news media begin mass-producing special helpful news supplements advising the public on how to avoid the massive crowds and traffic and heat.

8—Researcher Shere Hite releases her scientific new book, *Men Are Scum.* The South Florida news media continue to generate massive quantities of helpful hurricane-style news alerts concerning the upcoming papal visit and what the public should do to avoid massive crowds and traffic and heat and crime.

9—In Washington, D.C., ground is broken for the $25.4 million Presidential Polyp Museum. South

Florida experiences an epidemic of hernias suffered by residents attempting to pick up newspapers filled with helpful papal supplements informing them how to cope with massive crowds and traffic and heat and crime and disease and death.

10—It is a glorious moment for South Florida as Pope John Paul II is greeted by an estimated crowd of 3,000 soldiers garbed in festive camouflage outfits, frowning warily at 1,500 news media personnel crouching on the ground to confirm that the manhole covers are, in fact, welded shut.

12—In the ongoing hearings, Senator Joseph Biden pledges to consider the Bork nomination "with total objectivity," adding, "You have that on my honor not only as a senator, but also as the Prince of Wales."

17—The market-savvy McDonald's Corporation, capitalizing on the popularity of the movie *Fatal Attraction,* introduces a new menu item, Boiled McRabbits.

21—Professional football players go on strike, demanding the right to "have normal necks." Negotiations begin under the guidance of mediator Mario Cuomo.

28—Tensions ease in the Persian Gulf as a Delta Air Lines flight, en route from Boston to Newark, successfully lands on the U.S. carrier *Avocado.*

October

1—Senator Joseph Biden is forced to withdraw from the Democratic presidential race when it is learned that he is in fact an elderly Norwegian woman. On the Republican side, the spectacularly Reverend Pat Robertson announces his candidacy for president, buoyed by strong popularity among humor columnists.

8—Three hundred prominent law professors sign a petition stating that Supreme Court nominee Robert Bork has a "weenie beard."

12—Hurricane Floyd, packing a wind estimated at 14 miles per hour, lashes South Florida, wreaking more than $67.50 worth of havoc. Governor "Bob" Martinez, after touring the devastated area via golf cart, pledges that he will request federal disaster relief, then campaign against it.

15—In an effort to establish that she is not a bimbo, Jessica Hahn appears nude in *Playboy* magazine. We are pretty sure we must have made this item up.

19—In Norman, Okla., a renegade automatic bank teller known to its followers only as "The Leader" sends a message out on a special data-transmission line to New York. Within seconds, Wall Street is gripped by the worst computer riot in history.

20—The Wall Street computers continue to rage out of control, threatening that if any attempt is made to subdue them, they will start electrocuting investment bankers. Tragically, it turns out that they are only bluffing.

22—As the stock market is brought under control, major brokerage firms run expensive prime-time TV commercials reassuring the public that this is a good time to get back into the market, prompting the public to wonder how come these firms didn't spend a few bucks last week to warn everybody to get the hell *out.*

23—The Senate rejects Bork. President Reagan, informed of this by his aides, angrily responds: "Who?"

25—The Senate Transportation committee recommends the federal speed limit be raised on highways going through boring or ugly areas, so drivers can get through them quicker. "In Indiana, for instance," the committee says, "it should be 135 miles per hour."

29—The Minnesota Twins win the World Series. President Reagan, as is the custom, calls up manager Tom Kelly and nominates him to the Supreme Court.

November

1—In the ongoing heroic effort to trim the federal budget deficit, House and Senate conferees agree not to order appetizers.

7—Totally true item: The *Herald* refuses to publish an episode of the comic strip "Bloom County" because it contains the quotation, "Reagan sucks." To explain this decision, the *Herald* runs a story containing the quotation, "Reagan sucks." Several days later, in response to a letter from an irate "Bloom County" fan, the *Herald* prints an explanatory note containing the quotation, "Reagan sucks."

8—Canadian Prime Minister Brian Mulroney, large chunks of his scalp falling off, angrily demands the United States do something about "acid rain."

10—Don Johnson announces he is leaving Miami, dealing a severe blow to the area's hopes to repeat as winner of the Biggest Cockroach Contest.

12—In continuing media coverage of the "character issue," presidential candidates named Bruce "Dick" Babbitt and Albert "Dick" Gore, Jr., state that they have tried marijuana, but no longer use it. "Now we just drink gin till we throw up," they state.

13—George Bush reveals that he tried to smoke marijuana, but nobody would give him any.

15—In their continuing heroic deficit-reduction efforts, House and Senate conferees agree to continue working right through their 2:30 racquetball appointment.

17—In Geneva the final obstacle to a superpower summit is removed as U.S. negotiators agree not to notice the mark on Soviet leader Mikhail Gorbachev's forehead.

22—In ceremonies marking his retirement as secretary of defense, Caspar Weinberger is presented with a pen-and-pencil set, manufactured by the General Dynamics Corporation for $352.4 million.

24—The city of Cleveland, Ohio, announces that it has developed tactical nuclear weapons, and does not wish to hear any more jokes.

29—The world financial community's faith in the U.S. economy is restored as heroic House and Senate conferees hammer out a breakthrough compromise deficit-reduction measure under which $417.65 will be slashed from the $13.2 million pastry budget of the Federal Bureau of Putting Up Road Signs with Kilometers on Them.

30—In a presummit public relations gambit designed to show that he is a normal human, Mikhail Gorbachev is interviewed by Tom Brokaw, who, clearly nervous, addresses the Soviet leader as "Premier Forehead Mark."

December

1—For the first time, all 257 presidential candidates appear in a televised debate, which is beamed via satellite to a nationwide TV audience consisting of Mrs. Brendaline Warblette of Elkhart, Indiana, who tells the press that, after viewing the debate, she leans toward "What's his name, Cuomo."

2—In a widely hailed legal decision, the judge

in the bitter divorce dispute between Joan Collins and Peter Holm orders them both shot. Mikhail Gorbachev appears on *Jeopardy*.

5—In a cost-cutting move, financially troubled Eastern Airlines announces that its domestic flights will operate without engines. "Most of them never take off anyway," explains a spokesman.

8—In Washington, the long-awaited U.S.-Soviet summit meeting gets off to an uncertain start as President Reagan attempts to nominate Soviet leader Mikhail Gorbachev to the Supreme Court.

9—The summit concludes on a triumphant note as, in the culmination of 10 years of negotiations between the superpowers, Gorbachev and New York Governor Mario Cuomo sign a historic agreement under which both sides will move all of their mid- and short-range long-term strategic tactical nuclear weapons 150 feet to the left.

12—Michael Jackson, angered over persistent media reports that he has had extensive plastic surgery, strikes a *People* magazine reporter with one of his antenna stalks.

15—Under intense pressure from the United States to reduce the trade deficit, Japanese auto manufacturers agree to give their cars really ugly names.

18—*Playboy* magazine offers Tammy Faye Bakker a record $1.5 million if she will promise never, ever to pose nude.

23—*Motor Trend* magazine names, as its Car of the Year, the new Nissan Rat Vomit.

27—Oscar C. Klaxton, an employee of the U.S. Department for Making Everybody Nervous, wins a $10,000 prize for dreaming up the concept of a deadly "hole" in an invisible "ozone layer."

28—Cleveland declares war on "Chad."

31—The year ends on a tragic note as an Iowa farmer backs up his tractor without looking and accidentally kills an estimated 14 blond 43-year-old Democratic presidential contenders named Dick. Knowledgeable observers suggest, however, that this will have little impact on anything.

Air Bags for Wind Bags

Every now and then I like to suggest sure-fire concepts by which you readers can make millions of dollars without doing any honest work. Before I tell you about the newest concept, I'd like to apologize to those of you who were stupid enough to attempt the previous one, which, as you may recall, involved opening up Electronic Device Destruction Centers.

The idea there was that consumers would bring their broken electronic devices, such as televisions and VCRs, in to the destruction centers, where trained personnel would whack them (the devices) with sledgehammers. With their devices thus permanently destroyed, consumers would then be free to go out and buy new devices, rather than have to fritter away years of their lives trying to have the old ones repaired at so-called factory service centers, which in fact consist of two men named Lester poking at the insides of broken electronic devices with cheap cigars and going, "Lookit all them *wires* in there!"

I thought the Electronic Device Destruction Center was a sure-fire concept, but apparently I was wrong, to judge from the unusually large amount of explosives I received in the mail from those of you who lost your life savings and, in some cases, key organs. This made me feel so bad that I have been sitting here for well over five minutes wracking my brains, trying to think of an even *more* sure-fire money-making concept for you.

One promising concept that I came up with right away was that you could manufacture personal air bags, then get a law passed requiring they be installed on congressmen to keep them from taking trips. Let's say your congressman was trying to travel to Paris to do a fact-finding study on how the French government handles diseases transmitted by sherbet. Just when he got to the plane, his mandatory air bag, strapped around his waist, would inflate—FWWAAAAAAPPPP—thus rendering him too large to fit through the plane door. It could also be rigged to inflate whenever the congressman proposed a law. ("Mr. Speaker, people ask me, why should October be designated as Cuticle Inspection Month? And I answer that FWWAAAAAAAPPPP." This would save millions of dollars, so I have no doubt that the public would violently support a law requiring air bags on congressmen. The problem is that your potential market is very small: There are only around 500 members of Congress, and some of them are already too large to fit on normal aircraft.

But fortunately for you, I have come up with an even *better* money-making concept: The "Mister Mediocre" fast-food restaurant franchise. I have studied American eating preferences for years, and believe me, this is what people want. They don't want to go into an unfamiliar restaurant, because they don't know whether the food will be very bad, or very good, or what. They want to go into a restaurant that advertises on national television, where they *know* the food will be mediocre. This is the heart of the Mister Mediocre concept.

The basic menu item, in fact the *only* menu item, would be a food unit called the "patty," consisting of—this would be guaranteed in writing—"100 percent animal matter of some kind." All patties would be heated up and then cooled back down in electronic devices immediately before serving. The Breakfast Patty would be a patty on a bun with lettuce, tomato, onion, egg, pretend-bacon bits, Cheez Whiz, a Special Sauce made by pouring ketchup out of a bottle, and a little slip of paper stating: "Inspected by Number 12." The Lunch or Dinner Patty would be any Breakfast Patties that didn't get sold in the morning. The Seafood Lover's Patty would be any patties that were starting to emit a serious aroma. Patties that were too rank even to be Seafood Lover's Patties would be compressed into wads and sold as "Nuggets."

Mister Mediocre restaurants would have a "salad bar" offering lettuce, tomato, onion, egg, pretend-bacon bits, Cheez Whiz and a Special House Dressing made by pouring ketchup out of a bottle, tended by an employee chosen on the basis of listlessness, whose job would be to make sure that all of these ingredients had been slopped over into each other's compartments.

Mister Mediocre restaurants would offer a special "Children's Fun Pak" consisting of a patty containing an indelible felt-tipped marker that youngsters could use to write on their skin.

Also, there would be a big sign on the door that said:

DEPARTMENT OF HEALTH REGULATIONS!
ALL EMPLOYEES MUST WASH HANDS
BEFORE LEAVING THIS RESTAURANT!

If you're a Smart Investor who would like to get a hold of a Mister Mediocre restaurant franchise before the federal authorities get wind of this, all you need to do is send me a fairly large amount of money. In return, I'll send you a complete Startup Package consisting of an unsigned letter giving you permission to use the Mister Mediocre concept. You will also of course be entitled to free legal advice at any time. Like, for example, if you have a situation where your Drive-thru customers are taking one bite from their patties and then having seizures that cause them to drive over pedestrians in a fatal manner, you just call me up. "Hey," I'll advise you, for free. "Sounds like you need a lawyer!"

Iowa's Safe But You'll Be Sorry

Here are some helpful summer vacation Travel Tips, designed to help you make sure that your "dream vacation" will be just as fun and smooth and fatality-free as it can possibly be.

This is an especially good time for you vacationers who plan to fly, because the Reagan administration, as part of the same policy under which it sold Yellowstone National Park to Wayne Newton, has "deregulated" the airline industry. What this means for you, the consumer, is that the airlines are no longer required to follow any rules whatsoever. They can show snuff movies. They can charge for oxygen. They can hire pilots right out of Vending Machine Refill Person School. They can conserve fuel by ejecting husky passengers over water. They can ram competing planes in midair. These innovations have resulted in tremendous cost savings, which have been passed along to you, the consumer, in the form of flights with amazingly low fares, such as $29. Of course certain restrictions do apply, the main one being that all these flights take you to Newark, New Jersey, and you must pay thousands of dollars if you want to fly back *out.*

And now, for those of you who are planning to take your vacations abroad this summer, we have these words of reassurance from the travel industry, which by the way will be wanting all the tour money up front this year: Relax! There is no need to be worried about the fact that most foreign countries are crawling with violent anti-American terrorists with no regard for human life! Experts do advise, however, that you take the simple common-sense precaution of renouncing your U.S. citizenship and wearing a turban. Also, while in public places abroad, you want to make a point of making loud remarks such as: "Say! I speak English surprisingly well, considering I am not a U.S. citizen!" and "Unlike a U.S. citizen, I'm wearing a turban!"

Most Americans, however, plan to "play it safe" this year and vacation near the exact geographical center of the United States, as far as possible from the Libyan navy. Come July, we could have millions of people clotted together in Iowa, looking for public toilets. So I thought it might be a good idea to find out what Iowa has in store for us, attractionwise. I called up their tourism bureau and spoke to a nice woman named Skip Strittmatter, who told me that they have a whole list of 25 Top Tourist Attractions in Iowa, including Des Moines, the Mississippi River, ethnic festivals ("We're one of the top states in ethnic festivals," says Skip Strittmatter), and late in July a big bicycle ride across Iowa on a bicycle. "It's quite famous," says Skip Strittmatter, who also notes that you can bet on dog races in both Council Bluffs and Dubuque.

Another major reason to be attracted to Iowa is the annual Riceville Mosquito Shootout. This is still the truth. Riceville is a small town on the Wapsipinicon (Indian for "white potato") River, the result being that the town has mosquitoes, a fact which it has turned into a Tourist Attraction by having an annual event wherein they distribute roughly 400 cans of Raid, generously donated by the manufacturer, Johnson Wax, to the townspeople. Then, at a prearranged time, they sound the tornado siren and everybody rushes outside and blows the hell out of the local mosquito population, which doesn't return for sometimes up to a week and a half, depending on rain. The Shootout is preceded by a picnic where they give away mosquito-related prizes, including one year a working telephone shaped like an insect, generously donated by Johnson Wax. The dial was on the bottom.

I got all this information straight from the man who conceived the whole Mosquito Shootout concept, M. E. Messersmith, editor and publisher of the Riceville Recorder. He tells me that more and more non-Riceville people are showing up at the Shootout every year, and I think you should definitely make it the cornerstone of your vacation plans, if they decide to have it again, which they probably will, only they haven't set a definite date. I asked Messersmith if there were any other attractions in the Riceville area that people might want to visit after they experience the Shootout, and he quickly reeled off a lengthy list including beautiful farmland, a lake with fish in it, farms, a nine-hole golf course, crops of different kinds, a bowling alley, and agriculture. Plus, Messersmith noted, Riceville is "just 40 minutes away from the world-famous Mayo Clinic," which I suppose would be mighty handy if your touring party got trapped for any length of time in a giant cloud of Raid.

I don't mean to suggest, by the way, that Iowa is the only safe and fun place to go this summer. I'm certain Kansas has also cooked up plenty of attractions. My recommendation is: Take an extra day, and see both. And let's not forget some of the other fine natural attractions we have here in the U.S.A., such as Theme Land, Theme World, ThemePark World, ThemeLand Park, ThemeLandWorld Park, and Six Flags over AdventureParkLandTheme World. All of these fine attractions offer Fun for the Whole Family, such as food, rides, food, and Comical Whimsy in the form of college students wearing costumes with enormous heads. These would make ideal disguises for terrorists.

Europe on Five Vowels a Day

Americans who travel abroad for the first time are often shocked to discover that, despite all the progress that has been made in the past 30 years, many foreign people still speak in foreign languages. Oh, sure, they speak *some* English, but usually just barely well enough to receive a high-school diploma here in the United States. This can lead to problems for you, the international traveler, when you need to convey important information to them, such as "Which foreign country is this?" and "You call this toilet paper?"

To their credit, some countries have made a sincere effort to adopt English as their native language, a good example being England, but even there you have problems. My wife and I were driving around England once, and we came to a section called "Wales," which is this linguistically deformed area that apparently is too poor to afford vowels. All the road signs look like this:

LLWLNCWNRLLWNWRLLN—3 km

It is a tragic sight indeed to see Welsh parents attempting to sing traditional songs such as "Old MacDonald Had a Farm" to their children and lapsing into heart-rending silence when they get to the part about "E-I-E-I-O." If any of you in our reading audience have extra vowels that you no longer need, because for example your children have grown up, I urge you to send them (your children) to: Vowels for Wales, c/o Lord Chesterfield, Parliament Luckystrike, the Duke of Earl, Pondwater-on-Gabardine, England.

But the point I am trying to make here is that since the rest of the world appears to be taking its sweet time about becoming fluent in English, it looks like, in the interest of improving world peace and understanding, it's up to us Americans to strike the bull on the horns while the iron is hot and learn to speak a foreign language.

This is not an area where we are strong, as a nation: A recent poll showed that 82 percent of the Americans surveyed speak no foreign language at all. Unfortunately, the same poll showed that 41 percent also cannot speak English, 53 percent cannot name the state they live in, and 62 percent believe that the Declaration of Independence is "a kind of fish." So we can see that we have a tough educational row to hoe here, in the sense that Americans, not to put too fine a point on it, have the IQs of bait. I mean, let's face it, this is obviously why the Japanese are capable of building sophisticated videocassette recorders, whereas we view it as a major achievement if we can hook them up correctly to our TV sets. This is nothing to be ashamed of, Americans! Say it out loud! "We're pretty stupid!" See? Doesn't that feel good? Let's stop blaming the educational system for the fact that our children score lower on standardized tests than any other vertebrate life form on the planet! Let's stop all this anguished whiny self-critical *fretting* over the recently discovered fact that the guiding hand on the tiller of the ship of state belongs to Mister Magoo! Remember: *We still have nuclear weapons.* Ha ha!

Getting back to the central point, we should all learn to speak a foreign language. Fortunately, this is easy.

HOW TO SPEAK A FOREIGN LANGUAGE:

The key is to understand that foreigners communicate by means of "idiomatic expressions," the main ones being:

GERMAN: "Ach du lieber!" ("Darn it!")
SPANISH: "Caramba!" ("Darn it!")
FRENCH: "Zut alors!" ("Look! A lors!")

Also you should bear in mind that foreign persons for some reason believe that everyday household objects and vegetables are "masculine" or "feminine." For example, French persons believe that potatoes are feminine, even though they (potatoes) do not have sexual organs, that I have noticed. Dogs, on the other hand, are masculine, even if they are not. (This does not mean, by the way, that a dog can have sex with a potato, although it will probably try.)

PRONUNCIATION HINT: In most foreign languages, the letter "r" is pronounced incorrectly. Also, if you are speaking German, at certain points during each sentence you should give the impression you're about to expel a major gob.

OK? Practice these techniques in front of a mirror until you're comfortable with them, then go to a country that is frequented by foreigners and see if you can't increase their international understanding, the way Jimmy Carter did during his 1977 presidential visit to Poland, when he told a large welcoming crowd, through an official State Department translator, that he was "pleased to be grasping your secret parts."

When You Grotto Go

The travel rule I wish to stress here is: *Never trust anything you read in a travel article.* Travel articles appear in publications that sell large expensive advertisements to tourism-related industries, and these industries do not wish to see articles with headlines like:

URUGUAY: DON'T BOTHER

So no matter what kind of leech-infested, plumbing-free destination travel writers are writing about, they always stress the positive. If a travel article describes the native denizens of a particular country as "reserved," this means that when you ask them for directions, they spit on your rental car. Another word you want to especially watch out for is "enchanting." A few years back, my wife and I visited The Blue Grotto, a Famous Tourist Attraction on the island of Capri off the coast of Italy that is *always* described in travel articles as "enchanting," and I am not exaggerating when I say that this is one Travel Adventure that will forever remain a large stone lodged in the kidney of my memory.

We never asked to see The Blue Grotto. We had entered Italy in the firm grip of one tour, which handed us over to another in such a way that there was never any clear chance to escape, and the next thing we knew, they were loading us into this smallish boat and telling us we were going to see The Blue Grotto. They told us it was Very Beautiful. "But what *is* it?" we said. "It is Very Beautiful," they said.

So our boat got into this *long* line of boats, each containing roughly 25 captured tourists sitting in the hot sun, bobbing up and down and up and down and up and down and up and down, and soon we were all thinking how truly wonderful it would be to go sit in a nice, quiet, shady sidewalk cafe somewhere and throw up. We were out there in the sun for *two hours,* during which time—I cannot emphasize this point too strongly—we continued to bob up as well as down. We agreed that this had damn well better be one *tremendous* grotto they were taking us to.

When we got close to it, all we could see was this *hole* in the rock at the bottom of a cliff, and it became clear that they intended to put us into even *smaller* boats, boats that would bob violently on dry land, and take us *into this hole.* So at this point an elderly woman on our tour told the tour leader that maybe she and her husband better not go along, as her husband, a very nice man named Frank, was a stroke victim who had some trouble getting around, but the tour leader said, in a word, no. He said the way the system was set up, *you had to see The Blue Grotto.* He said there was *no other way out.* He said it was *Very Beautiful.*

At this point I am going to interject a seemingly irrelevant fact, which you will see the significance of later on: Also on the boat with us were three recently divorced women from California who had been drinking wine.

So finally our boat was next to the hole, and they had us climb down, four at a time, into the tiny boats, which were rowed by surly men with low centers of gravity who smelled like the Budweiser Clydesdales. The rowers were in a great impatient hurry to load us into the boats, such that if my wife and I had not been right there to grab Frank, the stroke victim, by his shirt, he would have been—this is not an exaggeration—pitched right directly into what travel writers traditionally refer to as the Sparkling Blue Mediterranean Waters. So we scrambled in after him, and so did his wife, and we all went bobbing off, away from the main boat, toward The Hole.

I have since read, in travel articles, that because of the way the sunlight bounces off the bottom, or something, The Blue Grotto is a Natural Wonder Transfused with a Blue Light of Almost Unearthly Beauty. It looked to us more like a dank cave transfused with gloom and rower-perspiration fumes and the sound of the official Blue Grotto Rower's Spiel bouncing off the walls. The spiel has been handed down through the generations of rowers from father to son, neither of whom spoke English. The part I remember is: "You pudda you handa inna da wadda, you handa looka blue." We didn't want to put our hands in the water, but we were about to do it anyway, just so we could get out. This was when our boat got hit by the wave that ensued when one of the recently divorced California women decided that it might be fun, after being out in that hot sun, to leap out of her boat and go swimming in the famous Blue Grotto.

Well. You cannot imagine the stir of excitement *this* caused. This was clearly a situation that had not been covered in Blue Grotto Rowers Training School. Some of the rowers attempted to render assistance to the woman's boat, which was sort of tipping over; some of them were trying to get the woman out of the water, which she was against ("Stop it!" she said. "You're hitting me with your goddam *oar.*"); and some of them continued to announce, in case anybody was listening, that if you pudda you handa inna the wadda, you handa looka blue. I think I speak for all the passengers on my boat when I say I felt exactly the way Dorothy did when she realized that all she had ever really wanted was to go back to Kansas.

We finally got out of there, back into the sunlight. Frank's skin was the color of Aqua-Velva. His wife was saying, "Are you OK, Frank?" and Frank, who could not talk, was clutching the side of the boat with his good hand and giving her what he probably hoped was a reassuring smile, but which came out looking the way a person looks when he pulls a hostile Indian arrow out of his own shoulder. You could just tell that, no matter what his doctor gave him permission to do, he was never, ever again, for the rest of his life, going to travel more than 15 feet from his Barca-Lounger. The rower wouldn't let us out of the boat—he literally blocked our path with his squat and surly body—until we gave him a tip.

Someday, this rower is going to come to the United States, and I will be waiting for him. I am going to take him to Disney World, which any travel writer will tell you is a Fantasy Come True, and I am going to put him on the ride where you get into a little boat and nine jillion dolls shriek at you repeatedly that *It's a Small World after All,* and when he is right in the middle of it I am going to hurl *Fodor's Guide to Florida* into the machinery so he will be stuck there forever. Wouldn't that be *enchanting?*

Ground Control to Major Tomb

I have good news and bad news on the death front. The good news is that within a very short time, sooner than you dared hope, you can have your ashes leave the immediate solar system. The bad news is that it may soon be impossible to purchase your casket needs wholesale in Wendell, Idaho.

We'll start with the good news. I don't know about you, but I was starting to wonder if the space program was ever going to produce any practical benefits. Oh, I realize it produced Tang, the instant breakfast drink, but my feeling about Tang is that I would consider consuming it only if I were stuck in space and had already eaten everything else in the capsule, including my fellow astronauts.

So I was very pleased when the Reagan administration gave the OK to an outfit called the Celistis Group, which plans to send up a special reflective capsule filled with the ashes of deceased persons, each packed into a little container about the size of a tube of lipstick. Your container would have your name on it, and of course your Social Security number. God forbid you should be in a burial orbit without your Social Security number, in case there should be some kind of tax problems down the road and the IRS needs to send an unintelligible and threatening letter to your container.

What I like about this plan is, it's a chance for the common person, a person who does not happen to be a United States senator or a military personnel with a nickname such as "Crip," "Buzz," or "Deke," to get into the space environment. And the negative aspect, which is to say the aspect of being in a lipstick tube, is I believe more than outweighed by the fact that, according to the Celistis Group people, if you take the Earth orbit package, you'll be up there for *63 million years.* Plus, your capsule, as I pointed out earlier, will have a highly reflective surface, which means your Loved Ones will be able to watch you pass overhead. "Look," they'll say. "See that little pinpoint of light? That's the capsule containing Uncle Ted! Either that or it's an early Russian satellite, containing a frozen experimental dog!"

And that's just for the Earth Orbit Package. If you can wait a couple more years, and pony up $4,600, you can get the Escape Velocity Package, which will take you right out of the Solar System, such that your remains, as Celistis Group Vice President James Kuhl explained it to me, "will be sailing forever through deep space, etc."

My only concern here is this: Let's just say this particular capsule, a couple of billion light years from Earth, gets picked up by those alien beings Carl Sagan is always trying to get in touch with. And let's say they open it up, and they see all these tubes resembling lipstick, which is a concept they would be familiar with from intercepting transmissions of "Dynasty," and they naturally assume we are sending them, as a friendly gesture, a large supply of cosmetics. I don't know about you, but where I come from, we like to think of our dear departed ones as being with their maker at last and resting in eternal peace. We are not comfortable with the concept of their being smeared upon the humongous lips of Jabba the Hutt.

But other than that, I think the whole idea is terrific, and I urge all of you who feel that you or a loved one may at some future date be dead, to look into it. Please note that you should not contact the Celistis Group directly, because, as Mr. Kuhl explained it to me, "We enter the picture after the cremation has taken effect."

This means you have to deal with your local funeral director, which you will find a very interesting experience, because funeral directors, at least the ones I've dealt with, generally manage to make you feel like a Nazi war criminal if you don't purchase one of the better caskets. Never mind that they're just going to set fire to it; somehow, you'll get the message that, OK, sure, they can use a plain old el cheapo $900 pine box, if you're comfortable with the idea of having your loved one's ashes spend 63 million years mixed in with the ashes from a common, sap-filled softwood of the same type used to make Popsicle sticks, whereas all the other loved ones in the entire reflective capsule will be mixed with, at the very least, walnut. If that's what you want, fine.

So I think those of us who are not bog scum will want to purchase a higher-quality casket. This is why it's such a shame about the situation out in Wendell, Idaho. That's where Roger King, who's a woodworker, has got himself into this big hassle with the funeral directors because he's trying to sell caskets directly to the consumer. He has a showroom, right in Wendell, where he has some caskets on display, in addition to furniture, and he claims he charges a third to half as much per casket as a funeral director. "We've got a pine for $489," he said, "and a solid walnut for $1,500."

So naturally the Idaho funeral directors association fired off a letter to the state, claiming that King was selling caskets without a license. This of course would be a violation of the law designed to protect the public from buying caskets from unlicensed people, which as you can imagine would lead to who knows what kind of consumer tragedies. I don't even want to think about it. And I'm not making this up.

So then King sued the funeral directors, claiming they were discouraging people from buying his caskets. When I talked to him, he had sold only two in about six months, and he sounded kind of desperate. He had even started running radio casket advertisements, which is something you might look forward to if your travel plans call for you to be in the

Wendell area. But to be brutally frank, I doubt that Roger's going to make it in the direct-to-the-consumer casket business. This means you're going to have to continue purchasing your caskets retail, from your local funeral director. Be sure to ask him about the space burial plan. My guess is he'll somehow manage to suggest that, if you really *cared* for the deceased person, you'll want the Escape Velocity Package.

Where Saxophones Come From

TODAY'S SCIENCE TOPIC IS: THE UNIVERSE

The universe has fascinated mankind for many, many years, dating back to the very earliest episodes of "Star Trek" when the brave crew of the starship Enterprise set out, wearing pajamas, to explore the boundless voids of space, which turned out to be as densely populated as Queens, New York. Virtually every planet they found was inhabited, usually by evil beings with cheap costumes and Russian accents, so finally the brave crew of the Enterprise returned to Earth to gain weight and make movies.

To really understand the mysteries of the universe, you should look at it first-hand. The best time to do this is at night, when the universe is clearly visible from lawns. As you gaze at it, many age-old questions will probably run through your mind, the main one being: Are you wearing shoes? The reason I ask is, recently I was standing barefoot on my lawn, and I got attacked on the right big toe by a fire ant. This is an extremely ungracious style of insect that was accidentally imported into the southern United States from somewhere else, probably hell. I once saw a TV documentary wherein a group of fire ants ate a *cow*. When a fire ant attacks your toe, he is actually *hoping* you'll fight back, so the other fire ants can jump you, after which the documentary makers will beat you senseless with their camera tripods. They all work together.

But we are getting off the track. When we gaze upward at the boundless star-studded reaches of space, we should be thinking about more than ants in our lawn: We should also be thinking about snakes.

FEDERAL PORNOGRAPHY WARNING: The Attorney General Has Determined That the Following Paragraph Contains Explicit Sexual Words, Which Could Cause Insanity and Death.

I used to think snakes were bad, until I got this document from an alert reader named Rob Streit, who is a member of the Chicago Herpetological Society ("herpetologist" is Greek for "alert reader"). This document is a sales brochure from an outfit in Taiwan that I am not making up called "Kaneda Snake Poisonous Snake House" (Cable address: "SNAKE"). Do not be misled by the name. The folks at the Kaneda Snake Poisonous Snake House do not think that you would be so stupid as to purchase a poisonous snake. They think you might be so stupid as to purchase *snake penis pills.*

To quote the brochure: "Made of 5 species of the penises, livers, and galls of the snakes processed by modern scientific ways. The pills possess the efficacy to strengthen the kidney in order to increase the ability of reproductive function and keep the energy as well as the physical healthy, is a kind of good nutriment."

Sold me! My only question would be: "What?" I mean, until I got this document, I was unaware that snakes *had* penises. Where do they *keep* them? In special little cases? Then how do they *carry* them? These are some of the mysteries that make it so fascinating to think about today's Science Topic, which is: The Universe. (Really! Go back and check!)

The big mystery, of course, is: Where did the universe come from? Although this question baffled mankind for thousands of years, we now know, thanks to reading science books to our son, that the universe was actually formed 4.5 billion years ago this coming Saturday when an infinitesimally small object, smaller than an atom, smaller even than the "individual" butter servings they give you in restaurants, suddenly exploded, perhaps because of faulty wiring, in a cataclysmic event that caused the parts of the universe to go shooting out in all directions and expand at an incredibly rapid rate, an expansion that continues to this day, especially in the case of Raymond Burr. According to this hypothesis, after a couple of million years, various weensy particles began clumping together to form stars, planets, saxophones, etc., which is why we refer to this as the "Big Band" theory.

The Big Band theory is now widely accepted in the scientific community, although it still has a few technical bugs in it, such as that anybody who took it seriously would have to have the IQ of soup. There is no way you could fit everything in the universe into a little dot. I base this statement on my garage, which contains approximately one-half of the things in the universe, because my wife refuses to throw them out, scrunched together at the absolute maximum possible density, so that if you try to yank any one thing out, all the other things, attracted by gravity, fall on your head. From this we can calculate that the universe was roughly twice the size of my garage when it (the universe) exploded.

We certainly hope this has cleared up any lingering questions you may have had regarding the universe. We are looking forward to bringing you equally thoughtful discussions of other interesting Science Topics. We are also looking forward to receiving our order from the Kaneda Snake Poisonous Snake House.

The Secrets of Life Itself

I propose that we pass a federal law stating that the government will no longer pay for any scientific research if taxpayers cannot clearly see the results with their naked eyes. I don't know about you, but I'm getting tired of reading newspaper articles like this:

"LOS ANGELES —A team of physicists at UCLA announced yesterday that they have made a major scientific breakthrough with the discovery of an important new subatomic particle. This was the team's eighth major particle this month, giving them a three-particle lead over MIT.

" 'These particles are very difficult to detect, even with the aid of enormous federal grants,' said Head Physicist Dr. Ernest Viewfinder. 'But we definitely saw an important new one. At least I saw it, and Dr. Hubbleman here thinks he did, too.' Dr. Viewfinder said he could not show this particle to newsmen because it was 'resting.' "

I'm starting to wonder whether the physicists are pulling some kind of elaborate scam here. I'm starting to wonder if they don't sit around their $23 million atomic accelerators all day, drinking frozen daiquiris, and shrieking "There goes one now!" and then laughing themselves sick. Maybe it's time we laypersons asked some hard questions about this idea that all matter consists of tiny invisible particles whizzing around. I'm willing to believe that uranium does, because physicists have demonstrated that they can use it to vaporize cities. But I'd like to see them do this with some kind of matter that the layperson is more familiar with, such as cheese. I have examined cheese very closely, and as far as I can tell it consists of cheese. I have obtained similar results with celery.

Then you have your biologists, always getting into *Newsweek* by claiming they've isolated an important new virus. By way of "proof," they show you this blurred photograph that looks like, yes, it could be an important new virus, but it also could be an extreme closeup of Peru or Anthony Quinn. The biologists always promise that just as soon as they get a few million more dollars they're going to give us a cure for the common cold, but we veteran laypersons tend to hang on to our nasal spray, because we know that all they're really going to give us is more photographs of Anthony Quinn.

Another invisible thing biologists love to talk about is DNA, which is of course the Key to Unlocking the Secret of Life Itself. Biologists have learned that the public, particularly the journalist public, will take anything they do seriously, as long as they claim it has something to do with DNA. Not long ago biologists managed to get two rats on national TV news by claiming they had the same DNA molecules inside them, or something like that. Of course you didn't see any DNA molecules; you saw these *rats,* being broadcast to the nation as if they were the Joint Chiefs of Staff.

I have here in front of me a recent front-page newspaper story about a biologist who claims that he isolated the genes of an animal called a "quagga," which used to live in South Africa before it became extinct. The story says the biologist got the genes from the skin of a stuffed quagga in St. Louis, and that there are 25,000 different gene fragments, each of which is being reproduced in a separate culture of bacteria. So what we have here is a biologist telling reporters, with a straight face, that he has 25,000 dishes containing pieces of genes that they cannot see, which belong to an animal that they never heard of, which exists only in stuffed form in St. Louis. And instead of spitting into the dishes and striding disdainfully from the room, the reporters take notes and actually put the story in the newspaper.

And don't get me started on astronomers, with their $57 million atomic laser telescopes, and their breakthrough photographs of "new galaxies" that look remarkably like important viruses, and their "black holes," which are of course invisible to the layperson because they suck up all the light around them. Of course. In fact this very phenomenon probably contributed to the extinction of the quagga.

I say it's time the government stopped giving money to the particle-and-virus crowd, and started giving it to scientists who will do experiments that the public can understand and appreciate. Mister Wizard comes to mind. Think of what he could do with several million federal dollars:

"NEW YORK —Mister Wizard announced that he has successfully demonstrated the existence of gravity by dropping a mobile home onto Long Island from a height of 60,000 feet. 'To my knowledge,' Mister Wizard told reporters, 'this is the first time this has been done, and we intend to look at slow-motion videotapes over and over in hopes of furthering our understanding of what happens when gravity causes a mobile home to strike Long Island at a high rate of speed.' He added that 'in the very near future' he will attempt to determine 'what happens when you pump 300 gallons of grape juice into a cow.' "

Heat? No Sweat

The best way I know of to deal with heat is to wait until the middle of a major jungle-style heat wave, when if you lie still for more than 20 minutes patches of fungus form on your skin, when birds are bursting into flames in midair and nuns are cursing openly on the street, then go down to Sears and try to buy an air conditioner. Or, if you already have an air conditioner, you can try to get somebody to fix it.

But as of the last heat wave, we didn't have one, and after about the fourth or fifth day my wife was getting that look where, later on, the neighbors tell the homicide detective: "We knew she was feeling emotional strain, but we had no idea she owned a scythe." So I went down to Sears and joined the crowd of people thrusting credit cards at the appliance salesperson, who was of course being extra surly and slow. Who could blame him? Throughout spring, he had stood alone in Major Appliances, an outcast, wearing a suit whose fabric originated outside the immediate solar system, drumming his fingers on a washer until he had drummed little finger holes right through the lid, and we had all strode right past him. And now we were clustered around him like Titanic passengers hoping to obtain lifeboat seating.

CUSTOMER: Please please PLEASE can I buy an air conditioner?

SALESPERSON: That depends. Will you be wanting the service warranty?

CUSTOMER: Yes of course.

SALESPERSON: Just one?

CUSTOMER: No, no, of course not. Several service warranties. Eight service warranties.

SALESPERSON: Well, I don't know . . .
CUSTOMER: And these two dishwashers.

Wise consumer that I am, I bought the air conditioner with the maximum number of "BTUs," an electronic measurement of how heavy an air conditioner is. To get it into the house, my wife and I used the standard husband-and-wife team lifting system whereby the wife hovers and frets and asks "Can I help?" and the husband, sensing from deep within his manhood that if he lets a woman help him, all the males he feared in tenth grade gym class, the ones who shaved because they actually had to, will suddenly barge into the house and snap him with towels, says "No, I'm fine," when in fact he also senses deep within his manhood that he is on the verge of experiencing a horrible medical development that would require him to wear a lifetime helpful groin device.

To install my air conditioner, all I had to do was get a hammer and whack out a large permanent metal part of our window that was not shown in the official Sears instruction diagram, then plug it in, using of course a plug adaptor, which you need to void any potential warranty. This particular air conditioner is one of those new "energy-efficient" models, which means that rather than draw electricity from the power company, which would cost money, it operates by sucking power out of all the other appliances in the house. You can actually see them get smaller and writhe in pain, when it kicks in. More than once we have been awakened in the dead of night by the pitiful shrieks of the toaster, which has been with us for many years and does not understand what is happening.

Sometimes my wife expresses concern about "overloading the circuit," a term I suspect she read in one of her magazines. In the past decade or so, the women's magazines have taken to running home-handyperson articles suggesting that women can learn to fix things just as well as men. These articles are apparently based on the ludicrous assumption that *men* know how to fix things, when in fact all they know how to do is *look* at things in a certain squinty-eyed manner, which they learned in Wood Shop; eventually, when enough things in the home are broken, they take a job requiring them to transfer to another home. So I looked at our air conditioner, which appeared, in what feeble brownish light the lamp was able to give off, to be getting larger and chuckling softly, and I gave my wife a reassuring home-handyman speech featuring the term "ampere," which I believe is a BTU that has broken loose from the air conditioner and lodged in the wiring.

If you cannot install air conditioning, I suggest you perspire. Perspiring is Mother Nature's own natural cooling system. When you're in a situation involving great warmth or stress, such as summer or an audience with the queen, your sweat glands, located in your armpits, rouse themselves and start pumping out perspiration, which makes your garments smell like a dead rodent, which is Mother Nature's way of telling you she wants you to take them off and get naked. Of course the average person cannot always get naked, let alone the queen, so many people put antiperspirant chemicals on their armpits; this forces Mother Nature to reroute the perspiration to the mouth, where it forms bad breath, which is Mother Nature's way of telling you she is basically a vicious irresponsible slut.

One final note: Do not be tempted to beat the heat by drinking alcoholic beverages. A far better route is to inject them straight into your veins. No, ha ha, seriously, the experts tell us that alcohol actually makes us *warmer!* Of course, these are the same experts who tell us, during cold weather, that alcohol actually makes us *colder,* so we have to ask ourselves exactly how stupid these experts think we are. My common-sense advice to you is: If you must drink alcoholic beverages, fine, but for your own sake as well as the sake of others, take sensible precautions to insure you don't spill them on your clothing, which is already disgusting enough.

Blowing the Big Game

A recent consumer near-tragedy has demonstrated once again, as if we needed any more demonstrations, why the federal government must act immediately to prohibit the sale and possession of plaid carpeting. I feel especially strong about this issue, because the near-tragedy in question involved an eight-year-old girl named Natalie who happens to be the daughter of two friends of mine, Debbie and Bill. They have agreed to let me tell their story in exchange for a promise that I would not reveal that their last name is Ordine (pronounced "Ore-dean").

Our story begins a few months ago, when Bill bought Natalie two birthday presents, one of which was a gumball machine. Natalie of course immediately got a major wad of gum stuck in her hair and chose to correct the problem personally, without any discussion with a parent or guardian, by getting some scissors and whacking off a large segment of the right side of her hair, but that is not the near-tragedy in question. I mention it only so you'll grasp that when it comes to buying birthday presents for an eight-year-old, Bill has no more sense than a cinder block. This is why, as the other present, he bought Natalie a popular children's dexterity game called Operation, in which you attempt to put little humorous simulated organs into a humorous simulated person without setting off a buzzer.

Ordinarily, there would be nothing wrong with this, but it happens that Bill and Debbie have a carpet with large plaid squares on it. So as most of you have no doubt already guessed, on the afternoon of her class Christmas play, Natalie invented a game whereby she would put the little plastic heart of the Operation game into her nose to see how many squares of carpeting she could blow it across. Which is fine, provided it is done in the context of an organized league with uniforms, coaches, etc., but Natalie was doing this all on her own, and the result is that she got the heart stuck up her nose. You hate to have this kind of thing happen, because it's not the kind of problem that will just go away by itself, like, say, a broken leg. No, if you want to deal with a heart stuck up your nose, you pretty much have to expose yourself to an assault by Modern Medicine.

So Debbie called the Emergency Room, which has of course heard of every conceivable thing being stuck in every conceivable orifice and consequently told Debbie that this was nothing to worry about, plus they were busy with some real emergencies, so Natalie should go ahead and be in her class play and come in later that evening. So Natalie performed with the heart in her nose—she was one of the Rough Kids Who Wouldn't Go to Sleep on Christmas Eve—and then went to the hospital, where the doctor tried to get the heart out with forceps, but of course couldn't reach it. So he decided to keep Natalie overnight and operate the next day, which he did, and of course he couldn't find the heart.

"What do you mean, you can't find the (bad swear word) heart?" is the parental concern Bill recalls voicing to the doctor before he (Bill) stomped off in search of a small helpless furry animal to kick in the ribs. Meanwhile, the doctor ordered a CAT scan, which is the medical procedure that evidently requires the destruction of rare porcelain figurines because it costs $810, and which of course showed no trace of the heart. So the doctor concluded that the heart must have gotten into Natalie's digestive system, and everything would be fine and nobody should worry about it.

The bill for this medical treatment was of course $3,200. Bill and Debbie, when they are not whimpering softly like the radiation victims in *The Day After,* admit they find the whole episode somewhat ironic, seeing as how it began with a game that has a medical theme. But as Bill points out, the difference is that "in real life, the doctor gets the bucks no matter what happens. In the game, you actually have to do it right."

I should point out that the heart was, in fact, in Natalie's digestive system. We know this because Debbie conducted a Stool Search, which I will not discuss in detail here except to say that if anybody should have been paid $3,200, it is Debbie. Also, here's a useful tip from Debbie for those of you consumers who for some reason might wish to conduct your own stool searches at home: *Make use of your freezer.*

Natalie, the victim, is fine now, and will never ever ever ever put a heart of any kind in her nose again for at least several months. Bill says she took the heart to school in a Ziplock bag so she could tell her classmates the whole story. "She really spread the word about the dangers of putting pieces of games in your nose," said Bill. "She became real evangelistic, sort of like a reformed alcoholic, or Chuck Colson."

None of this would have happened, of course, if Bill and Debbie, who are not bad parents, really, did not have plaid carpeting. And who knows how many other unsuspecting parents have exactly the same consumer menace lurking in their family rooms? How do we know that some child is not at this very moment inserting a pretend organ into his or her nose to see how far he or she can shoot it? This child might bear in mind that the current record, held by eight-year-old Natalie Ordine, who got her name in the newspaper and everything, is only two big squares, which should be easy to beat.

The Swamp Man Cometh

Summer is almost here, boys and girls, and do you know what that means? It means it's time to go to . . . SUMMER CAMP! Neat-o, right boys and girls?! Let's hear it for summer camp!! Hip-Hip . . ."

(Long silent pause)

Listen up, boys and girls. When Uncle Dave says "Hip-Hip," you say "Hooray!" in loud cheerful voices, OK? Because summer camp is going to be A LOT OF FUN, and if you don't SHOW SOME ENTHUSIASM, Uncle Dave might just decide to take you on a NATURE HIKE where we IDENTIFY EVERY SINGLE TREE IN THE FOREST.

I happen to know a lot about summer camp, because, back when I was 18, I was a counselor at a camp named "Camp Sharparoon." There is some kind of rule that says summer camps have to have comical-sounding Indian names and hold big "powwows" where everybody wears feathers and goes whoooooo. Actual Indians, on the other hand, give *their* summer camps names like "Camp Stirling Hotchkiss IV" and hold dinner dances.

Camp Sharparoon was a camp for youths from inner-city New York who were popularly known at the time as "disadvantaged," which meant they knew a LOT more about sex than I did. I was in charge of a group of 12- and 13-year-old boys, and when they'd get to talking about sex, I, the counselor, the Voice of Maturity, the Father Figure for these Troubled Children, would listen intently, occasionally contributing helpful words of guidance such as: "Really?" And: "Gosh!" There were times I would have given my right arm to be a disadvantaged youth.

Talking about sex was one of our major activities when we went camping out overnight in the woods. We counselors mostly hated camping out, but we felt obligated to do it because these kids had come from the dirty, filthy streets of the urban environment, and it seemed that they should have the opportunity to experience the untamed forest wilderness. Of course, the untamed forest wilderness contained infinitely more dirt and filth than the urban environment, not to mention a great deal of nature in the form of insects. This is why we built the urban environment in the first place.

Nevertheless, we'd set off into the woods, carrying our bedrolls, which we took along so the campers would have a safe place to go to the bathroom. Bed-wetting was a problem on camping trips, becuase the campers would never go out to the latrine at night. They were concerned that they might be attacked by the Swamp Man, who, according to the traditional fun campfire story we wise mature helpful counselors always told at bedtime to put the camper in the proper emotional state for sleep, was this man with slime in his hair and roots growing out of his nose who would grab you and suck your brains out through your eye sockets. So we generally woke up with at least one bedroll dampened by more than the dew, if you get my drift.

Fortunately, the campers always handled this potentially embarrassing situation with enormous sensitivity and tact. "VICTOR PEED IN HIS BED!!" they would shriek, their happy voices shattering the stillness of the forest morn, alerting the tiny woodland creatures that it was time to flee unless they wished to become the subjects of primitive biological experiments involving sharp sticks and rocks. Heaven help the toad that wandered into our campsite. One minute it would be a normal toad, maybe two inches high, and the next minute, having become the subject in the Two Heavy Flat Rocks Experiment, it would be a completely different style of toad, no thicker than a wedding invitation but with much larger total square footage.

You ask: "Well, why didn't you, as the Voice of Maturity, stop them from doing this horrible thing?" To which I reply: (a) If God had wanted us to be concerned for the plight of toads, He would have made them cute and furry. (b) As the old saying goes: "A disadvantaged youth who is crushing a toad with a rock is a disadvantaged youth who is not, at least for the moment, crushing the skull of another disadvantaged youth."

You must realize that these campers needed to work off a great deal of nervous energy caused by eating nothing, breakfast, lunch, and dinner, but Kellogg's Frosted Flakes. The raccoons always got everything else. When I hear scientists claim that, after human beings and game-show contestants, dolphins are the smartest animals on Earth, I have to wonder what kinds of designer chemical compounds they (the scientists) have been snorking up their noses, because anybody who has ever dealt with raccoons knows that they are far more intelligent than we are. My campers and I would spend hours rigging up these elaborate Crafty Old Woodperson devices whereby you hung your food between two trees so the raccoons couldn't get it. The raccoons would watch us on closed-circuit TV from their underground headquarters, laughing themselves sick, and as soon as it got dark they'd put on their little black masks and destroy our devices instantly using advanced laser technology.

If we ever decide to get serious about space travel, what we need to do is convince the raccoons somehow that campers have placed food on Jupiter. The raccoons will find a way to get it.

Well, boys and girls, looks like Uncle Dave got so caught up in telling old "war stories" that he completely forgot about you! That's one of the great things about camp, boys and girls: It leaves you with so many memories that will stay wedged in your brain until you die! Possibly on your way to the latrine.

Clan of the Cave Rhinoceros

Play review: *The Cave People,* written and performed by the Rose Valley School Kindergarten class, featured ROBERT BARRY as one of the woolly rhinoceroses.

As is true of most serious dramatic works, *The Cave People* works on several levels: on one level, it is the story of a group of primitive people who sit outside their cave while various animals run by; yet, on another level, it is the story of a group of primitive people who go *inside* their cave and get trapped by a giant rock.

But I am getting ahead of myself. For if one is to truly understand this work, one must first examine the philosophical underpinnings of its creators, the Rose Valley School Kindergarten Class, which has devoted several months to studying the Origins of Man, interrupting this effort only for Story Time, Music, Lunch, Cleanup, Rest Time, Sharing Time, Free Time, painting Pictures to Go on the Refrigrator, Running Around Pretending to Be Jet Robots, Trying to Remember Where Your Sweater Is, and Snacks.

As a result of this course of study, the class developed several concepts, which were posted on the bulletin board over near the Really Tall Tower Made from Blocks. These concepts reveal a wide diversity of opinion about the Origins of Man, ranging from the traditional Judeo-Christian Biblical concept:

"This is Adam and Eve. They ate the bad fruit. They went back to God. They didn't have any clothes."

To the less-conventional Big Bird and Oak Tree concept:

"In the beginning of the world there was a big bird and an oak tree. The big bird had a coconut, and the moon was out."

And yet from this eclecticism of belief has emerged *The Cave People,* a work that has not only a strong sense of cohesiveness, but also has a great big gray cave made out of papier-mâché standing right next to the piano, which is sort of holding it up.

As Act One opens, some Cave People are sitting in front of the cave, and almost immediately the theme of Animals Running By is established by two woolly rhinoceroses, portrayed by Owen Smith and ROBERT BARRY, running by and making a noise like a 33 rpm recording, played at 45 rpm, of a bull elephant with its private parts caught in a trash compactor. And although the audience was unable to see the faces of these two fine young actors directly due to the fact that they were wearing yarn-covered paper bags over their heads, the power of their performance, especially that of the lead rhinoceros, ROBERT BARRY (the one who did not have his arm stuck through the eyehole), was such that even veteran drama critics such as myself were moved to take upwards of 20 color photographs.

This was followed by deer running by wearing antlers and brown underpants and waving at their parents, which set the stage for a moment of powerful drama as the dreaded saber-toothed tiger, played superbly if somewhat blindly by Matt Dorio with something on his head, came prowling by, bonking into things, causing the Cave People to poke each other with their spears and laugh. "They were really scared," explained the narrator.

The Getting Trapped in the Cave by a Giant Rock theme is then introduced by means of having the Cave People go inside the cave, then having the giant rock, which had been held up by a piece of yarn, fall down and almost block the entrance. In fact it probably *did* block the entrance, in rehearsal, although in the actual play, the piano player had to shove the giant rock over with her left hand, but she did this with a very natural and convincing motion. Just then *another* group of Cave People emerged from behind the piano and had the following realistic primitive dialogue with the ones that were trapped:

PEOPLE OUTSIDE THE CAVE *(in unison)***:** You guys inside! Push hard on the rock!

PEOPLE INSIDE THE CAVE *(in unison)***:** OK!

This is followed by an absolutely stunning bit of staging as the Cave People all push on the giant rock and, as if by magic, it rises *straight up in the air.* Believe me when I tell you that there was not a dry set of underwear in the audience at this point.

The Animals Running By theme is then reintroduced as the dreaded saber-toothed tiger bonks its way back on stage, and the Cave People stab it about 50,000 times with their spears until it is, in the words of the narrator, "totally dead." The theme of Getting Everybody Back Onstage is then established as the Cave People invite the deer and the woolly rhinoceroses to help them eat the tiger. In the cheerful words of the narrator: "They all sat down, roasted him, ripped him apart, and had a delicious meal." The concept of the meal being delicious was dramatically reinforced by having the Cave People say: "Yummy!" and "This is a delicious meal!" Of course, the woolly rhinoceroses, being unable to speak, could only pat their stomachs in a satisfied manner, but they did this in such a convincing and moving way that even veteran critics wanted to rush right up and give them a great big hug.